English Reformations

English Reformations

Religion, Politics, and Society under the Tudors

CHRISTOPHER HAIGH

CLARENDON PRESS · OXFORD

OXFORD

UNIVERSITY PRESS

Great Clarendon Street, Oxford OX2 6DP

Oxford University Press is a department of the University of Oxford.
It furthers the University's objective of excellence in research, scholarship,
and education by publishing worldwide in

Oxford New York

Auckland Cape Town Dar es Salaam Hong Kong Karachi Kuala Lumpur
Madrid Melbourne Mexico City Nairobi New Delhi Shanghai Taipei Toronto

With offices in

Argentina Austria Brazil Chile Czech Republic France Greece
Guatemala Hungary Italy Japan Poland Portugal Singapore
South Korea Switzerland Thailand Turkey Ukraine Vietnam

Oxford is a registered trade mark of Oxford University Press
in the UK and in certain other countries

Published in the United States
by Oxford University Press Inc., New York

British Library Cataloguing in Publication Data

Data available

Library of Congress Cataloging in Publication Data

Haigh, Christopher.
English reformations: religion, politics, and society under the
Tudors/Christopher Haigh.
p. cm.
Includes bibliographical references and index.
1. Great Britain–Politics and government–1485-1603. 2. Great
Britain–Social conditions–16th century. 3. Great Britain–Church
history–16th century. 4. Great Britain–History–Tudors,
1485-1603. 5. Reformation–England. I. Title.
DA315.H28 1993 942.05–dc20 92-21515

ISBN 978-0-19-822162-3

19 20

Printed in Great Britain
on acid-free paper by the
MPG Books Group, Bodmin and King's Lynn

For Alison

Preface

I began to write this book in January 1988, in Sydney. I had begun to think about it in September 1971 in Manchester, as I planned a new special subject for my students. We were to look at 'Resistance to the Reformation in England', from the fall of Wolsey to the collapse of the Revolt of the Northern Earls. We were to ask how much opposition there was to religious change, what it achieved, and why ultimately it failed. I wish to thank all those Manchester students who helped me tackle these problems, especially Alison Bartholomew, Susan Brigden, Steven Ellis, Jenny Hetherington, Susan Taylor, Patricia Turner, and Stephen Thompson. It was a hugely enjoyable course to teach, in a lively and innovative department.

It seemed to me in 1971 (as it does even more strongly after twenty years of further work) that the story of reformers and victors is only part of proper Reformation history; I hoped to add the resisters and the losers, and those who just watched it all happen. I wanted to construct a version of the English Reformation which integrated the dynamic of high politics with the variety of local responses. I found some of what I was looking for in over twenty record offices, in the act books of Church courts and visitations, and in the churchwardens' accounts of nearly two hundred parishes. I am grateful to archivists and librarians from Chichester to Durham, from Exeter to Norwich—and in Sydney. Closer to home, I thank the Governing Body of Christ Church for three periods of research leave, to trail around record offices and write the book—and the staff of Christ Church Library, especially the ever-patient John Wing. Christ Church has been a warm-hearted and supportive place to work.

In 1972 a Mancunian lady complained to the vice-chancellor of the University that he was letting a Roman Catholic lecture on the Reformation; he replied that there was no reason why he shouldn't, and in any case I wasn't. Her anger now seems quaint, but, more recently, when a fellow-historian had the same assumption corrected, he exploded, 'Then why does he write such things?'. I have no real idea, and readers must judge for themselves. No doubt it is naive to suppose it is because that is what the evidence has told me—but it certainly feels that way! A childhood Methodist, a teenage Presbyterian, a briefly Catholic first marriage, ten years of determined atheism, ten more of indifference, and now a kind of Anglican agnosticism in the serenity of Christ Church Cathedral; if readers find anything helpful here, they are welcome to speculate. Perhaps such a well-travelled spirit can sympathize with all viewpoints; perhaps such temporary allegiances betray understanding of none. Perhaps—as I hope—one can use what one has learned and try to write good history.

It has been exciting to be a Reformation historian through the 1970s and 1980s, as 'revisionism' disrupted cosy pigeon lofts and china shops. There has been a lot to learn, and a lot to unlearn. Geoffrey Elton has made me defend myself every step of the way, and I have a thick file of challenging letters which forced me to think and rethink. I do not suppose he will like this book very much, but if the ideas hold together it is his own fault! Many others have provided encouragement, ideas, references, argument, and cold common sense; in particular, I thank George Bernard, John Bossy, Margaret Bowker, Susan Brigden, Patrick Collinson, David Cressy, Cliff Davies, John Guy, Felicity Heal, Ralph Houlbrooke, Ronald Hutton, Sybil Jack, Ian Kershaw, David Loades, John Morrill, Frank O'Gorman, Glyn Redworth, Bill Sheils, Margaret Spufford, David Starkey, Robin Storey, Alison Wall, Jenny and Patrick Wormald, and the anonymous readers for Oxford University Press. At OUP, I am grateful to Ivon Asquith for inviting me to write the book, to Tony Morris for making sure I did, and to Anne Gelling for picking up the pieces once I had.

For twenty years I have been saying what I thought was wrong with the Reformation history I learned as a student. Perhaps what I have argued has seemed negative and destructive; I know it has caused some offence. This book finally offers a positive, alternative explanation of change, and now puts OUP's money where my mouth has long been. Rather than wrestle in almost every paragraph against other views, I have chosen to tell the story simply as I see it. I trust this makes for clarity, but the debate to which the book contributes is fully explicit only in the 'Introduction' and the 'Bibliographical Essay'. The book I might have written—'on the one hand, Dickens; on the other hand, Scarisbrick'—would have been tediously argumentative and twice as long, so I hope any who think their opinions have been disregarded will forgive me. I do not suppose I have written the last words on English Reformations—or any part of them: I hope I have advanced a debate that I have found illuminating and exhilarating.

I have tried to explain how Reformation happened in England (with a few examples drawn also from Wales), and to show how Reformation was experienced by people in the parishes. I have relied heavily (I hope not disproportionately) on years of study of churchwardens' accounts, though for brevity I have cited them in notes only when I have quoted directly from particular accounts. I have not written a comprehensive textbook version of English Reformations, describing in painstaking detail every issue others have thought relevant. I confess I have kept ruthlessly to what I think is important in explaining change, and readers will have their own lists of neglected topics; humanism, monasteries, and the wayward career of

Thomas Cranmer head mine. I trust this concentration will appear as self-discipline rather than self-indulgence. The writing has taken three and a half years, crammed between tutorial and administrative responsibilities, much of it in time stolen from what might have been a private life. I thank my wife, not only for her help but for her patience, which has been tested far.

Christ Church, Oxford   C. A. H.
Michaelmas 1991

Contents

PROLOGUE

The Religious World of Roger Martyn

ROGER MARTYN lived at Long Melford in Suffolk through much of the sixteenth century. He died there in 1615, aged 88. Towards the end of his long residence he wrote a brief description of 'the state of Melford church and of Our Lady's chapel at the east end, as I, Roger Martyn, did know it'.[1] It is a nostalgic evocation of village religion, as remembered from his childhood in the 1530s. The church's interior had been dominated by the great rood or crucifix, standing high in the rood-loft between nave and chancel, and flanked by images of the Virgin Mary and St John the Evangelist. On the front of the loft, facing the congregation, the twelve apostles were painted, and the roof above was decorated with gilded stars. Beyond the rood was the high altar; to the left of it was a large statue representing the Trinity, patron of the church; to the right were images of saints. Above the high altar stood a gilded carving of Christ's passion, closed behind painted doors except on high feast days. In the aisle was the Jesus chapel, maintained by the Martyn family; on its altar was a crucifix with the two thieves, to the left an image of Christ, and to the right a *pietà*, an image of the Virgin bearing her crucified son.

The church inventory of Long Melford for 1529 supplies further detail of the church and its services. There were at least twenty-three images in the church—statues of SS Andrew, Anthony, Christopher, George, and John the Baptist, of SS Anne, Catherine, Margaret, and Mary Magdalene, and of others—each with a decorated cloth hanging before it. For the image of the Virgin there were rings and gorgeous coats, one reserved for holy days. Some of the parishioners were members of guilds which supported devotion to the images of the Trinity, Jesus, the Virgin Mary, and St Peter, and a fraternity of the young men of the parish made gifts to the church. The church had thirteen silver and gilt chalices for its masses, including 'the best chalice, gilt, 133½ ounces'; most of the chalices had been presented by clergy or parishioners. There were fifteen copes, the best 'a cope of red velvet branched with gold, with a suit of the same called the best suit'; there were eleven mass books, and twenty-seven antiphonals, graduals, and processionals for liturgical singing by the priests and choir, and crosses, cloths, monstrances, and banners for the parish processions.[2]

Martyn lovingly recalled the festivals of the Church's year. On Palm

Sunday there was a parish procession around the churchyard, with the consecrated host, a communion wafer, carried under a canopy borne by four yeomen of the village; the church bells were rung, the choir sang, and as the procession returned to the church porch flowers and holy bread were strewn over the choirboys. On Maundy Thursday candles were set in a painted frame before the Easter sepulchre, where the sacrament was reserved. On Good Friday the priest sang the Passion service from the rood-loft, standing next to the rood which had been veiled through Lent. On St Mark's day and at Corpus Christi there were processions round the green with the consecrated sacrament, bell-ringing, and singing. The choir was rewarded for its efforts with dinner at Melford Hall three times a year. In Rogation week there were great celebrations, as well as three days of beating the bounds of the parish and prayer 'for rain or fair weather, as the time required'. There was ale and a parish dinner on Rogation Monday; a breakfast of cheese at the rectory and later ale at the manor house chapel on the Tuesday; and ale at Melford Hall on the Wednesday.

On the eve of St James's day there was a village bonfire, with a tub of ale and bread for the poor. There were bonfires and ale in front of the Martyns' house on Midsummer eve and on the eve of Saints Peter and Paul; for the St Thomas's eve bonfire, the family provided mutton pie and peascods, as well as the usual bread and ale, 'and with all these bonfires, some of the friends and more civil poor neighbours were called in' to dine by candlelight with Roger's grandfather, as a taper burned before the image of St John the Baptist in the hall. It was, as Martyn painted it, an idyllic picture. No doubt it was overdone, a merry Melford in the past, where merriness is always to be found. For when Roger Martyn wrote it had almost all gone. The delightful church remained, but was almost unrecognizable inside: no rood, altars, nor images; no gilded stars, no organ, and probably no choir. There were no guilds, no processions or celebrations on festivals, and though the bounds had to be beaten at Rogationtide the entertainments had probably been dropped. Martyn had kept some sorry relics: a crucifix, the organ, and a bell; 'I will that my heirs, when time serve, shall repair, place there, and maintain all these things again.'[3]

Martyn had lived through a series of Reformations, which had shattered the parish religion of his childhood—though he still hoped they would be reversed. There had been three legislative Reformations, in 1530–8, 1547–53, and 1559; together they had, partly for political reasons, changed the constitution, worship, and prescribed beliefs of the English Church. The authority of the pope in Rome had been rejected, and replaced by a royal supremacy; the independent jurisdiction of the clergy had been broken. The church services of Martyn's childhood had been banned, most significantly the mass, in which the communion wafers and wine had changed their substance at the priest's consecration into the holy body and blood of

Christ. The villagers of Long Melford were now told that their eternal salvation depended not on the intercessions of the Church and charitable works, but on predestined faith in the justifying sacrifice of Christ on the cross. Alongside these political Reformations, there had been a Protestant Reformation, an evangelical movement in which new believers sought to persuade Catholic neighbours to share their commitment; sometimes it was with the more or less enthusiastic support of the state, and sometimes, as in 1525–32, 1539–46, and 1553–8, against active official opposition.

A combination of government coercion and individual conversion drove traditional Catholicism from the churches, and replaced it with a Calvinistic Protestantism. For Roger Martyn, and for others, the Reformations were disastrous: he had resisted the new Protestantism, his own religion was proscribed, and he became a member of a secret Catholic sect. For a few (including some in Long Melford) the Reformations had brought spiritual freedom: heretics who had long rejected the superstitions of Catholicism found their scepticism endorsed, first by preachers from the universities and finally by the state. For many, no doubt, the Reformations brought changes which were mainly external, from passive observance of Catholic ritual to passive hearing of sermons and psalm-singing, though adjustment from the familiar to the novel may have been worrying. But for others, there was a real spiritual reorientation: from a Catholic mental universe of supportive saints and saving sacraments to a Protestant one of justifying faith nurtured by sermons and Bible-reading. And for all—those who objected, those who welcomed, those who merely watched, and those who struggled to adapt—the Reformations had shaken and altered much that they had known.

Long Melford was a prosperous cloth-producing village, its wealth displayed by the grandeur of its church—though some of its poorer workers had joined an anti-tax rebellion in 1525. In Roger Martyn's childhood, the parish was in the spiritual charge of William Newton, a Cambridge graduate and a pluralist with ecclesiastical offices in East Anglia. He was responsible for providing sacraments and pastoral care, though he usually did so through a curate as deputy. In 1535 Newton's annual income from Long Melford was £28. 2s. 5d., more than three times the average income of English priests (and perhaps ten times that of an agricultural worker). Newton was rector of the village, which meant that he received the full value of his benefice: various small fees, about £5 a year from farming the rectory's glebe land, and about £20 from tithe, a 10 per cent tax on his parishioners' incomes, paid in cash or kind. Roughly two-thirds of all parish benefices in England were rectories; the rest were appropriated to support monasteries or colleges, which took the profits of the rectories and paid substitute vicars or curates to serve the parishes. Vicars were much less well paid, and so less likely to be graduates; Newton's neighbour John Lee had £9. 6s. 8d. from the vicarage of Acton, and at Little Waldingfield Christopher Greening had only £4. 18s. 10d.[4]

Long Melford church was also staffed by four chaplains. Three were chantry priests, paid from fixed endowments bequeathed by local notables; in 1535 Edward Turrell had £7. 5s. a year, John Skurre £6. 6s. 8d., and Thomas Hore only £4; Hore was 'the Lady priest', serving the recently built chapel of the Virgin Mary 'at the east end'. Their main duty was to celebrate masses for the salvation of souls nominated by their founders, usually those of the founder, family and forebears, those to whom the founder owed prayers, and sometimes 'all Christian souls'. The object was to reduce by prayer the time of suffering spent by souls in purgatory, a middle-place of expiation, neither heaven nor hell, and help them to eternal bliss with God. In some parishes a chantry priest was also required to teach at a school funded from the endowment. The Melford chantrists were also responsible for assisting in the daily worship of the parish church, with the help of John Wood, a stipendiary chaplain with £6. 13s. 4d. a year by the gift of a parishioner. Often there were additional clergy, employed by guilds to pray for members, paid for a year or two to pray for a soul, or picking up occasional fees from those who asked for special masses.

Some of the land in Long Melford was owned by the great Benedictine monastery of St Edmund at Bury. The abbot, one of the most powerful men in East Anglia, probably came from the parish, and he was certainly related to the wealthy Smith family of Melford clothiers. There were 840 religious houses in England and Wales, and St Edmund's was among the richest: its net income in 1535 was £1,660,[5] when the average was only about £200. It was a large and complex business; it received rents from its properties (including £128 from Long Melford), tithe from its appropriated rectories, and various fees and obligations from clergy and laymen. It paid an army of officials and servants: lay bailiffs to collect its rents and stewards to hold its manor courts; lay craftsmen and servants to maintain the establishment and work the demesne land; clerical vicars and curates to serve its appropriated churches. It offered hospitality to travellers, education to local boys, and charity to the poor. But its prime duty was worship; it existed to praise God, and to pray for the welfare of the living and the dead, especially its own members and benefactors. The abbey had sixty-two monks in 1535, though the average membership of all religious houses was only a dozen.

Long Melford was one of the 1,148 parishes in the diocese of Norwich, which in Martyn's boyhood was ruled by the old and blind Bishop Richard Nykke. The bishop was a great lord; like St Edmund's Abbey, the bishopric had estates and rectories, and like Abbot Reve the bishop sat in the House of Lords. In the diocese, his formal duties were confirmation of children, ordination of clergy, institution of priests to benefices, and supervision of orthodoxy, morals, and pastoral care in the parishes. Nykke had been an energetic disciplinarian, determined to maintain the authority of his office and repress misconduct among his clergy and heresy among the laity. Through his diocesan courts, Nykke's judges enforced canon law, the law of the Church—which regulated marriage, defamation, and probate of wills, and enforced church attendance, payment of tithes and dues, repair of church fabric, sexual morality, and orthodox beliefs. The officials of the diocese and its archdeaconries held regular visitations of the parishes, when priests and churchwardens were questioned to reveal breaches of the law. Offenders were given penances, and obedience enforced by suspension from the Church's sacraments or excommunication from the Christian community.

There were eighteen English dioceses, and four in Wales, each with its own bishop, courts, and bureaucracy. York, Durham, and Carlisle formed the northern province of York, with its own archbishop. The rest, including Norwich, constituted the larger province of Canterbury, under its archbishop. William Warham, archbishop from 1504 until his death in 1532, achieved prominence by service to the Crown in law and administration, as many other bishops had done. Above all, the archbishop had to be a manager: managing the estates of Canterbury, the work of its courts, the dispensing of patronage, the collection of taxes, the relationships between his suffragans, the Church's dealings with the king and the pope, and the meetings of the Canterbury Convocation. He called Convocation, the provincial parliament, into session; he chaired the Upper House of prelates; and he supervised the debates of archdeacons, deans of cathedrals, and representatives of the parish clergy in the Lower House. In their two Convocations of Canterbury and York, the churchmen granted taxation of the clergy to the Crown, and made laws which bound both clergy and laity.

The Church in England and Wales was a huge and complex organization. All 2,500,000 men, women, and children were members, like it or not, and subject to discipline by the clergy. Everyone was bound to attend church on Sundays and festivals, to fast on appointed days, and to make confession to a priest and receive communion at least at Easter. All those with wages, profits, or produce were bound to contribute to the upkeep of their parish priests and churches. There were roughly 9,500 parish churches, staffed by an average of probably four priests each (some of them in subsidiary chapels within large parishes),[6] and there were other priests who said masses for cash and found occasional work where they could. So there were perhaps 40,000 secular priests, and also about 10,000 priests in the regular orders of monks and friars; and there were subdeacons and deacons progressing towards priesthood, and as many as 2,000 nuns. The Church professionals must have numbered more than 60,000 men and women in all, roughly one in forty of the population; the priesthood certainly totalled 50,000, about 4 per cent of all males. The Church was an all-embracing institution, and its clergy were everywhere.

In some respects the Church was not a distinct national body; it was simply Long Melford at prayer and nearby Acton and Little Waldingfield at prayer, no more than a loose federation of parishes. Each local community of priests and people co-operated together in their work and their worship, and the church was the village centre for meetings and jollities as well as for services. The ordinary chaplains and parishioners of Long Melford may have had much more in common with each other than either had with their superiors, Bishop Nykke or the duke of Norfolk. Perhaps the laypeople did not often conceive of 'the Church' as a separate hierarchy of authority and sphere of activity. But in other ways the Church, and specifically its ordained clergy, was discrete. The priests were distinguished (in theory) by the discipline of celibacy, and they had corporate identity and privileges. The clergy were not taxed by parliament, but voted their own levies in Convocation; their crimes were not punished by the secular courts, but by their own bishops; they had exempt jurisdictions or sanctuaries, where fugitives could escape the king's justice; their courts enforced laws made by clerics, rarely limited by statute.

But the Church was too rich and powerful to be allowed to go its own way. Kings of England needed its wealth, especially in time of war—when they also needed its supportive propaganda, through preaching and prayers. Religion, which prescribed the obligations of the people and promised divine punishment for disobedience, was far too important to be left to the priests. Kings employed churchmen as lawyers, bureaucrats, and diplomats, because they were educated and could use Latin, the language of international relations. Kings wanted access to ecclesiastical patronage, so their servants could be rewarded by appointment to rich livings, and be paid from Church tithe or endowments, while working on royal business. So the Crown supervised nominations and elections to the most important ecclesiastical offices: asking popes to provide or cathedral chapters to elect particular bishops, suggesting suitable abbots or priors for monastic communities, persuading patrons to present favoured candidates to benefices; the Crown's wishes were rarely flouted. The formal power of the monarchy over the Church was limited; in practice it was considerable, and long had been.

But kings had to watch the constitutional boundaries of Church and state, for encroachments—accidental or deliberate—by the clergy might weaken royal authority or compromise essential interests. So the Crown offered writs of prohibition, which could transfer suits from Church courts to its own; and writs of praemunire, which could block litigation in Church courts on matters thought subject to royal jurisdiction. The monarchy, and the lay lawyers, insisted that Church property and patronage were bound by common law and the royal courts. The king's responsibility for national security and public order made the conduct of the clergy a matter for his concern, but the clerical privilege of exemption from secular punishment (called benefit of clergy) limited his direct power over them. Cases of treason had always been excluded from benefit, but if other crimes seemed to increase then the privilege might appear a bar to proper law enforcement. However, suspicious kings were not jealously eyeing the jurisdictions of the Church, nor were wily clerics usurping the proper functions of secular government. There was a potential for friction, but it was rarely made real.

Henry II had tried to define the relationship between Church and state in 1164, which produced a dramatic clash with Archbishop Becket, but though the king made a humble submission after Becket's murder, he got most of his way. In 1297 there was a confrontation between Edward I and Archbishop Winchelsey, over royal taxation of the clergy; but it had been provoked by the pope, not English churchmen, and there was a speedy resolution in the king's favour. Archbishop Stratford claimed in 1341 that Edward III was infringing the privileges of the clergy over jurisdiction and taxation, and he excommunicated Crown servants; but there was a compromise solution, and both sides backed down. Thereafter, there was no serious conflict until 1531; there were disputes over abuse, but no struggles over principle. The leaders of the Church in England were themselves royal officials, with no interest in constitutional crises, and the political reality was that a king could coerce the clergy when he had the backing of the lay magnates. In the main, therefore, the bishops recognized royal authority, and in return kings supported the churchmen against heresy and lay critics of their wealth.[7]

The ecclesiastical hierarchy stretched up from Long Melford to Rome: rector of Long Melford, archdeacon of Sudbury, bishop of Norwich, archbishop of Canterbury, Roman cardinals and curia, and at last the pope, Vicar of Christ and supreme pontiff of the universal Church. The authority of the papacy over the English Church had been contentious in the past. Innocent III had ordered suspension of all church services in England in 1208, and had excommunicated King John, to impose Stephen Langton as archbishop of Canterbury. Thereafter, popes lost their tussles with kings of England. In 1296 Boniface VIII had forbidden royal taxation of the clergy, but was unable to sustain his prohibition. Clement VI's numerous provisions of clerks to English benefices had been countered by the Statute of Provisors in 1351, and there were further restrictions in 1391; churchmen had themselves protested against papal intrusion. When Martin V appointed Bishop Beaufort as his special representative (legate *a latere*) in 1417, the nomination was rejected by both Henry V and Archbishop Chichele. But later popes were content to maintain their powers by exercising them as kings wished: they provided Crown nominees to benefices, and took their taxes in return.

The papacy had become, for the English, not much more than a symbol of the unity of Christendom. Since the pope usually did as the king asked in his realm, it was the king who really mattered. Some of the laity paid Rome small taxes as Peter's pence, and some of the clergy paid a levy of a year's income on provision to a benefice. The king had a representative at Rome as a cardinal protector, to ensure that royal candidates were provided to English benefices; the pope might also promote a leading churchman in England as a cardinal, usually to flatter the king or gain his assistance. The pope was the apex of a legal and administrative bureaucracy: some canon law cases went to Rome on appeal, and some English people—including their kings—sought dispensations from the pope to relax rules of the Church, especially to permit uncanonical marriages. A few enthusiasts trooped off to Rome on pilgrimage, particularly in jubilee years, and some did not like what they saw there. But papal authority was neither loved nor hated: it was not important enough for such strong emotions. It was not a political issue; it was a minor fact of ecclesiastical life.

In the century before the birth of Roger Martyn, there were only minor adjustments of the relations of king, pope, and clergy. But we should not think of a static 'pre-Reformation Church', waiting meekly to be challenged by the inexorable forces of modernization. There were changes, and some of them had strengthened the position and reputation of the Church. The usurping Lancastrian, Yorkist, and Tudor dynasties needed endorsement from the Church, and may have been reluctant to offend its senior clergy. The expansion of lay education produced laymen to replace clerks in royal government—which reduced the Crown's use of benefices to support its servants, increased the residence of incumbents, and may have improved pastoral care in the parishes. The recruitment of clergy had slumped in the late fourteenth century, but by the mid-fifteenth it was booming, probably because of energetic lay endowment of masses, and the improved reputation of priests. Criticism of churchmen had become associated with heresy and threats to the social order, and there was little lay complaint about clerical wealth between the Parliament of 1410 and that of 1529.

When there was denunciation of the worldliness of priests, it usually came from the clergy themselves: from moral reformers such as Thomas Gascoigne, chancellor of Oxford University in 1444–5, or from humanist scholars such as John Colet. In 1496 Colet had returned from study in Italy, and lectured in Oxford on St Paul's Epistles. He brought a new style of scriptural exegesis, applying the methods of Renaissance classical scholarship to the biblical text, and a renewed fervour for the re-creation of primitive Christianity. At Oxford in 1498 Colet condemned the Church's compromises with the world and its values, and demanded that bishops and priests should eschew royal service and the race for profits and promotion. In 1510, as dean of St Paul's, Colet preached the same message to the Canterbury Convocation: the clergy were guilty of 'pride of life', 'lust of the flesh', 'covetousness', and 'worldly occupation', and they must reform themselves before they could be effective Christian pastors.[8] His improving sermon has often been used by historians as crucial evidence for the condition of the English Church before the Reformation, as a demonstration of why reform was needed and so why the Reformation came. But we should be careful.

Colet asked Convocation for 'the reformation of ecclesiastical affairs, for never was it more necessary and never did the state of the Church more need your endeavours'. He was wrong, however. There is very little evidence that the conduct of the clergy was worse than it had been in earlier centuries, and a good deal to suggest that it was much better. Colet's cry for reform was not provoked by a decline in the morals or commitment of priests; rather it stood in a long tradition of Christian protest against the contamination of God's priests by man's ambition. Before Colet there had been Gascoigne in the fifteenth century, Langland in the fourteenth, Grosseteste in the thirteenth, and Bernard of Clairvaux in the twelfth; all critics of clergy who followed the ways of Mammon rather than the path of Christ. The cry for moral reform is a constant theme in Christian history, not the precursor of crisis, and it is unwise to read realities from the claims of crusaders. Colet was not a proto-Protestant, disgusted with the ecclesiastical structure and the sacramental system; he was a high clericalist, anxious to maintain the privileges of priests by raising their prestige.

Colet recognized that 'the diseases which are now in the Church were the same in former ages', and admitted that canon law had provided remedies. 'The need, therefore, is not for the enactment of new laws and constitutions, but for the observance of those already enacted'. He told the bishops in 1510 that they should accept only well-qualified candidates for ordination as priests and for institution as incumbents, and ensure that parish clergy fulfilled their pastoral duties. The bishops must devote themselves to diocesan work, and their revenues to religious projects, not to high living and grand building. They should ensure that religious orders followed their rules and withdrew from the world, and that Church courts did not seek profits for their officers. If churchmen would only follow the will of God and the canon law, then the laity would esteem them better and their rights and revenues would be secure. In some respects Colet's programme was pie in the ecclesiastical sky: the king would not permit free election of bishops by cathedral chapters, and the laity could not be kept out of clerical appointments. For the rest, however, Colet was describing good episcopal practice.

In the Convocation of 1510 were bishops who needed no advice from John Colet on how to run a diocese. We know that Blythe of Lichfield,

Fisher of Rochester, Mayhew of Hereford, Nykke of Norwich, Oldham of Exeter, Sherburne of Chichester, and Smith of Lincoln were energetic administrators, determined to maintain clerical discipline and the quality of pastoral care. They were already doing what Colet wanted, and more. Although William Warham's attention to Canterbury was distracted by his responsibilities as primate and lord chancellor, he took part in a careful diocesan visitation in 1511–12 and employed effective deputies, such as Cuthbert Tunstall. In 1510 Fox of Winchester was busy as lord privy seal, but in 1516 he withdrew from government and threw himself into diocesan business. Only three dioceses in the southern province in any way deserved Colet's criticism. Bath and Wells and Worcester were both held by absentee Italians, hired by the king as his representatives in Rome, though Bath and Wells at least had an experienced Church bureaucrat as its vicar-general, managing the diocese as effectively as most bishops. The one disreputable English bishop on the bench of 1510 was Stanley of Ely, and he would be replaced in 1515 by the impressive Nicholas West.

James Stanley was the only bishop who may have heard Colet's sermon red-faced and wriggling, for he embodied the defects the preacher condemned. He had 'pride of life': as a son of the first earl of Derby, he advanced through the hierarchy from childhood by family influence. He exhibited 'lust of the flesh': he had three children (apparently by his housekeeper), and established them among the gentry of north-west England. He had shown 'covetousness', with a string of the most lucrative benefices in England. He followed 'worldly occupation', living as a great lord and hunting with neighbours and retainers. He was a negligent and absentee bishop, wintering in Lancashire with his brother, the second earl; a magnificent builder, especially at Manchester; and in all respects a man of secular interests who happened to be in orders. He was also a unique case: step-brother of Henry VII, and the one noble's son promoted bishop by Henry VII or Henry VIII. He lived as an aristocrat because he was an aristocrat, foisted on the Church by family connection and royal patronage. But if the bishops of 1510 included one great sinner, they had a saint too: John Fisher of Rochester.

Some of Fisher's own sermons echoed the themes of Colet. The clergy 'were wont, and indeed ought still, like lights to the world to shine in virtue and godliness', but 'now there cometh no light from them but rather an horrible misty cloud or dark ignorance'.[9] Like Colet, Fisher had a high view of the priesthood and its privileges; like Colet, he believed that only the ministrations of a virtuous priesthood could bring the laity to Christ and through him to salvation. And, like Colet, he feared that the worldly clergy of his day did not proclaim Christ's call for repentance with proper evangelical fervour. Fisher's theology and his spirituality stressed the prevalence of sin and the necessity of repentance to avoid God's fearsome punishment. He was conscious of the deficiencies of the clergy not because they were acute or worsening, but because *any* defects threatened the salvation of men and women. It was Fisher's pastoral concern to save souls which made him such a critic of the priests, not the realities of clerical life. And it was concern for souls which made him a first-class diocesan, fulfilling the episcopal ideal set before Convocation by Colet.

The Church in early Tudor England was richly varied. It was a moral and spiritual force—not as moral or as spiritual as the idealists wished, but declaring Christ's message and pursuing salvation for souls. If there was a James Stanley to bring scandal, there was a John Colet to denounce him and a John Fisher to set saintly example. The Church was also a great national institution, with rights and privileges, laws and jurisdictions, property and employees. It had formal relations with the king, the pope, secular courts, and civic authorities; there were opportunities for friction and occasional clashes of interest, but officials muddled through and got on with their business. And the Church was a collection of parish communities: Roger Martyn, his family, and their neighbours received the sacraments in Long Melford church from William Newton and his assistants. No doubt there was some local contention between priests and people, as there was between lay villagers; no doubt Martyn's picture of decorous worship and seasonal jollity was overdrawn. But the Church in each community was what its people made it, for better or worse.

When Roger Martyn was a small child, the English Church—and Long Melford church—seemed impregnable. Like all human institutions, it could benefit from improvement; and there were improvers enough: preachers, scholars, and administrators. But it faced no great challenges. The Crown was not plotting to seize the Church's jurisdiction, and the lawyers were not plotting to grab all the business of its courts, though neither would refuse what gains fell their way. The nobility and gentry were not planning an attack on the property of the Church, though they were unwilling to give it more and would not protest if it had less. There was no general reluctance to pay the Church's tithes, or Long Melford's tithes, though farmers and workers did not queue to give more than they must. A few heretics denied parts of the teaching of the Church, some of them in Long Melford, but they had been around for a century and more without causing much trouble. And whatever the difficulties the Church faced, little and usually local, it was secure, for it offered the sinners of England security in this world and eternal bliss in the next. When Roger Martyn was a small child, there were no Reformations on any visible horizon.

INTRODUCTION

Interpretations and Evidence

THE title of this book has been chosen quite deliberately: it is *English Reformations*. It is not *The* English Reformations. That would claim that the only English Reformations which ever were took place in the Tudor period, and suggest that they formed a complete and effective process. But the various (and varied) Reformations in sixteenth-century England were haphazard and had only limited success, at least by comparison with Protestant aims: they did not make Church or people emphatically Protestant, and there remained much still to be done. There were to be later energetic attempts at more complete Reformation: in the mid-seventeenth century, when more Protestant forms of Church government and worship were proposed; and in the late eighteenth century, when Methodists and Evangelicals offered a more fervent faith to those whose Protestantism was nominal or minimal. So the book is not a study of *the* once-and-for-all English Reformations. Rather, it examines *some* English Reformations, some of the campaigns to change the constitution of the national Church and the beliefs of its people; it asks how they happened, what they achieved, and why they were unable to do more.

Nor is the title *The Reformation in England*. That would assert that what happened in England was simply a local manifestation of the wider European movement, an integral part of 'the Reformation', in which Martin Luther's personal rebellion became a widespread revolt against the authority and superstition of the Roman Church. Now, of course, there are senses in which this is true. English protesters borrowed ideas from Luther, Zwingli, and Calvin: they became Protestants, consciously part of a broader Protestant cause. Religious change in England took place within a context of religious division and disruption on the Continent, which made it much safer for Henry VIII to go his own aberrant way. But English Reformations did not happen because of Luther, and they did not follow any general Continental pattern. The Catholic Church in England was not corrupt and worldly as in Germany. Luther's ideas had only slight impact in England before Henry—for his own, decidedly un-Lutheran, reasons—turned against the pope. And if Henry found it briefly convenient to deal with Lutheran princes and Lutheran theologians, he also found it necessary to burn Lutherans (and especially Zwinglians) for heresy.

In some cities of Germany and Switzerland, Reformation came with enthusiasm and violence; altars and images were cast down and smashed by rioting mobs, eager to destroy the symbols with which priests had kept them in awe. In England (and especially away from London) it was different: altars and images were carefully removed on government orders, by masons and carpenters paid by churchwardens, and the altars and images were often kept safe, in case of future need. On the Continent, princes and city councils declared themselves for 'the Reformation': they swept away papal power and clerical privilege, they seized Church property, they introduced vernacular services and Bibles, and they prescribed Protestant and proscribed Catholic beliefs—often in weeks, months, or a very few years. In England, it was different: change was piecemeal, and it took twenty years to get from the first real attack on Church jurisdiction in 1532 to the first Protestant church service in 1552; and then it was almost all undone by Queen Mary. Only in 1559 did an English regime opt for a full Reformation, and still there were theological, liturgical, and legal loose ends to be tied up.

These English Reformations took some ideas from *the* Reformation; they could happen as they did because they coincided with it. But they were not *the* Reformation, exported across the Channel and installed in England by Luther, Calvin, and Co. Ltd. Whatever such English Reformations had in common with Reformation on the Continent, they were not the same thing: not *the* Reformation, declared by reformers and demanded by crowds. The term 'Reformation' is applied by historians to a set of historical events, often treated as if it was an inexorable process: a theological attack on Catholic doctrine, the abolition of papal authority, the reduction of priestly power, the suppression of monasteries and chantries, the abolition of the mass, the introduction of simplified Protestant worship, the enforcement of Protestant ideas, the conversion of people from Catholic to Protestant loyalties. In England, such events did not come in swift and orderly sequence, as consecutive steps of a pre-planned programme or a protest movement: they came (and went again) as the accidents of everyday politics and the consequences of power struggles.

There were soon people in England who wanted wholesale Reformation: scholars such as Hugh Latimer and William Tyndale, and London merchants such as Humphrey Monmouth. There were also those who were hostile to any ecclesiastical reform at all, fearing it would prove the thin end of the schismatic Lutheran wedge: John Fisher and Thomas More had been critics of clerical defects, but the example of Germany turned them into defenders of every last religious ditch. But between the absolute Protestants and the absolute Catholics were the pragmatists. Bishop Tunstall abandoned the pope without much sign of qualm, but he baulked at restrictions of clerical privilege and episcopal power. Bishop Gardiner accepted the abolition of monasteries, persuading himself they deserved to fall, but he fought for the mass and especially the doctrine of Christ's real presence in the eucharist. Henry himself was apparently willing to jettison any inconvenient belief, but he could not stomach justification by faith and he would not give up the real presence. And there was Archbishop Cranmer, whose theological views shifted so subtly and secretly that analysis of them is a historical industry in itself.

From a modern perspective, such men may seem hypocrites, *politiques*, and cowards: perhaps in some measure they were. But they lived in confused and dangerous times, when ideas and power structures were unstable. Tunstall and the rest did not make unprincipled selections from the Reformation package, picking out what suited them and rejecting the rest. The future had not yet happened! Participants did not know that they were in 'the Reformation', they did not know that the Lutheran schism would be final, they did not know that the Catholic Church would reform its practice but retain its theology: they did not know, and could not yet know, what was to be Catholic and what was to be Protestant. So they did not elect for or against 'the Reformation' in one great do-or-die decision; rather, they made a number of lesser choices in particular contexts: for or against Cardinal Wolsey in 1529, for or against the independent canon law in 1532, for or against the Aragon marriage in 1533, for or against papal authority in 1534, for or against higher taxes on churchmen in 1535, for or against the smaller monasteries in 1536, and so on. If Reformation is to be understood as it happened in England, it must be broken up, or deconstructed.

The religious changes of sixteenth-century England were far too complex to be bound together as 'the Reformation', too complex even to be 'a Reformation'. England had discontinuous Reformations and parallel Reformations. There were three political Reformations: a Henrician political Reformation between 1530 and 1538, much of it reversed between 1538 and 1546; an Edwardian political Reformation between 1547 and 1553, almost completely reversed between 1553 and 1558; and an Elizabethan political Reformation between 1559 and 1563—which was not reversed. These political Reformations could not make England Protestant; statute by statute, however, they gave England Protestant laws and made popular Protestantism possible. What made English people Protestant—some English people Protestant—was not the three political Reformations, but the parallel evangelical Reformation: the Protestant Reformation of individual conversions by preachers and personal contacts, the Reformation which began in London, Cambridge, and Oxford from about 1520, and was never completed. So England had blundering Reformations, which most did not understand, which few wanted, and which no one knew had come to stay.

This is not how historians have usually seen things. They have often preferred to bundle Reformation events together into one big event: 'the Reformation'. And big events have to have big causes. So 'the Reformation' was the result of great progressive movements: the rise of anticlericalism, the rise of the modern state, the rise of rationalism (and humanism, and Protestantism), the rise of the middle class, the rise of capitalism, together with the decline of feudalism, the decline of monasticism, the decline of clerical power, the decline of Catholicism. Or so it has seemed. But there are two main problems with this approach. One is methodological: it is simplifyingly whiggish. A whig version of history is teleological; it finds the origins of the known result, explains by alleged modernizing forces, and shows how the bad old past became the brave new future. England abandoned superstitious Catholicism, and took up sensible Protestantism, as progress had determined it would. So whig history charts the corruption and decay of Catholicism (which must have decayed, because it lost), and so it charts the growth of popular Protestantism (which must have been popular, because it won).

This technique is seductively easy: it defines significant change, helps us to organize an explanation, and gives principles for selection of relevant evidence. The complex interactions of simultaneous events can be reduced to a series of progressive forces or 'factors', which can then be illustrated by appropriate examples wrenched from specific contexts. One part of Reformation was a reduction in the power of churchmen: Why did this happen in sixteenth-century England? Because of hostility towards them, anticlericalism, which is proved by literary criticisms of priests, by refusals of tithe, by rejections of the authority of Church courts. It is rarely asked who criticized, or refused, or rejected, or when, where, and why they did so; it is rarely asked if criticism, refusal, or rejection was typical, or frequent, or increasing. Since historians seek explanations for a Reformation cataclysm, they look for pre-Reformation troubles, and they pile up the troubles into evidence of mounting crisis. Calm, co-operation, and contentment are ignored, for they do not offer forces for the future. This is a highly selective approach to the past: it exaggerates conflict, accelerates change, and gives a one-sided story of protest and victory.

Whiggish history concentrates on the achievement of progress: the defeat of superstition, obscurantism, and regimentation, the victory of realism, rationalism, and freedom. These reflect, of course, modern, western, liberal values, and perhaps the men and women of sixteenth-century England saw things differently: one person's superstition may be another's spirituality, and one person's freedom another's guideless anarchy. Whiggish progress was marked by the step-by-step implementation of 'reform', which meant the abolition of the old and the imposition of the new. Since, by definition, the old is always passing away and the new always coming to be, reform was easy: history was gently nudged along. Thomas Cromwell drove out the pope and the monks, and brought in the English Bible. Thomas Cranmer put down saints and purgatory, and introduced the *Book of Common Prayer*. Somehow, Mary Tudor got in the way and progress was halted, but she guaranteed her own failure by popish cruelty and a Spanish marriage. Elizabeth picked up the Protestant pieces, regained the ground lost after Cromwell and Cranmer, and made a land fit for Protestant heroes: Francis Drake, Philip Sidney, and Richard Grenville. It was a doddle!

Or was it? Change will appear straightforward if history is reduced to a sequence of reforms, ignoring reactions, reversals, alternatives, and contexts. Change will seem easy if its opponents are left out of the story, or treated as silly old fogeys destined for defeat. But such distilled history is an illusion; it is not how the past was. Religious change was not made by Cromwell, Cranmer, and Elizabeth; it was made by Cromwell and the duke of Norfolk, Cranmer and Stephen Gardiner, Elizabeth and Mary Queen of Scots: those who got in the way as well as those who pushed forward. It did not happen only in London; it happened (or happened slowly) in Lancaster, Lewes, Lichfield, Llandaff, and Long Melford in Suffolk. Reformations were not the work of theologians in Cambridge and law-makers in Westminster alone; they were also the work of those who sat bewildered in pews or befuddled in alehouses, those who grumbled as well as those who greeted. Reformations were made by Catholics as well as by Protestants, because the Reformations came out of the clashes between them. So whiggish history employs a defective method, and it yields an over-simplified, unbalanced, and misleading version of English Reformations.

It is also an inaccurate version, for the evidence no longer sustains it. The whig history of Reformation has been founded on two sorts of printed evidence: the criticisms made by Protestants and the laws passed by parliaments. The cause of Reformation was established from the complaints of early protesters such as Thomas Bilney, Simon Fish, and Hugh Latimer; they argued that the Catholic Church was corrupt, worldly, and superstitious, therefore it had to be reformed. The priests had cheated the people with gimmicks and false promises of salvation; their fraud must be exposed, and the people offered biblical truth: Protestantism was the answer. The process of Reformation was established from the statutes which carried through reform, from the Acts against clerical abuses in 1529, through the Acts against Roman jurisdiction in 1532–5, the Acts against monasteries in 1536 and 1539, the Acts against the popish mass in 1549 and 1552, and finally the crowning legislation of 1559 with the 'Elizabethan settlement': end of story. The evidence of protest showed why England wanted Reformation; the evidence of legislation showed how it got Reformation.

But we can now know hugely more about the realities of Tudor religion and politics, and much of it cannot be crammed into a one-sided whiggish scheme. Especially since about 1960, there has been an intensive study of the unpublished manuscripts in national and local record offices, prompted by improved organization of archives, by expansion of higher education, by wider availability of research grants in the 1960s and 1970s, by a democratic fashion for grass-roots history, and by the pioneering example of a number of major historians. Now we do not need to take our account of what the 'unreformed' Church was like from Fish and Tyndale, nor from the allegations in the 1532 Commons' Supplication against the Ordinaries. Now we can examine the workings of the Church courts through consistory act books, depositions books, and cause papers: the records of what the courts actually did, not the charges of those trying to discredit them. Now we can study religious life in the parishes through visitation reports, last wills, and the annual accounts of churchwardens: the records of what happened in churches, not the claims of those who thought parish religion so much nonsense.

Of course, we do not solve our historical problems by a simple shift from *The Supplication for the Beggars* written by Simon Fish to the Long Melford accounts compiled by Roger Martyn. All historical evidence requires critical assessment and realism in its use, Roger Martyn's evidence as much as Simon Fish's. The administrative records of institutions give a slanted and partial view, just as the propaganda of Protestants does. Churchwardens' accounts tell us only what churchwardens spent, not what they thought, and certainly not what the rest of the parishioners thought. Wills indicate only what those rich enough to make them left to churches and churchmen at death, and not why they did so or what they had done about religion in life. Visitation presentments show us only what clergy and parishioners admitted, not what they had actually done, or not done. Consistory records deal only with disputes and offences which got to court, and not with problems sorted out locally or kept quiet for fear or favour. But, used with care and good sense, these sources can add new dimensions to our understanding of the Tudor Church, its relationship with its people, and their practice of religion.

It is now possible for historians to tackle seriously issues which have hitherto been guessed at or ignored. We can now see conventional Catholic religion from the perspective of those involved in it, and not merely from the standpoint of those who rejected it. When we worked from the mocking criticisms of Fish and Jerome Barlow and others, it was easily supposed that in early Tudor England traditional devotions—prayers to saints, offerings to images, membership of religious guilds, endowed masses for souls, festal plays and processions—were collapsing. But wills and accounts seem to show that this was not so; if there were sceptics, there were many more enthusiasts and probably even more conformists. When we studied the Church courts from the denunciations of rival lawyers, it was easily supposed that the authority of the courts was onerous and their judgements despised. But the proceedings of the courts suggest this conclusion was misplaced: there were alehouse radicals who scoffed at officials, but the volumes of business and the conduct of litigants imply that the courts were useful and their resolutions respected.

It is also now possible for historians to study Reformation as it actually happened, and not only as it was commanded. It has often been said[1] that the English Reformation 'was an act of state'. And so, in large part, it was (or they were). But an act of state is only the start of a process of enforcement, response, and perhaps ultimately obedience. When historians worked from the legislative record of statutes and proclamations, it was tempting to suppose that what the law said was what people did, since there was then no way to test the question. Reformation was therefore a list of official pronouncements, the stages by which 'Catholic England' became 'Protestant England'. However, the study of local administrative records enables us to examine the imposition of new regulations and compliance with them. We have long known that in 1538 royal injunctions ordered every parish to acquire an English Bible for its church, but we can now tell when some parishes did so, and it was rarely in 1538. We can now try to chart not only the making of rules but the enforcement of rules, and see English Reformations as struggles between state and people as well as struggles between Catholics and Protestants.

The recent attempts to get at the grass roots of Reformation history are frustrating and perhaps futile. Can we ever know what 'people' thought? Does it matter anyway? The answers are, 'No, we cannot', and 'Yes, so we must try'. There were no public opinion polls in Tudor England, and in a fragmented and localized society there was no coherent public opinion to measure. There is no form of evidence which will tell us unequivocally what people believed; but there are several sorts of evidence which, taken together and used circumspectly, can show how behaviour and attitudes shifted in some groups and communities. Every parish was unique: it had its own successions of priests and squires, its own relationships with bishops and magnates, its own links with towns and traders; its own reasons to change or stay the same. So every parish had its own Reformation: English Reformations indeed! But we need not conclude that everywhere was different so nothing general can be said. We may recognize regional similarity while remembering local singularity; we may observe broad national trends while noting that rates of change varied area by area. We must try to say something, no matter how cautious we have to be.

It is sometimes suggested that even if we could know what 'the people' thought and did, it would not matter. History was made by princes and politicians: 'people' were consumers, the victims of history, and it is naïve and rather left-wing to suppose otherwise. But in the history of the Reformations, 'people' mattered in at least three ways. First, because the Reformations were about what 'people' should think and do. Both Catholics and Protestants cared about souls; they thought their own truth would help souls to heaven, and their enemies' error would send souls to perdition. What 'people' thought was an issue for Bishop Edmund Bonner and for Bishop Nicholas Ridley, because they were Christian pastors as well as ecclesiastical politicians. It was an issue for them, and it must be an issue for historians who want to comprehend them. Secondly, 'the people' mattered to governments, since there was constant risk of disorder or rebellion if surly subjects were provoked by insensitive policies. If we have no sense of what various sorts of 'people' thought, we can never understand political decisions. Even bluff King Hal had to rule with his subjects in mind, or they might refuse to pay his taxes, join his armies, and obey his laws.

Thirdly, 'people' mattered in these Reformations because they were there and they took part. Sometimes, some rebelled: in 1536, 1549, 1554, and 1569 there were major risings caused partly by religious discontents; there were lesser but potentially dangerous disorders in 1537, 1541, 1548, and 1570. Sometimes, and especially in London, some actively advanced the cause of Reformation, pulling down images in 1547, mocking the mass in 1548, pulling down altars in 1550. Some were converted by Protestant proselytizing; some were outraged by such heresy, resorting to personal violence or informing to authority. And everywhere, always, people obeyed or did not obey the rules of Reformation or de-Reformation, and their obedience or disobedience is Reformation history. The English Reformations were not composed simply of the books of Tyndale, the statutes of Cromwell, the sermons of Latimer, and the liturgies of Cranmer, nor of the six wives of Henry VIII and the 280-odd martyrs of Bloody Mary. They also included the responses of millions of men, women, and children, whose names we will not know, but whose presence and participation are facts of history. We cannot put them all in, but we may not leave them all out.

The evidence yielded by the record offices does not demolish a whiggish version of English Reformations. Rather the new material puts the old into context: it adds perspective and balance. It enables us to put into our history those pieces which the whig approach had left out: Catholic loyalty and unthinking conservatism, hatred of heresy and distrust of novelty, petty resistances and reluctant conformities, the relief and enthusiasm which greeted restoration of old ways, the bewildered adjustment to renewed demands for change. And we can get the forces of whiggish progress into proportion; we can see the criticism of priests alongside the fervour for what they offered; see Lollard and Protestant dissidents tilting at formidable

Catholic devotions; see the risks that Henry VIII, Somerset, Northumberland, and Elizabeth took; see even more dramatically the faith and heroism of those who died at the Marian stakes, for what in worldly terms should have seemed a lost cause. But all this will make explanation of religious change much more difficult: 'the rise of Protestantism' and 'the decline of Catholicism' will no longer serve. They are not even descriptions, much less explanations.

This book will not attempt to explain Reformation by use of great background causes. Those which have been cited in the past seem to offer little help nowadays. Some have been massively exaggerated: the early impact of anticlericalism and Protestantism, for example. Some, such as the various rises of capitalism, the middle class, and the modern state, seem to have been long-term features of human history, rather than specific causes. Some have dubious relevance to Reformations in England or anywhere else—such as the humanism and rationalism which were as evident (or not) in countries which retained their Catholicism as in those which embraced Protestantism. All are clumsy generalizations, difficult to relate to the myriad details of complex change. The book will not offer detachable explanations of a great English Reformation event; instead, it will seek to tell the story of all the lesser events which in sum became some English Reformations.[2] It will try to give an account of changes as they happened, one by one; it will try to show how one event led to another, not because of a predetermined sequence, but because of the choices of participants. It will examine the making of political decisions, and their enforcement.

English Reformations were about changing minds as well as changing laws, but it was the changing of laws which made the changing of so many minds possible. The religious history of England would have been very different if its rulers had not decided to break with Rome, and finally to break with Catholicism. There would have been a Protestant movement without the backing of the state; there was a Protestant movement before it got the backing of the state. But it is hard to see how it could have captured the Church without the state's endorsement, and it is hard to see how it could have gained that endorsement if the chances of politics had not favoured the piecemeal advance of anti-Catholic measures. At best, perhaps, Protestants might have become an opposition Church of French Huguenot proportion, a dangerous minority which could fight but not win civil wars. At worst, they might have been crushed by persecution, like Evangelists in Italy and Spain. It was politics which made the difference, politics which provided the dynamic of change, politics which made English Reformations instead of the Reformation in England.

The explosion of historical research which took place after 1960 has revealed very much more about the workings of central politics and government, mainly by drawing on the vast archives of the Public Record

Office. Tudor government was far more complicated than a simple sequence of Council advice, royal resolution, parliamentary approval, and institutional enforcement. We now know—or think we know—about the making of political decisions, the exercise of political influence, the building of political careers, and the fall of political leaders. We understand much more about the life of the Court, and the kinds of personal and factional pressures which might be exerted upon kings, queens, and ministers. We know something of what lay behind the Reformation statutes: the political calculations, the drafting and redrafting of bills, the determined manipulation of parliamentary opinion, the amendments adopted to get legislation through. And much of what has been discovered suggests the fluidity and contingency of political choices and events. For rulers, decisions were hard to reach and harder to sustain; for ministers power was hard to achieve and harder to retain. No wonder there were English Reformations—reversed and reversible.

The petty machinations of Court politics acquire national significance when their consequences are imposed upon millions of people. Political victories—Cromwell over More in 1532, Norfolk over Cromwell in 1540, Hertford over Gardiner in 1546, Warwick over Arundel in 1550, Mary over Northumberland in 1553, Cecil over Norfolk in 1569, Leicester over Sussex in 1579—influenced the religious experience of men, women, and children across the land. For it is likely that most of those who lived in Tudor England experienced Reformation as obedience rather than conversion; they obeyed a monarch's new laws rather than swallowed a preacher's new message. Even the preacher's freedom to convert was circumscribed by official policy; underground proselytizing at risk of persecution would be far less effective than public preaching of an official gospel. Religious change was governed by law, and law was the outcome of politics. The Reformations were begun, defined, sustained, slowed, and revitalized by political events. So the core of a study of English Reformations must be a political story. And that story begins in 1530.

PART I

A Church Unchallenged

❧ 1 ❧

Parishes and Piety

IN 1530 the London printer Robert Redman published a best-seller. It was *A Work for Householders, or for them that have the guiding or governance of any company*. Despite its unpromising title, the book went through two editions in 1530 and three more in 1531; by 1537 it had been printed eight times. A convenient little handbook of practical family religion, *A Work for Householders* was one of the most popular new publications of the decade. It had been written by Richard Whitford, a scholar-monk at the fashionable Bridgettine house of Syon in Middlesex. Whitford's earlier writings had been specialist works of piety for monks and nuns, but his new book had been drafted for the household of a lay friend; this friend had seen its sales potential, and encouraged publication. Whitford was an instant success. As well as *A Work for Householders*, in 1530 he also published his own adaptations of short works of private devotion by St Bonaventura, Bernard Sylvester, and St Bernard, the last reprinted twice in the following year. 'The old wretched brother of Syon', as Whitford called himself, was in demand at the bookshops.

Richard Whitford's striking popularity continued for some years. In 1531 he brought out *A Work of Preparation unto Communion*, and perhaps also *The Following of Christ*, a new translation of the *Imitatio Christi*, which went through five editions in its first year alone. In the same year, the enterprising Robert Redman put together *A Work of Preparation* and *A Work for Householders*, with Whitford's translations of St Bernard's 'Golden Epistle' and St Bonaventura's 'Crossrow', in a collected edition, which also sold well and was reissued twice. The printers must have pestered poor Whitford for other books, but *The Pipe or Tun of the Life of Perfection* (1532) was too obviously designed for enclosed religious orders and it flopped. Then in 1534 he published *A Daily Exercise and Experience of Death*, successfully adapted from an earlier composition for the nuns of Syon. It was his last work for the wider market, and was soon reprinted twice. In all, at least thirty-two editions of these and similar pious books by Whitford sold out in the years 1530–8. He had been a major publishing phenomenon.[1]

Whitford was not alone, and other monks shared his literary appeal. In 1528 Whitford had edited *The Pomander of Prayer*, a manual first drafted by 'one of the devout fathers of the Charterhouse of Sheen'. *The Pomander* was deliberately published 'for the unlearned that lack knowledge of Holy Scripture', and they apparently bought it: there were further editions in 1530, 1531, and 1532. It was a sensible, down-to-earth guide, showing the laity 'how and under what manner they might order themself in prayer'.[2] Whitford's Bridgettine colleague William Bond had published some more demanding works, *The Pilgrimage of Perfection* in 1526 and *The Directory of Conscience* in 1527; though he died in 1530, the year of Whitford's first success, he achieved posthumous popularity with a reprint of *The Pilgrimage* in 1531 and two further editions of *The Directory* in 1534. Another Syon brother, John Fewterer, organized the publication of the anonymous *The Mirror of our Lady* (dedicated to the monastery of Syon) in 1530, and published his own *The Mirror or Glass of Christ's Passion* in 1534.

Alongside these works of advice and devotion produced for a lay audience, other pious publications achieved success about 1530. *The Rosary of our Lady*, associated with the growing use of the rosary in England, was first printed in 1525 and reissued in 1531 and 1537. The *Jesus Psalter*, an aid to devotion which had been widely used in manuscript, was first published in print in 1529 and reissued in 1532 and 1534. The *Primer*, a standard medieval collection of Latin and English devotions for use at home or in church, now had remarkable sales: it had sold thirty-seven editions between 1501 and 1520, but from 1521 to 1530 it went through another forty-one editions, six of them in 1530 alone, and twenty more reprints by 1535. Some printers of the *Primer* tried to capture a larger share of the market in 1531 by adding to it a moral treatise called 'The Manner to Live Well'. Other works sold well too: lives of the saints, collections of prayers, manuals of devotion, meditations on the Passion of Christ. The demand for religious literature, especially aids to personal piety, was truly enormous and apparently insatiable.

The tremendous popularity of Whitford and his colleagues may be ascribed partly to the novelty of their writings. The literate laity had long been offered edifying tales of the saints, but they had not hitherto been told in print how to organize their own devotional lives. *The Pomander of Prayer* was a practical guidebook to prayer: it gave suggestions on what to pray for, on how to maintain concentration during prayer, and on the fasting and charitable works which should accompany prayer. Whitford's *A Work for Householders* had a wider range: it offered advice on how to live a Christian life in the layman's world, from making the sign of the cross on waking to kneeling for prayer and recollection at bedtime. Its emphases were realistic: the Christian man was to discipline his life by following an occupation, to teach the faith to his household, to honour his parents, to be reverent at mass; he was not to swear, not to make use of charms or witchcraft, not to entice women by false promises of marriage.

But although Whitford's medium was novel, his message was entirely traditional.[3] *A Work for Householders* gave in book form the moral and religious instruction which the priests had long offered in sermon and confession; it stands in a tradition of teaching which in England went back to Archbishop Pecham's Lambeth decrees of 1281, and beyond that to the Lateran Council of 1215. Pecham, and the authors of later manuals on the duties of parish clergy, had required priests to teach and explain to parishioners the Lord's Prayer, the Creed, the Ten Commandments, the Seven Principal Sins, the Seven Works of Mercy, and the Seven Sacraments: exactly the domestic curriculum recommended by Whitford. Pecham's guidance for curates was printed ten times in 1516–34, and set the pattern for pastors. John Mirk's *Festival* (a collection of model sermons printed twenty-four times between 1483 and 1532) provided a simple exposition of the Lord's Prayer in English, and was usually printed with four additional sermons on the essentials of the faith as set out by Pecham. Mirk's 'Instructions for Parish Priests' expected the clergy to check at confession that parishioners could recite in English the Lord's Prayer, the Hail Mary, and the Creed.

Richard Whitford had established the most systematic and determined programme for implementing the spiritual syllabus defined by Pecham. Where Pecham had wanted the elements of the faith taught in church four times a year, Whitford wanted them taught at home every day, preferably by use of his own book. The householder was responsible for teaching his children and servants the Lord's Prayer, the Hail Mary, and the Creed, and he should hear each of them recite once a week. He was advised to have Whitford's expositions read aloud at every meal, or at least once a day. When these had been thoroughly learned, 'Then must you teach them to know by order the precepts or Commandments of God, the names of the seven principal sins, and of their five wits', and explain them by Whitford's commentary. Whitford also urged the conscientious literate Christian to 'gather your neighbours about you on the holy day, specially the young sort, and read to them this poor lesson'—*A Work for Householders*.[4]

We do not know how far Whitford's readers followed his prescriptions; perhaps it was not very far. Certainly he expected that those who tried would have a difficult time, and that those who knelt to pray at night in shared bedrooms would be mocked for their piety; but 'Fie, for shame that any Christian should be so cowardous' as to pray in secret. However, we do know that Whitford's book was extremely popular, which suggests that the traditional pattern of Christian living he advocated was highly esteemed. Christians should daily cross themselves *In nomine Patris et filii et spiritus sancti*; they should seek aid from their favourite saints; they should 'hear mass quietly and devoutly, much part kneeling', using psalters or rosary beads (as an Italian visitor had noted Londoners doing in 1500); they should seek blessings from priests and godparents; they should prepare carefully for confession, and make sure they understood the penances imposed. Richard Whitford's Christian of 1530 was to be much the same as John Mirk's Christian of 1400, a pious and obedient Catholic; and that, it seems, was what Whitford's many readers wanted.

The massive sales of *A Work for Householders* from 1530, and the popularity of other devotional aids at about the same time, suggests that Catholic Christianity was secure in early Tudor England. The only hint in Whitford's book that the orthodox faith faced any challenge was a passing warning that 'good devout Christians' should take no notice of heretics who denied the sacrament of penance.[5] Yet in 1528 a series of trials in the courts of the bishop of London had revealed a network of heretical groups, importing forbidden books from the Continent and supporting their own wandering evangelists. In the following year Cardinal Wolsey had been thrown from power by an aristocratic coup, and the first session of a new Parliament had passed three statutes undermining the position of the clergy. In 1530 the king's lawyers compiled a collection of documents which sought to prove that the English Church was subject to the authority of the king, not the pope, and a proclamation excluded from England any papal bulls which infringed royal sovereignty. Was Richard Whitford blind to these early stages of the English Reformations?

Whitford knew that something was amiss. In his preface to *The Pomander of Prayer*, he had complained, 'charity and peace is almost extinct, faith dispersed, hope dissolved, virtue and pity outlawed, sanctity annulled, priesthood distained, religion decayed'. In truth, this was just the age-old complaint of preachers and religious writers, that piety was in decline and the godless were about to triumph. The sales of Whitford's own books were to prove him wrong. But the state of ecclesiastical politics was more ominous: 'What division is among the princes and heads of the Church, I report me unto you, I do fear me to the great hurt and oppression of the people.'[6] If there was a threat to orthodox Catholicism in England, it was from the competing machinations of princes, popes, and politicians, which unexpectedly led to national schism and national heterodoxy. The threat was not of any internal decay, or a progressive alienation of a disaffected laity, or even the growth of hostile intellectual and social movements; these things had hardly begun to happen by 1530.

Catholic Christianity before England's break with Rome was flourishing; we must not assume that the Reformations prove otherwise. For it was the break with Rome which was to cause the decline of Catholicism, not the decline of Catholicism which led to the break with Rome. Before the intrusion of political considerations which had little to do with religion, early Tudor England was not heading towards a Reformation. The popularity of manuals which offered aids to orthodox piety is one indicator of traditionalist strength, though it tells us only about the book-buying minority. For a broader-based view, we might look at the religious life of the parishes, where we find massive evidence of energetic commitment to conventional devotions. From the evidence both of the wills of the dying, which suggest the proportions of laypeople who made gifts to their churches, and of churchwardens' accounts, which show how churches were decorated and cults maintained, our conclusion will be the same. In England, late medieval parish religion was not just a going concern, it was an expanding business with good prospects for the future.

It is now well established that early Tudor laymen and women, from affluent aristocrats to those who had barely anything to leave, generally made bequests to religious causes and especially to the parish churches. Professor Scarisbrick has studied roughly 2,500 wills of the first half of the sixteenth century from all regions of England (though with an emphasis on the midlands); he found that all but a tiny proportion of testators left something to religion, and that at least 60 per cent made gifts to the maintenance and services of their own church. Professor Jordan has examined the volumes of money given to charitable causes in the period 1480–1540. He calculated that 70 per cent of the money left to charity went to religion in Lancashire, Somerset, and Yorkshire; 60 per cent in Buckinghamshire, Norfolk, and Norwich; 48 per cent in Bristol and 45 per cent in London. Mrs Bowker has looked at wills from three counties in the diocese of Lincoln; she discovered that about 85 per cent of testators made bequests to their parish church in the 1520s, and about 75 per cent in the mid-1530s. Dr Attreed's examination of wills from the north of England in the years 1525–40 suggests that 75 per cent of testators left gifts for the running of the parish church, and 16 per cent made bequests specifically for church repairs.[7]

Most of this largesse passed into the hands of parish churchwardens and the wardens who administered parish guilds and special funds. Since rich benefactors usually paid for something identifiable, such as a new cope or a new service book, it was the small gifts of the poor which contributed to the running expenses of each church—and they could not suffice. The bulk of ordinary parish income came from the rents of property bequeathed in the past, and from the more-or-less voluntary payments of the living: in collections for the Paschal candle, in the gatherings from parishioners on Hock Monday and Hock Tuesday, in the profits of the sale of specially brewed ale, and in individual subscriptions to particular projects. Sometimes wardens would impose a compulsory rate or 'cess', especially if major building was envisaged, but parishes appear usually to have managed on giving enforced only by pious obligation and social pressure. By such informal means, churchwardens could raise from small and poor communities the money which sustained elaborate public devotions.

The little moorland village of Morebath in Devon had only thirty-three households assessed for Peter's Pence in 1531, but its parish life was energetic and its devotion in its church remarkable.[8] The finances of the parish were organized in ten funds or 'stores', six of them administered by their own wardens and four by the churchwardens or 'high wardens of St George'. There were elaborate mechanisms for transferring surpluses between funds, and additional accounts were established for special purposes, as in the 1530s, when the parish was saving to buy a set of black vestments. Revenues came from four sources: from the profits of the sheep-flocks kept for the stores, from the church ales organized by the high wardens and the wardens of the Young Men's Guild, from collections such as those by 'the Maidens' wardens', and from benefactions. Between 1520 and 1540 the parish received gifts and bequests from seventy-seven donors, totalling, the vicar estimated, over £40 in cash, as well as equipment for church services; little wonder the parish said an annual 'dirige for the benefactors of the church'.

The poorest parishioners seem to have given what they could. In 1526 Alice Obleye, a servant, bequeathed 4d. to the store of St George, 4d. to the store of Jesus, 4d. to the store of St Sidwell, and 2d. to the alms light. The vicar himself contributed; in the first years of his incumbency, in the early 1520s, Christopher Trychay gave money towards the making, gilding, and equipping of an image of St Sidwell, the glazing of windows, and purchase of a set of white vestments; in 1530 he added matching white vestments for the deacon and subdeacon. The seven bequests of 1531 were mainly earmarked for a new image of the Virgin Mary, and Katherine Robbins left an elaborate set of beads, 'the which beads must hang upon the new image of Our Lady every high day by her mind'; she also bequeathed ten shillings and a sheep to St George's store, a sheep to the store of Jesus, a sheep to Our Lady's store, and another sheep to the store of 'St Maryn of Marley'; then she made the churchwardens her executors, and gave the church half the residue of her estate.

The parishioners of Morebath always had some new, and often expensive, project afoot. In 1529 the statue of Jesus was painted, St Sidwell's image gilded, and 'an image of the Nativity of Our Lady with her appurtenances' ordered; when the Virgin's image was completed and gilded in 1531, the wardens commissioned from the same carver a new image of St George on horseback, promising him a bonus 'if he do well his part'. In 1533 a tabernacle for the new image of the Virgin was gilded, as was the image of Our Lady of Pity. In 1534 the new St George was gilded and erected in a costly gilded tabernacle, new seats were installed in the church, and an altar newly carved. In November 1534 there was a setback: a thief broke into the church and stole St Sidwell's silver shoe and a chalice, 'so upon this the young men and maidens of this parish drew themself togethers and with their gifts and provision they bought in another chalice without any charges of the parish'. In 1535 a new carver was asked to provide a crucifix with Mary and St John, for the rood-loft; in 1536 the crucifix was gilded, and in 1538 Mary and John and the roof above the rood. A new cope was purchased in 1539, and thereafter the wardens saved for the new black vestments.

A picture of harmonious co-operation would be unconvincing, and there were certainly frictions. In 1531 there was a dispute over the appointment, payment, and duties of the parish clerk, and a more acrimonious row on the same subject in 1536. The proposal to buy black vestments seems to have been a pet project of the vicar, and certainly it took a suspiciously long time to raise the money. It is not suggested here that Morebath was a shining beacon of Christian charity, but that as a community it had real pride in its church and saints. The females of the parish took a full part in church life: the Young Maidens' Guild collected for 'Our Lady's light'; women served as wardens of the stores, and sometimes as high wardens; and women often left jewellery for the images of the Virgin Mary and the virgin martyr Sidwell, and money towards the candles on their altars. In 1528 Joan Hillier gave the church a candlestick, 'upon the which candlestick she doth intend to maintain a taper before St Sidwell, trimmed with flowers, to burn there every high and principal feast'. The piety of Morebath is striking, but it is unusual only in that it was carefully recorded, by a vicar who supervised the accounts and listed benefactors.

An obsessive devotion to saints was a characteristic of West Country religion. At Ashburton there were regular repairs and repaintings of images, and an elaborate new rood-loft in 1522–3, an improved St George in 1526–9, a new St Thomas Becket in 1529, and a St Christopher in 1538. Elsewhere, images were maintained within a broader concern for a church and its worship. In the Somerset parish of Yatton, the wardens paid for the gilding of the Blessed Virgin and St James in 1529–30, and had a new tabernacle carved for the image of Thomas Becket. Becket had been gilded in 1514, at the end of a programme of painting the church and its images; there was further gilding and painting in 1537, with scaffolding for the gilder to work on St John. Revenue at Yatton was from ales, gatherings, and bequests, and the level of giving increased markedly when major projects were planned. In 1524–5 a new stone cross was set up in the churchyard, with a head commissioned from a mason at Bath. In 1527 a new organ cost £15, plus 5s. for carriage from Bristol to Yatton. In 1529 the parish had one of the bells recast for £19, and two more recast in 1531–3. Lavish new vestments and a cope were bought for £30 in 1534, and a cross for the altar of St James.[9]

The saints played their part in the worship of all churches, and often in the financial arrangements too. At Wing in Buckinghamshire (as at

Morebath and Ashburton), there were separate funds to supply candles before the altars, for Saints Katherine, Margaret, Thomas, and Mary Magdalene, as well as Our Lady's altar and the holy rood, and an additional fund of the 'torchmen'. The church's inventory of 1527 shows that it was splendidly equipped with plate, vestments and service-books. There were, for example, five silver chalices, two gilt chalices, and three parcel-gilt chalices, and 'six vestments with their albs and all things purtaining thereto—one of blue velvet and another of green, the third of blue damask branched, the fourth of red satin with a tunicle to the same of the same sort for a deacon, the sixth of white satin'. Even this was not enough to satisfy parochial pride, and in 1538 the wardens raised almost £2 in donations and bought an organ, altar-cloths, and other service equipment from the suppressed abbey of Woburn.[10]

The inventory for the parish church of Bassingbourne, Cambridgeshire, in 1498 shows another well-stocked church, with lavish provision of plate and vestments, and thirty service-books. The running of the church was financed by church ales and benefactions, and assistant clergy were funded by the guilds of the Trinity, the Holy Cross, and St John the Baptist. In 1511 the churchwardens organized a play of St George, which was attended by parishioners of twenty-five neighbouring villages, and with the profits they commissioned an image of St George; this was erected by 1520. The church of Sherborne in Dorset paid its way mainly from a Whitsuntide ale run by 'the king of Sherborne', but there were also revenues from bequests, pew rents, and offerings for candles. The annual inventories of this prosperous parish show a massive and expanding store of liturgical equipment, which by 1542 extended to twenty-two copes and fourteen sets of vestments. Besides the Whitsun ale, the high point of the Sherborne year seems to have been Corpus Christi day, when the consecrated host was carried in procession in a decorated shrine, and a play was performed in a tent in the churchyard.[11]

It should not be supposed that an energetic parish life was confined to villages and small country towns. The incomplete churchwardens' accounts of St Andrew's Canterbury[12] also show the parishioners anxious to maintain and improve their church and its worship. Regular income came from rents of parish property, the collections on St Andrew's day and at Easter and Hocktide, and the annual gift from 'the brothers and sisters of the Cross light', and there were occasional revenues from collections for special projects, from bequests and gifts, and from compulsory rates. In 1504 fifty-five people were assessed for between 4d. and £2 to pay for pews in the church, and some of the wives held a collection towards the cost of the necessary bolts. In 1508–9 a rood-loft was built at a cost of £24. 6s. 8d., plus £4. 1s. 4d. 'for the making of the stairs going up to the rood-loft' and a good deal of incidental expenditure. Most of the money for the rood-loft was raised by a rate paid by forty-eight parishioners, and the cost of an organ in 1513 was also met by rating.

But the giving at St Andrew's was not always forced. In every year there were the usual voluntary collections towards church expenses, especially the 'gatherings' by the men on Hock Monday and the women on Hock Tuesday. The inventory of 1485 lists elaborate equipment, with many of the items marked as the gifts of individuals. Among the silver plate there were four chalices, two candlesticks, two basins, two cruets, a pax, a chrismatory, and a monstrance 'to bear in the sacrament on Corpus Christi day'. In 1505 a new bell was purchased and a pulpit installed, without the need for a rate. In 1513 the women of the parish collected again towards the making of more pews, and in 1515 seventeen of them bore part of the cost of a cover for the font. One parishioner contributed £2 for the painting of two images in the rood-loft in 1518, when the parish also paid £4. 13s. 8d. for a new antiphoner. In the following year William Petyte bequeathed £20 for 'a new suit of copes'; the money was duly 'paid for a new blue suit bought at London'.

In the capital, too, the accounts of St Mary at Hill give the same impression of parochial and devotional vitality.[13] Although property rents produced a good proportion of the church's income, there were also gifts and bequests, parish collections for the rood light and Paschal candle, and Hock Monday and Hock Tuesday 'gatherings' as in any country parish. Some of the income was spent on communal celebrations. On Palm Sundays the parish mounted a play about the Old Testament prophets at the north door of the church. In 1525 the stage was repaired, and in 1531 the wardens paid for the hire of costumes and the making of false beards. In the 1520s, as there had been for decades before, there were parish processions on St Barnabas's day and Corpus Christi day; five dozen flower garlands were bought to be worn by the clergy and choristers and to decorate the three processional crosses, and parishioners carried torches. On these festal days the rector and churchwardens shared the cost of bread, ale, and wine for the choristers.

At St Mary's there was clearly a concern to maintain the appearance of the church and the quality of its services. In 1497 the rood-loft was moved, with a general refurbishment of the images; there were payments for repairs to the figures, for new crowns, and for 'painting and gilding of the rood, the cross, Mary and John, the four Evangelists and three diadems'. In the same year the liturgies for the new feasts of the Transfiguration and the Name of Jesus were copied into the service books. In 1504 new pews were installed for the women in the congregation, and in 1513 additional pews were set up for the men. Also in 1513, there was a reform of arrangements for the use of vestments and service equipment, especially for the six chantry priests, 'so the choir may be the better kept'. In 1515 the women collected £9. 10s. for a splendid new altar-cloth 'of white and red cloth of gold'. The altar cross and processional crosses were repaired in 1527–8, images were painted, and a goldsmith renewed the gilt on the candlesticks and censers.

Churchwardens' accounts show some variations in the sources of local revenue and the patterns of parish expenditure. St Mary at Hill owned rental property, St Andrew's Canterbury raised church rates, Morebath sold wool from its sheep, and Sherborne sold ale brewed by its 'king'. There was more enthusiasm for new images at Ashburton, Morebath, and Yatton than there was in Canterbury or London; perhaps urban churches had long since acquired as many images as could decently be accommodated. There was more attention to the festal calendar and liturgical niceties in London and Sherborne than in West Country parishes; perhaps the villages had less tradition of civic celebration. But the similarities between parishes seem more striking than the differences. Everywhere congregations were busy raising large sums of money, often in enjoyable ways, for the decoration of their churches and the maintenance of dignified worship. And in many places they made heavy investment in fabric improvement and new building.

The magnificent steeple at Louth was built from 1501 onwards, at the huge cost to a small town of £305. It was probably with relief as well as pride that the parishioners celebrated its completion in 1515, with a service, *Te Deum laudamus*, bell-ringing, and free ale all round. From 1520, St Andrew Undershaft in London was rebuilt; the richer parishioners contributed cash or building materials, and the poor offered their labour. At Great Dunmow in Essex in 1526, the building of the tower was financed by a collection; the largest subscription was £3. 6s. 8d., the smallest 1d., and a few refused to help. The Great Dunmow tower was a poor thing compared with Louth's, costing only £18. 15s. 9d., but then the parish paid £21. 8s. 6d. for a peal of bells and raised another £48 by collection for an organ. In 1533–4 the parishioners of Solihull rebuilt and extended their nave; some of them provided the timber, and others carried it to the church. The people of Sherborne found a neat solution to their desire for a grander church; in 1542 they bought the church of the suppressed abbey for £180, which they raised by selling the stone and lead of their old church and pawning their silver plate.[14]

From all parts of the country there is documentary and architectural evidence of extensive church building. In Somerset, the parish church of Long Sutton was completely rebuilt, and dedicated anew in 1493. In the same county, west towers were built in the early sixteenth century at Huish Episcopi, Shepton Beauchamp, and Whitestaunton. Martock church was given two new bays, a richly carved and painted nave roof, a north aisle, and two side chapels about 1513; Tintinhull's tower was extended and given a turret in 1516; Cleeve's tower was added in 1533; and St Mary Seavington was reconsecrated in 1543 after extensive rebuilding. There was widespread rebuilding in Cornwall and Devon, especially in the 1520s. In Suffolk the peak years for church building seem to have been in the later fifteenth century, but in the 1540s there was building work on at least eleven of the churches in the east of the county. Perhaps most remarkable of all is the building activity of Lancashire, where in the first half of the sixteenth century there was major work on a quarter of churches and thirty-eight completely new parochial chapels were built to serve outlying villages.[15]

All this costly activity suggests that local communities took great pride in their churches. Very large numbers of laymen and women had contributed, according to their means, to building projects. But parish churches were not the only religious institutions which received the loyalty—and the lucre—of the laity. Historians have only recently come to realize the great number and significance of religious guilds or fraternities.[16] These were primarily associations formed to provide funerals and prayers for deceased members, but many acquired other religious and social roles. The larger guilds, as at Abingdon, Chesterfield, Hull, Maidstone, Taunton, and Worcester, supported schools or almshouses for their members, and many others owned a guildhall for feasts and meetings. Those which could afford to employed their own priests to say masses for the souls of departed members, and those which could not kept bede rolls of the names of those for whom members should pray; probably all guilds maintained a candle before the image of a patronal saint or the rood.

The greatest of the guilds, such as Our Lady's in Boston and Holy Trinity in Coventry, had nation-wide membership and large resources. In the mid-1520s, Our Lady's Guild had an annual income of over £900 from property and subscriptions; it supported seven priests, twelve choristers, thirteen bedesmen, and a grammar school, and its papal privileges included remission of sins for all those who attended its services on the feasts of the Virgin and made offerings.[17] In the middle of the scale was the parish guild of St Peter at Bardwell in Suffolk, which served as a social club as well as a religious fraternity. Most of the adults of the village were members, and it had its own guildhall, with fine cutlery, a cook, and musicians for special occasions. Most common were the smallest fraternities, such as the Plough Guild at Kirton-in-Lindsey, the 'torchmen' at Wing, the 'brethren of the crosslight' at St Andrew's Canterbury, or the Young Mens' Guild at Morebath, which probably did no more than support candles in the churches and perhaps pay parish priests to read bede rolls of members.

Religious guilds were thus extremely varied; they were also extremely numerous. In London, eighty-one fraternities are known to have existed after 1500, and probably thirty of them were new groups. In Norwich twenty-one fraternities were recorded between 1510 and 1532, and in 1542 the small fenland town of Whittlesey had ten. Professor Scarisbrick has calculated that there were about a hundred and twenty fraternities in early sixteenth-century Lincolnshire, more than a hundred in Northamptonshire, and equal densities in East Anglia. These guilds retained their popularity, at least until 1530. The Palmer's Guild at Ludlow was recruiting at the rate of over two hundred a year between 1505 and 1509; the less fashionable Corpus Christi Guild at Boston gained about ten new recruits a year in the 1520s. Twenty-seven new members (at 3s. 4d. a time) joined the High Cross Guild at Stratford-upon-Avon in 1529–30, and fifty-three dead friends and relatives were enrolled to secure prayers for their souls. The Corpus Christi Guild at Coventry and the Holy Trinity Guild at Sleaford both recruited well in the 1520s, but then they slumped in the 1530s.

The larger guilds were certainly in decline after 1530, but probably because of the economic difficulties of the towns rather than any lack of enthusiasm for fraternities. The parish fraternities in the countryside, not dependent on urban rents, seem to have held their own, at least for a while. At West Tarring in Sussex, a county where guilds were not numerous, a new fraternity of St Mary was established in 1528 to support a priest in the parish church; it was still attracting benefactions a decade later. In Somerset, where fraternities were common, testators continued to make bequests to their guilds, until the government confiscated the assets in 1548. The High Cross Guild at Stratton in Cornwall supported its own chantry priest, kept a bede roll, and paid for obits by the vicar. It continued to attract new members from among local people, though its popularity waned from 1540; then in 1547 it gained twenty new recruits, anxious to get on the roll before the authorities closed it down.[18]

Fraternities were probably at their most popular in the 1510s and 1520s. In Norwich, only 6 per cent of testators had made bequests to guilds in the period 1370–1439, but 22 per cent made them in 1490–1517, though in 1518–32 the percentage fell to 14. Between 1393 and 1415, about 8 per cent of London testators had made gifts to guilds, but in the 1520s about a quarter did so. The large suburban parishes of London were especially likely to have successful fraternities, and probably 10 per cent of parishioners joined their local guild. The motives of the recruits to guilds were sometimes mixed. In Coventry guild membership was part of the career pattern of civic officials; ambitious young craftsmen joined the Corpus Christi Guild, and then graduated to the more prestigious Holy Trinity Guild in middle age. In Norwich, the fraternity of St George was the preserve of town dignitaries and East Anglian gentry, and it held a great procession with the mayor and alderman on its feast day. But most fraternities offered few social or economic advantages, and the benefits available were primarily religious.

Membership of a fraternity was one of the many ways in which men and women secured prayers for their souls. The widespread provision of prayers for the dead, to assist them from purgatory into heaven, suggests a general commitment to traditional religion. From a modest obit, or annual mass for named beneficiaries, to the perpetual endowment of a chantry priest to offer daily masses for the founder, the power of paid prayer was harnessed to the salvation of souls. In Devon and Cornwall, 70 per cent of testators in the 1520s left money for prayers of one kind or another. In the north of England between 1525 and 1540, 39 per cent of testators specifically asked for prayers at death, and 34 per cent for masses after death. In the archdeaconry of Huntingdon in 1529–30, 60 per cent of wills made bequests for prayers for the dead, though in the archdeaconry of Lincoln only 22 per cent did so. Professor Scarisbrick suggests that in the mid-1530s two-thirds of all will-makers made some formal arrangement for prayers or masses after death, and that most of the others expected prayers from their friends and relations. And parish evidence from Bristol suggests that wills alone seriously under-record the real provision for prayers.[19]

In some of the towns, it seems that the demand for endowed prayers had already peaked. Among richer Londoners, 43 per cent of will-makers had wished to endow masses in 1479–86, but only 36 per cent in 1523–5. In Norwich, 24 per cent of testators had made bequests for masses in 1370–1439; 44 per cent had done so in 1490–1517, but then 38 per cent in 1518–32. These shifts were slight, however. In York the last perpetual chantry was established in 1509, but the city alderman continued to augment existing chantries and it seems that economic difficulty rather than religious scepticism explains any contraction of demand for masses. In the rest of Yorkshire, enthusiasm for chantries was unabated, and fifty-nine chantries were endowed after 1500, despite the high cost and legal difficulty of making such foundations. In Lancashire, too, chantry-endowment continued; there eight chantries were established in the 1490s, seven in the next decade, eleven in the 1510s, and ten in the 1520s. After a statute of 1532, designed to conserve the Crown's feudal income, it was illegal to found perpetual chantries, but temporary endowments remained popular.[20]

Although there were variations from place to place, the overall demand for masses, and therefore for the priests to say them, was huge. Between 1490 and 1517, the citizens of Norwich endowed a total of 444 years of daily masses for the dead, and founded perpetual chantries for five priests, creating work for probably twenty-one additional priests.[21] With more chantries, more fraternities, more payments for prayers, more altars to popular saints, more chapels for outlying villages, came a need for more priests. The trends in ordinations to the priesthood suggest that from about 1450 there was a considerable expansion in the demand for clergy; there was certainly a large increase in the supply. In the diocese of York, for example, the number of secular priests ordained in a year rose from a low point of seventy-five in 1453 to a peak of 363 in 1508. The 1508 figure was a unique one, and the annual average was then about two hundred; but the Church in the North was recruiting more than twice as many ordinands each year at the beginning of the sixteenth century as it had done a century earlier.[22]

The ordination registers of the dioceses of Hereford, Lichfield, and Lincoln suggest similar patterns, though recruitment in London remained sluggish. Laymen were becoming priests in unprecedented numbers, and if ordinations fell back in the 1520s from the peaks of the previous decade it was only a relative decline from a very high level.[23] As never before, the laity were providing both the men who became priests and the posts which sustained them. For in addition to the compulsory funding of incumbents through tithe, laypeople were making voluntary endowments and payments to support additional priests. In the North and East Ridings of Yorkshire in 1526–7 there were 238 incumbents, 101 chantry priests, and 510 stipendiary priests; most of the 611 assistant clergy would have been funded by the laity on a voluntary basis. In the archdeaconry of Chester in 1541 there were more than 250 assistant clergy, over two-thirds of them paid by lay donations. In the diocese of Winchester in the same year there were 75 additional priests supported by individual gentlemen, 19 more paid by parishioners, and 9 funded by fraternities.[24]

The churches of England were well staffed in the early sixteenth century. There were many small country parishes served by single parish priests, but the larger parishes of the west and north and the town churches often had substantial staffs. In 1522 Holy Trinity church in Coventry was served by a vicar, two chantry priests, and eleven stipendiaries; St Michael's church had a vicar, six chantrists, and eighteen stipendiaries. At Holy Trinity Hull in 1525 there were twenty-five chaplains; the little Yorkshire parish of Bubwith had five priests, Bridlington had seven, and one parish in Newark had fifteen. These were exceptional cases, of course, but there were on average two priests for each parish in the dioceses of Lincoln, Canterbury, and Rochester.[25] There was some risk that the additional chaplains would become clerical drones, mere 'mass priests' who made no contribution to parish life. But even chantrists were expected to take part in the round of worship, and many of them acted as assistant curates in busy parishes.[26] There were many priests in England in about 1530, but not too many.

So in 1530, when Richard Whitford first published *A Work for Householders*, the conventional religion of late medieval England was at its most luxuriant and energetic. Two editions of *A Work* sold out in that year, and six editions of the ever-popular *Primer*.[27] In the archdeaconry of Lincoln, 93 per cent of testators made bequests to the cathedral, 76 per cent to their parish churches, 29 per cent to other churches, 22 per cent to the friars, 22 per cent to masses for souls, and 14 per cent to fraternities. In the Devon parish of Morebath, the vicar donated two sets of white vestments to the church, and the wardens made payments towards the new images of the Virgin and St George which were on order. At Cranbrook in Kent, the church's aisle was rebuilt, funded by a collection from parishioners. In Lancashire, a new chapel was built at Colton and a new chantry endowed at Croston. At Stratford-upon-Avon the living and the dead were recruited to the High Cross Guild in good numbers. And in Norwich, in April 1530, the rich grocer Robert Jannys made his will, witnessed by his parish curate and two other priests.[28]

Jannys wished to be buried in the chancel of his parish church, before the image of his protector, St George. He left £5 to the high altar for forgotten tithes, and asked his executors to buy two new copes for the church. He made meticulous arrangements for his funeral, and for prayers to be said across the city. He left money to the monks, friars, nuns, anchorites, and poor of Norwich, and contributed towards the running costs of his parish church for the next twenty years. He bequeathed £6 a year for twenty years for 'an honest priest and a good choir man to sing and pray for me and my friends and them that I am bound to pray for, in the church of St George', and £10 a year for ever to found a chantry and grammar school at his birthplace. His executors were also instructed to spend another £40 a year for twenty years 'for my soul and all Christian souls'. In all, Jannys left about half of his wealth to be used on religious causes and prayers: £800 to provision for souls, £420 to endow masses, about £160 to religious orders, £65 and the two copes to parish churches, £20 and some land to anchorites.

There is a very wide range of such evidence to suggest that the ordinary religion of English parishes was in a healthy and vigorous state in the early sixteenth century. Not everything was perfect, of course. In some of the towns, the revenues of fraternities were under pressure and the endowment of prayers had begun to wane. In the mid-1520s, the booming recruitment of priests faltered, though this was probably because of fears of over-supply and perhaps the impact of clerical taxation. These were minor setbacks caused mainly by economic disruptions, and they were not significant. If Londoners became marginally less likely to pay for prayers, they became very much more likely to pay for manuals of private devotion of a distinctly traditionalist tone. The English were investing heavily—perhaps more heavily than ever before—in their religion. There is nothing here to indicate that we are on the eve of a Reformation, or that there was any decay of conventional piety. The political Reformation in England was not preceded by a collapse of Catholic Christianity, or even by any real contraction, but by a consolidation of its considerable strength.

2

The Priests and Their People

IN 1530, the year when Richard Whitford published his devotional best-seller and Robert Jannys gave half his wealth to religion, the English Church nevertheless faced problems. John Stokesley, the newly appointed and energetic bishop of London, conducted a personal examination of curates in his diocese.[1] He assessed their educational and pastoral qualifications to serve as parish priests, and of the fifty-eight curates whose examinations survive only fourteen were declared adequate. Twenty-one priests, including two Frenchmen and an Irishman, were banned from service in the diocese because of their ignorance, and sixteen others were suspended as unsuitable; one curate resigned, and four were told to undertake further study and present themselves for re-examination later. Stokesley's survey seems to confirm the criticisms of parish priests by some contemporaries and many later historians; only a quarter of London curates were thought to be satisfactory, and two-thirds were found in some way inadequate. It was apparently a damning indictment of the capital's clergy.

In the same diocese in the same year, another of the Church's difficulties was demonstrated by disputes at the parish of Hayes in Middlesex.[2] There were mounting arguments over tithing customs, which eventually divided the parishioners into two parties, one led by the lessee of the rectorial tithes and his brother the vicar, the other group by a local alehouse-keeper. The opponents of the vicar organized a fee-strike at Easter 1530, and at harvest-time they assessed their own tithe corn and allowed their cattle to trample over the lessee's share. Thereafter matters got worse, with provocative behaviour on both sides, threats to the vicar and his curate, and a near riot during mass. Archbishop Warham tried to reimpose discipline on the parish by calling the offenders before his court, but his authority was rejected and the curate's vestments were stolen to prevent church services. The archbishop and the vicar, Henry Gold, finally had to take the case to the royal court of Star Chamber, and have the ringleaders of the opposition sent to prison.

The findings of Bishop Stokesley's inquiry and the troubles of Henry Gold must be set alongside the evidence we have seen of eager lay participation in traditional devotions. Such examples may suggest that although laypeople were in the main content with their religion, they were not content with their Church. The inadequacies of the clergy must have been only too obvious to the laity, and it is likely that laymen objected to the tithes and fees extracted by churchmen. Criticism of clerical defects and resistance to clerical demands—in short, anticlericalism—may thus explain the apparently inexplicable: how it was that the Catholic English nevertheless had a Reformation. But we must beware of exaggerating the significance of ecclesiastical difficulties, in a search for the origins of the Reformation. Some priests were unsatisfactory, since the clergy were fallible humans, not inspired saints; some exactions were irksome, since enthusiastic taxpayers have always been rare. It is not enough to find that there were problems—of course there were problems: we need to know how common and how divisive they were.

The London investigation in 1530 tells us very little about the real qualities of the priests, and even less about the laity's response to them. The examinations survive for only about half of the City curates, and the bishop may have concentrated on those thought to be insufficient; certainly he was examining curates, rather than the better-educated incumbents. Stokesley himself was a notable scholar who had impressed Erasmus, and his intellectual standards may have been unreasonably high; four of those to be dismissed for ignorance were university graduates! The expectations which city parishioners had of their curates were probably rather different from those of this former Oxford philosophy don. In 1530 Stokesley was a new broom in the diocese, anxious to be seen to be doing something after criticisms of parish clergy in Parliament and Convocation. His objectives were probably to impose his authority on the diocese, to cut a figure as a reformer, and to frighten his clergy into greater pastoral effort. When the bishop had made his point he could relax a little; at least a dozen of the curates banned from the diocese were in fact allowed to keep their posts.

Most of the evidence we have gives a much more favourable impression of the parish clergy than does Stokesley's unrealistic report, and much of it suggests that laypeople were content with their priests. When churchwardens and other parishioners were invited to complain of their clergy at the visitations of bishops and archdeacons, they did so remarkably infrequently. At Cardinal Morton's visitation of Suffolk in 1499, from 489 parishes there were only eight allegations of sexual laxity against priests, and only two priests were suspended for their ignorance. Forty-eight incumbents were found to be absent from their benefices, but in all but two cases they had appointed appropriate deputies and there was no suggestion of pastoral neglect.[3] At Archbishop Warham's visitation of 260 Kent parishes in 1511–12, six priests were suspected of sexual offences (and another pestered a woman without success), and four priests were said to be ignorant. There were complaints of pastoral neglect from about one-fifth of the parishes, but that was rarely the fault of individual priests, and only eleven men were wilfully negligent.[4]

It was much the same in the huge diocese of Lincoln, which sprawled across nine Midland counties. At visitations of over a thousand parishes between 1514 and 1521, only twenty-five accusations of sexual misconduct were made against priests. We do not know how many of the Lincoln clergy actually offended against the rule of celibacy, but we do know that only in this small number of cases did churchwardens object sufficiently strongly to make a charge. It seems that what parishioners expected from their clergy was, above all, the proper fulfilment of liturgical and pastoral responsibilities, and it was negligence in this respect that was most likely to be reported. There were seventeen complaints that services were not conducted regularly, twelve that rituals were carelessly performed, seven that priests had failed to preach or visit the sick, and five that they were too old or infirm to perform their duties. But these are remarkably few reported failures from 1,006 Lincoln parishes and probably 2,000 serving priests. Though reformers might criticize, parishioners seemed satisfied.[5]

It is, perhaps, surprising just how well the parish clergy fulfilled their pastoral tasks. There was, after all, no formal preparation for priesthood. Probably 90 per cent of priests had acquired all their learning at a local school, their liturgical training by assisting at a parish altar, and their pastoral skills by observation, supplemented by private study of the handbooks for parish clergy. Those who attended the universities found little in the syllabuses which related to parish work. By the early sixteenth century young men were offering themselves for ordination in unprecedented numbers, and some Jeremiahs thought standards had declined. Thomas More claimed that once 'few men durst presume to take upon them the high office of a priest, not even when they were chosen and called thereunto. Now runneth every rascal and boldly offereth himself for able.'[6] But it was not the greater presumption of candidates which led them to ordination, nor even greater piety; it was probably the enhanced clerical career opportunities brought by new fraternities and endowments.[7]

There were examinations before ordination, handled by diocesan officials and cathedral clergy, but it was difficult to hold back the flow of ordinands and hard to be thorough when queues were long. Examiners seemed reluctant to reject any who could reach minimum standards, and there was little attempt to be more selective as supply boomed. Candidates were supposed to establish their family background, age, and financial support, and to be questioned on their morals and knowledge of the faith: the Creed, Commandments, sacraments, and the liturgy. It is probable that, when in larger dioceses two or three examiners had to deal with a hundred or more candidates at each ordination, the tests were not searching; and there was no investigation whether an ordinand had any real vocation for clerical life. But examination of priests before institution to a benefice was apparently stricter, and was sometimes conducted by the bishop himself. Several bishops instituted candidates only on condition that they undertook further study; in 1526 Bishop Longland found the vicar of Waterperry near Oxford unsuitable even on re-examination, and removed him from the benefice.[8]

The bishops relied upon regular discipline rather than careful selection to keep their clergy up to the mark, and they were generally successful. They aimed especially to ensure that the demands of parishioners for proper pastoral care were met. When the diocese of Canterbury was visited in 1511–12, church fabric and services were the main areas of investigation. Almost a quarter of the parishes had some defects in church buildings or equipment, often the fault of monastic appropriators. Those responsible were called before the archbishop's commissary, and timetables for repair were imposed. In a fifth of Canterbury parishes there had been some neglect of services or pastoral care, and again monasteries were sometimes responsible. At West Langdon and at Lydden, for example, Langdon Abbey had failed to provide resident priests to serve the cures, and the abbot was ordered to supply properly paid curates. At other parishes, such as Sholden, Stone, and some of the Dover churches, services were neglected because poor stipends could not attract priests, and the archbishop tried to negotiate increases. With benefices vacant, fears that there were too many priests were presumably unfounded.

Canterbury diocese was especially likely to have pastoral problems, for its parishes were small and there was a high rate of appropriation, so clerical incomes were low. In other dioceses the difficulties were sometimes less obvious, but episcopal supervision was no less vigorous. Bishops used the temporary confiscation of revenues to enforce the proper serving of cures, and sometimes deprived defaulters of their benefices. In the diocese of Norwich, Bishop Nykke sequestrated the fruits of forty benefices between 1507 and 1516, twenty-three of them because the cures were not properly served and five because of dilapidation of buildings. After his visitation of the diocese in 1532, Nykke deprived nine incumbents for negligence. Bishop Boothe of Hereford imposed ten sequestrations in 1521–5, nine of them for neglect of cures and one for neglect of fabric through non-residence. In the archdeaconry of Winchester, at least twenty-one sequestrations were in force in 1527, most of them for faults in fabric or pastoral care.[9]

Such negligence was not often the fault of resident priests; if nothing else, pressure from their parishioners ensured that resident clergy did their duty. Neglect of cures was usually because monastic rectors failed to supply vicars or because absentee incumbents did not provide curates. Bishops did their best to tackle these problems. In 1520 Bishop West of Ely cited five religious houses to answer charges of neglect of their churches, and when representatives failed to appear the livings were sequestered. In the diocese of Exeter, Bishop Veysey sequestered five monastic rectories in the 1520s, and in 1524 he warned a number of institutions to make the prescribed gifts to the poor in their appropriated parishes. The impact of non-residence by incumbents was also monitored. In Lincoln diocese between 1514 and 1521, about a quarter of parishes reported the absence of their incumbents, but in only a very small number of cases did neglect ensue as absentees provided curates rather than face sequestration of revenues.[10]

Most English dioceses appear to have been well run in the early sixteenth century, and the supervision of parochial care was a high administrative priority. In the diocese of London under Bishop Tunstall, his vicar-general kept a careful watch on absenteeism, and few incumbents were non-resident without official permission and proper substitutes. There was also a check on absentees from other dioceses. In September 1523 the vicar-general discovered that a chantry priest at St Michael's Queenhithe was also incumbent of Downham in Norwich; the priest was given four weeks to leave the diocese of London, and forbidden to serve there again. In the same year six other offenders were driven from the diocese, and there were similar cases in succeeding years.[11] It was not very different in the dioceses of Ely, Exeter, Hereford, Lincoln, Norwich, and York. So it seems that parish clergy were caught between the discipline of their bishops and the demands of their people. Whatever their motives for seeking ordination, however slight the tests of their suitability, most of them were forced to be hard-working pastors.

The vast majority of conscientious priests fitted easily into parish society. Many of them were local men, serving in or near their birthplaces; this was certainly so in country districts, and was even true in the city of Norwich. About one in ten of the sons of early Tudor Norwich citizens became a priest, and about a fifth of Norwich families had a son in the Church. So priests were not a race apart; they were sons, brothers, cousins. Despite the rhetorical stereotypes of lecherous curates and idle monks, the individual priest was usually a man of prestige and generally trusted. Over half of all wills were witnessed by parish priests, and in testamentary disputes a priest was assumed to be fair and impartial.[12] High ordinations suggest that priesthood was esteemed; recruitment had been much lower a century before, when clergy were much criticized. In any form of collective village action, whether negotiation with a landlord, riot over enclosure, or full-scale rebellion, the clergy were usually to the fore, not only because they were literate but also because their presence gave legitimacy to a cause. Parish priests were leading members of each community, usually responsive and respected.

It would therefore be surprising if disputes such as that which we have seen rocked Hayes in 1530 were at all common. Priests and parishioners had to get along together, and the reasonable requests of conscientious clergy were unlikely to be refused. Hayes was not a typical parish, and Henry Gold was not a typical vicar. The patron of the benefice and lord of the manor was Archbishop Warham, who in 1516 had presented his kinsman, the archdeacon of Canterbury, to the rectory of Hayes. The archdeacon never resided at Hayes, and leased the rectory to Thomas Gold, a sharp Middle Temple lawyer. In December 1529 Gold presented his brother Henry to a vicarage at Hayes, and then the trouble began. It seems that Thomas Gold tried to use his legal expertise to increase the profits on his lease, and his relationship with the archbishop to pressurize the parish. Henry Gold, a former fellow of St John's College Cambridge and chaplain to the archbishop, was a less than committed pastor; he later explained his failure to preach to parishioners as reluctance to cast pearls before swine.[13] The Golds deserved all the trouble they got.

Other aggressive tithe-owners caused resentment, and drove parishioners to resist. At Barfreston in Kent in 1511, the rector, Henry Tankerd, ignored tithing customs and demanded higher rates of personal tithe and tithe on young animals. He tried to force objectors into conformity by denying them holy bread and holy water, and seeking bonds for good behaviour from the justices. Tankerd seems to have united his parish against him: 'he is so malicious against them that they cannot suffer it but must depart their habitation', the churchwardens claimed. When relations between rector and people had so obviously broken down, Archbishop Warham had little choice but to remove the cantankerous cleric. At Chilham in Kent, the vicar had also been making unreasonable tithing demands, 'that no vicar of no time of mind was wont to have'. Robert Pele had sought a higher tithe on young animals, a tithe from old (as well as the usual young) wood, and a charge on every cart or plough. In response, the parishioners had established a common fund to fight him, and had recruited local notables in support of their cause.[14]

It would not be difficult to multiply such cases, especially from the 1510s on as inflation began to bite, and force the hard-pressed or the greedy to seek higher tithe. But historians have too often selected dramatic anecdotes from the court records, without placing them in their context. In fact, tithe suits in the ecclesiastical courts were remarkably rare. In the 250 parishes of the diocese of Canterbury there were fourteen tithe suits in 1482 and four in 1531; from its 1,148 parishes, Norwich diocese had ten cases a year in the early 1520s; Winchester had two suits from its 339 parishes in 1527 and three in 1529; and the 650 parishes of Lichfield diocese yielded only ten cases in 1525 and four in 1530. Few of these suits were the outcome of bitter clashes between incumbents and whole parishes; most were brought by a rector against one or two defendants, and the root of a case was often disagreement over the ownership of tithe rather than anyone's reluctance to pay. Tithe cases did not become common in the courts until the 1540s, when new economic pressures strained parish relationships.[15]

Of course, tithe disputes in parishes were more frequent than tithe suits in the courts, though rectors were criticized for their readiness to resort to litigation. But if disagreement over tithing had been at all common, there would surely have been many more tithe cases. It is not suggested here that the payment of tithe in the early sixteenth century was any more popular than the payment of income tax in the twentieth, but that the necessity of tithe, like that of tax, was generally recognized. Arguments arose not over the principle of tithing, but over the rules for assessment and the method of collection. Tithing was a complex business, and in parishes with mixed agriculture and small industries assessment must have been a constant process of negotiation. But to suggest that this often led to bitterness would be misleading, for when incumbents and parishioners had to live together there were strong pressures towards agreement. Even the institution of legal proceedings did not always signal a breakdown in bargaining. Clergy used suits as incentives to settle, and a good proportion of tithe cases ended in compromise.[16]

The few tithe cases which dragged at length through the courts and did cause real resentments were those in which the incentive to compromise was low: where the rector was a monastery or an absentee. Although religious houses were no more likely than other rectors to initiate tithe suits, they were particularly likely to be involved in long and contentious ones. The abbot of Whalley fought five men of Marsden near Colne through the courts of the archdeacon of Chester and the Duchy of Lancaster between 1532 and 1534, and called in the earl of Derby and the Duchy Council to help ensure victory. The law, as well as political influence, seem to have been on the abbot's side, and it is significant that the Marsden five got no support from fellow parishioners; they had to forge signatures on a document claiming the custom of the parish was on their side. But it was an expensive and bitter battle, with violence against the curate, accusations against the abbot of malicious prosecution, and a persistent refusal by the five to obey the decrees of the courts, both secular and ecclesiastical.[17]

Monastic appropriators had less need to make the tithing concessions which were wise for the resident incumbent, and so had absentees, whose curates might take the brunt of any local hostility. In 1532 the non-resident rectors of the London parishes of All Hallows Lombard Street, St Benet Gracechurch, St Leonard Eastcheap, and St Magnus sought to overturn recent tithe agreements and sued their parishioners in the Court of Arches for higher rates. The parishioners responded by appeals to the Common Council of London, the king's secretary, and Star Chamber, and defeated their rectors by a threat of praemunire. If appropriators and absentees had less call to compromise, so too did their parishioners, who felt no loyalty to distant tithe-owners and would fight them without qualm. The most persistent problems of tithe-resistance by Londoners arose in the parishes of notorious absentee pluralists, especially in John Palsgrave's St Dunstan in the East and Maurice Griffith's St Magnus.[18]

London posed particular problems in tithe assessment, and the common interests of citizens may have aligned them against their rectors, though not necessarily against priests in general. If the tithing of wood and animals posed difficulties in country areas, they were slight compared with the complexities of tithing profits, rents, and wages in towns. From 1453, tithe in London was regulated by a bull of Pope Nicholas V; householders paid tithe based on the rental value of property, and others were to make token offerings at Easter. But this agreement was breaking down by the 1520s, as rent increases made higher payments due and as higher prices discouraged the poor from making what were in effect voluntary payments. The Common Council imposed a new settlement in 1528, but as this favoured the rich against poor householders there was reluctance to pay at the new rates. Royal arbitrators proposed compromise rates in 1534, which were to apply to personal tithes as well as rents, but disputes continued and there was no definitive settlement until 1546.[19]

Lay–clerical relations were more difficult in London. In a sprawling and expanding metropolis, parish boundaries meant little and there was presumably less community loyalty to a particular church and its incumbent; fraternities may have counted for more. Rich city benefices went to well-connected absentees and busy administrators, leaving pastoral care to the curates. Laymen were well organized in their companies and Common Council, and likely to get their way in any political showdown. But the problems of London should not be exaggerated. The quarrels over tithe were between different groups of the laity as well as between parishioners and incumbents, and most Londoners had some conscience over tithe; 70 per cent of testators made bequests 'for my tithes and oblations by me forgotten or negligently withholden, if any such be, in discharging of my soul', or some such formula. Only one-third of city parishes produced tithe litigation between 1520 and 1546; on average, it was one case for each parish every eight years, just as in Lancashire in 1541–59.[20] Tithe conflict was not endemic; it was occasional, the product of particular circumstances or aggressive individuals.

But tithe was not the only, or even the most divisive, financial demand of the clergy. It is usually supposed that the mortuary, called a 'dead corpse present' in some places, was an insensitive and offensive exaction. There is some evidence to suggest that both priests and people thought themselves badly treated over mortuaries. About 1509 the bailiffs and leading citizens of Kingston upon Thames signed a protest that their vicar, the absentee diplomat Nicholas West, had broken local custom 'in taking of mortuaries otherwise than hath been taken and used time out of mind'.[21] In 1511 the monks of Dover complained that the mayor and officers of the town were withholding mortuaries due to the priory from the parish of St Martin's, but this may have been a bargaining ploy in a struggle over jurisdiction and the fees were paid within a month.[22] Also in 1511 there began the London *cause célèbre*, the case of Richard Hunne, who refused to pay a mortuary on behalf of his dead infant son. However, as we shall see, it was a year before Hunne was sued, and then in suspicious circumstances.

In Lancashire in 1514 John Cokeson of Sefton refused to give a 'fat ox' to the rector as a mortuary for his late wife, arguing that she had died in another parish. The rector, a grasping member of a powerful local family, had the ox seized and impounded Cokeson's cattle to teach him a lesson. The mortuary was simply one issue in a running conflict: Cokeson's wife had already been dead for seven years, and he was in debt to the rector on another matter. There was apparently some disagreement over mortuary customs at Lancaster in 1524, when the vicar and four local men drew up a sliding scale of fees based on the wealth of the deceased. In 1526 there was a long wrangle between the abbot of Whalley and the parishioners of Walton-le-dale: the abbot demanded mortuaries for the first time and the parishioners refused to pay. The Lichfield consistory court finally dismissed the case when the defendants produced a testimonial from their neighbours that mortuaries had customarily never been given in their village.[23]

Arguments over mortuaries were, like arguments over tithe, the occasional products of particular contexts: an innovating outsider at Kingston, a trouble-making sea-lawyer in London, or an aggressive abbot at Walton-le-dale. At Dover and at Sefton, mortuaries were mere weapons in wider local conflicts, and at Lancaster the issue was settled amicably. The abbot of Whalley certainly tried to maximize income, but the house was unusually generous in its charity. Mortuaries were not an attractive impost, but they were not a major problem and they rarely provoked litigation. Suits may have been more common in the archdeaconry of Leicester in the 1520s, but the evidence is scrappy and less than conclusive. There were only eight mortuary cases in the court of the archdeacon of Chester between 1502 and 1529, and only about one a year in the courts at Canterbury and Norwich. Mortuaries were, in some circumstances, refused, but it was not true that, as the lawyer-propagandist St German was to claim, 'there were few things within this realm that caused more variance among the people'.[24]

The records of diocesan visitations and court proceedings seem clear. Parishioners made few complaints about the learning, morals, or commitment of their clergy, and paid their tithes and mortuaries without undue protest. But it may be unrealistic to draw such a sketch of cosy Catholicism, to explain away every deficiency as a special case and every argument as an aberration. There were few neglectful parish priests, few grasping monastic appropriators, few greedy non-resident rectors, but added together these were more than a few occasions for dissatisfaction. Furthermore, what began as an isolated disagreement between individuals could bring a parishioner face to face with the Church as a powerful institution. As complainants against their priests and as defendants in tithe and mortuary suits, the laity appeared in Church courts, and there is some evidence these tribunals were distrusted. 'Spiritual persons cleave together like burrs, and will sooner do for a priest in an unjust cause than for a layman in a very righteous cause', it was claimed by some laypeople.[25]

It is not hard to produce examples of lay hostility towards Church courts and their sanctions. When John Cray of River heard he was to be presented at the Canterbury visitation of 1511 for absence from church services, he was not impressed: he 'sayeth that he setteth not a straw by the suspension of the commissary or official'. In the diocese of Lincoln at about the same time, one man tore up a citation to appear before the court of audience, and another called the chancellor a false judge. When William Bankes of Loughborough was given a particularly stiff penance in 1527 he told the court, 'I will not swear nor do no penance for you, nor ye shall not be my judge, for I do intend to go to a superior judge!' He was brought to heel only by excommunication and imprisonment, and after his submission he was paraded through the town while an apparitor proclaimed his disobedience to the Church.[26] However, such expressions of bravado or ill temper were rare, and it is clear that, in general, laypeople did set 'a straw by the suspension of the commissary'.

Willing co-operation with the processes of the ecclesiastical courts was widespread, though not universal. The apparitors of the diocese of London delivered as many as a thousand summonses a year, but in only one case a year, on average, did an officer encounter violence or abuse. In the diocese of Canterbury, in the late fifteenth century, three-quarters of defendants in instance suits appeared when first cited before the consistory; almost as many appeared to face office prosecutions before the archdeacon's court in the early sixteenth.[27] Those who had failed to appear were suspended from attendance at church services, and though some disregarded this prohibition it was enough to force most to conform. In the neighbouring diocese of Chichester, suspension remained a powerful sanction in the 1520s, and it was rarely necessary to proceed to the more drastic step of excommunication. Some defendants fled from the diocese to avoid suspension, and those suspended invariably submitted before the next court session.[28] It was to be different later, but before the 1530s the Church's sanctions were effective.

It was not only fear of suspension which produced co-operation with Church courts: it was also their utility. By comparison with most secular jurisdictions, the ecclesiastical court system offered cheap, speedy, and convenient methods of sorting out laymen's business. At least until the 1530s, the vast majority of litigation was promoted by, and concerned the interests of, the laity. Most instance suits related to lay matters of debt, marriage, slander, and testamentary provision; most office prosecutions arose from reports by churchwardens and parishioners, and related to the control of sexual behaviour (an issue of lay concern, not of priestly prurience).[29] It is true that instance business was in decline by the 1510s; as we shall see, the common lawyers recaptured the contract litigation they had lost in the mid-fifteenth century, and developed forms of action to deal with slanders alleging breach of secular law. But the loss of such business was apparently rapid only in London, where there were convenient alternatives to Church courts, and elsewhere the Church continued to provide vital legal services at a reasonable price.

It would be foolish to argue that the Church's courts made it popular. Legal fees are always too high, litigation always too lengthy, procedures always too complex, and judgements always unfair—to the losers. But it would also be foolish to suggest that the Church's courts necessarily made it *un*popular. Despite the claims to be made in 1529 and 1532, the courts gave probate of wills swiftly and cheaply, and most judges sought to settle disputes quickly and by agreement rather than to drag them out in the interests of fee income. The disciplinary powers of the Church were invoked by laymen to maintain socially acceptable behaviour in their communities, and a high proportion of the accused confessed or were convicted.[30] When in 1527 William Bankes of Loughborough was given his humiliating penance, for fathering two bastards on his niece, he raged against the judge; but perhaps his wife, his brother, their neighbours, the churchwardens who had reported him, and even his niece, thought justice had been done.

There were always a few malcontents who resented the authority of the Church and its clergy. At the Canterbury visitation of 1511 it was reported that Robert Trussell of Wichling was 'evil disposed toward the church', and had refused to pay his tithes and the rent for a pasture belonging to the parish; but he had recently served as churchwarden, and the new wardens seem to have been hounding him. When the vicar of Seasalter had asked for his tithe, Richard Port had responded with violence, and the vicar had prosecuted him at common law. There were trouble-makers at Milton. John Joye had told the vicar 'that he is as well occupied when he is about his tubs as the vicar when he is at mass', and William Valeys had said, 'a priest should say mass in a cruse or that he spend a halfpenny to buy a chalice'. But there was provocation: the vicar of Milton was a non-resident pluralist, and the parish priest had annoyed the townsmen by grazing cattle and horses in the churchyard.[31]

Worst of all was the situation revealed at Kennington in 1511; there

Richard Ricard and his friends terrorized the vicar and most of the parish. Ricard 'is so infest against priests that he is ever talking of them and ready to say the worst against them and their order', and at sermon times Thomas Fuller would heckle the preacher from the church porch. The gang had assaulted the vicar, threatened those who served at mass, and brought the services of the church almost to a halt. The campaign against the vicar may have resulted from his threat to report Ricard's sexual promiscuity; certainly Ricard had tried to prevent the wardens attending the visitation by accusing them of treason. Perhaps there was more to it, for Robert May (husband of one of Ricard's girl-friends) was an alehouse heretic. It was said he 'raileth against preachers', refused holy water and holy bread, and 'said it were as good to roast meat with the images of the church as with other wood, all is one thing'. But even Ricard's thugs dared not stand against the Church and their fellow parishioners. They all appeared before the commissary when cited, and Ricard went off to war to avoid finding compurgators.[32]

It was hard to defy the Church, for there was general support for its authority and rules. Heretics were at constant risk, not only from the prying of priests and apparitors but also from the suspicions of strangers and the hostility of neighbours. When Thomas Harding of Amersham abjured before Bishop Smith in 1511, he was made to wear the heretic's badge of a faggot. Four years later he secured release from this humiliation, on condition that he remained in Amersham, except for an annual pilgrimage to Ashridge. He observed these terms until 1522, when Bishop Longland reimposed the badge because of Harding's refusal to name heretics. Harding was, literally, a marked man. In 1532 he was seen reading a book in a wood outside Chesham, and reported to the officers of the town. His house was searched by angry townsmen, and an English Bible found hidden under the floorboards. After trial before Longland, Harding was burned at Chesham. According to John Foxe, an indulgence of forty days had been announced for those who carried wood to the fire, and people from miles around got their children to take faggots. There was a large crowd at the burning; though some bewailed Harding's fate many others rejoiced at his suffering and one man threw a block of wood at him.[33]

Most early Tudor heretics were descendants—often literal as well as spiritual—of the early followers of John Wycliffe: the Lollards. Wycliffe's condemnation of the wealth and privileges of the fourteenth-century clergy had attracted laymen hard-pressed by war taxation. His attacks upon the traditional sacramental doctrines of the Church (and especially his denial of transubstantiation of the bread and wine in the eucharist) had been much more controversial, but both materialist sceptics and seekers for less mechanical devotions had responded. Above all, Wycliffe's stress on the authority of the Bible, and the provision by his Oxford disciples of an

English translation, gave literate laypeople the opportunity of religious independence. But the Lollard moment had passed, and their Oldcastle rebellion in 1414 lost them any support among gentry and intellectuals. Some of the best evidence for Lollard survival lies in their manuscripts of the Bible and early tracts, but few of them were written (or even copied) after about 1430.[34] Lollardy was not crushed, but it was an unpopular heresy, and the bishops found willing lay allies when they mounted drives of persecution.

Even around Amersham, a Lollard centre, the faggot emblem was a badge of shame; there and in London convicted heretics tried to conceal their badges, or went without them. When the merchant Richard Hunne was suspected of heresy in 1512, the resulting loss of trade forced him to bring a slander action to try to clear his name. In 1515 the bishop of London claimed there was sympathy for heretics in the city, but the indignant Court of Aldermen sent a deputation to deny it. Seven years later, a Londoner began defamation proceedings when she was told, 'Thou art an heretic for thou tookest not thy rights at Easter'. A heresy accusation was a handy weapon against an enemy, and unpopular individuals were likely victims. In 1520 the miller of Clitheroe, who had been charging higher tolls, was reported to the halmote court: 'the said Nicholas behaves as if he were heretic and fanatic, and he is deemed among his neighbours not to hold the Catholic faith.' Also in Lancashire, in 1537 Thomas Hoskyn sued his wife's cousin after she had spread a rumour that he had refused to have his child christened.[35]

In this McCarthyite atmosphere of antagonism and distrust, Lollards formed frightened and introspective groups. Robert Bartlett confessed in 1521 that if an outsider came upon his Amersham Bible-study meeting, 'then they would say no more but all keep silence'. The Lollard parson of Horton in Buckinghamshire, Robert Freeman, was seen reading a book, so he rapidly closed it and hid it away in his bedroom. Before the vicar of Windrush near Burford introduced Roger Dods to his Lollard ideas, he swore him to secrecy.[36] Even the household unit was not necessarily secure. In about 1513, Thomas Collins of Ginge near Wantage admitted to his horrified son that he did not believe in transubstantiation; the mother just managed to dissuade young John from turning his father over to the authorities. Before the Bible could be safely read aloud in a Lollard family near Staines, the servants had to be sent out. Hatred of heresy could even override marriage vows: when Alice Doyly, an Oxfordshire gentlewoman, came under suspicion in 1521, her orthodox husband drove her from the house—or perhaps heresy was his excuse![37]

It is difficult to regard the Lollards as a major threat to the Church, or as evidence of any substantial disaffection from conventional religion. As Thomas More pointed out in 1533, if anyone surveyed the English dioceses 'except London and Lincoln he shall scant in any one of all the remnant find punished for heresy four persons in five year'.[38] The Lollards were not a big problem—but they were a problem, and they were ultimately to exercise an influence out of all proportion to their numbers. The main Lollard centres were, as More knew, the small towns and villages of the Chilterns, some parishes in the City of London, and parts of northern Essex. But there were also concentrations of heretics in Bristol and Coventry, and in the cloth townships of the Kentish Weald. There were scatterings of Lollards elsewhere, especially in the cloth-making villages of Gloucestershire, Wiltshire, and Berkshire, and in the Stour valley in Suffolk, though hardly any of them in the west, the Midlands, or the north of England.

But it is probably inaccurate to think in terms of a fixed distribution of Lollardy, for it was an amorphous and shifting phenomenon, subject to forceful external pressures. Bishop Alnwick's systematic investigations in the diocese of Norwich in 1428–9 produced a crop of sixty heretics from around Loddon and Beccles in Norfolk. Their leader and teacher, William White, was burned with two others in 1428, and over the next three years the rest were made to abjure and do public penance. These determined proceedings destroyed Lollardy as an organized movement in the area, and there was virtually no sign of heresy there until 1511.[39] There were secret Lollards, no doubt, but secrecy is a recipe for contraction, not growth. Archbishop Warham's persecution in Kent in 1511 was not quite as successful as Alnwick's, but five burnings and more than thirty abjurations forced the heretics of the Weald into obscurity for a decade and more. The strength of Lollardy in Buckinghamshire was eroded by the proceedings of Bishop Smith in 1511, and almost destroyed by Bishop Longland's energetic efforts in 1521–2.[40]

Smith had secured formal recantations from about sixty Chilterns heretics, and four more were burned; in addition he warned others that 'they should live among their neighbours as good Christian men should do'.[41] Longland's investigation was much more elaborate, and much more successful. He began by interrogating those who had abjured in 1511, and demanded names of heretics as evidence of their sincerity. Those accused were then questioned on their own heretical contacts, until Longland had the names of nearly 400 suspects from the area of Amersham, Chesham, and Missenden, and others from the Burford district west of Oxford. Four were burned for their heresy, and about fifty more recanted and did public penance. The impact of the campaign was dramatic; some of the known heretics were driven into poverty by public hostility, the economy of Amersham was undermined, and Buckinghamshire heresy was crippled. When Richard Saunders, one of the leading Amersham Lollards, died in 1524, he left an impeccably conservative will: he asked to be buried before an image of Thomas Becket, and endowed a year of masses for his soul.[42]

The evidence generated by Longland's proceedings, with other material, enables us to draw a social profile of Chilterns Lollardy. Richard Saunders was by far the richest man in Amersham, and both there and in the rural parishes Lollards were drawn from the middling ranks of society rather than from the poor. This seems also to have been true of the Coventry heretics who were dealt with in 1511–12, and in London Lollards were rich merchants as well as artisans. In Amersham, where Lollard influence may have been stronger than anywhere else in England, suspects formed about 25 per cent of taxpayers and perhaps 10 per cent of the total population.[43] The Chilterns heretics who were subjected to detailed interrogation all tended to name each other, suggesting a fairly restricted core group in each locality. There thus seems to have been a committed nucleus of Lollard families, which were related to each other, with a wider penumbra of sympathizers, and those who had picked up stray slogans. It was the determined few who attended Lollard Bible classes, taught each other to recite the Epistle of St James, and sometimes learned to read so that they could study the New Testament.

Informed Lollards, in the Chilterns and elsewhere, held beliefs they knew to be 'heretical' and which formed a coherent Wycliffite position. John Whitehorne, rector of Letcombe Basset in Berkshire, recanted seven articles of heresy in 1499. He had denied the real presence of Christ in the eucharist and the need for confession to a priest, and objected to reverence towards images; he had deliberately rejected the Church in which he served, claiming 'that the pope is Antichrist, and other ministers of the Church be his disciples'. Whitehorne was denounced again in 1508. He admitted that he had hidden heretical books in his church, and sheltered heretics who had escaped from prison in London. He was degraded from his orders, and handed over to the sheriff to be burned.[44] But others were less sure what heresy was. 'Lollards' may have been created from the sceptical and the misinformed by the lawyers and theologians who questioned them. It was claimed that some of those who abjured before Smith in 1511 were 'simple folk who could not answer for themselves, and therefore were oppressed by the power of the bishop'.[45]

Some heresy was a consciously adopted heterodox position; some was just an odd idea overheard in an alehouse. John Dissenger, a Rochester joiner, 'heard say in the city of London that we should not worship saints, but God only', and 'heard say that a man should not show his confessor all his sins that he had done'. Richard Flint of Topcliffe in Yorkshire did not make his confession in 1541 or 1542, 'saying the cause moving him to the same was that there was a saying in the country that a man might lift up his heart and confess himself to God Almighty'.[46] Some of those dealt with by Longland in 1521 may have been materialist sceptics rather than deliberate Lollards; about thirty had denied a real presence in the communion, and a similar number opposed veneration of images. One farm worker had declared, 'I thresh Almighty God out of the straw'; another man went off to light a candle to 'Block Almighty'. Paul Lomely of Gravesend scoffed in 1526 'that these priests maketh us to believe that the singing bread they hold over their heads is God, and it is but a cake!'[47]

It is hard to know the significance of heresy. In London and Bristol and Coventry, in Amersham and Great Marlow, Cranbrook and Tenterden, Colchester and Steeple Bumpstead, there were established Lollard communities; elsewhere there were scattered groups and individuals, and more widely still there were stray heresies and misconceptions. The detected Lollards may have been the tip of a more considerable iceberg, but the general hostility towards heresy suggests reporting rates were probably high and the submerged section of the iceberg therefore not very large. The old, blind, and irascible Bishop Nykke reported in 1530 on heresy in his diocese of Norwich: 'the gentlemen and the commonty be not greatly infect, but merchants and such that hath their abiding not far from the sea.'[48] Heretics were, like critics of Church courts, refusers of tithes, and complainers against the clergy, far from numerous, even by 1530. There were high levels of compliance with the Church's discipline and conformity to its beliefs; there were few signs of a future Reformation.

3

Books Banned and Heretics Burned

IN 1530 Nicholas Field, a Londoner who had recently travelled in Germany, addressed a small gathering of Chilterns Lollards at the house of John Taylor in Hughenden. He read to them from an English Bible, probably Tyndale's New Testament, and told them what he had seen and learned 'beyond the sea in Almany'. Pilgrimages, images, saints' days, fasting, and offerings to the church were unnecessary observances; services should be in the vernacular; and the eucharist 'was not, as it was pretended, the flesh, blood, and bone of Christ, but a sacrament, that is a typical signification of his holy blood'. The discussion which followed turned to the subject of purgatory: William Wingrave said there was no such thing, and tried to prove his point mathematically: 'If there were any purgatory and every mass that is said should deliver a soul out of purgatory, there should be never a soul there, for there be more masses said in a day than there be bodies buried in a month!'[1]

Also in 1530, John Ryburn, of nearby Princes Risborough, confessed the heresies he had acquired from the priest Thomas Lound, who had spent two years with Luther in Wittenberg. Ryburn too had learned that services should be in English, and, probably, that faith in Christ justifies: 'The blood of our Lord Jesus Christ hath made satisfaction for all ill deeds that were done or should be done, and therefore it was no need to go on pilgrimage.' James Algar got into trouble in 1530 too, for denying purgatory and instructing his executors not to use his money for the good of his soul.[2] Now some of these ideas would not be new to Buckinghamshire Lollards, and we only know what they remembered, not what Field and Lound had actually told them. But there are strong hints that justification by faith had been taught, the attacks on the Latin service and masses satisfactory may have derived from Luther, and the assertion that the eucharist was a sign perhaps came from Oecolampadius or Zwingli. Native English heresy was coming under new and potent influences.

Bishop Nykke of Norwich recognized as much. He did not suppose that heresy was a major threat in 1530, but he knew that it was a growing one. The Lollards had been a continuing but well-contained problem; if they had made some new converts, they had also lost adherents by persecution and more natural wastage. Although greater episcopal vigilance had made

Lollardy appear to expand from about 1496, it is unlikely that it had really done so, or at least, not by very much. The great heresy drives of 1511 had not revealed new centres of heresy, they had rediscovered old groups. But Nykke now identified new dangers: the spread of heresy in the University of Cambridge, and the importation of heretical books by merchants trading with the Continent. Nykke's fears were shared. In 1530 two new royal proclamations, apparently the work of Lord Chancellor More, denounced the spread of the Lutheran heresy, ordered secular authorities to assist the bishops in detecting suspects, and listed heretical books which were to be confiscated, including Bible translations and works by Luther, Bullinger, and Tyndale.

The English authorities had been shrieking against Luther for a decade, since the condemnation of his teachings by Leo X in 1520. Luther's books had been imported to England from 1518, and sold reasonably well at the Oxford bookshop of John Dorne in 1520, but they soon came under attack. In 1520 the confiscation of Luther's works was ordered in Cambridge and in London, and the Cambridge proctors supervised the burning of offensive books. In 1521 Cardinal Wolsey turned his attention, briefly but dramatically, to the problem of Luther. He organized a conference of Oxford and Cambridge theologians, and commissioned some of them to write against Luther.[3] On 12 May he presided at a public bonfire at St Paul's Cross, when Luther's books were cast into the flames and Bishop Fisher preached against their errors. Most strikingly of all, Wolsey persuaded Henry VIII to write a response to Luther. It is probable that the university theologians produced the first drafts, Thomas More sorted them into order, and Henry merely added the finishing touches. But the book, the *Assertio Septem Sacramentorum*, was published under Henry's name in July 1521.[4]

Bonfires and a royal refutation made for good propaganda, but there would have to be proper enforcement if the papal bull against Luther was to have real impact. In 1521 Wolsey circularized the bishops, drawing their attention to the forty-two Lutheran heresies condemned by the pope and asking them to seize books by Luther; he secured a proclamation ordering local officials to assist the bishops in tracking down heretics. John Longland, the new bishop of Lincoln, instructed his commissary at Oxford to search the bookshops for heretical works by Luther and others, and the 1521 campaign against heretics in the Thames valley was probably a product of the fuss about Luther.[5] In Norfolk, Bishop Nykke picked up a vicar who admitted he had read books by Luther, but claimed to have handed them over for burning in Cambridge. But when a formal denunciation of Luther was posted at Boxley Abbey in Kent in 1522, it was torn down by a priest, who then went off to hand out Lutheran tracts in the high street at Maidstone.[6]

For William Roper, a young student at Lincoln's Inn, the prohibition of

Luther's books was already too late. In some spiritual anguish at his own sin, he had found comfort in his study of Luther. By 1521 he had accepted justification by faith, and denied the efficacy of works and ceremonies in salvation. Roper discovered, as Luther himself had done, that justification in Christ freed the tender conscience from the treadmill of penitential works.[7] Thomas Batman, warden of St Bartholomew's hospital in Rochester, was another early convert to justification by faith. In December 1524 he was charged with upholding Lutheran heresies, including justification by faith alone, the ineffectiveness of good works, and the priesthood of all believers. By February 1525 there was further evidence against Batman; he had been telling people that in Germany priests now married, and that the laity were given both bread and wine in communion. But Batman was not only a new Lutheran; he held some ideas which seem to owe more to the Lollard tradition, such as hostility to the veneration of saints, to confession, and to the payment of tithes.[8]

In Cambridge, too, there were early readers of Luther's works. A circle of advanced thinkers met at the White Horse tavern, soon known to its critics as 'Little Germany'. The membership of the group was apparently fluid and remains uncertain; it probably included Thomas Arthur, Robert Barnes, Thomas Bilney, John Clark, John Frith, George Joye, Hugh Latimer, and George Stafford. But to think of this loose society as a Lutheran club would be wrong. Stephen Gardiner was involved in the discussions, admitting in 1545 that 'because there was not then in them malice, and they maintained communication having some savour of learning, I was familiar with such sort of men'.[9] Thomas Cranmer was then an impartial student of the issues Luther had raised, rather than a committed follower of his solutions. The group seems to have been characterized by a fervent biblical piety rather than by specifically Lutheran ideas. Bilney developed his theology by the study of Erasmus's translation of the New Testament, rather than by study of Luther—or that is what he claimed in 1527.[10]

Thomas Bilney seems to have endured the same sort of spiritual torment as Martin Luther and William Roper, and to have found his consolation, as they had done, in the love of Christ revealed in Scripture. In Erasmus's Latin translation of St Paul, Bilney discovered 'that Christ Jesus came into the world to save sinners, of whom I am the chief and principal'; this text 'did so exhilarate my heart, being wounded with the guilt of my sins and being almost in despair, that immediately I felt a marvellous comfort and quietness'. Such was his conviction of the saving power of the cross of Christ that the secondary aids of Catholic practice, the images, penances, and pilgrimages, were distractions, at best irrelevant and at worst idolatrous. Bilney communicated his fervour to others, and became a central figure in the Cambridge group. Latimer declared later that it had been Bilney who had brought him from obstinate popery to 'that knowledge that I have in the word of God', and Arthur, Barnes, John Lambert, and others were also moved by his enthusiasm.[11]

In 1525 the Cambridge men went public. Bilney secured a preaching licence from the bishop of Ely, and soon went further afield condemning images. On Christmas Eve 1525, Robert Barnes and, apparently, Hugh Latimer preached from Cambridge pulpits against the worldliness of the Church. Barnes, a doctor of divinity and prior of the Augustinian friars, was the most eminent member of the group. In somewhat Erasmian terms, he criticized the Church's preoccupation with jurisdiction and regulations above the preaching of the gospel, and condemned the arrogance and affluence of the bishops—with special reference to Wolsey. He was suspended from preaching by the vice-chancellor, and charged with teaching heresy; the university authorities were probably afraid of the wrath of the cardinal. At this point, however, Barnes was caught up in Wolsey's own propaganda ploys, and had fame (and Lutheranism) thrust upon him. Wolsey had planned another book-bonfire, and needed some sample heretics for the ceremony. Barnes was sent up to London for examination and trial.[12]

On 11 February 1526 Thomas Wolsey again presided in splendour at St Paul's, flanked by the assembled prelates of the English Church. Again Bishop Fisher preached vigorously against the pernicious doctrine of justification by faith alone; again Lutheran books were solemnly burned. But on this occasion Robert Barnes and four foreign merchants knelt through the sermon, in token of their submission to the truth, and carried penitential faggots in procession afterwards. Barnes was bemused by the whole proceeding, astonished to be held up as a Lutheran when he had done little more than criticize abuses.[13] But Wolsey needed a token English Lutheran for the day, and Barnes had cast himself as victim by his attack on the hierarchy. The Dutch merchants from the London Steelyard were a stroke of propagandist genius; they demonstrated that Lutheranism was a nasty foreign import, to be shunned by the right-thinking English. But perhaps the occasion aroused the curiosity and interest of Londoners. Even for heretics, all publicity is good publicity.

The organizers of the book-burning, Wolsey, Fisher, and Longland, were worried by the influx of heretical books. They had good cause, and the most influential, William Tyndale's translation of the New Testament, was about to arrive. Tyndale, like Barnes, had been an enthusiast for Bible-based preaching; like Barnes, he was driven by a bishop into the arms of the Lutherans. He had sought from Cuthbert Tunstall, bishop of London, funding for his projected English translation of the New Testament. When Tunstall refused, Tyndale obtained the patronage of a London merchant, Humphrey Monmouth, who had Lollard connections and was to be involved in the trade in Lutheran books. For six months Monmouth financed Tyndale's translating work in London, and when Tyndale went to Wittenberg in the spring of 1524 Monmouth continued his support. After an abortive attempt to print his translation in Cologne, Tyndale produced the first printed English translation of the New Testament at Worms, in March 1526. It was based on Erasmus's Greek text, but heavily influenced by Luther's German version. Copies were immediately smuggled into England.[14]

The unauthorized translation of the Bible into English had been banned by the English bishops in 1410, in an attempt to suppress the Wycliffite version; thereafter the Lollards had given Bible-reading a bad name. There was no chance that a Luther-based translation would escape the prohibition. In October 1526 Bishop Tunstall of London instructed his archdeacons to warn the diocese that all copies of the translation were to be handed in within thirty days, on pain of excommunication. He then summoned the London booksellers and forbade them to sell the Tyndale version; Archbishop Warham circularized his other bishops to require them to hunt down the New Testament and other forbidden books. There is little sign these measures had much effect: John Parkyns of St Andrew's Eastcheap was soon in trouble for saying, 'If I had twenty books of the Holy Scripture translated into English, I would bring none of them in for my lord of London, curse he or bless he, for he doth it because we should have no knowledge but keeps it all secret to himself.'[15]

The Tyndale Testament found a ready market, especially among old Lollards and young university men—helped by some assiduous salesmanship. In the autumn of 1526 Robert Barnes was under house arrest at the Augustinian friary in London, but was allowed visitors, even suspicious ones. His recantation had made him a public figure, and he was visited by two Lollards from Steeple Bumpstead in Essex, who hoped he would help them convert their curate. They showed him their Lollard manuscript Gospels, which he mocked: 'A point for them, for that they be not to be regarded toward the new printed Testament in English, for it is of more cleaner English.' Barnes sold them a copy of Tyndale's version for 3s. 2d., and told them to keep quiet about it. Robert Necton hawked New Testaments around London, Essex, and Suffolk; his usual suppliers were Simon Fish, a London lawyer, and Dr Robert Forman, parson of All Hallows Honey Lane, but when a Dutchman offered him two or three hundred copies at a knockdown price he was suspicious and refused to buy.[16]

The most active travelling salesman in Tyndale Testaments for Oxford was Thomas Garrett, Forman's curate at Honey Lane. Early in 1527 he had sought out the young men in Oxford with a reputation for literary interests, and thereafter had sold them Lutheran books and translations. He made contact with some of the 'Little Germany' group who had moved from Cambridge to Oxford in 1526, to help staff Wolsey's new college, and he became their supplier. One of the Cambridge imports, John Clark, held a Bible class in his room at the Cardinal's College, where he read from St Paul's Epistles to the younger students. All this was deeply embarrassing to the bishop of Lincoln and the commissary of Oxford. Searches were conducted early in 1528, and though Garrett fled in disguise he was tracked down by the proctors. Twenty-two Lutheran suspects were rounded up, and a large cache of buried books unearthed, including works by Bucer, Oecolampadius, Zwingli, and Wycliffe, as well as by Luther. Some of the accused did public penance for their heresy; some were allowed to go free; some were imprisoned in the cellar of Wolsey's college, where they grew sick and died.[17]

A few of the Oxford suspects were certainly Protestants later, and John Frith now fled to join Tyndale on the Continent. But the Cardinal's College circle, like the White Horse tavern set, was not committed to Luther. Some of the members were toying temporarily with radical ideas; Michael Drone soon abandoned novelties, and John Fryer was, much later, imprisoned for popery; others were attracted by Bible-based piety, without deserting orthodox ideas. Among the authorities, however, there was clearly concern that the universities would become centres for the wider preaching of heresy. In 1527 the bishops of Ely and Lincoln, ordinaries for the two universities, began to take oaths not to spread Lutheran heresies from suspect priests before they were instituted to benefices.[18] But it was impossible to contain heresy within the universities. Robert Forman, who had attended 'Little Germany' while president of Queens' College Cambridge, was already settled in a London parish and organizing the distribution of Lutheran books. And Thomas Bilney and Thomas Arthur had preached through London and East Anglia in the spring and summer of 1527.

Bilney had already taken an oath to eschew the heresies of Luther and others, but that did not restrain him, perhaps because he was really no Lutheran. He preached fearlessly in a number of London and suburban churches, and in Suffolk. In Ipswich he declared that he brought only the message of the Bible: 'Lo, here is the New Testament, and here is the Old. These be the two swords of our saviour Christ which I will preach and show to you, and nothing else.' His emphasis was upon the saving power of the cross of Christ, and he criticized the distracting devotions of contemporary religion. Christians should turn to Christ, and not seek help from saints; to do otherwise was 'as if a man should take and strike off the head and set it under the foot, and the foot to set above'. At the church of St Magnus in London he condemned offerings of money and candles before images, and suggested that kings should 'destroy and burn images of the saints set up in churches and other places'. It was powerful and provocative stuff.[19]

Bilney's preaching created quite a stir in East Anglia. His 'most ghostly' sermons in Ipswich attracted Lollards from Colchester; at Hadleigh his preaching influenced some of the clothworkers, and turned a cobbler from Eye against honouring images. Thomas Arthur had also drawn attention to himself, especially by his attacks on ecclesiastical jurisdiction and the number of its regulations. He used homely (not to say lavatorial) similes:

when he spoke of laws he brought a similitude of crosses set up against the walls in London that men should not piss there, that when there were one cross or few more men did reverence to them and pissed not there, but when there was in every corner a cross set then men of necessity were compelled to piss upon the crosses.[20]

It is not surprising that Wolsey decided upon a show trial, though the temptation to prove England's orthodoxy, at a ticklish stage in the negotiations with Rome for King Henry's divorce, presumably entered his calculations. He summoned Arthur and Bilney up from Cambridge, together with their ally George Joye; however, when Joye saw how many bishops had assembled for the trial he wisely fled.

Bishop Longland began proceedings at Westminster on 27 November 1527 with a sermon on the dangers of Lutheranism. The bishops were told that only the Church could interpret the Scriptures, and that heretics must be exhorted to accept its authority. Arthur and Bilney were then brought before two archbishops and eight bishops, including the leading heresy-hunters.[21] Arthur's proved a fairly straightforward case; he confessed to some of the opinions ascribed to him, agreed to abjure his heresy and was set free on condition that he preached no more. Bilney was a more troublesome defendant and as his case dragged on Wolsey lost interest and left the trial to Tunstall. Bilney was examined on thirty-four articles, drawn mainly from his recent sermons, and on some he gave perfectly acceptable answers. He agreed that Luther had been properly condemned for his heresy, and that the canons and festivals of the Church should be observed. He was less orthodox on the nature of the true Church, and he argued that pardons from the pope detracted from the sufficiency of Christ's sacrifice.

The crucial issue, the issue which had brought Bilney to public attention, was the veneration of images. On that question, probably to the surprise of the bishops, Bilney gave a carefully phrased but orthodox answer: he believed images might serve as 'laymen's books', and then they were not idols but symbols. In the light of what it seems certain he had preached about images, either he was now lying or he was concealing his view that in practice images always were treated as idols.[22] The court was, however, determined to convict him of heresy on images, and produced witnesses to his sermons at Willesden, Newington, and Ipswich. As the witnesses testified to what he had said, Bilney asked for the trial to be abandoned as he could not remember what he had preached. It appears that he was anxious to avoid a recantation on the subject of images, since it would imply abandonment of his faith in the centrality of Christ's atonement and a recognition of a role for saints in salvation.

Tunstall pressed Bilney to abjure seven articles, in which saints and images were prominent. He refused. In letters to the bishop, Bilney claimed he had preached no heresy, only the remission of sins through Christ. On 4 December he was declared a contumacious heretic, but Tunstall held the case open and did not complete the reading of the sentence. There were further attempts to get Bilney to recant. Wolsey obviously wanted a discredited conformer, not a determined martyr. With much anguish and on the advice of his friends, Bilney finally agreed to recant. He read the seven articles before the court on 7 December 1527, and was forbidden to preach except by special permission of a bishop. On 8 December he carried his faggot in procession at St Paul's Cross, and stood in shame before the preacher through the sermon. But the official treatment of Bilney may have backfired: in 1529 a London priest complained that the bishop would 'suffer no man to preach at Paul's Cross but flatterers and dissemblers, for they that say truth are punished as Bilney and Arthur was'.[23]

The bishops had silenced Arthur and Bilney, and shown that the public preaching of heresy (or criticism of the hierarchy) was a risky business. But they found it much more difficult to suppress the surreptitious trade in Lutheran books, and to prevent secret Lollard conventicles; Bishop Tunstall's proceedings in 1528 showed that the two dangers had already coalesced.[24] Tunstall had a stroke of luck when he picked up the old Lollard evangelist John Hacker. Hacker had been caught in Bishop Longland's drive against the Buckinghamshire heretics in 1521, and had abjured his heresy; when detected again in London in 1528, he sought to avoid burning as a relapsed heretic by turning king's (or rather bishop's) evidence. He described the meetings of Lollard conventicles, named his Lollard contacts over the previous six years, and made it possible for Tunstall and his vicar-general to uncover networks of book-distribution. Hacker's revelations were disastrous for the Lollard groups of London and Essex, but invaluable for historians.

The house of Thomas Matthew, a Colchester fishmonger, emerged as a centre for Lollard meetings and the distribution of books. Tyndale Testaments and other books had been provided for the Matthew group by Robert Necton, who got his supplies from London. John Hacker had addressed the conventicle, but the usual teacher there was John Pykas, a Colchester baker. Pykas had been introduced to heresy in 1523 by his mother, who had given him an English manuscript of the Pauline Epistles and told him to believe in them, not the sacraments of the Church. In 1526 he had bought a copy of Tyndale's printed New Testament from an Italian in London; he had read it through several times, and lent it out to his friends. In 1527 he had travelled to Ipswich to hear Bilney preach, and what he heard seems to have become the basis for his teaching at Matthew's house, elsewhere in Colchester, and in nearby villages. One of the members of his circle had been John Tybal, who had moved from Colchester to Steeple Bumpstead and established a heretical group there.

Tybal attempted to persuade the priests of Steeple Bumpstead, especially the curate, Richard Fox, to his views on the sacraments and purgatory. With a friend, Tybal had gone to London in September 1526 to seek advice from Robert Barnes, who was presumably drawn to their attention by his recantation at St Paul's. They had returned with a Tyndale New Testament and a letter from Barnes to Fox. Fox was duly converted, and became an undercover Lollard chaplain, using confession to try to influence his parishioners. He taught that Christ was not really present in the eucharist, and that images should be taken down from the churches; but John Lond was shocked by his opinions and threatened to carry wood to Fox's burning. The curate participated in the conversion of Thomas Topley, an Augustinian canon. Fox had induced Topley to read Erasmus's *Colloquies* and Wycliffe's 'Wicket', which had shaken his faith, and had brought the Cambridge friar Miles Coverdale to preach in the parish. Coverdale had dissuaded Topley from belief in transubstantiation, confession, and the veneration of images.

Evidence from the Essex investigations led often to London. John Hacker revealed a conventicle there which met at the house of a tailor, William Russell, in Bird's Alley near Coleman Street. Hacker, from Coleman Street himself, had attended its meetings for six years, teaching against the real presence, images, and pilgrimage. The Coleman Street circle included John Stacy, whose house was used as a base for the copying of Bible extracts, and John Sercot, a grocer who paid for the copying. Robert Necton of Colchester, purveyor of imported books across East Anglia, revealed that one of his London sources of supply was Robert Forman, rector of All Hallows Honey Lane. Dr Forman was found to have two sacks of Lutheran books, though he claimed he had collected them so that he could refute their heresies. Humphrey Monmouth, a London draper, was also exposed as a supplier of forbidden books, and had his own small Lutheran library. He was accused of holding an increasingly common mix of Lutheran and Lollard beliefs: 'that faith without works is sufficient to save a man's soul' and 'that we should pray to God and not to saints'.[25]

The London importers of heretical books brought most of their wares from Antwerp. There was a constant demand for the reprints of Tyndale's New Testament, with its Lutheran prefaces, and there was an increasingly wide product-range available. *Unio Dissidentium*, a selection of extracts from patristic writers which supported Lutheran principles, circulated quite widely among the English clergy. It had first been published at Cologne in 1522, and was republished many times at Antwerp from 1527, partly for the English market. Rowland Taylor studied *Unio* at Cambridge, and together with Latimer's sermons it led him into heresy. It was one of the books that Robert Necton had sold around East Anglia, and in March 1528 the curate of Kensington was dismissed when he was found to have *Unio* and Tyndale's New Testament. By 1533 it had reached as far as Dalton in north Lancashire, and the parish priest there was ordered to hand it over to the authorities.

Antwerp was so prominent partly because of its well-established trading links with London, and because it was the main base for the most prolific English Protestant translator and propagandist, William Tyndale. In May 1528 he published *The Parable of the Wicked Mammon*, which incorporated a sermon of Luther and gave an exposition of the doctrine of justification by faith. This was certainly an influential volume; in the spring of 1529 John Tewkesbury, a London leather-seller, admitted to Tunstall that he had been converted to the new religion by reading Tyndale's New Testament and *Wicked Mammon*.[26] In October 1528 Tyndale brought out *The Obedience of a Christian Man*, which denounced the English Church and defended Luther against the charge that his doctrines were subversive of good order. *The Practice of Prelates*, a slashing attack on the pride and corruption of Wolsey and the bishops, was issued in 1530. By December 3,000 copies were said to be in circulation, and Tyndale's brother and others were forced to do public penance in London for distributing it.[27]

Tyndale's earliest polemical works had combined positive statements of Lutheran positions with attempts to discredit orthodox religion and its institutions. Simon Fish, a London lawyer, adopted the negative approach in *A Supplication for the Beggars*, printed at Antwerp late in 1528. The tract took the form of a complaint of poor beggars, that all the alms of England had been taken by the rich beggars, 'bishops, abbots, priors, deacons, archdeacons, suffragans, priests, monks, canons, friars, pardoners, and summoners'. By their lands, tithes, oblations, fees, and mortuaries, the clergy had gained one-third of the realm's wealth. In return, all they did was to pray for souls in purgatory, but the doctrine of masses satisfactory had been invented simply to extract money from the laity. Priests protected their fraud by keeping the Bible in the obscurity of Latin, by prosecuting their critics for heresy, and by defeating challenges to their jurisdiction. Fish suggested that the king should confiscate ecclesiastical property and make the priests work; then king and country would prosper.[28]

It was a subtle piece of populist propaganda, which sought to show that Catholic doctrines had a financial cost and so to enlist economic motives for religious change. Thomas More, already commissioned by Tunstall to answer heretical books, recognized the danger of Fish's argument. He replied immediately in *A Supplication of Souls*, a counter-petition on behalf of the souls in purgatory dependent upon prayers for their release from torment. More's book, and a supporting *New Book of Purgatory* by John Rastell, provoked John Frith to enter the debate. Frith had fled from Oxford to the Continent when the Cardinal's College circle was broken up in 1528, and had joined Tyndale in the propaganda campaign. His *Disputation of Purgatory* was published at Antwerp in 1531, and achieved instant fame. Frith dismissed the doctrine of purgatory, on the grounds that it could not be found in Scripture and it diminished the saving power of Christ's blood. Salvation came not by prayers for languishing souls, but by divine grace through faith in Christ. The book was a trenchant statement of the central Protestant position.

The flow of books from Antwerp was well organized, and some of them were highly effective. When Richard Bayfield, a renegade monk, was examined in November 1531, he confessed that he had Tyndale's *The Practice of Prelates* and Frith's *Disputation of Purgatory*. More dangerously, he had read other books aloud at Lollard meetings: Tyndale's *Wicked Mammon*, *The Obedience of a Christian Man*, and his prefaces to the Pentateuch, and Antwerp editions of old Wycliffite tracts. Bayfield had himself smuggled books in through Colchester, including works by Tyndale and Frith, and by Luther, Melanchthon, Oecolampadius, and Zwingli.[29] James Bainham, a London lawyer and new husband to the widow of Simon Fish, was interrogated in December 1531. He admitted possession of Tyndale's *Wicked Mammon*, *The Obedience of a Christian Man*, *The Practice of Prelates*, and his 1531 *Answer unto Sir Thomas More's Dialogue*, as well as Frith's book on purgatory. He praised the works of Tyndale and Frith, and declared that 'the truth of Holy Scripture' had only recently been revealed after having been hidden for 800 years.[30]

John Foxe reports that a number of men were brought to abjure their heresies in 1531–2, after having been found in possession of banned books.[31] William King, servant, had hidden in his bed-straw at Worcester a New Testament, George Joye's protestantized English *Primer* and English *Psalter*, and Fish's translation, *The Sum of Holy Scripture* (a practical guide to the Christian life, built around justification by faith). Edward Hewet, servant, had read the New Testament and Frith on purgatory; William Lincoln, apprentice, had books by Tyndale and Frith, and an Antwerp print of the Lollard *Examination of Master William Thorpe*. John Medwell, servant, had a New Testament, *Wicked Mammon*, and the Thorpe *Examination*. John Mel, of Boxted in Essex, had Tyndale's New Testament and Joye's *Psalter*, and William Smith, tailor, had the New Testament and an edition of the Lutheran will of William Tracy. Michael Lobley had gone to Antwerp, and bought *Wicked Mammon, The Obedience of a Christian Man,* Frith's book on purgatory, and his translation of Luther's *Revelation of Antichrist.*

The spread of heretical books had not been stopped by Wolsey's ceremonial conflagrations or by Thomas More's contentious counter-propaganda. After More became chancellor, in October 1529, the emphasis shifted, from burning books to burning those who bought them and those who held to their ideas. Thomas Hitton, carrying Tyndale's New Testament and Joye's *Primer* from the Continent, was picked up in Kent and burned at Maidstone in February 1530.[32] Richard Bayfield, importer of books and teacher of Lollards, was burned in London in December 1531; John Tewkesbury, in trouble again, suffered two weeks later. Thomas Bennet, an Exeter schoolmaster and old Cambridge friend of Bilney, was burned in January 1532; he had put a poster on the door of the cathedral declaring, 'The pope is Antichrist, and we ought to worship God only and no saints.'[33] James Bainham at first abjured his heresy, but then publicly withdrew his recantation and was burned on 30 April 1532. It seems that this burst of flames, and especially the Bainham case, provoked concern in the political nation; and the burning of Thomas Bilney was a public-relations disaster.

After Bilney's recantation in December 1527 he spent a year in prison, and was allowed to return to Cambridge in 1529. But he was much troubled by his own betrayal of the truth. In 1531 he announced that he was going 'up to Jerusalem', and set off for Norwich, taking Tyndale Testaments with him. He preached in Norwich and to gatherings in the fields around, apparently condemning the invocation of saints and the veneration of images, as he had done in 1527. He was proceeded against as a relapsed heretic by Thomas Pells, chancellor of Norwich diocese, and there was really nothing to save him from the fire. But Bilney was apparently anxious to die in communion with the Church. He sought absolution from the chancellor and was allowed the eucharist, which must surely mean that he had made a private recantation. He went to his execution on 16 August 1531, but what happened at the stake is confused and controversial. It seems that he quietly read an abjuration drawn up by Pells, but when asked to make an open recantation before the crowd he was ambiguous at best.[34]

The burning of Bilney was immediately a contentious issue. Pells and his bishop were both aggressive clerics, and may have been unpopular in Norwich; Bilney was a local boy, and had excited some sympathy. It was far from clear to all townsmen—as it has been far from clear to all historians—that he really was a heretic. The clergy claimed that he had recanted, and produced the abjuration drafted for him; the laity declared there had been no audible recantation. There was a political complication, too; Bilney had tried to appeal from the Church to the king, and the mayor of Norwich, Edward Rede, may have feared the repercussions. To protect himself, Rede compiled his own account of the affair, and had it signed and sealed by the city aldermen; he may have intended to raise the issue in Parliament. It was perhaps to forestall such unfavourable publicity that Thomas More launched a Star Chamber investigation. He concluded that Bilney had been properly tried, and had formally recanted. But the issue remained contested, and in 1532 More had to publish his own version of Bilney's death in *The Confutation of Tyndale's Answer*.

But it should not be assumed that the burning of heretics was generally resented, or that their cause had much appeal. When Thomas Bennet went to the stake at Exeter in 1532, he was threatened with a blazing furze-bush on a pike and told, 'Ah! whoreson heretic! Pray to Our Lady and say *Sancta Maria, ora pro nobis*, or by God's wounds I will make thee do it!' The crowd raged against him and threw sticks and furze into his fire. When Thomas Harding was burned at Chesham in 1532, children took wood to the fire and some of the crowd delighted to see him suffer. Before James Bainham's burning in 1532, he feared most for his wife: 'for my sake she shall be an approby unto the world, and be pointed at of every man on this sort, "Yonder goeth the heretic's wife!" '[35] Dr John London tried to persuade his nephew from heresy in 1534, and the family shame was a major argument.

Your mother, after that she shall hear what an abominable heretic she hath to her son, I am well certain (he said) that she will never eat more bread that shall do her good. Alas, he said, remember that hitherto there was never heretic of all our kin.[36]

Known heretics, even those who had abjured, were ostracized and ill-treated. When Humphrey Monmouth got a reputation as 'a Scripture man', his poor neighbours in Barking refused to take charity from him, or to borrow money. In 1528 John Hig, a Dutch Lutheran living in London, abjured his heresy; later he petitioned for release from his faggot badge, since no one would employ him wearing it. In 1531 Richard Hilles sought employment from Thomas Cromwell, because other merchants refused to deal with him, and in 1536 he was hated by his neighbours when he would not contribute towards candles before the images. Hilles was harassed by his churchwardens, until he finally left the country in 1539.[37] In 1535 a couple of Hugh Latimer's Wiltshire parishioners lost their cattle; their neighbours said it was a proper punishment for their heresy. William Senes of Rotherham got the rough end of the earl of Shrewsbury's Catholic tongue in 1537: 'Come near, thou heretic and kneel near! . . . Thou art an heretic, and but for shame I should thrust my dagger into thee!'[38]

Some of this hostility was a knee-jerk reaction to anyone labelled a heretic, but some was a more specific response to those who traduced conventional pieties. As Richard Hilles found, critics of saints and their images could have a hard time. Though there were mockers of images, we know of them only because they were disliked and denounced. John Hewes was reported in 1531 for scorning a man who knelt in the street at Farnham in Surrey when a crucifix was carried by: ' "Thou art a fool!", said he, "it is not thy maker, it is but a piece of copper or wood!" ' Grace Palmer, of St Osyth's in Essex, was turned in by her neighbours in the same year for telling them not to go on pilgrimage to images, 'for there you shall find but a piece of timber painted', and for refusing to contribute to candles for images.[39] Those who prated and preached against images were attacking a lively element in popular devotion. Bilney's drive against images in 1527 was apparently provoked by the erection of a great new rood at the London church of St Magnus.

It seems that Lollard and later condemnation of images had little impact upon popular attitudes. In 1516 there was a dramatic demonstration that images and miraculous stories could still move masses—and queens and cardinals. The convulsions suffered by Sir Roger Wentworth's daughter were apparently alleviated by a vision of Our Lady of Ipswich. When the child was taken on pilgrimage to the shrine at Gracechurch, the rumour brought 1,000 people to escort her. The image achieved a temporary cure, until the parents delayed a promised return visit; the fits came again, and a further pilgrimage was made to the shrine, this time with 4,000 in attendance. The girl was cured of her fits, urged the people to be 'more steadfast in the faith', and relieved her brother of a similar affliction. A local notable reported the story to Henry VIII. Queen Katherine and Cardinal Wolsey went on pilgrimage to the shrine in 1517, and Gracechurch gained a new fame. In 1526 Wolsey obtained a new indulgence for pilgrims, and in 1529 Thomas More told the story in print, as proof that miracles could still happen.[40]

There was a minor miracle at Rickmansworth, Hertfordshire, in 1522, which was similarly publicized by Wolsey with an indulgence.[41] It was claimed that incendiarists had broken into the church at night, and set fire to ornaments, images, and the organ. The church sustained a good deal of damage in the fire, but, it was reported, the reserved host and the rood were miraculously untouched. Wolsey and Bishop Longland sought to raise money for the church's restoration fund by offering remission of 140 days of penance for all those who contributed, but they also took full advantage of the publicity. The conflagration was blamed on heretics, who had thereby shown themselves to be sacrilegious vandals, and the survival of the host and the rood formed God's judgement of their attacks on transubstantiation and veneration of images. But it is striking how rare such acts of iconoclasm were—and they were usually carried out in the safety of darkness, which suggests fear of communal retribution.

There was a brief and localized outbreak of iconoclasm in the Stour valley region in 1531–2, which may have been a response to the Bilney affair. Two images of St Petronilla were pulled down in different churches, an image of St Christopher suffered similarly, and a couple of roadside crosses were thrown over. More dramatically, in 1532 the famous rood of Dovercourt was carried off at dead of night and burned. There is some evidence that the escapade was organized as revenge for Bilney's burning, by a priest who had preached with him at Hadleigh. He escaped, but three of those responsible were caught and hanged in chains.[42] Pious pyrotechnics were, however, most unusual and are not evidence of any wider rejection of images. There were individual sceptics, and it was reported in 1533 that some London citizens pricked images with pins to see if they would bleed.[43] But, as we have already seen, the cult of saints and their images remained lively in the parishes. There is barely any sign of a general decline in devotion to saints, until the government itself endorsed the heretics' condemnation of images.

If the radical campaign against saints and images was broadly ineffective, so too was the attack on purgatory and prayers for the dead. Since indulgences did not play a big part in English religion, Luther's detraction had a mainly academic impact. There were some shifts in fashion and forms of provision for souls, but no lessening of determination to secure prayers for them. The purchase of huge numbers of funeral masses already seemed a vulgar excess; instead, testators sought continuing flows of masses from endowed priests, whom they expected to assist in parish work. From about 1520 there was a slight decline in the volume of masses endowed, but not yet in the proportion of testators who made provision for them; this suggests the explanation was economic and not religious. It was not until the late 1530s that benefactions for masses declined at all significantly, and then from fears for the future of endowments rather than from real doubt of the efficacy of prayers for the dead. It was the thieving of Henry VIII which was to undermine endowed masses in England, not the theology of Martin Luther.

The Lutheran call remained a lonely voice in a hostile wilderness. In October 1530, William Tracy, a Gloucestershire gentleman, made his will.[44] It was very different from that of Robert Jannys, the Norwich grocer who had sought so many prayers. Tracy began in an unusual, and purposely provocative, way:

First and before all other things, I commit myself to God and his mercy, believing, without any doubt or mistrust, that by his grace and the merits of Jesus Christ, and by the virtues of his passion and of his resurrection, I have and shall have remission of all my sins and resurrection of my body and soul.

Tracy had certainly been influenced by the Lutheran doctrine of justification by faith alone, and he broke decisively with the usual pattern of will-making. He did not ask for the assistance of Mary and the saints, and he made no provision for prayers for his soul; he expected salvation only through faith in Christ, not through mediators or masses.

Tracy's will achieved instant fame. It was copied by his son, and circulated among heretics in manuscript; soon it was printed in Antwerp with a commentary. It was examined for heresy by the Oxford theologians in November 1530, and by the clergy in Convocation in February 1531. Tracy's body was then exhumed, and burned as the corpse of an unrepentant heretic. The episode showed both the propaganda skills of the Lutherans and the determination of the churchmen to crush dissent. But in 1530 what was most significant about Tracy's will was its singularity: hardly anyone wrote (and few thought) as Tracy did. The habit of commending the soul to the care of Mary and the saints remained almost universal among will-makers until well after 1530, and then the practice was abandoned only slowly. The habit of endowing masses, or at least leaving money to the poor or to relations 'to pray for me', remained very widespread.[45] There was no sign as yet that the future lay with William Tracy rather than with Robert Jannys.

4

Church Courts and English Law

In 1530 William Tracy's Lutheran will was a case of heresy, to be considered by the Oxford theologians; by 1532 it had become a constitutional *cause célèbre*, and a case of ecclesiastical excess. The will was discussed in Convocation in 1531, and Tracy's son Richard, common lawyer and member of the House of Commons, was summoned before the assembled clergy. The document was condemned as heretical. Copies of the will became recommended reading among heretics, and one was found in the possession of Thomas Phillip, a prisoner in the Tower of London. In January 1532 it was reported to Convocation that Thomas Browne of Bristol had made a will like Tracy's, and an exemplary gesture was then thought necessary. Archbishop Warham instructed the chancellor of Worcester diocese to have Tracy's body exhumed, since a declared heretic was unworthy to lie in consecrated ground. But the chancellor, Dr Parker, went too far: he burned the body for heresy.[1]

Now William Tracy had been convicted of heresy by the Convocation of Canterbury, and a corpse could hardly recant, so burning might be thought the proper, if macabre, punishment for inevitable obduracy. But it was a penalty which should have been carried out only by the secular power, after the issue of a writ by the lord chancellor to the sheriff of Gloucestershire. The Church had ignored due legal process, and apparently shown itself careless of constitutional niceties, and this at a time when the energetic pursuit of heretics was beginning to cause concern. Critics of the clergy had been handed a potentially powerful weapon. Tracy's son mobilized his legal and political connections, and tried to get a witch-hunt going against leading clerics, offering the prospect of heavy fines for the government if it pursued all those involved. Thomas Cromwell, the royal secretary, took over the case, and the unfortunate Parker was called before the king. Parker pleaded that he had acted under orders, and blamed the now dead archbishop; he was nevertheless forced to pay £300 to get a pardon for praemunire.

The Tracy case assumed political importance because it encapsulated a number of contentious topics. It seemed to show that, as common lawyers had been arguing for half a century, the Church had to be brought under the control of the common law. It seemed to show that the Church was waging a campaign of repression against its critics which threatened the lives (and even the corpses) of prominent laymen. And it seemed to show that the king was not master in his own realm, that the clergy were, as Henry himself had complained just two days before the order for the exhumation, 'but half our subjects'.[3] The related problems of the Church's legal independence, the clergy's wilful aggression, and the king's sovereignty assumed new importance in the changed circumstances after 1530. But they could become so significant because the contentions of 1530 and after put new perspectives on old issues: especially the attempt to clip the Church courts in the reign of Henry VII, the death of Richard Hunne in 1514, and the clash over benefit of clergy in 1515.

The common lawyers' criticism of the jurisdiction of the Church had two roots. The first was simple and sordid: competition for business. The volume of litigation in the courts of King's Bench and Common Pleas collapsed in the late fifteenth century. The combined business of the two courts had fallen to half of its mid-century level by the 1490s, while the number of lawyers in need of work had been increasing. The 'missing' litigation had mainly moved to the court of Chancery, because the common law courts had not yet provided effective legal remedies for complex commercial disputes. It is not certain that legal business had been directly transferred to the Church courts, but it is not surprising that common lawyers thought it had. From the 1450s, the consistory court of Canterbury dealt with a growing volume of debt and breach of contract business (under the guise of 'breach of faith' suits), which peaked in 1491. The Canterbury consistory also heard an increasing number of defamation cases, many of which could—or should—have been dealt with at common law, cases which reached their peak in 1485.[4] But by then the common lawyers were fighting back.

It would be too cynically reductionist to argue that common lawyers merely coveted the business of ecclesiastical courts. For a second root of their criticism lay in the increasing coherence and confidence of common law thought.[5] By about 1450 the Inns of Court had established formal structures of legal moots and readings, at which legal questions were regularly debated. By about 1485, writers on common law were attempting to formulate the underlying principles of their law, and to consider its relationship with other legal systems. Many lawyers, by a convenient but convincing argument, had concluded that common law and statute were superior to ecclesiastical canons. In 1485 Chief Justice Hussey declared that the king of England was superior to the pope in his own realm; in the same year, an Inner Temple barrister suggested that new Church legislation would be invalid if contrary to the existing law of the land. The lawyers' combination of practical self-interest and theoretical self-justification proved powerful—and dangerous to churchmen.

By the mid-fifteenth century, some defendants before the Church courts were seeking to frustrate processes against them by arguing that ecclesiastical judges encroached on the rights of the king.[6] Their lawyers cited the 1393 Statute of Praemunire, which had been designed to inhibit proceedings against English bishops in the papal courts at Rome, and which the clergy had then supported. But the Act was now interpreted as an attack on the jurisdiction of Church courts in England. In 1465 it was held that the English Church courts came within the meaning of 'Roman court' in the 1393 Act, so that statute could be pleaded against them. And in 1496 the King's Bench judges agreed that a suit in an ecclesiastical court for a temporal cause was a case of praemunire, an offence against the king. Over the same period, the common lawyers developed the use of a second weapon against ecclesiastical usurpation of secular business: the writ of prohibition. Cases in Church courts concerning debt and contract were sometimes (and especially under Henry VII) challenged by prohibitions, in the hope of gaining advantage for defendants by switching suits to Common Pleas.

Writs of praemunire and prohibition were generally sought by litigants in the ordinary course of legal battles. But from the 1490s, and especially after the death of Lord Chancellor Cardinal Morton in 1500, the king's lawyers used praemunire in a deliberate campaign to limit the work of ecclesiastical courts. As attorney-general to Henry VII, Sir James Hobart prosecuted churchmen for the illegal exercise of ecclesiastical jurisdiction, and as a justice of the peace in East Anglia he encouraged defendants from Church courts to make praemunire charges against clergy. John Ernley, Hobart's successor as attorney, began praemunire actions against ecclesiastical judges who had heard debt cases, thus challenging the Church's competence in a major field of litigation. This attempt to secure a clearer distinction between the roles of secular and ecclesiastical courts was precisely what the common lawyers were seeking. In 1514 it was argued by John Hales at Gray's Inn that temporal and spiritual courts should have parallel, not overlapping, jurisdiction, and that spiritual judges, who had no knowledge of trade and finance, should keep out of such issues.[7]

Under the pressure of these attacks, the business of the Church courts declined. Suits for the recovery of debt dwindled in the Canterbury consistory, and under the leadership of Chief Justice Fyneux the common law courts developed new forms of action to deal with lucrative commercial cases. The common law was slower to provide any alternative to the Church for defamation suits, though lawyers had long argued that secular defamation—accusing a man of felony rather than fornication—was not the business of the clergy. In 1508, however, the first slander suits for calling a man a thief were heard in King's Bench and Common Pleas.[8] The common lawyers' defamation business built up only slowly, for they were no more obviously competent to deal with slanders than were churchmen; but in 1512 the consistory court of the diocese of London apparently abandoned litigation involving secular defamation. The losses of the canon lawyers were the gains of the common lawyers: the combined business of King's Bench and Common Pleas increased by one-third for 1501–10, compared with the preceding decade.

It is possible that the efforts of Hobart and Ernley should be regarded as part of a concerted royal attempt to break the remaining independence of the English Church.[9] Henry VII secured a tame episcopate by using royal service as the criterion for promotion and nominating lawyers rather than theologians; then he ensured that they behaved by demanding huge recognizances. Lord Chancellor Morton obtained bulls from Rome which brought suffragan bishops more firmly under his own jurisdiction, and which modified the ecclesiastical privilege of sanctuary—after the king's judges had held that sanctuary could not apply to traitors. Henry issued licences for the appropriation of benefices and the suppression of monasteries, hitherto normally granted by the pope. In 1489 and 1497 there were statutory restrictions upon benefit of clergy, limiting the immunity of clerks from secular penalties. There were few appeals from England to Rome, and in 1500–9 bishops invoked the support of the secular power against excommunicates less frequently than at any time since the reign of Henry III.

But it would be an error to see in the reign of Henry VII any major clash between Church and state. Henry VII's episcopal appointments policy was only a continuation of Edward IV's, and seems odd only by comparison with Henry VI's unusual nomination of theologians.[10] Recognizances for good behaviour were taken from bishops only as they were taken from all men of power. Encroachments on sanctuary and benefit (with papal approval) were part of a wider drive to restore public order after a period of political and social unrest, rather than deliberate attacks on a rival jurisdiction. There were few praemunire prosecutions while Cardinal Morton was chancellor, and the campaign was concentrated in the period after 1500, when the weaker clerics Deane and then Warham held the great seal.[11] The praemunire charges were not specific sallies against churchmen, but part of a broader effort to raise royal revenue by prosecutions of all kinds. The years of the praemunires were also years of the relentless pursuit of penalties through King's Bench by one of Hobart's clerks. Henry VII ruled the clergy as he ruled the laity, by harassment and penny-pinching.

It is only from the warping perspective of the Reformation that Henry VII's treatment of the Church seems at all remarkable—only when we put together the ecclesiastical implications of otherwise disconnected royal policies. Of course some clergy, on the receiving end of Henry's measures, thought their jurisdiction was under sustained attack. When Bishop Nykke faced a praemunire in 1505, he wanted to fight back; he complained to Archbishop Warham that

The laymen be more bolder against the Church than ever they were. If your Lordship help not, having the great seal in your hand, and other your subjects can nothing do. If your Fatherhood would favour me, I would curse all such promoters and maintainers of the praemunire in such cases as heretics and not-believers in Christ's Church.[12]

Warham, however, was no clerical militant, and he remained cautious of secular jurisdictions. It is noticeable that, in the court proceedings which followed his visitation of 1511, he and his commissary were most careful to send disputes to common law if there was any question of property involved.[13]

But, once Henry VII was safely in his grave, Warham was not supine. The overall weakening of the Church's political and legal position under Henry VII was partly reversed, as Warham and his colleagues took advantage of the leading role of ecclesiastics in the government of the young Henry VIII. Warham's summons of the clergy to the Canterbury Convocation of 1510 warned of the need to defend the Church against lay hostility to its rights. A bill 'for the liberties of the English Church' was introduced in the House of Lords in 1510, probably in an attempt to secure statutory backing for the 'charter of liberties' granted by Edward IV in 1462. The bill passed the Lords, but was apparently amended unacceptably in the Commons and was dropped. The bishops had signalled their aims; these were, if they really had sought confirmation of the charter, clerical immunity from abuse of praemunire procedures and from trial in secular courts.[14] The praemunire problem had, for the moment, been solved by the death of Henry VII; immunity from trial, however, would mean the overthrow of a 200-year compromise and was an unrealistic goal. But the churchmen were on the attack.

The bishops had worked themselves into a fine state of political paranoia. Like Nykke of Norwich, some saw criticism of the legal position of the Church as heresy; the arguments of the common lawyers therefore made the Church appear beleaguered by heretics, and senior clergy fought back. It was no coincidence that persecution of heretics was more frequent from 1496, as prohibitions and praemunires became more common, and no coincidence that a nation-wide drive against heretics followed the Convocation of 1510. There was a real problem of heresy, but the bishops reacted to it so vigorously because they were determined to reassert their authority. Between 1510 and 1512 there were campaigns against heresy by Bishop Fitzjames in London diocese, Warham in Canterbury, Smith in Lincoln, Blythe in Lichfield, and Nykke in Norwich, and less systematic proceedings in other dioceses. The king issued commissions to back the investigations, and there were several burnings of heretics for perhaps the first time in half a century. In November 1511 Erasmus and his friend Ammonio were joking about the effect of the burnings on the price of fuel in England.[15]

As the bishops responded by repression, other clergy advocated reform. In his sermon at the opening of the 1510 Convocation, John Colet, dean of St Paul's, suggested that the privileges of the Church should be earned rather than enforced. He argued that worldliness among the clergy was a greater danger than heresy among the laity, and that the laity must respect the clergy as men before they would respect their rights as priests. Colet was probably correct that the clergy showed 'pride of life' in their search for preferment and 'covetousness' in their demand for tithes and fees. Priests, after all, shared the workaday vices of humanity.[16] It may even be that the clergy appeared more materialistic, as unprecedented recruitment sharpened competition for benefices. For all his commitment to humanist reform, Colet was as much a clericalist as the bishops, and hoped to defend the clergy's status by raising their reputation. But in political terms perhaps Bishop Fitzjames was right that Colet had to be silenced, even if the threatened heresy charge in 1513 was a clumsy and distasteful way of gagging him.

John Taylor, prolocutor of the Lower House, advanced much the same argument as Colet in his own Convocation address of 1514.[17] He admitted that defects among the clergy had weakened the Church's ability to defend its liberties against laymen, and criticized the bishops for slack discipline. But this was apparently a minority view. More common was the conspiracy theory of Christopher Urswick, arch-pluralist and diplomat. In 1514 Urswick warned the prior of Canterbury that some laymen were trying to undermine the power of the Church, to escape punishment for their own moral laxity. Critics had seized upon individual lapses among priests and presented them as characteristic of the whole clerical body, so that the moral authority of the Church was weakened. The Church must now resist the encroachments of the laity. Bishop Nykke agreed; in 1515 he warned the bailiffs of Ipswich that local questioning of his authority 'savoureth of heresy', and as there had been recent burnings his threat was obvious.[18]

It was this mixture of clerical aggression and defensiveness which produced the case—or rather the cases—of Richard Hunne, merchant tailor of London.[19] In March 1511 Hunne's baby son died in the parish of St Mary Matfellon, and, when the parish priest made the customary demand for the child's christening robe as a mortuary, Hunne refused. It seems that the matter was to have been left there, for the clergy often exercised discretion in the collection of mortuaries. But in November 1511 there was a dispute before the mayor's court between Hunne and a friend, and the rector and churchwardens of St Michael Cornhill, over title to a tenement. In a year when churchmen were on the look-out for opponents of their authority, Hunne had twice cast himself in that now-dangerous role. The next we know is that Hunne was cited late in April 1512 before the archbishop's Court of Audience, for refusal of the mortuary. This suggests that some London clergy now wanted to settle the mortuary issue, and perhaps make an example of Hunne, before the highest court available, not before the usual London commissary court or diocesan consistory.[20]

Hunne denied that a mortuary had been due (on what grounds, we do not know for certain), but in May 1512 Cuthbert Tunstall, Warham's chancellor, decided for Thomas Dryffeld, the rector of St Mary Matfellon. Whether Hunne then paid up is not clear; what followed suggests he did not. On 27 December 1512 he attended vespers at St Mary's; it was not, incidentally, his parish church, and he may have been looking for trouble. The priest, Thomas Marshall, refused to continue service until Hunne left the church, calling out, 'Hunne, thou art accursed and standest accursed!' This claim that Hunne was excommunicate may reflect either Hunne's disobedience to Tunstall's decree or that he was already under suspicion for heresy. As soon as the next legal term began, in January 1513, Hunne sued Marshall in King's Bench for slander, alleging that his credit had been ruined and his business damaged by what had been said in church. He also sued out a writ—against Dryffeld, Marshall, proctor, advocate, summoner, and witnesses—alleging that the original mortuary case had been a praemunire offence.

Richard Hunne was making himself a considerable pain in the collective ecclesiastical neck. He was also raising some very important issues. His King's Bench slander case was an interesting suit, for it straddled the newly emerging borderline between ecclesiastical and secular defamation: was the charge that Hunne was excommunicate an ecclesiastical defamation (since to stand excommunicate was a spiritual offence) or a secular defamation (since the very worldly matter of Hunne's livelihood was affected)? The case was not decided, but its implications were immense: potentially, it undercut the Church's jurisdiction in defamation, for any slander might have secular consequences. The significance of the praemunire action is less obvious, for we do not know the grounds of Hunne's challenge. He may have impugned the Church's right to hear a case involving property, or he may simply have attacked the jurisdiction of the archbishop's court over his case.[21] But Hunne had certainly reopened the whole praemunire dispute, which the clergy hoped had been laid to rest with the body of Henry VII.

So it is not surprising that Hunne was charged with heresy, especially as there is a good deal of evidence that, besides his provocative attitude to ecclesiastical jurisdiction, he really did hold heretical opinions.[22] Indeed, there is a suggestion—made by Thomas More—that Hunne had sued for a praemunire to forestall heresy proceedings. The slander case was repeatedly adjourned, and the praemunire suit swung back and forth. After the allegation in Hilary term 1513, the defendants replied in Easter denying the competence of King's Bench, and probably at the end of Michaelmas Hunne countered the defendants' reply. The case was then adjourned from term to term. Archbishop Warham may have initiated heresy proceedings against Hunne in Convocation early in 1514; Hunne was apparently arrested in October, after a search had revealed a Wycliffite Bible in his house, and held in the Lollards' Tower at St Paul's. He was examined by Bishop Fitzjames at Fulham on 2 December, and returned to prison; on the morning of 4 December 1514, he was found hanging in his cell.

For the Church, this was a most embarrassing outcome. It might appear that a powerful critic had been deliberately murdered to wreck his praemunire challenge; indeed, that may be what had really happened. Fitzjames and his chancellor, William Horsey, claimed that Hunne had killed himself, and proceeded to provide a motive for the suicide by convicting him posthumously of heresy. The judges—Fitzjames and three other bishops—were probably right that Hunne was a heretic, or, at least, that if he had come to trial alive he would have been convicted. When examined on 2 December, Hunne had been charged with denying that tithe was due to the Church, criticizing the worldliness of the clergy, defending a known heretic in 1511, and possessing an English Bible and heretical books. He seems to have made a qualified admission of guilt. At his post-mortem trial, it was also alleged that he had denied the real presence in the eucharist and veneration of saints; witnesses deposed that he had had an English Bible and defended Bible translation. His body was burned on 20 December, under a writ from Lord Chancellor Warham.

But in February 1515 a London coroner's jury found that Hunne had been murdered, and named Chancellor Horsey and two gaolers as the killers. It had certainly been a suspicious suicide: there were signs of a struggle, and that the suicide had been rigged (though the coroner's report survives only in an edited version published in 1539). One of the gaolers, Charles Joseph, had fled into sanctuary and then tried to concoct an alibi for the night of Hunne's death. He was arrested in January 1515, and when the alibi was broken he confessed to the murder and accused Horsey and William Spalding, the other gaoler. This is, however, a tainted accusation, for Joseph had been a summoner in the diocese of London until he was sacked by Horsey in October 1514.[23] Thomas More claimed Hunne killed himself because he faced conviction for heresy, but it seems, on balance, that Hunne was murdered by Joseph and Spalding—perhaps deliberately, but more probably while he was being softened up for further examination. Joseph, a defendant in Hunne's praemunire case, had some motive for over-enthusiastic interrogation.

It is difficult to believe that Dr Horsey could have been directly involved—and certainly not in a premeditated murder. Even if there was a risk that Hunne would win his praemunire suit (which is unlikely), Horsey would surely have realized that a dead Hunne would only damage ecclesiastical interests. He would certainly have known that a live Hunne would be convicted of heresy, and that Hunne would either burn, or he would recant and be thoroughly discredited as an opponent. But, except for the purposes of Protestant polemic on the one hand and vindication of Thomas More's honesty on the other, it does not much matter whether Horsey killed Hunne—or, indeed, whether Joseph or Spalding or Hunne himself did. What matters now is that, in the context of the clerical campaign to recover rights thought to have been lost under Henry VII, Hunne seemed a victim of ecclesiastical oppression. Until 3 December 1514, convicting Hunne of heresy could have strengthened the Church's jurisdictional claims; from 4 December, with Hunne a martyr for secular interests, its bargaining position was much weaker.

It was widely believed that churchmen had deliberately murdered a critic to protect their privileges. The papal agent in London reported early in March 1515 that the citizens were furious with the clergy, and there seems to have been much sympathy for the plight of Hunne's widow and children. Bishop Fitzjames pleaded with Wolsey to keep Horsey from trial, since Londoners were now so sympathetic towards heresy that any jury would, he said, 'cast and condemn my clerk though he was as innocent as Abel'. But his accusation leaked out, and the Court of Aldermen sent a deputation to deny any favour for heresy.[24] Horsey's fate had become a national issue, for by an unfortunate coincidence the question of benefit of clergy had been raised in a way which made it appear that the clergy were closing ranks to protect one of their own. In February 1515, while the coroner's jury was still considering the death of Hunne, the abbot of Winchcombe had preached at St Paul's Cross against punishment of clergy by secular courts. The priests were again trying to defend, even extend, their privileges.

It had been the custom in England, since before 1315, for clerks accused of criminal offences to be tried by a secular court, and, if convicted, handed over to a bishop for punishment, the 'benefit' being exemption from secular penalties. Churchmen had long contested this arrangement, and had claimed that clerks should be tried, as well as punished, by other clerks in ecclesiastical courts. In 1462 Edward IV's charter of liberties had granted clergy the right of trial before their own courts. But it seems that the secular courts took no notice, probably because the procedure of indictment by a grand jury led to trial in a secular court, and no alternative mechanism had been created. Convocation had continued to protest that the charter was ignored, and it is likely that the 1510 bill 'for the liberties of the English Church' had claimed separate trials for clerics. But while the clergy were seeking to extend their benefit, in practice it had been curtailed. In 1489 and

1497 statutes had restricted the right of those in minor orders to plead their clergy, and in 1512 there was a further limitation.[25]

It was enacted that convicted murderers and robbers should not be permitted benefit of clergy unless they were actually in holy orders, as ordained subdeacons, deacons, or priests. There was presumably objection from the prelates in the House of Lords, since the Act was passed with a proviso that it was to remain in force only until the next parliament. But in May 1514 Leo X's bull *Supernae dispositionis* had declared that in some matters laymen had no jurisdiction over churchmen. Abbot Kidderminster's sermon at the beginning of the Parliament of 1515 sought to prevent the renewal of the 1512 statute by applying the pope's bull and the text 'Touch not mine anointed'. He denied there was any distinction between holy orders and lesser orders, so that all clergy were exempt from secular punishment. More fundamentally, he argued that the statute was void because it contradicted the law of God and the liberties of the Church, and all those who had participated in its passage were subject to the censures of the Church. Kidderminster had challenged the legislative authority of parliament.[26]

The clergy were not united on the issue of benefit. At the Convocation of 1514, Dr John Taylor had defended the 1512 Act as a necessary consequence of the misbehaviour of clergy. And when a Commons delegation asked the king to convene a conference on the problem, his theologians and canonists spoke up for the Act. Dr Henry Standish denied that the statute was against the laws of God and the liberties of the Church, and claimed it was in the public interest. Against Kidderminster's appeal to the papal bull, Standish argued that the decree had not been formally received in England and was therefore not binding: a claim with good medieval precedents. But the majority of senior clergy were opposed to Standish. When the Commons asked the bishops to force Kidderminster to renounce his views in public, they replied that they were bound to maintain them with all their power, perhaps endorsing Kidderminster's claim that canon law could override parliamentary statute. The dispute was threatening to become a major constitutional crisis; and worse was to come.

During the prorogation of Parliament from April to November 1515, Standish had continued to argue his case in lectures and sermons. But some of the bishops apparently decided to try to silence him, as Colet had been silenced in 1513. When Convocation met in November, Standish was summoned on suspicion of heresy to answer on four articles: whether a secular judge could try clerics; whether minor orders were holy; whether a decree of pope and clergy was binding on a country where custom had been contrary; and whether a king could penalize a bishop who failed to punish offenders as required. Although the articles arose from the immediate debate on the 1512 Act, their implications were far-reaching. The bishops and their canonists were claiming that canon law was independent of king and parliament, and were again asserting that clergy were exempt from secular jurisdiction—not simply from secular punishment, as Kidderminster had first suggested, but from secular trial too. Their stand, if accepted, meant that Horsey would not only escape temporal penalties, he would also escape temporal courts.

Against the common lawyers' argument that canon law was overridden by common law and statute, the canonists were now asserting that common law and statute were overridden by canon law—which they were apparently identifying with the law of God. The king's lawyers and judges met at Blackfriars to consider the issues raised by the Standish case, and the judges attempted to intimidate the churchmen by declaring that those who had participated in citing Standish before Convocation had committed a praemunire. This was an ominous, and probably decisive, development, for by threatening their endowments it forced the bishops to compromise. When Henry VIII called a meeting at Baynard's Castle of both houses of Parliament, his Council, and the judges, Cardinal Wolsey had little choice but to offer a partial retraction on behalf of his colleagues. But the leading bishops—Wolsey himself, Fox, and Warham—continued to maintain that trial of clerks before secular judges contravened the law of God and the liberties of the Church, and asked the king to allow the matter to be decided at Rome. Henry refused.

The bishops had made a serious tactical error, by appearing to challenge the authority of the Crown as well as the authority of the common law: they had driven Henry into the arms of the lay lawyers. It was perhaps at this time, when both lawyers and churchmen were urging him to abide by his coronation oath, that Henry revised its text. He restricted the promise to maintain the liberties of the Church to those 'not prejudicial to his jurisdiction and dignity royal'.[27] At the Baynard's Castle meeting, he stood upon his considerable dignity and declared that

By the ordinance and sufferance of God we are king of England, and the kings of England in time past have never had any superior but God alone. Wherefore know you well that we shall maintain the right of our crown and of our temporal jurisdiction as well in this point as in all others.[28]

Henry was claiming an imperial authority, a sovereignty independent of external powers and internal constraints. He had, indeed, been sporting the emblem of an arched 'imperial' crown since 1511 at least.

The king was not, however, saying anything very new, or anything very significant—though it did sound good. Bishop Stafford had declared in 1397 that Richard II was an emperor in his own kingdom, and kings of other realms made the same claim for themselves. In 1485 Chief Justice Hussey had, as we have already seen, asserted that the king was answerable only to God, and Henry VII had used the imperial crown emblem on coins. In practice, there was no incompatibility between grandiose imperial theory and amicable relations between Crown, Church, and papacy.[29] What mattered was not the slogan Henry VIII used but the action Henry VIII took; and now he did nothing. Wolsey, however, engineered a skilful settlement. There was no praemunire charge against the bishops, and they quietly abandoned the demand for separate clerical trials. Convocation dropped its proceedings against Standish, and the Crown accepted Horsey's plea of innocence. However he was fined £600 and sent off to exile in Exeter. Parliament was dissolved, and the 1512 statute lapsed. Finally, Wolsey secured a decree from Leo X in 1516 that all orders up to subdeacon must be taken simultaneously, so the problem of criminous clerics in minor orders would gradually disappear.

At the end of the Parliament of 1515, the clerk wrote in his journal that 'in this Parliament and Convocation there arose the most dangerous dissensions between the clergy and the secular power over the liberties of the Church'.[30] No doubt that was how it seemed in December. The Hunne and Standish affairs may have presented the clergy as ruthless defenders of existing privileges and arrogant claimants of more. Certainly the death of Hunne made the assertion of clerical rights more sinister, and the assertion of rights made the death of Hunne seem part of a pattern of aggression. But there is, again, a risk that we see events from the misleading perspective of the later Reformations, and imagine monolithic institutions locked in determined combat. It is not clear that the death of Hunne was blamed on 'the Church' or 'the clergy'; perhaps it was blamed on Horsey and his minions. It is unlikely that it was much of an issue outside the London merchant community. Nor is it clear that benefit of clergy was a divisive issue unless the clergy made it so; after 1515 the problem virtually disappeared from the political agenda.

The 'dangerous' Parliament of 1515 was followed not by the dangerous Parliament of 1529 but by the Parliament of 1523, when men had more to think about than criminous clerks. But it would be a mistake to suggest, as some have done, that the English Reformation had really begun in 1515, though it was somehow delayed until 1529 by Wolsey's machinations.[31] It is true that the controversial issues of 1515 were cleverly defused by Wolsey; but the issues of 1515 were not the issues of 1529, or of 1532. The mini-crisis of 1515 was produced not by a lay attack upon the Church, but by the prelates seeking to press further the reassertion of authority begun in 1509; it was produced by clericalism, not anticlericalism. The disputes about clerical immunities were almost as much within the clergy as between clergy and laymen. Above all, in 1515 the king had no interest in asserting greater control over the Church, and once he was assured that the churchmen did not threaten his prerogative he let the matter rest. If 1514–15 was a dress rehearsal for 1529–32, then it was *Hamlet* practised without the prince of Denmark.

In October 1514, when Hunne was arrested for heresy, Thomas Wolsey was the newly promoted archbishop of York. In November 1515, as Convocation proceeded against Standish, Wolsey was made a cardinal, at the king's request. In December, as soon as the parliamentary session had ended (and after his defence of clerical interests), he succeeded Warham as lord chancellor. In May 1518 he was made papal legate *a latere*, special emissary from the pope to the king; in July he was given the bishopric of Bath and Wells, to hold with York—the first time sees had been held in plurality since the mid-eleventh century. Wolsey secured successive extensions and expansions of his legatine commission from Rome, until he held delegated powers which could override, or at least challenge, virtually all other ecclesiastical jurisdictions. His determination to erect an independent legatine administration brought him into conflict with his brother bishops. In 1519 Warham complained that because of Wolsey's claims he would soon 'have nothing left for me and my officers to do, but should be as a shadow and image of an archbishop and legate, void of authority and jurisdiction'.[32]

Except for a debate over sanctuary in 1519–20, after 1515 disputes over the boundaries of ecclesiastical jurisdictions were within the Church rather than between the Church and the secular power; they arose from the ambitions of Wolsey. The feeding of his overweening arrogance was certainly a motive for the grand commissions he sought, but his public justification was the need for a centralized reform programme. The cardinal himself embodied many of the ecclesiastical evils he claimed to abhor, his multitude of responsibilities prevented sustained concentration, and his designs were frustrated by wrangles over jurisdiction. But Wolsey really was a reformer.[33] In 1518 he chaired a conference of bishops which produced a sensible package of reforms. Bishop Fisher repeated some of Colet's strictures of 1510, attacking the worldliness of priests and especially the spending of the people's tithe on luxurious living.[34] The new episcopal decrees covered the morals of the clergy, the duties of incumbents, the selection of deputies for absentees, and the work of middle-rank administrators. They were moderate measures, but they soon encountered resistance.

The constitutions produced by the bishops were not binding, as there had been no representative Convocation, so they were put to local synods of the clergy for confirmation. All went well in the diocese of Hereford, where meetings in the archdeaconries of Hereford and Shropshire accepted the decrees. At the synods of the Lincoln archdeaconries of Oxford and Northampton, too, opposition does not seem to have been significant. But in the archdeaconries of Bedford, Huntingdon, and Leicester, the decrees were rejected. At Huntingdon one priest argued that the bishops had no power to make regulations affecting the lower clergy without their involvement and consent; the other priests present agreed by voting the proposals down. At Leicester it was suggested that the bishops had deliberately organized consultation through local synods, so that opposition would be fragmented. In each archdeaconry, the resistance came especially from the graduate clergy, those who profited from non-residence and would lose most from stricter controls.[35]

Wolsey made further attempts at reform by legislation. He issued comprehensive constitutions for the province of York in 1518, he tried to regulate the behaviour of sanctuary-men in 1519, and in 1519 he obtained sweeping powers from Rome for reform of the secular clergy. The religious orders also endured his attentions: the Augustinian canons were given new constitutions in 1519, the Benedictines had new statutes in 1522, and in 1525 Wolsey embarked on a more systematic rationalization of monasteries. But the Benedictines complained that their new regulations were unrealistic, and if strictly enforced would empty their houses. In 1525 there was local resistance in Kent and Suffolk to Wolsey's suppression of minor monasteries, and some of the clergy—especially the monks—regarded his policy as sacrilegious. In 1526 Henry Gold, Warham's chaplain, preached against the closure of monasteries; it was not the religious orders which needed reform, he suggested pointedly, but clergy in high places who busied themselves in politics.[36]

For all the complaints, however, Wolsey's reforms brought nothing very new. The constitutions issued for York in 1518 were merely re-enactments of much earlier legislation, including Pecham's decree of 1281 on the teaching duties of parish priests. But perhaps that was enough: there had been no decline of clerical standards, and there was no need for emergency measures. As Colet had argued in 1510, the faults in the Church were as they had always been, and the existing canon law already provided for them. 'The need, therefore, is not for the enactment of new laws and constitutions, but for the observance of those already enacted.'[37] And that was exactly what Wolsey's bishops tried to secure. In the diocese of Chichester, Bishop Sherburne revitalized administration, tightened the discipline of the clergy, and sought to ensure that the laity fulfilled their religious duties. In the dioceses of Ely, Lincoln, Norwich, Rochester, and Winchester, energetic bishops imposed firmer controls on the selection and behaviour of their clergy; the same was probably true in Exeter, Hereford, and Lichfield.[38] Colet was now dead, but perhaps his advice had been heeded.

In some part, these reforming bishops responded to the pattern of Christian life and priesthood propounded by Erasmus and Colet. In larger part, they responded to the practical pressures of huge numbers of candidates for ordination and preferment. Perhaps more, they reacted to the legatine challenge of Wolsey; he was claiming new powers to reform, and their own authority was best preserved by undertaking reform themselves. But, above all, they and their junior colleagues resisted what they saw as a hydra-headed lay challenge. The old Lollard heresy, the early influence of Lutheran ideas, the lawyers' attacks on ecclesiastical jurisdiction and litigation, the Londoners' sympathy for Hunne, the exaggerated lay complaints against lax and immoral clergy—all served to provoke the bishops to stifle criticism, defend privileges, and improve conditions. Repression and reform went together. In 1528 Archbishop Warham congratulated Bishop Longland on his 'fervent zeal for reformation to be had as well of heretical doctrines as of misbehaviours in manners': if others had tried as hard, 'the dignity of the Church had not been had in such contempt as it is now'.[39]

The bishops' vigorous encouragement of education was the product of their commitment to reform, which to them meant both the eradication of heresy and the improvement of clerical standards. In 1516 Bishop Fox established Corpus Christi College Oxford, to the glory of God and the Virgin, 'and for the extirpation of heresy and error, and the augmentation of the orthodox faith'. Six bishops shared in the foundation of five university colleges between 1496 and 1525, and five of them drafted or supervised college statutes which emphasized the training of priests by preaching and theological study. Some of the new colleges were planned as centres of the humanistic 'new learning', to contribute to an intellectual as well as an educational reform. At a lesser level, fifteen local schools were founded by eleven bishops between 1490 and 1525; some of them were deliberately designed for the teaching of candidates for ordination. Though their motives were mixed, the commitment of many bishops to Catholic reform, as well as clerical privilege, is clear—and Wolsey himself made two major reformist foundations.[40]

Protected by a lord chancellor less nervous of the common law than Warham had been, the Church courts regained some of their business and their authority. In the diocese of Canterbury, the decline of debt litigation prompted court officials to maintain their fee income by devoting more effort to disciplinary work. The overall instance business of the Canterbury consistory increased in the early 1520s, after thirty years of erosion, and even debt and contract litigation picked up again. In the diocese of Durham, secular defamation remained a major category of business in the consistory. In Chichester diocese, Sherburne's reorganization of the courts produced greater speed and efficiency; instance business recovered, and office prosecutions tripled. But while the business of the ecclesiastical courts revived, that of the common law courts stagnated and then collapsed. The combined litigation of King's Bench and Common Pleas had recovered to 67 per cent of its mid-fifteenth-century level in 1501–10, but then it fell to 56 per cent in the 1510s and 35 per cent in the 1520s. Some lawyers were squeezed harder than ever.[41]

It is unlikely that the recovery of the Church courts took much business away from the common law courts. It was the equity courts of Chancery and Star Chamber which were responsible. It is also unlikely that the common lawyers as a group lost very much, as some of them handled Chancery and Star Chamber suits. But the jurisdictional boundaries between courts were once more matters for debate, and the position of the Church was inevitably an issue. The ecclesiastical courts had apparently beaten off the challenges of Hobart and Hunne, canonists had claimed that their law was superior to statute, clergy sat in judgement in Wolsey's expanding conciliar courts; the interests of the common law now seemed at risk. It is not surprising that criticism of Church courts sharpened as they reasserted their authority, nor that their competence was again challenged. In November 1530, Christopher St German published the second dialogue of his legal text *Doctor and Student*. It was in English, not Latin or law French, and designed to influence educated opinion.

St German had already argued that private property was of human institution, and therefore to be regulated by the laws of men, not those of God. In the second dialogue, he showed that the existing range of canon law could not avoid touching upon property: on the probate and execution of wills, on the property of heretics, on the tithes and goods of the Church itself, for example. The Church had gone beyond its proper jurisdiction, and its rules concerning property were *ultra vires* and not binding. In effect, St German wished to restrict the canon law to narrowly spiritual matters, ceremonies and sacraments.[42] St German was no revolutionary theorist: he was drawing on established legal thought; but he was making it more explicit and public and so, for the Church, potentially more dangerous. The danger would become a reality only if Henry VIII had reason to join an attack on the Church; and in 1530 he had. In October 1530, when *Doctor and Student* II was in the press (and William Tracy was making his Lutheran will), Henry had been persuaded to proceed against the whole English clergy for praemunire.

✦ 5 ✦

Politics and Parliament

IN 1530 the English Church was suddenly confronted with an unexpected and unwonted challenge. In July, the attorney-general filed praemunire indictments in King's Bench against eight bishops and six other ecclesiastical officials. It was alleged that, by entering into compositions with Wolsey for the exercise of their jurisdiction, they had implicated themselves in an illegal assertion of his legatine powers. By September it was rumoured that another 200 clergy would be indicted, and by 21 October Henry VIII had agreed that the whole clergy of England should be charged.[1] The rule of Wolsey had given the common lawyers a powerful weapon against ecclesiastical jurisdiction, and the king was apparently willing to let them use it. The penalties for praemunire offences were loss of property and life imprisonment. Henry could hardly imprison all the clergy, but they were now at his mercy. It seemed that, in an unexpected fall from power in 1529, Cardinal Wolsey might bring the authority of the English Church crashing down with him.

This perilous position was reached in the autumn of a year when the future of the Church had appeared secure, if not untroubled. As we have already seen, the laity were buying orthodox religious books in unprecedented quantity, and they were giving money for their parish churches and for prayers at levels only a fraction down from recent peaks. In the 1520s laymen had entered the priesthood in numbers only ever exceeded in the previous decade, and there were few signs of local friction between priests and people. The clergy's provision of sacraments and pastoral care gave little cause for complaint, and the Church imposed its discipline with general support. The old Lollard heresy had been revitalized by the emergence of evangelists from the universities and the arrival of Lutheran books from Antwerp, but the heretics had so far made little progress. There was still a widespread hostility towards heresy, and in 1530 Henry VIII had twice instructed secular officials to assist the episcopal campaign against heretics. There had, it is true, been a political crisis in 1529, but it had not been the first stage of a Reformation.

The disruptions of 1529 were not the product of deep-seated division between clergy and laity: there was no such division. They were rather the consequences of a chance conjunction of circumstances, which brought temporary danger to churchmen but which determined no disaster. The Parliament of 1529 legislated to control some ecclesiastical fees and some clerical pluralism, but it did so in moderation. Common lawyers had been anxious to trim the power of the Church, and they seem to have taken the lead in the Commons, but they were followed only because of tensions created in the late 1520s. The lawyers had their chance only because Wolsey had been disgraced, and a Parliament called at a time when the king wanted churchmen intimidated. And Henry was hostile not because of a developing notion of imperial sovereignty, but because of a developing affection for Anne Boleyn; a developing worry over the royal succession also played its part. So the recovery of ecclesiastical authority which had taken place under Wolsey was not wrecked by lay intransigence: it was halted by the machinations of a talented woman, and of the politicians who used her charms for their own advancement.

Henry VIII was first attracted by Anne Boleyn early in 1526, when he was most vulnerable.[2] The king had found the solace of his wife insufficient as early as 1514; his mistress Elizabeth Blount bore their son in 1519, and was passed on to a Lancashire gentleman in 1522. Elizabeth Blount was then succeeded by Mary Carey, married sister of Anne Boleyn; Henry apparently left her to her husband in 1525. Since Henry had also ceased sexual relations with Queen Katherine in 1525, he was open to other allures. He was also concerned for the succession. Henry and Katherine's only surviving child, Mary, had been born in 1516; there had been a miscarriage in 1517, a still birth in 1518, and no further pregnancy. For a king to have but one legitimate heir was worry enough; for that heir to be female was, given patriarchal and feudal concepts of competence and authority, a national nightmare. Henry again offered Mary in marriage to the Emperor Charles V, so his daughter would at least have a powerful husband—but Charles refused her. The king's bastard son was then created duke of Richmond in June 1525, as a male candidate for the throne.

Henry's quest for Anne began with courtly dalliance and grew to passionate devotion. We do not know whether Henry decided to divorce Katherine of Aragon because he had fallen for Anne, or whether he fell for Anne when he had already decided to divorce Katherine. Probably the two processes of decision went together, encouraged by Anne's refusal to become a mere mistress, a refusal which suggests Anne knew she could realistically aim for marriage. Anne offered the twin fulfilment of regal duty and personal joy—if Henry could dispose of Katherine, and there was no reason to suppose he could not. Indeed, Henry had his argument ready to hand, for he had apparently already begun to doubt the validity of a marriage which had not produced the necessary male heir. Two biblical texts from Leviticus were said to forbid a man's marriage to his brother's widow; Henry had married the wife of his dead brother Arthur.[3] Enticed by the prospects of a new wife and a son who would surely follow, Henry easily convinced himself that he was free to marry Anne—when the Church could be brought to agree.

Henry's first attempt to have his marriage annulled was carried out in secret. At the end of May 1527, Cardinal Wolsey and Archbishop Warham heard pleadings from the king's proctor against the 1505 dispensation issued by Pope Julius II to permit Henry and Katherine to marry within prohibited degrees. But on 1 June 1527 came news that ravaging troops of the Emperor Charles V had sacked Rome and made Pope Clement VII their prisoner. It had been likely that Katherine would appeal to Rome against an annulment granted by Wolsey; now, with the pope a puppet of Katherine's nephew Charles, it was certain her appeal would be upheld. So Henry had to seek a divorce which would not be overturned on appeal to Clement. It was initially hoped that this could be achieved as part of Wolsey's master plan to establish a papacy in exile at Avignon: the confined Clement would delegate his pontifical authority to Wolsey, who would then solve the diplomatic problems of Europe and the marital problems of the king of England. It was a grand scheme, but pope, cardinals, emperor, the king of France and, finally, even the king of England failed to co-operate.[4]

The secret divorce strategy was not secret for long. There were soon rumours around London, Katherine was warned, and the imperial ambassador told Charles what was afoot. On 22 June 1527 Henry informed his distressed wife that she was not a wife at all—though he continued to treat her as a queen. The search for a divorce seems to have completed Henry's commitment to Anne: his (undated) love letters to her suggest it was about this time that they finally determined to marry.[5] Wolsey went off to France, on the first stage of his mission to acquire papal powers. But, in impatience, Henry sought to bypass the cardinal by sending a direct emissary to the pope, asking for what was effectively a dispensation for bigamy. Wolsey, though, managed to scotch this foolish tactic. Wolsey probably did not yet know that Henry planned to marry Anne, and he saw the divorce as part of his diplomatic revolution, shifting England from an imperial to a French alliance: the king would divorce a Spaniard and marry a Frenchwoman. The cardinal's error soon became clear.

In August 1527 Henry began to shower Anne with gifts of jewellery; in September he sought a papal dispensation to marry her if the Aragon marriage was annulled. Since Mary Boleyn had been Henry's mistress, he was related to Anne in the first degree of affinity, exactly the relationship between Henry and Katherine; so again a dispensation was needed. (There was a certain embarassment in seeking a dispensation from the pope to marry Anne while claiming the dispensation to marry Katherine was against the law of God; but Henry was a literal-minded man, who thought the Leviticus prohibition of marriage to a brother's wife did not apply to a sister's lover.) Henry's agent William Knight was once more instructed to keep his mission secret from the cardinal. When Wolsey discovered that Henry was again acting independently (and ineptly), and heard the king had been told he was not pursuing the divorce with vigour, he rushed back to England. But he found that, in his absence, his political position had been undermined: Anne was recognized as favourite, and had formed an alliance with Wolsey's aristocratic enemies.[6]

Henry VIII did not turn irrevocably against the cardinal, and Anne Boleyn dared not become an open enemy, but Wolsey's situation was now insecure. His near monopoly of patronage and political advice had been broken, and replaced by an unstable competition for influence. Anne's position gave her allies—especially her father Viscount Rochford and her uncle the duke of Norfolk—a line of communication to the king. They were able to jockey for power with Wolsey, and to restrict his freedom of action. Wolsey was forced to improve his own communications with Henry. He sought to surround him with reliable clients, and packed the Privy Chamber with his own henchmen; Sir Richard Page and Thomas Heneage were added to Sir John Russell. Anne retaliated by persuading Henry to appoint her own relations—her brother George Boleyn and her cousin Francis Bryan—to the Privy Chamber. There was also a third group in the Privy Chamber: Henry's old friends the marquis of Exeter and Sir Nicholas Carew, who complicated matters further by their support of Queen Katherine and antagonism towards Wolsey.[7]

In the spring of 1528 'the matter of Wilton' provided a clear demonstration that the pattern of politics had changed.[8] The death of Cecily Willoughby, abbess of the lax and fashionable Benedictine convent of Wilton in Wiltshire, raised a minor issue of patronage, which became part of a major struggle for power. A majority of the nuns appear to have backed the succession of the prioress, Isabel Jordayn, who was expected to reform the convent and impose stricter standards. But a slacker minority supported Eleanor Carey, sister of Anne Boleyn's brother-in-law William Carey, confident that her family influence would protect them from an exacting Jordayn regime. Anne and William persuaded Henry to agree to Eleanor's promotion, and Wolsey had to acquiesce despite his preference for Isabel. But then Eleanor's scandalous past became known: she had had affairs with two priests, and had borne children. Henry dropped his favour of Eleanor, and Wolsey took advantage of his legatine authority to nominate the reformer Isabel Jordayn as abbess.

But Henry was unwilling to offend Anne more than was essential, and her allies in the Privy Chamber had probably been lobbying. Henry had had to deny Anne's suit for Eleanor, but he did not have to accept Wolsey's nominee. He told Anne that 'to do you pleasure' he would order that Isabel Jordayn be not appointed, and that a third candidate be found. The king wrote three times to Wolsey to insist on a third course, but Wolsey stood by his choice. Perhaps he saw it as a matter of religious reform; more likely it was a trial of strength with Anne. In the event, Wilton had its stricter abbess and Wolsey had his way, but at a high political price. Henry was furious at the cardinal's disobedience, which seemed to confirm the allegations that Wolsey could not be trusted to serve the royal interest. When Wolsey claimed he had not known of the king's wishes, Henry bluntly accused him of lying:

Ah, my lord, it is a double offence, both to do ill and to colour it too; but with men that hath wit it cannot be accepted so. Wherefore, good my lord, use no more that way with me, for there is no man living that more hateth it.[9]

The Wilton affair was more than a noise about nuns. It showed Wolsey that he could thwart Anne only at the risk of alienating Henry, and it showed Henry that he could not wholly rely on Wolsey. The cardinal was now in an almost impossible position. He had to get Henry an annulment to retain the king's favour, for failure—even delay—would be construed as disloyalty. But the annulment was proving difficult to obtain, and Henry could not quite understand why. The problems were both legal and political. Henry's favourite argument, that Julius II's dispensation for the Aragon marriage was invalid because no pope could dispense from the law of God, was unlikely to succeed. This was partly because the dominant opinion among canonists was that marriage to a brother's widow was not forbidden by God, and partly because a pope would not willingly declare that a predecessor had acted against divine law. So Wolsey had to rely on a subsidiary argument, that there were technical deficiencies in the original dispensation: somewhat slim grounds for divorcing the aunt of that emperor whose army menaced the pope.

Wolsey was forced to seek a method of dissolving the Aragon marriage which would prevent any appeal by Katherine to the pope. He therefore pressed for a decretal commission from Clement VII, a commission which declared the law as it applied in the case, left Wolsey to establish the facts, and prohibited any appeal against his decision. English commissioners warned Clement that Wolsey's position in England depended on the grant of a commission, and hinted that Henry's loyalty to Rome was being jeopardized.[10] The pope replied in April 1528 with a commission which gave Wolsey almost what he wanted; but almost was not enough to guarantee Henry a new marriage and public acceptance of any heir. At length, in October 1528, Cardinal Campeggio arrived in London, carrying a decretal commission for himself and Wolsey to hear the case as legates. But it did not block all loopholes, and Clement had ordered that it was to be shown only to Wolsey and the king. Wolsey, however, soon recognized that it was the best that could be had from a pope very much more afraid of Charles V than of Henry VIII.

When Wolsey warned Campeggio and Clement that he was at risk if Henry did not have his divorce quickly, he was not exaggerating. And when he warned that papal authority was at risk too, he was exaggerating only a little.[11] In December 1528 Katherine had been sent away from Court, and Anne Boleyn had moved to a suite adjoining the king's. By January 1529 at the latest, Anne had concluded that Wolsey sought to frustrate, not achieve, her marriage to Henry, and was scheming with Norfolk, her father, and the duke of Suffolk. Anne's supporters were telling Henry that an annulment would only be achieved by ignoring the papacy. Anne showed him a copy of Tyndale's *The Obedience of a Christian Man*, which argued that princes were subject to God alone.[12] Members of Henry's latest mission to Rome bullied the pope with threats that Henry would follow the example of the Lutheran princes in Germany. They criticized Wolsey in their reports to Henry, and told him that the pope would do nothing to help.[13] But the Boleyn faction had not completely broken Henry's confidence in his cardinal; he continued to hope for something from Wolsey's wizardry, and pressed the two legates to hear his divorce case.

The legatine court opened at Blackfriars on 18 June 1529, though Katherine spoiled the early proceedings by announcing that she had already appealed to Rome. In the following sessions her counsel, led by Bishop Fisher, argued vigorously for the validity of Julius II's dispensation, and Henry's case was bogged down in technical detail. But it was soon too late for the king—and for Wolsey. On 21 June Charles V's troops had routed the French at Landriano, and removed any possibility that French military pressure might free the pope from imperial coercion. Clement told a confidant, 'I have quite made up my mind to become an imperialist, and live and die as such':[14] he would give Henry no annulment. On 16 July Clement VII formally revoked Henry's suit to Rome. On 31 July Cardinal Campeggio, knowing a revocation document would be on its way from Rome, adjourned the case for the summer. The duke of Suffolk thumped the table and declared bluntly, 'By the mass, now I see that the old saw is true, that there was never legate nor cardinal that did good in England!'[15]

Wolsey's enemies guessed that their opportunity had come as soon as Katherine appealed to Rome. Lord Darcy collated their evidence against Wolsey in a paper dated 1 July 1529, a comprehensive indictment of the cardinal's regime in Church and state. On ecclesiastical matters, it was objected that Wolsey had exercised papal authority contrary to the royal prerogative, overridden the jurisdiction and rights of other churchmen, and misused Church revenues and property. There was obvious outrage that 'the abomination, ruin and seditions and erroneous violations used at the pulling down of abbeys by his commissioners and servants, and the great robberies and spoilings, may be weighted to the worst act or article of Martin Luther's'.[16] Although the complaints were couched in terms of righteous conservative indignation, Darcy's draft programme for a parliament was ominous:[17] the overthrow of Wolsey was to be followed by an exclusion of cardinals and legates from England, a reduction of fees charged by the clergy, and an attack on ecclesiastical property. Here were echoes of John of Gaunt's campaign in the 1370s. If the king were converted to such a policy, the clergy would be in trouble.

It seemed there was no one to save Wolsey, for he had alienated all possible support. Even his fellow clergy were against him—and no wonder. His assertion of legatine authority, and especially his claim to the probate of wills, had brought him into conflict with the other bishops. His unprecedented tax demands had provoked hostility from the lower clergy, both in the Lower House of Convocation in 1523 and in the parishes in 1525. As we have seen, conservative common lawyers had been angered by his expansion of the work of equity courts, and perhaps by his deflection of their attack on ecclesiastical litigation. Some of the nobility had been enraged by his arrogance and autocratic rule, and some had disagreed with his foreign policy, especially the new alliance with France. There was particular opposition in London, with resistance to his financial exactions, resentment of his treatment of City companies, and fear that his cold war with the emperor would disrupt the cloth trade. But, despite all, Wolsey still had one friend, and the one who really counted: Henry.

The aristocratic conspirators and their allies had to work hard to destroy Wolsey. Norfolk, Suffolk, and Rochford surrounded the king and kept Wolsey away during the summer progress; Stephen Gardiner, the new secretary, answered Wolsey's letters to Henry coldly. The king was persuaded to order writs for a new parliament, which might be used against the cardinal. Wolsey finally managed to gain an interview with Henry in mid-September, through the mediation of Campeggio. But although Henry's kindness to Wolsey worried the enemies, it was clear that they had almost managed to turn Henry against him. Anne Boleyn had been campaigning openly against the cardinal, and some of her allies had been advocating a drastic solution to Henry's various problems. They proposed that the overthrow of Wolsey should be combined with the confiscation of Church property and the abolition of papal authority, so the divorce could be settled in England. Henry was being offered considerable inducements to dispose of Wolsey: a massive gain of property, and a marriage to Anne Boleyn.[18]

Although Henry did not accept the whole Darcy programme, he agreed to the dismissal of Wolsey. On 9 October 1529, first day of the legal term, Wolsey was indicted in King's Bench for praemunire, having infringed jurisdictions in England by exercise of his legatine authority. On 17

October he was ordered to surrender the great seal. But Henry sent him a ring, in token of continuing friendship. With Parliament due to meet on 3 November, Wolsey probably calculated that he had better seek punishment from the king than await the wrath of Lords and Commons. On 22 October he formally acknowledged his guilt of praemunire, and on 30 October submitted himself to the king's mercy; his lands and goods were declared forfeit. But Wolsey was not finished, and for a year the possibility—at times the likelihood—of his recovery hung over those who had brought him down. He was not imprisoned, but allowed to retire to his house at Esher, and on 18 November Henry reversed part of the sentence for praemunire. Wolsey's influential enemies then laid forty-four further charges against him,[19] and petitioned Henry to ensure that Wolsey never again wielded power. Yet still Henry showed him signs of favour.

So the dominating issue which hung over the first session of the new Parliament was not the divorce of the king or the reform of the Church; it was the cardinal: his rule, his future, and the safety of those who stood against him. There were energetic attempts to keep the anti-Wolsey bandwagon rolling, and to show the king the level of hostility to the cardinal. In mid-October the London Court of Aldermen had instructed the livery companies to produce a programme for Parliament, and the Mercers' Company suggested five grievances arising from Wolsey's regime. Four of the articles related to trade and the law, but a fifth was couched as a broad attack on probate charges, mortuaries, and ecclesiastical court fees.[20] It is true that probate fees hit merchants hard, since they were calculated on the value of goods (which merchants had) rather than lands (which they did not). But probate fees had been a dead parliamentary issue for a hundred years. Rather, complaints which implicitly raised the Hunne case and the work of Wolsey's legatine courts owed as much to the campaign against the cardinal as to any genuine and general grievances.

On the first day of the Parliament, copies of Simon Fish's *A Supplication for the Beggars*, with its denunciation of clerical wealth (shades of Wolsey again), were distributed in the streets of London. In his speech at the opening ceremony, the new chancellor, Thomas More, drew attention to the cardinal's misdeeds, noting that as yet he had suffered only 'gentle correction' and 'small punishment'.[21] The groups which had particular grievances against Wolsey—lawyers and merchants—were especially well represented in the House of Commons, and their complaints were soon aired. Edward Hall remembered later that the early discussions in the Commons were of probate, mortuaries, pluralists, non-residents, and priests who served as stewards or traders.[22] A provocative petition to the king was drafted, asking how the bishops could justify clerical pluralism, holding of secular office, leasing of secular property, and trading; mainly issues which Wolsey's career had made prominent. A substantial case was being erected against Wolsey, in addition to the praemunire charge he had admitted.

It is clear that the cardinal's enemies were throwing as much mud as they could in his direction, and some of it was splashing over other churchmen. But there may have been some real feeling that the clergy, and not just the cardinal, had to be cut down to size. Perhaps it was true that, as Hall claimed, Wolsey's dominance in the kingdom had encouraged the pretensions of the priests, at least in London. In 1528 the citizens had again seen clerical aggression in action. On behalf of the whole city clergy, one of Wolsey's chaplains and six other priests had protested to the Common Council against lay evasion of tithe, and demanded an improvement in the terms of assessment. They insisted that personal tithe should now be paid as a duty, and not, as it had come to be, a voluntary offering. The Common Council was probably reluctant to risk a confrontation with Wolsey, and made limited concessions to the priests, publicized by bills set up in churches informing the laity of their obligations. It is unlikely that the new terms made much difference to the tithe paid, but the clergy had scored a victory over the citizens.[23]

All in all, it seems that the complaints expressed in the House of Commons in 1529 were the product of recent circumstances and particular interests rather than of deep-seated grievances. In the summer of 1528 there had been a severe outbreak of the sweating sickness in London, which had closed the law courts and brought, as the French ambassador remarked, more business to the priests than the doctors.[24] The high mortality naturally led to more mortuaries and more probate fees, and it may have been the number rather than the level of these charges which led to trouble in the following year. In some parishes mortuaries were already levied on a sliding scale rather than a flat rate, and incumbents often exempted the poor. In most dioceses, probate fees were still charged on a scale drawn up in 1341, and the wills of the poor were given probate without fee. But when the Mercers protested against mortuaries and probate, and when the comptroller of the king's Household (a long-standing opponent of Wolsey) made outrageous allegations about the fees the cardinal had collected, the rest of the Commons were willing enough to follow.[25]

A Commons committee of lawyers considered the issues raised in debate, and drafted proposals for reform. They considered complaints about mortuaries, probate, pluralism, Church court fees and other administrative charges, heresy proceedings, and the right of Convocation to make laws which bound laymen. But from this rag-bag of issues they proceeded only with the first three, the least contentious and most closely related to Wolsey. The draft mortuaries bill apparently caused no difficulty; it passed the Commons, and in the Lords the prelates did not resist. Hall reported that the bishops admitted some priests had been greedy, but thought they acquiesced 'because it touched them little'. Perhaps they recognized that the bill would make slight difference to practice in many areas. But the bill to limit probate fees did affect the bishops, and in the Lords they 'both frowned and grunted'.[26] Having just reclaimed their full probate revenues from Wolsey, they would not willingly see them denied by the Commons!

John Fisher, bishop of the poorest English see and a stickler for the rights of the Church, led the protest. He denied that the bills from the Commons were honest attempts to reform real abuses, for the clergy were already dealing with defects. Rather, they were deliberate invasions of clerical privilege, and the preliminary skirmishes of an attack on Church property. The real motives of the Church's critics were economic: 'If the truth were known, ye shall find that they rather hunger and thirst after the riches and possessions of the clergy, than after the amendment of their faults and abuses.' There was a good deal of truth in Fisher's analysis, for the bills did not reflect widespread grievances and they came from sectional interests. The final Probate Act helped none but the rich; the poor were exempted from fees, but that had happened anyway, and the new scale of fees threw heavier burdens on middling groups while reducing payments by the prosperous. But Fisher went too far: he warned the Lords of what had happened in Germany, and declared that 'all these mischiefs among them riseth through lack of faith'.[27]

In the Commons, Fisher's attack was interpreted as an accusation of heresy, and seized upon as an opportunity to enlist the support of the king. Speaker Audley led a delegation to complain to Henry, who summoned Fisher to explain himself. Fisher, with a phalanx of bishops to back him, stood by his defence of the Church, but claimed he had meant it was the mischiefs in Germany, not in the Commons, which 'riseth through lack of faith'. King and Commons were not convinced, but there the matter rested. We do not know what part Henry and his advisers had played in the early proceedings in the Commons, but all the signs are that from this point onwards business was carefully managed, if only because the Crown was having trouble with its bill to cancel royal debts. Lords and Commons now appointed joint committees to consider mortuaries and probate, and when they failed to reach agreement the king had new compromise bills drafted. The principles of mortuary and probate charges were not challenged, and there was no hostile criticism of clerical practice. The prelates abandoned their resistance, and the bills passed.

The Commons bill against pluralism also provoked conflict, again defused by royal interference. The pluralities issue arose from the scandalous cases of Wolsey and his bastard son, and perhaps from Wolsey chaplains who had the best London benefices. Although a fifth or a quarter of benefices were held in plurality, adequate curates were almost always supplied and neglect very rarely ensued.[28] Indeed, where there was pastoral neglect it was usually the fault of monastic appropriators,[29] but that stick could not be used to beat Wolsey. A reduction of pluralism would make no difference to pastoral care: it would simply make some curates into incumbents. The bill which the Commons passed was bitterly resisted by the prelates in the Lords, since it interfered with the regulation of clerical discipline. Once more the king broke the deadlock, if only because he would lose if his own clerical servants could not be funded by pluralism. He ordered a joint committee of eight members of each House to hammer out a compromise bill in Star Chamber. It was not a compromise the bishops liked; but they accepted it, perhaps encouraged by the knowledge that the king had exempted praemunire offences from the general pardon.

The pluralities bill was emasculated by amendments. The final statute was so hedged about with provisos that it can have made very little difference in practice: any priest with influence enough to secure two benefices would surely have qualified under the Act. If pluralism had really been a grievance of the laity, it should have been the Commons rather than the prelates who objected to the legislation! The later history of the Pluralities Act does not suggest there had been seething resentment of pluralism and a determination to crush it. The legislation on mortuaries, probate, and pluralism was to be enforced in the Exchequer Court, with informers offered half of the fine on each offender. But in 1530–5 there were only 210 prosecutions of clergy, most of them brought by trouble-makers and only fourteen of them pressed to a conclusion in court; in the 1530s Londoners cited only seven of their priests for breach of the statutes. But perhaps it was the principle rather than the practice which mattered to the lawyers in the Commons: clergy were now punished under secular laws for infringements of discipline.

It is possible to write an outline narrative of the 1529 parliamentary session only because we have the chronicle of Edward Hall, who sat in the Commons. But Hall was a lawyer and Protestant sympathizer, whose account was written later to show the defects of the Church, the growth of lay criticism, and the role of the king in reform. He imposed a Reformation perspective on the session, and probably exaggerated the significance of ecclesiastical issues. The six-week session, after all, produced twenty-six statutes; nine were on economic matters, four on criminal law, four on land law, three were private Acts, one was the general pardon, and one—surely the most contentious of all—cancelled the loans owed by the king. Only three statutes dealt with the clergy, though one of the criminal statutes restricted sanctuary.[30] Four very damp reforming squibs did not make the first explosion of the Reformation. Taken as a whole, the parliamentary business of 1529 was not a consequence of hostility to the Church; it was a consequence of the rule of Thomas Wolsey.

The Church had flaws, and therefore some critics; its leaders had offended vested interests, especially London lawyers and merchants, and therefore it had enemies. The policies and the excesses of Wolsey had united the enemies, and given their slogans a spurious validity. And now his failure in the divorce offered opportunities to discredit the Church with his abuses and to discredit him with the Church's. In the circumstances of 1529, surely, it is surprising how little, not how much, the critics achieved: the clergy escaped almost unscathed, though they did not see it that way. The committee of lawyers produced only three bills on peripheral issues. Perhaps they lacked confidence that more drastic proposals would be supported in the House; perhaps they were intimidated by Fisher's charge of heresy; perhaps they guessed that the king would allow no more. When there was conflict with the prelates, Henry intervened to achieve compromise rather than to coerce the clergy into submission. Henry did not encourage, nor did he permit, a frontal attack on the churchmen; for all its attractions, he had not been converted to the Boleyn strategy.

But that is not what he told the pope and the foreign ambassadors; they were to think that he had set the laity and heretics on the Church. In a deliberately dramatic and ominous gesture, Henry had replaced Wolsey as chancellor not with another cleric (though Warham may have been offered his old job), but by a layman, Thomas More. A few weeks later, Henry had dined with Chapuys, the new imperial ambassador, and taunted him with hints of horrors to come. He argued that wars and heresies were the results of the vanity and ambition of popes and cardinals, and that Luther's criticism of clerical vices had been entirely justified. Luther was not all bad, and his heresy 'was not a sufficient reason for reproving and rejecting the many truths he had brought to light'. The need for Church reform was now obvious, and Henry would do his duty by rooting scandals from the English Church. To make the point of the conversation quite clear, he concluded with an attack on papal dispensations, claiming that if the pope could dispense for pluralism he could do so for bigamy—a new twist to an old Lollard argument.[31]

Henry's priority was still a marriage to Anne Boleyn, and the coup against Wolsey had done only a little to advance his cause. The attack on the cardinal, like the proceedings in Parliament and the threats to seize ecclesiastical property, contributed to the campaign to intimidate the pope. But it would take much more pressure than Henry was willing to exert to raise Clement's fear for the English Church above his fear of Charles V. Other approaches were needed. Since before the legatine hearing, Henry had had a small group of scholars working on arguments for his divorce: Edward Foxe, Stephen Gardiner, Edward Lee, John Stokesley, and Nicholas de Burgo. A little before Wolsey's fall, they were joined by Thomas Cranmer, who apparently suggested two related tactics. Cranmer thought that the overriding authority of the Levitical prohibition might be established by consulting the university canonists and theologians of

Europe; and, in case the weight of learned opinion did not persuade the pope, justifications for unilateral action in England should be sought.[32]

Henry's approval of the Cranmer plan sent teams of English agents scouring foreign libraries and badgering foreign faculties. The English universities were also consulted. In February 1530 the king asked Cambridge for an opinion on the validity of his marriage. The senior members as a whole were divided, but Stephen Gardiner, master of Trinity Hall, persuaded them to entrust a decision to a committee of theologians; on 9 March the Cambridge Convocation produced the required answer. Oxford proved more difficult. In February Archbishop Warham, the university's chancellor, asked for a unanimous opinion, but this could not be achieved. Warham then ordered the university leaders to ensure that their juniors did not block a decision, and Bishop Longland tried the Gardiner approach and asked that the theologians should decide. There was opposition from the arts faculty to any exclusion from the discussions, and opposition from the town to the divorce proposal; Longland and his companions were stoned by the women of Oxford. But, after direct orders from the king, the decision went to a committee; Convocation approved its recommendation on 8 April, and condemned the Aragon marriage.[33]

Henry's marriage had now become a matter for international debate, and a large number of learned studies were printed or circulated in manuscript. John Fisher wrote at least seven books on the subject; some were smuggled across the Channel and one of them was printed in Spain. One after another, the leading European canonists and theologians came down in favour of the marriage to Katherine, and denied that there were grounds for annulment. But Henry's agents had more success with the university faculties, partly through the distribution of bribes (or 'retainers') to impecunious academics. By the middle of 1530, university opinions in favour of an annulment had been obtained from Paris, Orléans, Bologna, Padua, and three others. But Angers had declared against Henry, the pope had silenced Perugia, the Venetian civil authorities had forbidden discussion; elsewhere Charles V's bribes were larger than Henry's. It was a helpful, but not a very impressive, collection, and certainly not the academic consensus which might have induced the pope to change his mind.

It seems clear that judgements on the Aragon marriage as yet bore no relationship to any emerging divisions between Catholics and Protestants, in England or in Europe. Since there seemed no prospect that the issue would be solved except within the framework of papal law and theology, it had no broader implications. Although John Fisher regarded defence of the marriage as necessary to the defence of papal authority, other Catholics did not see it that way. John Stokesley, who was to die bewailing his failure to oppose the royal supremacy, was a leading proponent of the divorce. Protestants did not turn against the marriage because they had turned against the pope; both Luther and Tyndale denied the marriage was contrary to divine law, and Tyndale thought the divorce a nasty plot by Wolsey to lead the king astray. In England, Henry's team of divorce scholars included future Protestants (Cranmer and Foxe), clear Catholics (Lee and Stokesley), and Stephen Gardiner, who gave up the pope without much sign of regret, but wished to preserve Catholic belief and practice.

While Henry's agents collected opinions from the universities of France and Italy, it was necessary to prevent the pope giving a pre-emptive decision. In February 1530 Henry sent a mission to Bologna to try to persuade Charles and Clement to agree to a divorce, but in the prevailing diplomatic climate there was no reason why either should make a concession. Indeed, on 7 March Clement finally gave in to pressure from Charles, cited Henry to appear in Rome for trial of his case, and threatened excommunication if he remarried without papal approval.[34] This was a disaster for Henry, and exactly what Wolsey had tried to avoid. Until then, even after the revocation to Rome, it had remained possible to seek a legal solution in England and hope that the pope would accept a *fait accompli*; that was what the pope's own advisers had suggested at the start of the whole business. But now it was too late: either the pope must find for Henry, or Henry must deliberately flout the pope—unless, that is, Henry would give up his hopes for Anne and a secure succession, and there was no sign of that. Clement VII had put his authority in England at risk.

The English did not know what to do. The duke of Norfolk suggested Henry should ignore the citation, marry Anne, and hope for the best. But Norfolk was nervous. In April 1530 he asked Chapuys what the emperor would do if Henry married Anne in defiance of the pope: would he invade England? Chapuys replied that no foreign invasion would be needed, for the English themselves would rebel against Henry; there had been enough evidence of popular sympathy for Katherine and hostility to Anne to make that a perfectly believable threat.[35] Somehow, it seemed, the pope had to be persuaded to grant a divorce. The leading English prelates and magnates thought to support Henry's cause were summoned to a grand Council on 12 June, and told to bring their personal seals. They were presented with the draft of a letter to the pope, demanding a divorce as essential to the interests of the realm. There seems to have been opposition to the hostile tone of the petition; it was redrafted, and eventually signed by six bishops, twenty-two abbots, forty-two peers, and a dozen household officers. The lord chancellor and most of the bishops were not asked.[36]

This was the last, desperate throw of a papalist strategy, and it failed. In September the pope replied that if Henry wanted a rapid solution he should send his lawyers to Rome so that they could get on with the case! It was clear that Clement would not be moved by political pleas; surely, he asked, Henry did not want the issue decided 'without regard had either to right or justice'[37]—the very idea! This response can only have contributed to Henry's growing determination to act without papal approval, and, indeed, to deny that papal approval was necessary. For by September 1530 Henry's divorce think-tank had produced just what the king needed: a collection of documents and precedents used to show that the English Church had provincial rights and independent jurisdiction, and that the English king had sovereign authority over Church and realm. Henry had been told of the arguments in August, and in September he was shown the collection, the *Collectanea satis copiosa*. He seized upon it eagerly, annotated its texts, and swallowed its evidence and its conclusions.[38]

Up to and including the petition of June 1530, Henry and his agents had pleaded and threatened to get an annulment from the pope. When Clement had been warned Henry might be forced to take matters into his own hands, that had been only a tactic to secure a favourable decision. But at the end of August 1530 Henry instructed his ambassadors at Rome to tell the pope that by ancient privilege no Englishman could be cited outside the realm to answer to a foreign jurisdiction. In mid-September he enthusiastically explained to the new papal nuncio that English suits had to be heard at home. The hope was that Clement would recognize England's newly discovered status, and Henry's agents were to search the Vatican library for evidence that earlier popes had done so. Clement should then grant that the divorce could be decided in England; if he did not, there remained the second argument of the *Collectanea*. On 25 September the duke of Suffolk and Anne's father, now earl of Wiltshire, told the nuncio 'they cared neither for pope nor popes in this kingdom', for the king 'was absolute both as emperor and pope in his own kingdom'.[39]

International political reality had brought Henry to recognize that he would get no help from Rome; spurious historical argument brought him to recognize that he did not need it. A solution to his problem should be found in England, if his subjects could be brought to co-operate. He summoned a meeting of clergy and lawyers in October, and put to them the *Collectanea*'s argument for provincial independence—which seems to have astonished them. He then asked whether parliament could and would enact that, despite the pope's prohibition, the divorce case could be settled in England by the archbishop of Canterbury. We do not know exactly who attended this meeting, nor who was brave enough to reply to Henry, but he was told it could not be done.[40] It was probably this refusal which persuaded the king and his closest councillors that he would have to assert firmer control of the English Church. A week later it was decided that the praemunire indictments against individual officials would be abandoned. Instead, the whole English clergy would be charged. Henry had taken a new and perilous course.

PART II

Two Political Reformations, 1530–1553

6

Divorce, Supremacy, and Schism, 1530–1535

HENRY VIII did not have much patience, and by the autumn of 1530 there was little left. He had wanted Anne Boleyn for four years, but his desires had been frustrated. He had sought a divorce since May 1527, but his cardinal, his canonists, and his diplomats had failed him. Wolsey's strategems, the intricate arguments from the royal advisers, and the king's own threats to Rome had made no progress against Clement VII's fear of the emperor. The pope had not granted an annulment, and it seemed unlikely that he ever would. By September 1530, Henry thought he had found an answer in the principles of the *Collectanea*, and Anne and her family were advocating a unilateral solution within England. But this new hope was challenged when the October meeting of clergy and lawyers advised that parliament could not empower an archbishop to act against the pope's prohibition. Henry was furious: he prorogued the expected parliamentary session, and began a campaign of intimidation to alter the October decision. He had been given a reason to attack the privileges and pockets of the English clergy.

But Henry VIII had not embarked upon a Reformation, and he had no clear strategy. He did not begin implementation of a preconceived plan; if he had had a plan, he would have pushed it through much faster. Henry had certainly been attracted by the ideas enshrined in the *Collectanea*, but he seems to have been uncertain of their implications and their usefulness. He received conflicting advice from his divided councillors, but none offered a safe solution.[1] The Boleyns, and their *arriviste* allies Thomas Audley and Thomas Cromwell, proposed to ignore Rome and seek a dissolution from an English court under parliamentary authority, but the October meeting had blocked that road for the present. Norfolk, Suffolk, and others hoped to get the king his divorce by threatening the pope and the English Church, but that approach had failed so far, and they were increasingly fearful that the threats might become painful realities. Thomas More, the marquis of Exeter, and Katherine's supporters wished to block the divorce and protect the Church. But they could hardly achieve their ends and retain royal favour, unless Anne went too far and drove Henry back to Katherine. No wonder the king was confused.

Henry himself was impatient for an annulment, but still cautious in the means he was willing to employ. He had been told that England had a jurisdictional independence of Rome and that he enjoyed a spiritual supremacy over the national Church, but he wanted the pope to accept these arguments and allow a local decision on the divorce. He saw in the *Collectanea* further grounds for papal agreement to a divorce, rather than new grounds for a separation from Rome. Though it is true that the ideas of the *Collectanea* led naturally to the 1533 Act of Appeals and the royal supremacy, Henry did not yet follow the lead. The king did not envisage schism, and still less would he countenance heresy. He had approved of Tyndale's *Obedience of a Christian Man* and had told the imperial ambassador that Martin Luther was not all bad; but in 1530 he had again banned their books, and he allowed More and the bishops to round up heretics. So Henry turned on his clergy not in pursuit of Protestantism or an autonomous Church of England, but because he could think of no better way to promote his divorce than to bully the priests.

The Convocation of Canterbury met in January 1531, amid well-publicized threats of a praemunire against the whole clergy.[2] The bishops began to discuss pastoral reforms and the disciplining of heretics, and, no doubt, waited for what the king had in store. They were soon told. Henry sent to the House of Lords a bill to pardon the clergy for their complicity in Wolsey's guilt. He then demanded a huge clerical subsidy of £100,000, claiming this would cover his expenses arising from the clergy's failure to pursue the divorce suit effectively. When Convocation tried to bargain and offered £40,000, it was reminded that the praemunire placed all ecclesiastical property at risk: the clergy promptly agreed to pay the £100,000. Convocation now proposed a grant in phased payments over five years, in return for a continued royal campaign against heresy and a pardon for the praemunire offence. Henry, however, seems to have feared internal revolt or foreign invasion if he divorced Katherine unilaterally, and he asked for immediate payment of the whole sum in case of war. The clergy refused.

Although in theory Henry had the churchmen at his mercy, he was reluctant to proceed to extremes, if only because there were major technical problems in pursuing the praemunire charge through King's Bench. He offered the clergy an inducement to settle, promising definition of clerical privileges if they agreed to instant payment in an emergency. The bishops may have seen this concession as a hint of weakness, and they sought to drive a harder bargain. Convocation petitioned the king to confirm the privileges of the English Church, define the limits of praemunire and give assurance it would not be used to curtail ecclesiastical jurisdiction, limit the impact of the three statutes of 1529, and continue the campaign against heresy.[3] This was far too much: the clergy had not been cowed, and were repeating their demands of 1510 and 1515, jurisdictional autonomy and freedom from statutory constraint. Henry wanted his money, but he also wanted a compliant clergy who would give him his divorce in England; he was not going to cramp his future strategy and guarantee clerical immunities.

It was probably the misplaced militancy of Convocation which drove Henry to change his tactics. The clergy had first been accused of praemunire for acceptance of Wolsey's legatine authority, but it seems that some royal advisers wanted to go further. When the clergy were finally pardoned, by a second bill introduced to the Commons, it was for praemunire in the illegal exercise of the jurisdiction of Church courts. The courts and law of the Church had themselves constituted an infringement of the laws of England and the prerogatives of the king. At some stage during the praemunire struggle, the grounds of the charge had been shifted; it was probably early in February. By themselves widening the whole question of jurisdiction, the clergy played into the hands of the Boleyns and their allies. They forced the king to protect the unitary principles of the *Collectanea* by attacking ecclesiastical independence. For if he acceded to Convocation's petition, he abandoned his own claim to spiritual supremacy—a claim which might prove necessary for the divorce.

So on 7 February Convocation was asked to make five amendments to the text of the original subsidy grant. The king was to be styled 'sole protector and supreme head of the English Church and clergy'; his responsibility for his subjects' souls was to be acknowledged; he was to be asked to defend only those privileges which did not conflict with royal power and English law; his pardon was to be sought on terms to be declared later in Parliament; and the laity were to be implicated in the clergy's guilt.[4] Such alterations would represent an endorsement of the king's supremacy as advanced in the *Collectanea*, and they signalled a broadening of the royal attack. Their presentation was followed by a month of haggling over the terms—verbal and financial—of the clerical grant. At first, there was particular hostility to Henry's claim to be 'supreme head', despite the persuasions of royal councillors: Audley, Cromwell, and Anne's brother Rochford. Twice the bishops sent delegations to try to see the king, and were told they must negotiate with the councillors and especially Rochford.

But Henry must have wanted the best compromise he could get, rather than a continuing confrontation. In the face of vigorous clerical resistance, the Boleyn party gave ground. They sought to minimize the significance of the offending title, and argued that Henry did not intend to meddle in matters spiritual. When they suggested that Henry claimed supremacy only 'as far as the law of God allows', Bishop Fisher asked that the caveat be incorporated in the text of the grant. Archbishop Warham seems to have persuaded the king that this was the only way to achieve agreement, and Henry accepted the inclusion of the proviso. It was a saving clause: it saved the king's face and Convocation's conscience. On 11 February Warham put the revised formula to his fellow bishops: they were to recognize the king as 'singular protector, supreme lord and even, so far as the law of Christ allows, supreme head of the English Church and clergy'. When Warham asked for comment, there was silence; when he announced he would take silence for consent, a bishop declared, 'Then we are all silent.'[5]

The Lower House of Convocation proved more difficult to manage. The prolocutor secured subscriptions to the new title, but there was no unanimity. Later, seventeen members signed protestations on behalf of the clergy of their dioceses.[6] They announced that they had granted the king nothing new, and that his title did not infringe the liberty of the Church or the authority of the Holy See. They denounced in advance anything that might be done in derogation of the canons of the Church and the primacy of the pope. But there was much less trouble over the remaining amendments to the subsidy grant, because the king's agents abandoned them or agreed to recast them in innocuous forms. Henry even agreed to accept payment of the subsidy in five instalments. The clergy were then given their statutory pardon for praemunire, though there were exceptions. Eight clerics were specifically excluded, mainly leading opponents of the divorce and organizers of the protest from the Lower House. And the pardon would apply to the northern province only if its Convocation also granted a subsidy and accepted the king's supremacy—so far as the law of Christ allowed, of course.

There was further resistance when the royal demands were discussed in the Convocation at York. Bishop Tunstall of Durham entered a formal protest against the 'supreme head' title in the Convocation register, and later wrote to the king to explain his reasons.[7] He accepted that the king had a temporal overlordship of the Church, but argued that the law of Christ allowed no extension of this authority into spiritual affairs. There was also a more general dissent in Convocation on behalf of the clergy of York and Durham. Among the lesser clergy in the parishes, it was perhaps the cost of the subsidy rather than the implications of any title which caused difficulty. When Bishop Stokesley tried to collect the tax from the London clergy in September 1531, he had a riot on his hands.[8] The poorer priests complained they could not afford to pay, and demanded that as it was the prelates who had got the Church into trouble they should pay the cost. It is significant that this clerical resistance was encouraged by London laymen, who had no desire to see their priests fleeced by the king.

Henry VIII finally got his money, or rather, about 80 per cent of it—all that was eventually collected. But that was really all there was to show for the praemunire manœuvres. For all its drama, the campaign of intimidation had made little progress. The pope was not moved by the threat to the English Church, and the clergy in England had conceded nothing that mattered—or mattered yet. The 'supreme head' title, especially with its qualification, would only mean what the king was willing to make it mean and what the clergy were willing to let it mean; so far that was not much. So both the Norfolk strategy of bluster and threat and the Boleyn strategy of unilateral action had failed to advance the divorce. Henry had threatened the Church with expropriation, but when the bishops had called his bluff he had settled for easy terms. He had pressed the clergy to endorse the principles of the *Collectanea*, in preparation for a divorce settlement without the pope, but when they refused to do so he had accepted their evasive formulae. There were limits to the coercion Henry was yet willing to apply, and he was not gaining much by consent.

In February 1531 the leading clergy had reiterated the stand taken at the Hampton Court meeting in October 1530: that there were areas of spiritual authority immune from royal or statutory control. It was that claim which had to be broken if the king was to make headway towards a divorce in England. His cause was assisted by Christopher St German, who in 1531 published through the royal printer his *New Additions* to *Doctor and Student*. 'The said additions treat most specially of the power of the parliament concerning the spiritualty and the spiritual jurisdiction', and it was a tract for the times. St German asserted the power of parliament over Church property and clerical discipline, so defending the three statutes of 1529 against clerical denials of their validity. More important, he argued that the king in parliament was 'the high sovereign over the people, which hath not only charge on the bodies but also on the souls of his subjects'.[9] The immediate problem of the divorce was not discussed, but for those who knew the issues the relevance of St German's claim, and the significance of its publication, was surely clear.

Also in 1531, the king made public his case for a divorce. On 30 March an embarrassed Thomas More appeared in the House of Lords. On the king's behalf he rebuked those who thought the divorce suit arose only from lust for a lady, and then had the opinions collected from universities in support of the royal case read aloud. After the proceedings had been repeated in the Commons, More told MPs to report what they had heard to the counties.[10] A few weeks later, the university judgements were printed in Latin, together with a revised Latin version of the Crown's submission to the divorce hearing in June 1529. In November 1531, the king's case was published in English translation, to show 'that it is so unlawful for a man to marry his brother's wife that the pope hath no power to dispense therewith'.[11] The king's canonists argued that such an incestuous marriage was so wicked that a bishop should annul it whatever the pope said, and the parties should separate even if threatened with papal excommunication. Henry's line of attack was well prepared.

But it was still far from clear that he would actually follow it. For all the publicity, propaganda, and threats of unilateral action, nothing decisive was done. At Rome, the king's lawyers struggled to delay a divorce hearing in the papal court, and to secure the pope's agreement to a decision in England. At home, Anne's domineering ways, the difficulties of the divorce case, and fear of Charles V produced growing criticism of Henry's desires. There were defections from the Boleyn camp, secret reconciliations with Katherine, mutterings among courtiers, and even Court sermons opposing an annulment. In Council, More, Exeter, and now perhaps Suffolk tried to persuade Henry to abandon the divorce, and seek a better relationship with the emperor. Henry himself sometimes seemed uncertain: in April 1531 he wailed to Norfolk that Katherine had never treated him as badly as Anne did.[12] Royal policy had ground to a halt. Parliament had been prorogued from 31 March 1531 to 16 October, but in mid-October it was prorogued again. Chapuys, the imperial ambassador, reported this was because the king's advisers could not decide what to do.[13]

There were plenty of ideas, but there was no agreement. St German contributed a parliamentary draft which proposed a 'great standing council' to review and reform canon law, bringing it into line with common law, and so destroying autonomous clerical jurisdiction. Audley drafted a bill which would empower an archbishop to reconsider the evidence submitted to the 1529 legatine court and pronounce a divorce, the policy which had foundered on clerical resistance in October 1530. Cromwell produced a draft which assumed that Convocation would grant an annulment, and dealt with the problem of enforcing the decision. But the events of February suggested Convocation would prove awkward, and Katherine had already appealed to Rome. The only policy which Henry was yet willing to endorse was further intimidation of the pope and the English clergy. When Parliament finally met in January 1532, the Lords were presented with a bill to cut off annates, the large payments made to the pope by new bishops for their bulls of confirmation. The unco-operative pontiff was to be hit in his coffers.

But this measure encountered massive parliamentary resistance. In the Lords, it may have focused on the provisions to combat papal retaliation: if the pope refused to approve bishops, they were to be consecrated anyway; if he pronounced an interdict upon the realm, it was to be ignored. The peers and prelates refused to sanction such disregard of papal authority, and Henry conceded a new clause which delayed implementation of the Act until he confirmed it by letters patent. The duke of Norfolk tried to hold his supporters together by a private meeting, where he asked them to defend the king's right to his divorce. Lord Darcy (recently the legman for the coup against Wolsey) replied for the majority: the question should be decided by the Church, without blackmail and bribery.[14] On 24 February Archbishop Warham made a formal protest in Convocation against any parliamentary statutes against the pope or the liberties of the Church. Henry himself had to appear in the Lords three times to overawe opponents, and the lay peers reluctantly gave in. On 19 March, the bill was given its third reading, but by a narrow majority and against the opposition of all the prelates and the earl of Arundel.

Resistance continued in the Commons, perhaps led (as over the Appeals bill a year later) by merchants fearful that Charles V might seek to protect his aunt's marriage by sanctions against English trade. Henry's business managers had to make further concessions: the bishops were to be permitted to make a token 5 per cent payment to the pope if the Act came into force, and there would be no further measures against Rome for a year. Finally, the king was able to force the bill's passage, ordering that those who opposed him should, quite literally, stand up and be counted. There was a formal division, probably the first ever: members who supported the bill were ordered to one side of the House, and the opponents to the other.[15] Not surprisingly, the ranks of the supporters were swelled by timid opponents. By 26 March 1532 the Annates bill had passed both Houses, but only as a result of the most intense royal pressure. And it went through in the midst of another political crisis, in which Thomas Cromwell pitted the Commons against Convocation.

Cromwell had been in charge of planning for the parliamentary session, and he supervised government business in the Commons. However, his legislative programme soon came to grief. Henry's financial needs had produced two important measures, but the request for a subsidy was opposed, and hostility forced the abandonment of a bill to reform uses (trusts used to evade the king's feudal prerogatives). In the Lords, as we have seen, the Annates bill was resisted, and Cromwell's competence as a parliamentary draughtsman and manager was in doubt. He was now forced into a desperate gamble. He began a bold policy initiative without the king's prior approval, in an attempt to break opposition to the Annates bill and advance the king's annulment. Cromwell engineered renewed criticism of the Church courts, and promoted a Commons petition to the king for reform of canon law and procedure. It is probably not a coincidence that the petition was presented the day before the Lords were to give the Annates bill its third reading, and that the Commons were asked to consider the same bill after having been reminded of the greed and oppression of those who had opposed it.

The origins and significance of the 'Commons' Supplication against the Ordinaries' are complex and controversial matters, and no certainty is possible.[16] But it seems that Cromwell took advantage of genuine concern over recent heresy proceedings to raise the question of prelatical power. He brought out drafts probably prepared by lawyers in the 1529 session, and revised them into a comprehensive indictment of ecclesiastical jurisdiction. The 'Supplication' dealt with those issues which might turn MPs against the

Church: costs and delays in litigation and probate, tithe and mortuary charges, and the alleged unfairness of procedures; it had several extraneous issues to broaden its appeal. But the political dynamite—and the political purpose—lay in the first article: that Convocation made laws which bound the laity without their consent, and conflicted with royal prerogative and the statutes of the realm. This cleverly brought together a long-standing complaint of common lawyers (recently sharpened by St German), one of the principles of the *Collectanea*, and a line of progress towards a divorce.

As the bishops were soon to point out, the specific complaints of the 'Supplication' were largely unjustified; the petition was tendentious, prejudiced, and inaccurate. But it served the professional interests and ideals of common lawyers, and contained just enough half-truth to make it effective. Above all, Cromwell's involvement made it look like a government measure, and MPs who had already opposed bills on uses and a subsidy perhaps supported it to show their loyalty. The 'Supplication' passed the Commons, and was presented by a delegation to the king on 18 March, with evident lack of enthusiasm. The delegation asked for reform, and then pleaded for an end to a Parliament which had already gone on too long. Henry was somewhat confused:

you require to have the Parliament dissolved and to depart into your countries, and yet you would have a reformation of your griefs with all diligence . . . therefore if you will have profit of your complaint, you must tarry the time or else be without remedy.[17]

He was not much impressed by the petition; the Commons should rather concentrate on his bill for uses.

The king's response suggests he had not been involved in the planning of the 'Supplication', and he now proposed to act as arbiter between Commons and Convocation. But, as in 1531, Henry was to be forced into a stance hostile to the clergy by the vigour of their resistance. Again, the manner of their self-defence played into the hands of their opponents. The prelates had already been irritated by continuing intimidation; on 8 February sixteen clerics had been charged to prove their right to certain petty jurisdictions, and in March Warham was threatened with praemunire for a technical offence fourteen years earlier. The archbishop prepared a ringing defence, in which he cast himself in the role of Becket and threatened retribution on those who challenged ecclesiastical liberties.[18] But what really riled the bishops was the challenge to their legislative power just as they were putting it to good use. In February 1532 they had compiled a new code of reforming canons on clerical discipline, pastoral care, and education, which had been submitted to the king for emendation and approval.

So when, after the Easter recess, Convocation composed its reply to the 'Supplication', it did so in self-righteous indignation, and, it seems, in confidence of royal support. A draft was produced by Bishop Gardiner, Henry's secretary, claiming that trouble had been stirred up in the Commons by men sympathetic to heresy, and that the clergy's right to make laws came from God and could not be limited.[19] It may have been sent to the king as a preliminary response. By 27 April, Convocation had formulated a fuller 'Answer of the Ordinaries', less aggressive in tone than Gardiner's version but no less determined in its resistance.[20] The 'Answer' denied that there was discord between clergy and laity, defended ecclesiastical jurisdiction and procedure, and declared that any faults were those of 'particular men and not of the whole order of the clergy, nor of the laws wholesomely by them made'. Unwisely, Warham inserted a protest against the recent Citations Act, impugning its validity as an encroachment on 'the liberty and privileges of the Church'. Gardiner and Warham had blundered, as soon became clear.

They had also been unlucky, for other matters had angered the king and made him sensitive to any issue with implications for his divorce. Henry's ministers had renewed their request to the Commons for taxation, saying they feared a Scottish invasion and border defences should be strengthened. Some MPs hinted that the realm was only at risk because the king's policies alienated other powers, and one proposed that the king be petitioned to take back Queen Katherine. Such action had to be forestalled, and the Commons deflected. On 30 April Henry summoned a delegation of MPs. First he ingratiated himself; he handed them Convocation's response, with an encouragement to further action:

We think their answer will smally please you, for it seemeth to us very slender. You be a great sort of wise men; I doubt not but you will look circumspectly on the matter, and we will be indifferent between you.[21]

Then he warned them off discussion of the divorce, which he said was a matter of conscience not convenience.

Henry had set the Commons on the churchmen, and it was partly a political tactic to keep them away from his divorce. But it seems also that Henry had been provoked by Convocation's reply. The assertion that the Church received its authority from God and so was exempt from royal or statutory control was offensive to Henry's considerable dignity, and threatened both his claim of a supremacy and his aim of a divorce. Henry was again forced to defend the ideas of the *Collectanea*. The bishops tried to assuage royal wrath with a more conciliatory defence of their legislative rights, which offered the king a limited role in approving new canons,[22] exactly as they had already sought his endorsement of their new decrees. The Lower House, however, showed no willingness to compromise; they refused to discuss a request for taxation, insisted on an unambiguous defence of the power to legislate, and asked for a delegation to the king to seek preservation of clerical liberties. A mission led by Bishops Longland

and Stokesley was sent to Henry on 8 May, but their efforts gained no concessions from him and prompted more specific demands.

On 10 May Convocation was told that the king required subscription to three articles of submission: all future legislation was to be subject to royal veto; existing canons were to be examined by a committee of clergy and laymen, which would annul objectionable laws; and all remaining canons were to stand by royal authority.[23] Henry had demanded that the Church surrender its legislative independence. The leading clergy held a series of crisis meetings, and planned to resist. A delegation was dispatched to consult the ailing Bishop Fisher, who had recently drafted a declaration 'That the bishops have immediate authority of Christ to make such laws as they shall think expedient for the weal of men's souls'.[24] Bishop Gardiner wrote a skilful letter to the king, in which he combined a recognition that the bishops might be proved wrong with a warning that

if it be God's authority to us allotted, though we cannot use it condignly yet we cannot give it away, and it is no less danger to the receiver than to the giver, as your Highness of your high wisdom can consider.[25]

So far, the crisis brought about by the Commons' 'Supplication' had followed the pattern of events in the praemunire clash of 1531. But now a crucial difference emerged: the king would not compromise. Perhaps the assertion of clerical independence had brought the true significance of the *Collectanea* principles home to Henry; perhaps another year of frustrations had sharpened his determination to secure a speedy divorce; perhaps he was simply tired of bishops saying no. On 11 May the king called in Commons representatives; he showed them a copy of the bishops' oath of obedience to the pope, declared 'they be but half our subjects, yea, and scarce our subjects', and encouraged MPs 'to invent some order that we be not thus deluded of our spiritual subjects'.[26] This dramatic interlude was probably designed to commend to the Commons a bill drafted by Cromwell to restrict ecclesiastical legislation as an infringement of royal sovereignty. If the prelates would not surrender their powers, the king would try to seize them by statute. However, the bill encountered opposition in the Commons, privately encouraged by Chancellor More.

Faced by the prospect of being deflowered by the king or devoured by the Commons, the prelates sought the best deal they could get from Henry. But their offer of a partial submission was met by a tightening of the king's three demands, and it seemed that the longer the bishops resisted the worse the terms would be. On 15 May the king ordered a prorogation, which effectively meant that the bishops had to settle on that day or face individually the consequences of their disobedience. Henry sent a group of councillors to bully the bishops, and Norfolk delivered the king's final terms, which contained very slight modifications to entice acceptance.

Archbishop Warham forced through the most convincing submission he could get. The Lower House was not consulted, since its response to earlier drafts suggested the final document would have been rejected. Instead, the 'Submission of the Clergy' was passed by a rump of the Upper House: three bishops (and a few abbots) approved it, three did so with reservations, and Bishop Clerk voted against.[27] Henry had made something of the supremacy he had been conceded the year before, whatever the law of Christ might allow.

On 16 May a humiliated group of three bishops and four abbots delivered their 'Submission' to the king at Westminster. Thomas Cromwell was there, to witness the ultimate success of his courageous coup. On the same day, Thomas More was, effectively, dismissed as chancellor. His resignation had been on offer for at least a year; now the king accepted it. Henry did not yet know how active More had been in encouraging opposition in the Commons, but he did know that More had, over the past few days, joined the bishops in defending the Church in the Lords.[28] In the garden at York Place, More returned the great seal to the king. With Gardiner in disgrace over the 'Answer of the Ordinaries', and now More out of office, Anne Boleyn, Cromwell, and their allies would have a freer hand. Four days later Henry passed the seal to Thomas Audley, who had co-operated with Cromwell in preparing the 'Supplication'. Soon Audley released a batch of heretics who had been imprisoned by More. It was an ominous change of direction.

With hindsight, the 'Submission' crisis of 1532 seems a decisive event. The Church had abandoned its jurisdictional autonomy, granting the king control over canon law and a route to a marriage with Anne Boleyn. Clerical resistance had been dramatically broken, and thereafter the bishops were much more co-operative. Those politicians who were willing to get Henry his divorce at any cost—and who may even have hoped to use it to achieve schism from Rome—had proved their effectiveness and gained royal favour. But in fact little changed; Henry did not deliberately seek a Reformation, and royal policy remained hesitant and uncertain. The death of Archbishop Warham in August 1532 removed another important obstacle to a divorce, but it was October before Henry decided to nominate Cranmer (one of the divorce advisers) and March before his consecration. Parliament had been prorogued until November, but later it was postponed until February. Then, in October, Anne accompanied Henry to a meeting with the king of France at Calais. This encounter may have convinced Henry that he could count on French support in his dealings with the pope, and he apparently decided to go ahead and marry Anne. Or perhaps she surrendered at just the right time.

In a slight adjustment of the usual order of things, Anne became pregnant in December and married Henry secretly in January 1533. By this time,

Cromwell and Audley were busy drafting legislation to make the marriage safe from papal interference. At first it was intended simply to forbid appeals to Rome against a local decision on the divorce, but Cromwell's drafts went much further. He enshrined the principles of the *Collectanea* in a polemical preamble, trumpeting that 'this realm of England is an empire', a unitary sovereign state competent to determine its own causes. But what began as a unilateral declaration of jurisdictional independence from Rome in fact became a rather narrower measure. In a lengthy process of drafting and redrafting, the original prohibition of appeals on matters of faith and morals was deleted, and the appeals bill was confined to temporal causes such as testaments, tithes—and divorces. We do not know why papal authority over 'corrections of sins' was preserved. Perhaps Henry was not yet willing to break from Rome, or perhaps it was intended to ease a controversial bill through Parliament.[29]

Certainly the draft which was put to a meeting of prelates and ecclesiastical lawyers in February 1533 provoked criticism. There was then some last-minute revision to reduce clerical objections, and intensive lobbying of bishops. The appeals bill was introduced to the Commons on 14 March, and it met considerable opposition. It was argued that the pope would retaliate by organizing a trade embargo against England, and a London MP proposed that the king be offered £200,000 to drop the bill. Opponents managed to prevent passage of the bill through the Commons for nearly three weeks, but resistance crumbled early in April as the end of session approached. This may have been the result of royal pressure: we know that when Sir George Throckmorton spoke against the bill he was summoned for interview with Henry and Cromwell.[30] The bishops presumably obstructed the bill in the Lords, but they were unable to delay it significantly and it had passed the House by the time the session was prorogued on 7 April. The king's new decisiveness was producing real results. It was now safe to seek formal annulment of the Aragon marriage. Thomas Cranmer, the new archbishop, petitioned Henry for permission to consider the case.

When Cranmer pronounced an annulment in May 1533, he did so on the basis of decisions already secured from compliant Convocations. Stokesley and Gardiner, anxious to recover favour with the king, pressed the royal case in the Canterbury Upper House, and only Fisher opposed with real determination. The theologians were asked to agree that marriage to a deceased brother's wife was against divine law and could not be allowed by papal dispensation; sixty-six assented and nineteen disagreed. The canon lawyers were asked whether Katherine's marriage to Arthur had been consummated; forty-four thought it had, and six thought not. After some vigorous arm-twisting by royal agents, the York Convocation gave similar results. On 23 May Cranmer declared the Aragon marriage invalid; on 28

May he pronounced the Boleyn marriage lawful. Anne was crowned queen on 1 June: after six years of effort, Henry had got his way. But the consequences were serious. In July 1533 the pope condemned Henry's marriage to Anne, and gave him until September to return to Katherine, or face excommunication.

Henry was now forced to protect himself; a combination of anger at papal threats and fear of their consequences produced further measures against Rome. He issued letters patent to bring the Annates Act into force, but this financial lever brought no concession from the pope. In the autumn a band of agitators who had been promoting public hostility to the Boleyn marriage was rounded up; their efforts had underlined the risk that rebellion would follow an excommunication.[31] The king of France had secured postponement of papal action against Henry, but it was now necessary to undermine the pope's authority still further. In December 1533 the Council ordered sermons against the pope, and issued a pamphlet designed to justify royal policy and assuage public fears.[32] It defended the divorce, and argued that fine weather, peace in Europe, and the safe birth of Princess Elizabeth showed God's favour. The bishop of Rome was said to have no more power outside his own province than any other bishop, and any excommunication of the king was unlawful and to be ignored. Henry was being pushed far beyond a repudiation of papal jurisdiction over his marriage.

But he was not yet willing to take his realm into schism. It was politic to have preachers and government pamphleteers attack papal pretensions, but Henry was slow to make formal rejection of the primacy of Rome. It was expected that the parliamentary session of January–March 1534 would see major ecclesiastical legislation, but there was only a little tinkering with the positions of pope and Church. The 'Submission of the Clergy' was given statutory force, and then ignored. A new Act declared it was no longer heresy to deny the 'pretended power of the bishop of Rome', so no awkward ecclesiastic could prosecute the king's preachers. The refusal of annates was now made permanent, and a bill was introduced to stop all other payments to Rome and transfer the granting of dispensations from the pope to the archbishop of Canterbury. But on the last day of the session, when the Dispensations bill had passed all its stages, the king required a final proviso giving him power to abrogate all or part of the Act if he wished—so the Act could be used as a lever rather than an axe.[33]

A more significant antipapal step was taken in Convocation, which declared that the bishop of Rome had no more authority within England than any foreign bishop. The Lower House voted down the pope by thirty-two to four—a suspiciously low turn-out—but we do not know what exactly happened in the Upper House. Cranmer chaired the sessions, Fisher was ill, and some sees were vacant. But a body that had defeated the king in

1531 and fought him hard in 1532 apparently capitulated to his will in 1534. Perhaps the bishops had been broken by persistent intimidation; in February 1534 Nykke had faced a fine of 10,000 marks for praemunire and Fisher life imprisonment for alleged concealment of treason. Perhaps they had been more eager to defend the immunities of the English Church than the authority of a distant—and a little disreputable—pope. Perhaps their training as lawyers and experience as diplomats and administrators had made them men of the world, who obeyed its powers and wished to preserve its order. Probably, like so many others, they were unwilling to risk too much for what seemed only a brief storm in a jurisdictional teacup.

Although the leaders of the Church conformed, there was enough muttering and moaning from local priests and people to worry king and Council. The 1534 Succession Act was a measure of official anxieties. The statute declared the Aragon marriage contrary to the law of God, confirmed the Boleyn marriage, and fixed the succession to the throne on the heirs of Henry and Anne. Any actions or writing against the new marriage were to be punished as treason, and any verbal criticisms as misprision of treason. The king's subjects were to swear an oath to uphold the Act, and those who refused were to suffer the penalties for misprision: life imprisonment and confiscation of property. The Succession Act was a gamble, since it might provoke resistance, but the odds were heavily in the king's favour. When asked one by one to take the oath, few would risk the punishment for refusal, and acceptance was a public endorsement of royal policy. The process of swearing began on 30 March, the last day of the parliamentary session; the members present from both Houses of Parliament took the oath without dissent.[34]

But on 23 March the divorce action had finally been decided at Rome: the Aragon marriage was deemed lawful, and Henry was again ordered to return to Katherine. By 13 April, when the clergy of London were summoned to take the succession oath at Lambeth, the news was well known. Nevertheless, all the city priests who were called to swear did so, except Nicholas Wilson. The royal commissioners also called in Thomas More and John Fisher, both of whom refused the oath. The dissentients went to the Tower. More reported to his daughter, 'though I would not deny to swear to the succession, yet unto the oath that there was offered me I could not swear, without the [jeopardizing] of my soul to perpetual damnation'.[35] He accepted the right of parliament to fix the succession; what he would not do was swear to uphold an Act which declared the Aragon marriage 'against the laws of Almighty God'. He believed that marriage to be valid, so there was a conflict of laws; but the law of the state could not override the law of the Church. It was a conviction which would lead him to execution.

Through the spring and summer of 1534, very many of the men of

England (and a few of the women) were asked to accept Parliament's—
rather than the pope's—judgement of the divorce. Almost all of them did
so, despite the general hostility to the Boleyn marriage. They seem to have
taken a more practical view than had Thomas More, that is, that the
marriage and succession had been fixed by statute, and national law was
enforceable law. It was not a surprising, or even a novel, position: the
English had adopted it in previous disputes with Rome, over alien priories
in 1346 and papal provisions in 1351. On 20 April the citizens of London
were called to swear the oath in their guilds; the wardens swore first, and
then put the oath to their members. No one is known to have refused. On
18 May, the oath was offered to ninety-two villagers of Waldingfield in
Suffolk; twelve signed the certificate, thirty-four made their mark, and the
rest were listed by the three commissioners as having sworn. The process
was not always without difficulty. At Ashleworth in Gloucestershire the
vicar would not co-operate in calling his people to sign; he refused to read
the summons 'either for king nor queen, but said he would it had been
burnt or ever it came there'.[36]

The widespread formal acceptance of official policy did not give king and
Council much confidence. When the religious orders and colleges were
asked to repudiate papal authority, the prestigious Franciscan Observants,
Carthusians, and Bridgettines resisted. Cromwell was receiving reports of
anger and agitation from all over the kingdom; now that Rome had declared
against Henry there was a risk of foreign invasion. The parliamentary
session of November–December 1534 therefore saw measures to strengthen
royal authority and resources. As well as a subsidy from the laity,
Cromwell obtained a massive extension of taxes on the clergy. To meet the
costs of government and defence, the king was given the first year's
revenues from appointees to spiritual benefices, and a tenth of their income
thereafter. The command which Henry had asserted over the Church was
now given statutory backing: he was declared 'the only supreme head on
earth of the Church of England', with power to govern the Church, 'any
usage, custom, foreign laws, foreign authority, prescription, or any other
thing or things to the contrary hereof notwithstanding'.[37]

Though the session is ill-recorded, it seems that there was no significant
parliamentary resistance to the Supremacy bill. It granted only a little more
than the clergy had already given, it recognized what was already fact, and
it neutralized the coming excommunication of the king. There was
Commons opposition to a savage Treasons bill, designed to enforce the
supremacy and stifle dissent, but the bill eventually went through as
drafted. The Treasons Act proved what Henry's revolution by stealth had
now come to. To the dismay of Londoners, on 4 May 1535 three
Carthusian priors, a learned monk of Syon, and the vicar of Isleworth were
butchered at Tyburn, for denying that the king was head of the Church. On

19 June three more Carthusians suffered in the same cause. On 22 June John Fisher, bishop of Rochester, was beheaded on Tower Hill before a shocked and silent multitude. And on 6 July Thomas More went to the block. He asked the crowd 'to bear witness with him that he should now suffer in and for the faith of the holy Catholic Church'.[38] It was no longer just a matter of a king's marriage, it was 'the faith of the holy Catholic Church'.

7

Religious Innovations and Royal Injunctions, 1535–1538

HENRY VIII had not exactly been dragged kicking and screaming to the royal supremacy, but nor did he stride purposefully towards it. In hesitant and stumbling steps he had asserted the claims his divorce had made necessary, and by 1534 he had been forced to make reality of the slogans he had been using since 1530: national sovereignty and monarchical supremacy. But however slowly and unwillingly Henry had achieved his supremacy, once he had it he found he rather liked it; it appealed to his self-importance as a king and to his self-image as a concerned Christian. What had been designed as a weapon to gain a new queen and implemented to protect the new marriage became an essential attribute of kingship. In the right circumstances Henry would no doubt have modified (or even abandoned) his supremacy, and his agents hinted as much to pope and emperor; but the more Henry grew into his new role, the more he exercised and enjoyed his new powers, the less likely right circumstances became. The king, it seems clear, actually *believed* he was rightful supreme head, and, as the sceptics found to their cost, he expected others to believe it too.

In part, proceedings under the new Treasons Act for denial of the supremacy were security measures, to silence dissent by execution or intimidation. But they were also part of a programme of conversion, to ensure that the king's subjects recognized his new-found authority—or died. The treatment of Fisher and More certainly suggests this.[1] Both had been sent to the Tower in April 1534 for refusing to take the succession oath; at best they were impotent and isolated symbols of resistance, at worst examples of the futility of non-compliance. They were not known to have denied the supremacy, and might have been thought harmless old deviants, rotting securely in prison. But it is a measure of both the king's nervousness and his determination that the two men were systematically interrogated on the supremacy in May and June 1535. More reported, 'the whole purpose is either to drive me to say precisely the one way, or else precisely the other'.[2] When the two sought refuge in silence, evidence of direct denial was produced by subterfuge or fabrication. They would not acknowledge the supremacy, and so they were eliminated.

The supremacy which Henry asserted was given an increasingly elaborate intellectual foundation, to reassure loyal subjects and refute objectors at home and abroad. The first serious defence was published in 1534 by Edward Foxe (late of the research group on the divorce), as *De vera differentia*, a brief examination 'of the true difference' between royal and ecclesiastical power. Foxe reshuffled the material of the *Collectanea*, and argued that national Churches had no independent jurisdiction and were under the authority of their kings. Richard Sampson, dean of Henry's chapel, offered an even shorter *Oratio* with a blunt thesis: God prescribes obedience to the king, the king prescribes obedience to the royal supremacy, and his subjects must therefore reject papal claims. Also in 1534, and for a less-educated audience, there was a racy *Little Treatise against the Muttering of some Papists in Corners*, which justified the supremacy from Scripture and tried to calm fears of novelty. *A Little Treatise* denied that Henry had sought the supremacy to gain his divorce, and appealed for national loyalty to a caring king.

The most substantial—physically and intellectually—of the supremacy tracts was published by Bishop Gardiner in 1535. *De vera obedientia* was probably written as a bid for the royal favour Gardiner had lost over the 'Supplication' in 1532, and it therefore reflected the views he thought would appeal to the king as well as those he hoped might convince doubters. The rock upon which his book stood was the assumption that Church and realm were two aspects of the same community, and owed obedience to a single head: an Englishman was the king's subject not only as a citizen, but also as a Christian. He mocked the doctrine of the two swords, spiritual and temporal, and the bishop of Rome's arrogation of the spiritual sword; he claimed that God had given kings care for the welfare of their subjects in divine as well as earthly things. The power and responsibility of the king had now been acknowledged by the English parliament, and was welcomed by the English people: 'All sorts of people are agreed upon this point with most steadfast consent, learned and unlearned, both men and women: that no manner of person born and brought up in England hath aught to do with Rome.'[3]

Gardiner admitted that he had not always recognized royal headship of the English Church, and his treatise was presented as a record of his own intellectual pilgrimage to the truth. In Paris, he told the papal nuncio a different story: that he had written the book under duress.[4] Perhaps both explanations were honest. Gardiner himself, and the senior ecclesiastics who published in support of the supremacy—Longland, Stokesley, Tunstall—were certainly threatened with royal wrath. In 1556 Edmund Bonner was taxed with the preface he had contributed to *De vera obedientia*; he retorted that 'Fear compelled us to bear with the time, for otherwise there had been no way but one'[5]—death. But while such men might have conformed in terror of a ruthless king, it is hard to believe that fear alone made them active and effective propagandists. For better or worse, Henry VIII had made himself head of the Church, and his bishops might properly have concluded that their duty was to preserve the order and stability of the Christian commonwealth by defending his rule. Perhaps too, as Gardiner claimed, there had been a slow conversion to a new truth.

There were, after all, respectable scriptural, historical, and practical arguments in favour of a royal supremacy, as Foxe, Sampson, Gardiner, and other writers demonstrated.[6] The papal primacy had been undermined by humanist scholarship and calls for reform; an edition of Lorenzo Valla's demolition of one of the pillars of papal authority was published in London in 1534. It was now easy to argue that popes had usurped their power, which should be reclaimed by kings. Stephen Gardiner had deployed the theory of a unitary realm expounded in the fourteenth century by Marsiglio of Padua, whose *Defensor pacis* was first printed in English in 1535 with money provided by Cromwell. A Paduan argument had been made English reality by king and parliament, and the jurisdictional separation between Church and state had been abolished. An impotent pope had been unable to solve the divorce crisis and help England towards a male succession, but parliamentary statute and unilateral action by the English Church had provided a local answer to a pressing problem. Perhaps there was little to be said for a tainted papal primacy, and a lot to be said for an untried but promising royal supremacy.

On his deathbed in 1539, Bishop Stokesley of London wailed, 'Oh that I had holden still with my brother Fisher, and not left him when time was!'[7] Stokesley had not stood with Fisher against the supremacy in 1535; indeed, he had been sent to Fisher in the Tower to persuade him to endorse it. In 1537 he had joined with Tunstall in publishing a defence of the supremacy. By 1539, however, with the wisdom of horrified hindsight, Stokesley had changed his mind—or at least his tune. By then, schism had led to heresy and sacrilege: the supreme head had sanctioned concessions to Lutheran doctrine, heretical preachers had gone unpunished, shrines had been desecrated, and the last of the monasteries were being closed. But Fisher in 1535 had had no special foresight denied to Stokesley. In 1535 it was not inevitable—it was not even likely—that the break with Rome would be followed by changes in religious belief and practice. Indeed, an energetic supreme head may have seemed a better bulwark against heresy than a distant and distracted pope in Rome. What mattered (to Stokesley if not to Fisher) was not the royal supremacy, but what Henry made of it.

It soon became clear, especially to bishops, that the king intended his ecclesiastical authority to be made real and effective. In June 1535 Thomas Cromwell, acting as the king's vicegerent in spirituals, sent out a circular letter to the bishops. They were ordered to preach in support of the supremacy, and to ensure that the clergy of their dioceses did likewise. They were also to insist that references to the pope were obliterated from all service books, and a stroke of the pen or a gummed slip over *papa* would not suffice! A week later, Cromwell issued another circular, to sheriffs and JPs, who were instructed to watch over the bishops and report any negligence in their obedience to orders.[8] The bishops were now on trial, and soon they were on probation. In September their authority was suspended for the duration of a royal visitation of the Church, to be carried out by Cromwell's own agents. In October Cromwell established a vicegerential court, to exercise aspects of the king's supremacy. This office then began to return jurisdiction to the bishops, but on new and restricted terms.

By his inhibition of the powers of the bishops, the king had broken their derivation of authority from the pope; by his return of jurisdiction by royal commission, he made them functionaries of the monarchy, serving at pleasure. Furthermore, the September suspension was more than a technical assertion of supremacy; it was a piece of political pressure. For when the bishops received back their authority in the autumn of 1535, they found some of their rights withheld, especially the right of visitation (and so the right to visitation fees) and part of the right of probate (and so, again, the fees). These powers were to be exercised by the vicegerential officers, for as long as the king wished—and his wishes were not known. So the incentive for bishops to behave themselves—to preach the supremacy and enforce it upon their dioceses—was strong: authority and income were unlikely to be restored to the obstructive or indolent. Bishop Longland of Lincoln was sufficiently energetic in his execution of the royal will to get himself denounced as a heretic by the rebels of 1536; in February 1537 the rest of his authority was returned. It took others rather longer to earn rehabilitation.[9]

The episcopate which had its authority suspended in September 1535 was very different from that which had faced Henry over the 'Supplication'. Although the bishops of 1532 had been divided over the king's divorce, they had been united in their defence of ecclesiastical independence and their hostility to heresy. By 1535 this was no longer true, partly through the influence of Anne Boleyn over appointments.[10] Cranmer, archbishop of Canterbury, was a Boleyn protégé, as were Salcot of Bangor, Goodrich of Ely, Shaxton of Salisbury, and Latimer of Worcester. Edward Foxe got the see of Hereford in return for his efforts for the divorce, and Richard Sampson was to get Chichester in 1536, doubtless a reward for his *Oratio*. All were at least willing exponents of the royal supremacy, and Latimer and Shaxton had been in trouble for heresy in 1531. The shift in direction was poignantly demonstrated at Rochester. After the execution of John Fisher, heresy-hunter and clerical champion, John Hilsey was appointed bishop. In

1534 he had imposed the supremacy on the Dominicans, from 1535 he recruited radical preachers for St Paul's Cross, and in 1538 he led the campaign against images and relics.

Such men were promoted in part because the supreme head needed reliable anti-papalists as his bishops, and they often sympathized with Lutheran ideas. But Henry was also in search of moderate reformers, who lacked vested interests in old abuses and loyalty to old superstitions. As the king had come to enjoy his status as supreme head, so he came to fancy himself as a reformer, for he had been educated as a humanist and was an admirer of Erasmus. He was not to be a passive English pope, titular head and consumer of revenues; the supremacy was to be an active instrument of reform; hence the announcement of a visitation. So Henry was vulnerable to the temptations of those, such as Anne, Cranmer, and Cromwell, who used the prospect of 'reform' to lead him into courses he might hitherto have rejected. In 1530, to limit the attractions of Tyndale and his heretical books, the king had promised his subjects a vernacular Bible in some distant future; but this was a ploy and nothing was done. In 1535, however, bishops and scholars were given draft translations of biblical books to correct. Stokesley refused to comply, declaring to Cranmer, 'I will never be guilty to bring the simple people into error.'[11]

When the pretensions of a would-be reformer, the persuasions of Anne and Cromwell, and the pressures of international diplomacy all pointed in the same direction, Henry might be brought to do the unthinkable: negotiate with Lutherans. In the autumn of 1535 England's diplomatic isolation seemed dangerous. Rome was planning a general council of the Church, which might declare against Henry's marriage and supremacy. The pope had drawn up a bull of deposition, though its promulgation had been delayed. Charles V's victories in north Africa had apparently left him free to contemplate a strike against England, to avenge his rejected aunt and enforce the pope's decision. Henry needed allies, and he needed to embarrass the emperor. He sent Gardiner to Paris to bribe Francis I to wage war against Charles—in Italy, The Netherlands, anywhere! He also dispatched a mission to Saxony, to cause trouble for Charles in his German back garden. The king's agents, Bishop Foxe, Nicholas Heath, and Robert Barnes (the 'heretic' of 1526), were to ask the Lutheran princes to oppose a general council, propose that Henry join the Evangelical League, and hint at theological concessions for an alliance.[12]

The Lutheran princes and their theological advisers tried to take advantage of Henry's need for friends; they asked for financial support and English adherence to the Protestant Augsburg Confession. From Paris, Gardiner warned against acceptance of the Lutheran terms, and then England's negotiating position suddenly improved. The death of Katherine of Aragon in January 1536 reduced the risk of an imperial invasion, and

Francis I's seizure of Savoy in February kept Charles V busy in Italy. Henry's willingness to make concessions immediately evaporated; in March he rejected the Lutheran demands, but agreed to continue to seek a theological accommodation. The English ambassadors and Lutheran theologians hammered out a draft agreement—the Wittenberg Articles—which moderated the line of the Augsburg Confession. But Foxe and his colleagues were uncertain whether Henry would accept the draft, and the Lutherans wished England to abandon the 'four abuses': clerical celibacy, communion in one kind, private masses, and monastic vows. On the insistence of Luther himself, the Germans refused further compromise, and the English emissaries returned home with an incomplete agreement.

It seemed unlikely that their labours would bear fruit, for the political climate in England had changed dramatically. When Foxe and Heath had left for Germany, the Boleyn–Cromwell alliance had been dominant. Anne's father was lord privy seal; her leading allies served as secretary (Cromwell), chancellor (Audley), and archbishop of Canterbury (Cranmer); and her supporters surrounded Henry in the Privy Chamber. The break with Rome had thrust Henry into the clutches of reform-minded politicians, as well as reform-minded bishops. But when the ambassadors returned to England, Anne and her Privy Chamber friends were dead. There had been a coup which could kill any chance of further reformation along with some of its leading political proponents. Anne had been the victim of a carefully staged plot, which had taken advantage of a weakening in her position.[13] Katherine's death and Anne's miscarriage in January 1536 had removed two reasons for Henry's continuing commitment to his hectoring wife. The conservative courtiers—friends of Katherine, enemies of upstart councillors, and haters of heresy—now had their chance, and they took it.

Nicholas Carew, the marquis of Exeter, and their allies groomed the pliant Jane Seymour as rival, and perhaps successor, to the shrewish Anne. She was taught to flirt chastely with the king, to arouse frustrated desires, to tell him of the hostility to his Boleyn marriage, and to ask him to restore Princess Mary to the succession. Canon lawyers were sounded on grounds for an annulment of Henry's marriage, and the imperial ambassador was recruited to assist.[14] Anne was to be rejected, and Henry seduced into a Seymour marriage, an Aragonese succession, an imperial alliance, conciliar rule, and a firm stand against heresy—or that was the hope. And the hope seemed certain of fulfilment, especially when the conservatives found they had the unexpected support of Thomas Cromwell. Perhaps Cromwell recognized Anne as a lost cause, and joined her enemies to avoid sharing her fate. Perhaps he had his own motives to remove her: she was an opponent of the imperial alliance he favoured and a rival power- (and patronage-)

broker. Perhaps he concluded that the only way to save the cause of reform from collapse with the cause of Boleyn was for a reformer to organize her destruction on his own terms.

Whatever his reasons, Cromwell acted decisively. On 29 April he had one of Anne's musicians arrested and, after intensive interrogation (if not more), the young man 'confessed' adultery with the queen. Cromwell used this information to secure Henry's agreement to further arrests; Anne, her brother Lord Rochford, and her Privy Chamber friends were sent to the Tower in the first days of May, all suspected of adultery. It is possible the king knew the allegations were nonsense, but wanted his queen removed by any means. It is even possible that Anne was guilty, at least of foolhardy flirtations. But it is most likely that Cromwell fabricated the 'evidence' out of courtly dalliance and servants' tittle-tattle, and Henry's impatience for Jane led him to believe a farrago. Archbishop Cranmer was horrified; he was not privy to Cromwell's plotting, and feared the fall of Anne would halt religious reform. He wrote bravely to Henry, hinting at Anne's innocence but preparing for her conviction:

Wherefore I trust that your Grace will bear no less entire favour unto the truth of the gospel than you did before; forsomuch as your Grace's favour to the gospel was not led by affection unto her, but by zeal unto the truth.[15]

Anne and her alleged paramours were tried for adultery and treasonous conspiracy to kill the king; all were convicted and executed. It was a bloody, but brilliant, coup. The divorce which Carew and the conservatives had planned would have left an angry Anne alive, and her allies still in influential positions; the adultery charge gave Cromwell a clean sweep of almost the whole Boleyn faction, and prevented a counter-coup. But Cromwell had not brought down Anne to put Carew and Exeter in power. When they moved on to the next stage of their plan, and pushed Mary forward as successor to the throne, Cromwell struck at them. He persuaded Henry that they were responsible for Mary's obstinate refusal to recognize her father as supreme head, and there were threats of treason charges. Mary submitted to save her friends, but Exeter and Sir William Fitzwilliam were dismissed from the Council and others were barred from Court. Cromwell was then free to pack the Privy Chamber with his own evangelical allies: Denny, Hoby, Sadler, and more. Henry was again surrounded by reformers, but they were Cromwell's reformers, not Anne's.

So the schemes which were first meant to prise the king from the hands of reformers ended by consolidating Cromwell's hold and weakening the conservative presence at Court. Although the diplomatic pressure upon Henry to favour religious change had slackened, the domestic political pressure now intensified. The draft articles brought from Wittenberg became the basis for an English formulary rather than an international treaty. At least since March, Thomas Cranmer had been leading discussions between prelates and theologians for a statement of post-papal English orthodoxy. He had prepared the ground by a concerted campaign of sermons at St Paul's Cross; he had preached first against Rome, images, and purgatory, and he was followed by, among others, Hilsey, Shaxton, Latimer, and Salcot.[16] In March the bishops discussed proposals from the German Lutherans, and Chapuys heard that they proposed to deny purgatory, fasting, and reverence to saints and images.[17] Cranmer's plans were then jeopardized by the Boleyn crisis, but by the time Foxe and Heath returned from Wittenberg the reformers had, thanks to Cromwell's ruthlessness, recovered.

The conservative clergy fought a rearguard action in Convocation. On 23 June 1536 the Lower House petitioned the bishops against sixty-seven heresies in circulation. It was a clever manœuvre, which sought to associate Lutheran and evangelical reforms with the vulgarities of Lollards and sceptics.[18] But it did no good. Bishop Foxe tabled proposals derived from the Wittenberg Articles; when they were bitterly resisted, the king himself intervened to force compromise before the summer dissolution. Henry wanted an agreement—or, at least, as much agreement as could be achieved. Finally, over a hundred prelates and divines subscribed to Ten Articles, which were endorsed by the supreme head and published in August as an authoritative statement of belief, 'much profitable for the establishment of that charitable concord and unity in our Church of England which we most desire'.[19] The Articles have been variously described by historians as a victory for Lutheran opinion, and as a Catholic resistance to theological innovation; they were both. In assumptions and form they follow the Wittenberg proposals; in practice and emphasis they are very different.

By comparison with the Lutheran Augsburg Confession, the Ten Articles were a compromised compromise.[20] The Lutherans had made concessions at Wittenberg, and the Wittenberg formulas were further diluted in London. The 'Ten' distinguished the essential and the prudent in religion, so the evangelicals could be contented by restricting the essentials and the conservatives calmed by accepting controversial traditions as prudent. As soon became notorious, the Articles discussed only three sacraments: baptism, the eucharist, and penance, all essential to salvation. Confession and absolution were necessary, and 'works of charity' were required as 'fruits of penance'. Christ's body and blood were present in the eucharist, and although the red-rag word 'transubstantiation' was not used, 'substantially' and 'very substance' were.[21] No doubt the restriction reflected the Wittenberg agreement and the opinions of Cranmer and others. But the omissions do not mean that Henry (much less the more traditionalist bishops) had surrendered four sacraments. For the Ten

Articles bear all the marks of a rushed interim statement, in which difficult issues were glossed over or shelved.

Perhaps the key article was on justification, an example of well-diluted Lutheranism. Justification was through the merits of Christ's passion, attained 'by contrition and faith joined with charity'; though faith was the mechanism of justification, works were the required accompaniment.[22] It was a convenient formula, which later proved useful to eirenic theologians and practical churchmen. Throughout the 'Ten', the core doctrine was certainly justification by faith, but it was not stated bluntly and was hedged about with safeguards for conventional practice. In the articles on 'laudable ceremonies', the use of images, ceremonies, and prayers to saints and for souls were defended, with mild criticisms of popular excesses, and insistence on the centrality of worship of Christ. Though Henry had sanctioned admission of a good deal of Luther into his Church (probably to quieten Cranmer, Latimer, and their friends), he did not intend it to make much difference in practice. Sacraments and ceremonies—and, doubtless, superstitions—were to continue as before. The Ten Articles had brought more Reformation, but only a little more.

Nevertheless, the king who had raged in print against Luther's heresy had now allowed his doctrine of justification to influence the official definition of English orthodoxy. Henry certainly wanted to keep open the possibility of alliance with the Lutheran princes if it became necessary. More important, as the preface to the 'Ten' makes clear, he wanted 'unity and agreement established through our said Church', and if this meant concessions to English evangelicals he would make them. The Articles were designed to end 'diversity of opinions' and impose uniformity. Henry ordered suspension of sermons for the summer to prevent contention over interpretation, and thereafter preachers were to read the Articles in church without comment. But it was also the opportunity to pose as a reforming Christian king which made the 'Ten' acceptable to Henry; the criticisms of popular excesses on saints, images, and purgatory were probably as important for him as the statement on justification. Indeed, the Ten Articles were not an isolated prescription of novel belief, but part of a package of moderate reforms.

A week after its agreement to the Articles, Convocation endorsed a restriction of the number of holy days. On 11 August 1536 the new rules were announced; because so many feasts were the product of superstition and the occasion of vice and idleness, the less important were abolished, especially those at harvest time. Later in August, Cromwell, as deputy of the supreme head, issued a set of Injunctions to the clergy.[23] In part, they drew together recent instructions: the clergy were to publicize the royal supremacy, the Ten Articles, and the abrogation of saints' days. They also put into practice some of the principles of the 'Ten': priests were not to extol images or pilgrimages, and should encourage parishioners to give to the poor rather than offer to images. They reinforced conventional canons on clerical discipline, and emphasized the duty of priests to teach their people the Lord's Prayer, the Creed, and the Commandments, as had been required since Pecham and described by Mirk. The only radical initiative—that rectors were to provide Bibles in Latin and English for the people to read in church—was quietly ignored by the bishops for a year or more, probably because of the northern rebellion in the autumn of 1536.[24]

Although established beliefs were safeguarded in the Ten Articles and there was little new in the Injunctions, the 'August measures' seemed to challenge traditional religion. This was largely because of the context in which they appeared: during the suppression of the lesser monasteries. But though the attack on the religious houses was a radical move, it was not, in origin, a religious one. It was cloaked in the language of spiritual reform, but the real motive was financial. In March 1536 the preamble of the suppression bill argued that the lesser houses were too corrupt to be improved, but the model 'great and solemn monasteries of this realm' needed more recruits; so the small houses should be dissolved and their inmates moved to larger ones (leaving the redundant property for the king).[25] This was nonsense. The reports of the royal visitation of 1535–6 did not suggest any moral distinctions between large and small monasteries, and when monks ejected from smaller houses asked to move to surviving houses there was no room for them. The king did not seek reform; he sought revenue.[26]

As in the 1370s, the financial problems of the Crown and the political difficulties of a minister led to proposals for the expropriation of churchmen. The cost of the Irish rebellion of 1534 had produced a draft plan for the confiscation of Church property, including a dissolution of smaller monasteries, and had given good reason for the new taxes of first fruits and tenths. In 1535 county commissions produced new assessments for the taxes, which showed the potential profit from confiscation. In 1535–6 the royal visitation produced some evidence of monastic vice and rather more of laxity; but there were just enough scandals to put before Parliament in justification of a suppression bill. The decision to raise money by dissolution was partly a consequence of the diplomatic pressures which also sent Gardiner to Paris, Foxe to Wittenberg, and Lord Howard to Stirling to seek alliance with James V. The bill declared the need to suppress corrupt communities, but its criterion was in fact financial; houses with an income of less than £200 a year were to go, unless exempted by the king. Abbots and priors were bought off with pensions, and monks were offered the choice of places in larger houses or licences to serve as secular priests. Nuns had no such option, and were to be relocated or sent out into poverty.

We know little of the bill's passage through Parliament. Cranmer's sermon campaign at St Paul's Cross had prepared the ground by attacking abbots and monks. Latimer in particular was playing Wycliffe to Thomas Cromwell's John of Gaunt. Cromwell's intentions soon became known, and he was pestered by nobles and gentry with pleas for monastic estates, though there were also calls for exemption of favourite houses. Hardly any abbots or priors attended the Lords to share in the diminution of their orders; either they were warned off or they had no stomach for what was to come. Perhaps the Council anticipated trouble in the Commons, for it seems that the king himself introduced the bill there.[27] But that and the selective use of salacious titbits of visitation evidence was enough to get the bill through. Anyway, seizure of monastic wealth in time of financial crisis had happened before, in 1295, 1337, and 1369. The suppression commissioners were soon at work, discharging monks, selling off domestic and farm equipment, and confirming leases. This process was a reason— perhaps *the* reason—for the rebellions of October 1536.[28] Some of the surviving monasteries gave their support to the rebels, and paid the price after the failure of the risings; they were forced to surrender their houses.

But there was as yet no policy for a total destruction of monasticism. Some religious were transferred to larger houses, some houses were allowed to buy exemption from suppression, and some were allowed to stand to accommodate the large numbers of monks and nuns who wished to maintain their vocation. The king himself refounded houses dissolved under the 1536 act, and if Cromwell was pursuing a wholesale expropriation he had not told Henry. There were enforced surrenders of individual houses, but it was not until the spring of 1538 that determined destruction began.[29] Then the worrying amity of France and the Empire reproduced the policy of 1536: concessions to the Lutherans and confiscations from the monks. In May the last formal exemption from suppression was granted, and the bishop of Dover turned what had begun as a visitation of the friaries into a systematic demand for surrender. In June, the 'king's new monastery' at Bisham, less than a year old, was invited to expire. By September 1538 Thomas Legh was applying the same techniques to Midlands monasteries, and other commissioners soon followed. The monks sought the best terms they could get by quailing co-operation. The few who resisted—the abbots of Colchester, Glastonbury, and Reading—were executed.

For Cromwell, Cranmer, and the preachers they patronized, the attack on the monasteries was another step in their evangelical programme. Monasticism was a pious fraud, founded upon the false doctrine of purgatory; monks were no more useful than images, relics, and prayers to saints. For Henry it was different. He might concede the practical need for negotiation with Lutherans or seizure of monastic endowments, but he had not abandoned belief in the sacramental system or the efficacy of masses satisfactory for suffering souls. It seems too that Henry was shaken by the

1536 Pilgrimage of Grace, when 40,000 of his subjects took arms against Cromwell and 'the heretics'. Fear of internal disorder now strengthened his distrust of innovation; he called a Great Council of nobles in January 1537, which apparently agreed upon Catholic concessions in religion.[30] The policies of Cromwell and Cranmer were not disowned—yet; but they were increasingly, and surprisingly, out of step with the king's own preferences. Perhaps, as in 1532 and 1536, Cromwell gambled that political circumstance would force Henry further down a road he had no wish to travel. For a time, the gamble succeeded, but there was now a price on Cromwell's head; the price was success.

Cromwell was, however, unable to deliver an acceptable religious formulary. Henry VIII now wanted a more substantial (and less Lutheran) statement of English orthodoxy than had been possible in the hurried and incomplete compromise of 1536. Between February and July 1537 Cromwell and Cranmer chaired a series of sometimes-acrimonious meetings of bishops and divines. Cromwell still pressed for radical solutions, and once brought in a Scottish Lutheran to harangue the bishops. As in 1536, Foxe seems to have done most of the drafting. Stokesley and the more traditionalist bishops insisted that the four sacraments passed over in the Ten Articles should be given their proper status, but Cranmer, Latimer, and others denied the four were sacraments at all.[31] The outcome, inevitably, was another compromise: it was agreed that there were seven sacraments, but some were more sacramental than others! Baptism, the eucharist, and penance had been instituted by Christ and conveyed grace to remit sins; matrimony, confirmation, holy orders, and extreme unction had been recognized by the Church and conveyed spiritual benefits. Both sides could claim a victory of sorts.

Stephen Gardiner later described the haggling which had taken place. The main protagonists were Stokesley and Foxe, and after 'much stoutness' between them,

then Bishop Stokesley would somewhat relent in the form, as Bishop Foxe did the like. And then, as it were in a mean, each part, by placing words by special marks, with a certain understanding protested, the article went forth; and so to a new article, and so from one to another. There is sometime as evident contradiction as if it had been saved by a proviso.[32]

In sum, the new agreement was rather like that of 1536: a basic text with Lutheran origins, heavily amended to meet conservative objections.[33] The sections on baptism, penance, the eucharist, justification, and purgatory were lifted from the Ten Articles, and the discussion of ceremonies was only slightly altered. The commentaries on the Creed, the Commandments, the Lord's Prayer, and the Hail Mary were taken, via William Marshall's 1535 Primer, from Luther's expositions and reworked to suit the time. Only the sections on the four 'found' sacraments were new.

The four 'declarations' bore the marks of recent ecclesiastical disputes. The statement on matrimony emphasized the Levitical prohibitions cited in Henry's first divorce. Confirmation was grudgingly (by evangelicals) accepted as a sacrament, but a tamed episcopate had no God-given keys to heaven: confirmation was expedient, but inessential to salvation. The section on holy orders was a lengthy attempt to reconcile a conservative defence of the authority of the priesthood with a necessary recognition of the power of the Christian prince. The Church might make rules on matters such as holy days, but these were not immutable and may be broken in necessity. The discussion of extreme unction was simply a botched compromise: the Scriptural basis and efficacy of the rite were undermined, but the sacrament was 'very necessary and expedient' and gave the recipient 'remission of his sins'.[34] Cromwell and Cranmer had failed to browbeat the traditionalists into acquiescence in a Lutheran formulary. It was soon being said in Kent that the agreement was a defeat for reformers, 'for of truth it alloweth all the old fashion, and putteth all the knaves of the new learning to silence'.[35]

Nevertheless, Cromwell and Cranmer had won too much. When in July the text was submitted for Henry to approve, he refused. He declared that he had no time to do more than glance at the volume, but at the petition of his bishops would licence its public reading for three years.[36] We do not know why he responded in this way. Perhaps he really was too busy, or too preoccupied with Queen Jane's advanced pregnancy. But it is hard to believe that this was true of a king always eager to pick theological nits, and the bishops would surely have delayed printing for royal approbation. It seems that Henry did not like what he had seen (even at a glance), but would let Cromwell and Cranmer have what they had got of their way for a while yet. *The Institution of a Christian Man* was published in September 1537; lacking royal authority, it soon became known as the Bishops' Book. Its preface, subscribed by twenty-one bishops and twenty-five lawyers and theologians, offered the text to Henry for correction; he was soon at work. He sent Cranmer 250 emendations. Some were footling, and mere changes in phrasing. Some were impossible, such as his attempts to rewrite the Lord's Prayer and the Ten Commandments. Some were significant.[37]

Many of Henry's interventions were designed to undermine the assertion that justification was through faith and by the merits of Christ. He insisted that grace was conditional upon works. When, for example, in the commentary on the first article of the Creed, the believer declared himself God's 'own son by adoption and grace', the king added 'as long as I persevere in his precepts and laws,'[38] and there were several similar interpolations. Cranmer replied with a long, and firm, account of the nature and effects of true faith, objecting to the king's conditional clauses. Henry also raised the status of the saints by reference to their 'mediation' rather than 'intercession', and elevated matrimony to the first rank of sacraments. He eliminated criticisms of images of God, and allowed that images might be honoured if they were not treated as gods. It is clear that, even though restrained by Stokesley and his allies, Cranmer and Cromwell had gone further in the Bishops' Book than the king had wished. But if Henry had intended an immediate revision of the new book, he soon found his hands tied by his diplomatic, and marital, isolation.

Jane had died in October 1537, after giving birth to Prince Edward. With embarrassing speed, Henry's agents were sent looking for a new wife, who would bring the reliable alliance of France or the Empire. But the princesses Henry considered were unwilling or unattractive, and both Francis I and Charles V found Henry's political terms too demanding. By February 1538 Henry still had no wife, England still had no ally, and Franco-imperial peace negotiations were going well. Courting princesses had to be accompanied by courting princes—Lutheran princes. Henry's ambassador to the Evangelical League asked for a delegation to be sent to England. The Lutherans arrived in London at the end of May, and soon found they had the English over a diplomatic, if not quite a theological, barrel. Charles and Francis signed a ten-year truce at Nice in June; in July they met at Aigues Mortes, and there was talk of a crusade against heretics. In England, therefore, two months of theological negotiating went well, despite Stokesley's obstruction. Thirteen articles of faith were agreed, most taken from the Augsburg Confession and the Wittenberg Articles, though with some crucial amendments.[39]

Protected by the threat from abroad, Cromwell planned further encroachments upon traditional religion. They were prefaced by dramatic propaganda shows, which were as much to persuade the king of the need for reform as to justify it more widely. In February the fraudulent 'rood of grace' from Boxley Abbey was hawked around Kent, shown to the Court at Whitehall, and finally destroyed at St Paul's Cross, where Hilsey preached against idolatry and pilgrimages. In May a friar was burned for heresy—the new heresy of believing the pope head of the Church and Fisher a martyr—in the same fire as the Welsh image of Davel Garthen. In July images of the Virgin from Walsingham, Ipswich, and elsewhere were burned at Chelsea by Cromwell, on the grounds that they had been objects of superstitious devotion.[40] All this was in preparation for the publication in September 1538 of Cromwell's second set of royal Injunctions.[41] In the main these were extensions of the 1536 orders, but some went much further. Images to which offerings or pilgrimage had been made were to be taken down, candles before images were now forbidden, and there were to be sermons against veneration of images and relics.

Cromwell also instructed each parish to acquire 'one book of the whole Bible of the largest volume in English' by Easter 1539, to be set up in church for the people to read. The Bible order of 1536 had been virtually ignored, because the bishops were slow to enforce it, because of its ambiguity, and because there was no approved English translation. In August 1537 Cromwell had licensed a Bible printed under the name of 'Thomas Mathew', a fiction by which the work of Tyndale was concealed, perhaps even from the king. Cromwell had also commissioned Miles Coverdale to produce a better version, in an edition which could be used in churches, though delays to the printing in Paris meant the 'Great Bible' was not available by the deadline. This time, however, Cromwell was determined to have his Injunctions obeyed. He had enough copies of the orders printed for distribution to every parish, and sent batches off to the bishops to be passed on to the curates.[42] But by then the political foundation for Cromwell's policy had begun to collapse. Henry had never been entirely convinced of the threat from his brother monarchs, and he refused the concessions the Lutherans demanded.

By August the Lutheran and English delegations had hammered out thirteen articles on the Church, justification, and the three sacraments agreed in 1536. However it is likely that Stokesley and Tunstall were expecting Henry to reject them. But then the negotiations stuck. The Germans wanted a declaration against the 'four abuses' they had condemned before. Monastic vows were fast disappearing as an issue, but the conservative bishops refused to give way on clerical celibacy, communion in one kind, and private masses. Henry himself entered the proceedings, producing with Tunstall a lengthy defence of the 'abuses', and, sure of royal support, the conservatives now insisted on the four sacraments they knew the Lutherans would not accept. Cranmer regarded this as a wrecking manœuvre, and he was probably right; but it was a ploy only possible because Henry was now willing for the talks to founder.[43] On 1 October the Germans stumped off, complaining that 'Harry only wants to sit as Antichrist in the temple of God, and that Harry should be pope. The rich treasures, the rich incomes of the Church, these are the Gospel according to Harry!'[44]

The failure to reach agreement with the Lutherans was another defeat for Cromwell and Cranmer, who had hoped Henry would abandon the 'abuses'. But the king was now in his heresy-hating mode, and so looking more favourably upon conservatives; the evangelicals were under acute political pressure. It was their need to show Henry that they were not soft on heresy, and that their rivals were tainted by popery, which explains the dramas of the autumn of 1538. Cromwell struck first against his conservative enemies. At the end of August he had Sir Geoffrey Pole, brother of the exiled cardinal, sent to the Tower; two months later, under intensive interrogation, Pole broke and gave evidence against friends and relations. On 4 November Lord Montagu and the marquis of Exeter went to the Tower; soon they were followed by Sir Edward Neville of the Privy Chamber, and eventually by Sir Nicholas Carew. Cromwell wove their well-known antipathy towards the supremacy and religious change into evidence of treasonous conspiracy, and they were executed. The last conservatives had been swept from the Privy Chamber.

But Cromwell needed heretics as well as papists. On 1 October he issued a heresy commission, which gave Cranmer and other reformers a chance to show their zeal against Anabaptists. Poor John Lambert, who had been a member of the Cambridge 'White Horse' group, was then sacrificed for the good of the cause. He was, effectively, set up by evangelicals, and turned over to Henry on a charge of denying the real presence.[45] On 16 November the king himself, dressed in the white of theological purity, presided at Lambert's trial, where ten bishops (including Cranmer) took turns to argue against the accused. Henry was hot against heresy and suspicious of reform. He shared in the drafting of a fierce proclamation, issued on the day of Lambert's trial, giving Anabaptists and sacramentaries ten days to get out of the country. The proclamation also forbade the printing or import of English books and Bibles without licence, insisted on belief in the real presence and observance of church ceremonies, and declared clerical marriage contrary to Scripture.[46] Lambert was burned, with outrageous cruelty, on 22 November 1538: a gruesome symbol that Harry had finally had enough.

8

Resistance and Rebellion, 1530–1538

HENRY VIII took part in the trial of the heretic John Lambert in November 1538 as a dramatic demonstration of his Catholic orthodoxy. The king told Lambert, 'If you do commit yourself unto my judgement you must die, for I will not be a patron unto heretics.'[1] The gesture was a reminder to the monarchs of Europe that, despite schism from Rome and suppression of monasteries, Henry was no heretic. It was also a warning to English evangelicals and Protestants that though the king would reform abuses he would not tolerate heresy, especially on the eucharist. And primarily it was a signal to Henry's Catholic subjects that he was, after all, one of them. The proclamation of 16 November pronounced the same message: by condemning the free circulation of the Bible, denial of the real presence, and the marriage of priests, Henry was endorsing popular hatred of the 'new learning' and its supporters. By the autumn of 1538 he really had no choice. He had to make concessions to that fear and resentment of religious change which had been a growing political problem for six years and more.

At Easter 1525, Elizabeth Barton, a teenage servant at Aldington in Kent, fell into a hysterical illness.[2] She claimed to see visions, and was told by the Virgin Mary that she would be cured. The recovery took place, as predicted, before the image of the Virgin at Court-at-Street, and was witnessed by a great crowd. Elizabeth's fame soon spread, and the image became the focus of pilgrimage. The case was investigated by a commission appointed by Archbishop Warham and headed by Dr Edward Bocking, a monk of Canterbury. The commission was impressed by Elizabeth; she was sent to a nunnery at Canterbury, and Bocking became her spiritual director. During Lent 1526 she made a well-publicized pilgrimage to Court-at-Street, and a huge crowd turned out to see the young visionary and the miraculous image. She continued to have trances, make prophecies, and give spiritual comfort and moral exhortation to those who visited her. So far, Elizabeth's story had been rather like that of Anne Wentworth a decade earlier: a sick girl, a wonder-working image, and the enthusiasms of a religious revival. But then she turned to politics.

Elizabeth's later visions were, as Cranmer noted, 'chiefly concerning the king's marriage, the great heresies and schisms within the realm, and the taking away the liberties of the Church'.[3] She became a leading campaigner against the divorce, passing reprimands from the Virgin and Mary Magdalene to those involved. In 1528 she threatened Wolsey with God's retribution if he proceeded with the divorce; she sent a similar message to the pope; and she told Henry to his face that he would be dead within a month if he divorced Katherine.[4] Her admirers—especially a coterie of Canterbury monks, friars, and laymen—spread her warnings more widely. She spoke out, too, against heresy, demanding the punishment of heretics and the burning of Tyndale's New Testament. It does not much matter (and we cannot tell) whether Elizabeth was a deluded seer or a deliberate fraud, nor whether those around her believed in her visions. Probably she thought she had a mission to save the kingdom from disaster, and her supporters no doubt encouraged her convenient cautions. What does matter is the impact they had and the danger they posed.

From the autumn of 1532, when Anne Boleyn was being fêted as queen-designate, the Barton group mounted a major drive to stop the divorce. When Henry passed through Canterbury, Elizabeth told him he must mend his wicked ways, for he was 'so abominable in the sight of God that he was not worthy to tread on hallowed ground'.[5] He should destroy the 'new learning', protect the authority of the pope, and give up Anne, or face God's vengeance. When the threats had no effect, Elizabeth's friends spread a story that an angel had seized the host from Henry at mass and given it to her; God had withdrawn his favour from the king, and shown it to the 'holy maid'. Bocking and his allies told such tales to Princess Mary, the marchionesses of Salisbury and Exeter, the countess of Derby, Lord and Lady Hussey, Bishop Fisher, and any number of monks, friars, and London merchants. Thomas More was subjected to a barrage of persuasions, from Dr Risby of the Canterbury Observants at Christmas 1532, Dr Riche of the Richmond Observants in Lent, and from Bridgettines soon after. He was induced to meet Elizabeth, and then visited by two Carthusians to see how he had responded.[6]

More was a marked man, and had to be careful. Others were swept away by enthusiasm, and it seemed the nun was putting backbone into resistance to the king. Henry Man, of the Sheen Carthusians, thought she had put a fire into some like the Holy Spirit in the primitive Church, so that thousands would not now bow the knee to Baal.[7] The 'holy maid' had been a threat to the king's divorce, and by the spring of 1533 she was an even more potent threat to public acceptance of Anne Boleyn as queen. Bocking and the other priests were preaching publicly on Elizabeth's revelations, and Bocking prepared a collection of her prophecies. His draft was copied out, and taken to a London printer; by mid-July there were 700 copies ready for distribution.[8] But all this activity had alerted Cromwell. The books were seized, and Elizabeth was taken for examination by Cranmer. In September her accomplices were arrested and interrogated. Once Cromwell knew of the vigour of the Barton circle's propaganda, he had to wreck their reputations. On 23 November 1533 he staged a public humiliation at St Paul's Cross, at which Elizabeth confessed fraud and a sermon was preached against her.

Elizabeth Barton and her main publicists were executed for treason in April 1534. Their destruction had become a political necessity, for the 'nun of Kent' had acquired considerable reputation and influence. Her agents had lobbied hard around the Court, and Elizabeth was taken up by a number of aristocratic ladies; the pregnant marchioness of Exeter had asked her to pray to the Virgin for a healthy child.[9] The nun's efforts bore fruit: the husbands of some of her patronesses were soon approaching the imperial ambassador, directly or through intermediaries, to express their horror at Henry's proceedings and promise resistance. The reports of Chapuys, the ambassador, suggest that there was general hostility among nobles to the divorce and the break with Rome, and a hope that Charles V would mount a crusade against Henry. Lord Hussey told Chapuys that the northern nobles were determined to remedy the ills of the kingdom; Lord Darcy claimed there were 600 peers and gentlemen in the north opposed to royal policy; and Lord Bray thought twenty lords and a hundred knights would take up arms to defend Katherine and Catholicism.[10]

There was much exaggeration and wishful thinking in all this. Darcy and Hussey enlarged their political significance by claiming to represent a powerful alliance, and tried to encourage imperial invasion by guaranteeing noble support. Some of those whose aid was offered to Chapuys, such as the earl of Derby, were also rising on Anne Boleyn's skirts, and probably hedging their bets against any Catholic crusade. Bray and others looked to Charles V for decisive leadership, but Charles was busy being decisive elsewhere. Chapuys sought to commend himself to his emperor by inflating his own role as mentor of the alienated aristocracy, and the man on the significant spot. But the nobles were divided by local rivalries and family disputes, and intimidated by Cromwell and the king. There was really no chance of a concerted national rising led by the nobility. When rebellion came in 1536 it was disorganized and regional, and most of the 'opposition' peers turned out loyally to serve in the royal army. Few did more than send cryptic messages and symbolic daggers to Chapuys, and those willing to talk to him were often too frightened to talk to each other.

Nevertheless, in 1534 and 1535 a substantial section of the nobility disliked official policy, and disliked it enough to talk treason to a foreign ambassador. There was genuine outrage against Henry's treatment of Katherine, the emperor, and the pope, and a fear that he was flirting with heresy. The malcontents included major magnates such as Abergavenny, Dacre, Derby, Northumberland, and Rutland; military men such as Darcy and Sandys; courtiers such as Hussey and Exeter, and they expected at least the benevolent neutrality of Norfolk, Suffolk, and Shrewsbury.[11] Given the right political circumstances—a real risk of invasion, a bad blunder by Cromwell—their distaste might have been decisive. We know that the circumstances never were exactly right—though they almost were in the autumn of 1536, when there was a rebellion which looked suspiciously like the rising envisaged in 1534 by Darcy and Hussey. But the absence of determined resistance by the peerage did not lessen the danger of Henry's position: many of his nobles were waiting their chance to have Cromwell's head and change Henry's mind.

Hussey had thought that an effective rebellion might be raised by the clergy preaching against a heretic king, and calling the people to serve under a banner of the crucifix. It was fear of such an outcome which led Cromwell to strike against the priests who were preaching up Elizabeth Barton, especially since their campaign coincided with a papal threat to excommunicate Henry. There were other priests, too, who were out on the stump against the divorce and its consequences. Dr Nicholas Wilson and Dr Edward Powell toured the north in 1532–3, preaching in defence of Katherine and Rome and attacking heresy. By Easter 1533 they were at Bristol with another firebrand, Dr William Hubardin, all three called in by conservatives to reply to Latimer's reformist sermons. There was then a pulpit war, which polarized an already divided town. Powell declared against 'he that putteth away his first wife and taketh another without assent and dispensation of the Church'; Hubardin claimed that the pope had authority over princes and whoever opposed Rome was a heretic. Latimer's allies complained to the Council, and Hubardin was bundled off to the Tower.[12]

It was often the regulars who preached against royal policy. At Easter 1534 the warden of the Southampton Observants called denials of papal authority 'grievous errors', and read from a book in support of the papal primacy. The prior of the Cambridge Dominicans 'preached against the king's grace's great cause and most defended the authority of the bishop of Rome'. The warden of the Benedictine college in Oxford preached regularly against the king. In March 1535 a friar in Kent warned his congregation, 'Masters, take heed, we have nowadays many new laws. I know we shall have a new God shortly!' At Easter a Franciscan at Herne defended pilgrimages, and failed to pray for the supreme head. At Norwich in April the Dominican prior declared the king could be head of the Church only 'in temporalities, and protector and defender of the same'. In August Cranmer preached at Canterbury against papal power, and then the Dominican prior replied that the Church could not err and its laws were the laws of God. In September a Kingswood friar was sent to Cromwell for sermons in support of Petrine authority, and in October the sub-prior of Lewes was in trouble for treasonous preaching.[13]

It is thus not surprising that Henry and Cromwell were determined to isolate and crush dissent from the religious orders. The secular clergy were asked to sign an acknowledgement that the bishop of Rome had no authority in England; the regulars had to swear that they would never call that bishop pope or pray for him; that they would pray for Henry as supreme head and Anne as queen; and that they renounced all canon law which conflicted with the laws of the land. Royal commissioners had great difficulty in putting this comprehensive oath to the Observants, and in August 1534 the Observant houses were closed down; some of the friars were sent to the Tower, others were put into custody with Franciscans, and the rest fled the country. The Carthusians were similarly obstructive; three of their priors were executed in May 1535, and three monks in June; two more were hanged at York in 1537, and another ten were left to die of starvation in Newgate; the rest were forced to submit. The monks and nuns of Syon also held out for a time: Richard Reynolds was executed with the Carthusian priors, and then the leading dissenter was Richard Whitford, the best-selling author of 1530.

It took courage to denounce the supremacy from the pulpit, and real heroism to do so before the king's commissioners. Most of those who spoke out against the king did so in private where they thought they were safe, or in the alehouse where they forgot the risks. There was certainly much muttering against Anne Boleyn, damned as the cause of all the trouble. In 1533 a Warwickshire priest called her a harlot and maintainer of heretics, and hoped she would be burned at Smithfield. A Lancashire cleric declared, 'I will take none for queen but Queen Katherine; who the devil made Nan Boleyn, that whore, queen, for I will never take her for queen!' At Cambridge in 1534, a servant said that Henry was a heretic, and 'this business had never been if the king had not married Anne Boleyn'. A woman at Watlington near Oxford told her midwife she was too good to help Anne, 'for she was a whore and a harlot for her living'; a lay brother of Roche Abbey thought she was not Anne the queen but 'Anne the bawd'. Anne was 'a goggle-eyed whore' to a Suffolk woman in 1535, and at Bridgwater an Irishman called for God's vengeance on Anne, 'for whom all England shall rue'.[14] Most of England did.

Henry's rejection of Rome provoked considerable concern, at least among the clergy. In 1533 the vicar of Rye threatened that the pope would put the realm under an interdict and the harvest would fail. In January 1534 a Colchester monk thought a pamphlet on the supremacy put out by king and Council showed them 'to be all heretics, whereas before, he said, they were but schismatics'. In 1535 a Yorkshire parson warned that an interdict was coming, 'and if it were conveyed in we should have no more Christian burial than dogs'. The king's policy had left England with no friends but the heretics: 'All realms christened have forsaken us but only the Lutherans', and Henry would have to use his taxes to buy Lutheran support.[15] There was widespread reluctance to erase the pope's name from service books, as Cromwell had ordered in April 1535: despite the difficulty of detection, there were reports of disobedience from Oxhill in Warwickshire, Stoke Dry in Rutland, Witnesham in Suffolk, Harwich in Essex, Croydon in Surrey, Dymchurch and St Paul's Cray in Kent, Kingsbury in Somerset, and from Northamptonshire, Wales, and Yorkshire.

Perhaps it was reverence for the pope that made priests unwilling to deface his name, or perhaps it was prudence. The abbot of Woburn kept copies of the papal bulls for when they might be needed again, and stopped erasure from books as 'it will come again one day'. The vicar of Stanton Lacy in Shropshire glued slips of paper over the pope's name, since 'they are but fools that so will destroy their books, for this world will not ever last'. It was a common view that the breach with Rome was but a temporary disruption. In 1535 Robert Augustyn, a London Carmelite, said that 'we should see a new turn of the bishop of Rome, if we did live'; at St Albans a priest in confession predicted, 'if it fortune the king to die, you shall see this world turned up-so down or clear changed'.[16] George Rowlands, of the Crutched Friars in London, told a penitent in February 1536, 'these things will not last long, I warrant you; you shall see the world change shortly'. Rowlands had advised his people to pray secretly for the pope:

But we may say nothing openly, for the knaves has our heads under their girdle; but we must be obedient unto our king and obey his commandment and take all things patiently. But be of good comfort, and the more shall be our meed, for I warrant you, this world will change shortly.[17]

A dispute between the king of England and the pope was, after all, nothing new. 'Remember how often in times past these ways hath been attempted, and what end the authors thereof hath come unto', Dr John London warned his nephew in 1536. London was horrified by his nephew's approval of attacks on Rome, which would bring shame to his college and family and disaster to himself:

Remember that this world will not continue long. For (he said) although the king hath now conceived a little malice against the bishop of Rome because he would not agree to this marriage, yet I trust that the blessed king will wear harness on his own back to fight against such heretics as thou art. And then thou shalt be known, and thy heresies shalt be known, and thy heresies shall fly in every man's mouth.[18]

Whether parish priests, confessors, or uncles, there was a whole army of clergy using secret persuasions on behalf of the pope and the old ways. In 1535 Robert Ward (who was a friar himself and ought to have known) summarized for Cromwell the arguments used by the mendicants:

Oh father (or sister), what a world is this, it was not so in your father's days. Ye may see here a parlous world. They will have no pilgrimages; they will not we should pray to saints or fast, or do any good deeds; our Lord have mercy on us. I will live as my forefathers have done, and I am sure your father and friends were good and ye have followed them hithertoward. Therefore, I pray you, continue as ye have done and believe as your friends and fathers did, whatsoever these new fellows do say, and do for yourself while ye be here.[19]

It is, of course, impossible to know how successful such surreptitious propaganda was. We know about the dissenters because some were turned in by those who heard them, from loyalist horror, fear of complicity, or hope of reward. But committed papalists were confident of general support. When Reynolds of Syon was examined in the Tower in April 1535, he claimed that all Christendom was on his side:

I dare even say all this kingdom; although the smaller part holds with you, for I am sure the larger part is at heart of our opinion, although outwardly, partly from fear and partly from hope, they profess to be of yours.[20]

John Hale, vicar of Isleworth, who died at Tyburn with Reynolds, thought much the same:

For this is truth, three parts of England is against the king, as he shall find if he need; for of truth they go about to bring this realm into such miserable condition as is France, which the commons see and perceive well enough a sufficient cause of rebellion and insurrection in his realm. And truly we of the Church shall never live merrily until that day come.[21]

Such troubles were predicted often enough: 'These new laws may be suffered for a season, but in time to come it will cost broken heads and set men together by the ears', Dr Richard Benger had warned in 1534,[22] and so it was to be.

But it was not suppression of papal authority that brought violent conflict, it was suppression of monasteries. Laymen did not fight for the papal primacy, nor for the liberties of the Church; they did not take risks to protect the clergy from royal taxes or royal visitation. But by the middle of 1536 there was more than an abstract principle and clerical privilege at stake: there were attacks on saints' days and pilgrimages, there were to be English Bibles in the churches—and there were royal officers throwing monks and nuns from their houses, paying off their servants, pulling lead from their roofs, and packing up cartloads of valuables for transport to London. When the commissioners at Exeter ordered workmen to pull down the rood-loft in the priory church, a mob of women, armed with spades and spikes, broke in to protect the images and drove a carpenter to jump from the tower. At Norton Abbey in Cheshire, the ejected canons raised several hundred of their neighbours and besieged the suppression commissioners in the abbey tower. The canons and their supporters celebrated by roasting an ox—but too soon: the victory party was spoiled by the arrival of the sheriff, and most of the revellers fled in the dark.[23]

There was similar—but more successful—resistance at Hexham in Northumberland at the end of September. The commissioners heard that the canons had raised men and guns to defend their house, and sent out a small party to reconnoitre. As the commissioners approached, the bells of town and priory were rung, and armed men were drawn up in the street. The priory gates were locked against the commissioners, and defended by armed canons, servants, and townsmen. Their leader called down, 'We be twenty brethren in this house, and we shall die all, or that shall ye have this house.' The royal officers, surrounded by armed townsmen and women, showed the canons the king's commission, but the canons claimed to have a crown confirmation of the priory and vowed to resist: 'afore any other of our lands, goods, or house be taken from us we shall all die, and that is our full answer.'[24] At this point the officers thought it wise to withdraw; as they left, the canons and townsmen marched out in twos, and formed up in ranks on the green until the king's men were out of sight. If the men of Hexham then had their victory celebration, it was deserved: the priory was now safe for several months.

Other religious communities sought exemption from suppression by more peaceful means. The convent of St Mary's Winchester offered the king 500 marks to avoid suppression, and recruited Sir Edward Seymour by granting him a manor to help their cause; the nuns paid their money and were reprieved. The bishop of Lichfield made offers to the king and Cromwell for the priory of Baswich near Stafford to stand, and eventually the house paid 200 marks. In Lancashire, the five houses threatened with liquidation were invited to make bids for exemption: four proposed 1,000 marks (£666 13s. 4d.) each, and the poorest 250 marks. Some of them were asked to increase their tenders. Conishead could only go to 1,100 marks and was dissolved; Cockersand doubled its bid and survived; £400 was paid to the Duchy of Lancaster, and the rest guaranteed by local gentry. At least thirty-four houses paid for exemption, giving about £7,000 in all. Cockersand gave most, Polsloe and Blanchland gave £400 each, and another thirteen gave £200 or more each. Some bids failed. Sir Simon Harcourt offered £100 to Cromwell, plus £20 from the house, and another £100 for the king, for the continuation of Ranton in Staffordshire, but the priory was closed down.[25]

Exemption from suppression was not a straightforward financial transaction; if it had been, many more monasteries would have survived. The houses allowed to stand were often those for which the royal commissioners had made a special case. The nuns of St Mary's Winchester had been commended as 'religious and in living virtuous', with 'great relief daily ministered unto the inhabitants of the said city'. Ulverscroft in Leicestershire paid 200 marks to the king, but only after the commissioners reported the canons were 'good, virtuous, religious, and of good qualities, as writers, embroiderers and painters, and living, and desireth the king's highness to establish them there if it may stand with his gracious pleasure'. Sometimes these intercessions worked, sometimes they did not. The nuns of Catesby in Northamptonshire were 'as religious and devout and with as good obedience as we have in time past seen or belike shall see', active in charitable works among 'his grace's poor subjects'; the canons of St James's Northampton were well liked in the town, and gave relief to the poor. Catesby was suppressed; Northampton (much richer) paid 500 marks and survived.[26]

Some communities were reprieved to accommodate the many monks and nuns who sought transfers when their own houses went down. This explains why several houses were exempted for paltry payments, and why about forty (mostly poor nunneries) escaped without paying at all. The 1536 statute had allowed the religious to choose between going out into the world or moving to a larger house. Especially among the nuns (for whom the world offered little), there was such a clamour for transfer that there was no room in the larger houses and some of the smaller ones had to be exempted. In Yorkshire all but three of the nuns wished to stay cloistered, and thirteen nunneries were reprieved to accommodate some of those who wanted to remain in religion. Those monks who left their orders could become secular priests, and many chose—or were persuaded—to do so. In Sussex over 90 per cent of the monks asked to leave (which suggests pressure from the commissioners), but elsewhere there was more commitment to the cloister: in the Midlands 78 per cent of monks wished to continue. In Lancashire, 80 per cent of monks asked to remain in religion and two-thirds were willing to move elsewhere to do so. Cockersand was exempted to lodge the Premonstratensians, but all the rest were thrown out anyway.[27]

Though some had been eager enough to break free, a large number of resentful monks and nuns were chased from their homes in the summer and autumn of 1536, especially in Lincolnshire and the north. They seem to have become the catalysts of revolt. There were already reasons enough for trouble. The harvest of 1535 had been bad, and that of 1536 was better but not good; subsidy collectors were busy raising the second instalment of taxes granted in 1534; and there may have been discontent over enclosure and rents in some areas (though the rebels turned against government, not landlords). The bishop of Lincoln's commissaries were enforcing the royal injunctions, and there were rumours that they would confiscate church plate and deprive unsatisfactory priests of their benefices.[28] On Sunday 1 October 1536 the vicar of Louth warned his congregation that the officials were due there next day and they must make preparation; the church plate was locked away, and a watch set to guard it. When the bishop's officers arrived at Louth on Monday, the townsmen rang the bells to signal revolt;

they seized the officers and members of the subsidy commission, and sent a party off to Legbourne Priory to arrest the suppression commissioners.

The priests of the deanery, who had gathered at Louth for the visitation, swore loyalty to Church and people and returned to their parishes to spread the news of revolt. It was much the same at Caistor next day, 3 October. The clergy gathered for the visitation, and the laity for the subsidy; the bells were rung, the priests joined the commons, more subsidy commissioners were seized and the clergy brought in the neighbouring parishes. The captured gentry were told that the commons wished the king to take no more taxes, suppress no more monasteries, and hand over Cromwell, Cranmer, and the heretic bishops for punishment.[29] At Horncastle, the commons were raised by the rector of Belchford, and the local gentry were brought in to join the revolt; on 4 October the mob there murdered the bishop's chancellor; it was said that the priests chanted, 'Kill him! kill him!'[30] The gentlemen at Horncastle drew up a list of demands, which added some of their own grievances to the popular concern for taxes and monasteries, and now they led the protest; perhaps this was to deflect the aggressive commons into peaceful petitioning. What had begun as a local riot over church plate was fast becoming an organized movement.

Those who joined the cause took an oath: 'Ye shall swear to be true to Almighty God, to Christ's Catholic Church, to our sovereign lord the king, and unto the commons of this realm, so help you God and Holydam and by this book.'[31] The priests were especially active as recruiters, and some led out their parishioners behind the church cross or the consecrated host. Some of the ejected monks were busy too, and several of the larger monasteries joined in. The abbot of Barlings sent supplies, and monks from Barlings, Bardney, Vaudey, and Kirkstead marched with the rebel force. By 8 October it was thought that 40,000 rebels were up, and there was a great muster at Lincoln. There the rebels approved demands drafted by the gentry: no taxation except in wartime; repeal of the statute of uses; the liberties of the Church to be observed; no suppression of monasteries; heresy to be purged; those responsible for oppression and heresy to be punished; and a pardon for the rebels.[32] But Henry would have none of them, and his refusal to negotiate put the nervous gentry on the spot. With some difficulty they persuaded the commons to disperse and wait for concessions from the king; by the 12th it was all over—in Lincolnshire that is.

But by the time the Lincolnshire revolt collapsed there was a much more serious rebellion further north. On 4 October Robert Aske, a Yorkshire lawyer, was persuaded to take the Lincolnshire oath.[33] On 6 October the commons of south-east Yorkshire began to rise, and on the 8th the commons of Beverley held a muster; on the 10th Aske took on the role of 'chief captain', and began to issue orders for recruitment and meetings. His emergence as leader is a mystery: perhaps he and his allies had stirred revolt among the commons; perhaps he had taken over a revolt he hoped would come; perhaps he aimed to persuade the commons into peaceful petitioning; perhaps he became a unifying figurehead, a name on orders, in the early days of inchoate disorder. His declaration of the purpose of the revolt (or 'Pilgrimage of Grace', as he had begun to call it) was copied and circulated:

For this pilgrimage we have taken it for the preservation of Christ's Church, of this realm of England, the king our sovereign lord, the nobility and commons of the same, and to the intent to make petition to the king's highness for the reformation of that which is amiss within his realm and for the punishment of the heretics and subverters of the laws.[34]

Revolt spread rapidly through Yorkshire and beyond, and, under Aske, the rebels began to converge on York; they were admitted to the city on 16 October, after Aske had promulgated the rebel articles: an end to the suppression, repeal of the statute of uses, reduction of taxes, and punishment of Cromwell, Cranmer, and the heretics.[35] Aske then marched his men to Pontefract, where Lord Darcy surrendered the royal castle and joined the rebel leadership; by now the main rebel army was about 30,000 strong, commanded by five lords and a host of knights. Aske, Darcy, and their followers then marched on to Doncaster, where they confronted a small royal force led by the duke of Norfolk and the earl of Shrewsbury. There was disagreement among the rebel commanders over their strategy: some of the military men wanted to defeat Norfolk and march on London, but Aske persuaded them to camp at Doncaster and petition the king for redress.[36] A truce was agreed between the royal and rebel armies on 27 October, and two northern gentlemen were sent to the king with the pilgrims' petition. Most of the rebel army then disbanded, but Aske and his fellow-leaders were now the effective government of the north.

Henry's first response to the rebel emissaries was a blunt refusal to make concessions, and a demand for the execution of ten ringleaders. But it was clear to Norfolk that this would reactivate the Pilgrims' army and produce a march on London. So Henry was persuaded to offer negotiations, and Aske summoned a rebel council at York to discuss the proposal. Eight hundred representatives of rebel areas met at York on 21–5 November, and after much debate they agreed to treat with Norfolk. A second conference was held at Pontefract on 2–4 December, to draw up a statement of grievances, and the religious issues were debated by a meeting of senior clergy on 4–5 December. The twenty-four Pontefract articles[37] were compiled from complaints sent in from all over the north, and were agreed by the assembly of representatives. They embraced many divergent interests: there were three economic articles (on rents, enclosure, and taxes); six on legal and administrative matters; six political articles (especially on the royal succession, the punishment of Cromwell and others, and the holding of a free parliament); and nine (most of them at the head of the list) dealt with religious grievances.

The rebels demanded suppression of heresies and punishment of heretics; restitution of the pope's spiritual supremacy; re-establishment of the monasteries and the Observant friaries; the freeing of the religious orders from first fruits and tenths; and restoration of the liberties of the Church. It has been suggested that this indictment of Henrician policy was the product of Aske's own religious idealism, and cloaked the economic grievances of the commons and the legal and political concerns of the leaders.[38] It is certainly true that religion produced slogans the divided rebels could all accept and confidence that they marched in God's cause; but it would be false to see the rebel banner of the five wounds of Christ as a flag of convenience. The secular demands were late additions to the basic religious grievances, rather than vice versa, and it was the local impact of Henry's Reformation which had produced rebellion. When the commons were active in rebellion, it was not in refusing rents or pulling down enclosures; it was in protesting at the abolition of St Wilfrid's day (as at Watton), or in demanding the celebration of St Luke's day (as at Kirby Stephen), or in forcing nervous priests to pray for the pope.

Above all, the commons had defended and restored monasteries. As early as mid-September four parishes in the Yorkshire dales had taken an oath to protect the monasteries, and on 28 September the men of Hexham had chased off suppression commissioners. The canons of Coverham and St Agatha's Richmond were restored to their houses on 11 October, and the monks of Sawley in west Yorkshire on the 12th; by the 16th the canons of Conishead in north Lancashire were back in their priory and appealing for support from local rebels. But the reoccupation of houses was soon posing problems, for there were obvious conflicts of interest between the restored monks and the lessees of confiscated estates. Robert Aske issued orders on 16 October which sought to regulate such disputes, and the monks were to give receipts for the supplies they needed. In all, the rebels restored at least sixteen of the twenty-six northern monasteries which had actually been dissolved.[39] Of course, this was not always a spontaneous action: it was alleged that the ex-monks of Sawley had persuaded the commons to put them into possession of their abbey, and the canons at Conishead and Cartmel seem to have done the same.

Sir William Fairfax claimed in January 1537 that the rebellion had been all the fault of the monks:

The houses of religion not suppressed make friends and wag the poor to stick hard in this opinion, and the monks who were suppressed inhabit the villages round their houses and daily wag the people to put them in again.[40]

Fairfax would have known: he was the lessee of Ferriby priory, which had been restored on 16 October when local men had called in Beverley rebels to help them. The canons of Knaresborough had been spreading rumours of new taxes from the earliest stages of the rising. The monks of Furness ordered their tenants to join the Pilgrimage, and threatened loss of lands for those who would not; the abbot of Holm Cultram vowed he would hang tenants who failed to turn out for rebel musters. The prior of Bridlington sent two of his monks and eleven tenants to Aske's army, and many houses gave money and provisions—Bolton, Byland, Guisborough, Rievaulx, and Whitby, for example. Some of the larger abbeys were reluctant to jeopardize their future by revolt, and had to be 'encouraged': the monks of Whalley took the Pilgrim oath only after threats to burn their corn, but thereafter they gave active leadership in east Lancashire.[41]

But despite the efforts of the monks—and of the many parish clergy who led their people off to join the rising—the Pilgrimage did not alter royal policy. When the rebel negotiators met Norfolk at Doncaster on 6 December, they were offered pardon and a parliament to consider their grievances, and they insisted that the restored monasteries should remain. But Norfolk had already told the king that of course he would not have to keep any promises made to rebels.[42] On 8 December Aske persuaded the Pilgrims to return home, and surrendered his authority as chief captain: the rebellion was over, except for disorders in January and February when the commons concluded they had been duped. These later troubles gave Norfolk and Henry an excuse for retribution, and the gentry who had joined the Pilgrimage now rushed to prove their loyalty by co-operation in the king's revenge. Forty-seven Lincolnshire rebels were executed, and 132 from the northern Pilgrimage, including seventy-four strung up by Norfolk under martial law.[43] It was a restricted retaliation, given that perhaps 50,000 men had joined the various rebel armies, and any number of others had been involved in local disruptions: it was all that could be risked in a tense situation.

The rebellions had been confined to Lincolnshire and the six northern counties; perhaps the religious orders had contributed more to poorer areas with inadequate parochial organization; perhaps decisive action by the king's commanders in the south contained the trouble; perhaps—as on other occasions—southerners were willing to let the north do the work and to wait for the benefits. But there was widespread sympathy in southern counties for the Pilgrim cause. At Windsor a priest tried to persuade those mustering for the royal army that any who joined the northern cause 'did fight and defend God's quarrel'.[44] In January 1537 there was an attempt to get a Cornish Pilgrimage going, and a banner of the five wounds was made to lead the people in defence of saints' days. At Walsingham in April there was a plan to rise against the local gentry and defend the priory from suppression; it was a serious business, which ended with eleven executions. In June a group at Fincham in Norfolk planned to follow the example of the men of the north and of Walsingham; four were executed. Later in 1537 a Wiltshire rector thought 'it was unhappy that the northern men had not hold their way, for if they had it would have been better for us all', but he was unpopular with his neighbours and they turned him in.[45]

Some of the concerns which caused rebellion were certainly shared in the south. The rumours about the future of parish churches and property which worried Lincolnshire and Yorkshire also circulated in Buckinghamshire, Cornwall, Northamptonshire, and Shropshire. In 1537 the parishioners of Aylesham in Norfolk sold their church lands, and tried to sell their cross and plate before the king could get his hands on them. One of the churchwardens of Thame in Oxfordshire told the congregation after a service that the king was to seize crosses and jewels, and it would be better if they organized their own sale, 'and thus the king shall not have all his mind'.[46] It was fear of the king's intentions that prompted the resumptions and conversions of chantry lands which became common from 1536. In 1538 a chantry priest of Ipswich was accused of selling endowments and retorted, 'I would rather sell than the king should have it.'[47] Henry was fast becoming an unpopular king. When told of the execution of Anne Boleyn, the rector of Freshwater on the Isle of Wight rejoiced that the despoiler of the Church was made a cuckold in his own house, and a Kentish priest declared that Henry now persecuted the Church just as Nero had done.[48]

The northern fear of a rising tide of heresy was also found in the south. In 1535 a London Franciscan trusted all those 'of the new learning' would be executed, and hoped for the same fate for Henry and Anne as their supporters. At Sturminster Newton in Dorset in 1536 the incumbent warned against 'these abominable heretics that readeth the New Testament in English'; in Kent in 1537 a priest declared 'he had liefer that all the New Testaments in English were burned than he would buy any or look upon any'.[49] In towns such as Bristol, Exeter, Gloucester, Rye, and Salisbury there was vigorous resistance to reformist preachers, derided as 'heretic knaves'. From Gloucester in June 1536 the sheriff protested against disruptive preachers, and asked Bishop Stokesley and the duke of Norfolk to warn Henry that the preachers were going too far; in 1537 he petitioned Norfolk to have the 'whoreson heretic' Bishop Latimer silenced.[50] When Hilsey preached at St Paul's Cross he was called 'knave bishop and heretic', or 'heretic and Loller', and news of his sermons was carried to horrified villagers.[51] But these were the enthusiasts the king relied upon to explain and implement reform, and their provocations brought discredit to his policies.

The Injunctions of 1536 and 1538 seemed royal waves in the offensive heretical tide. There were reports of disobedience to the first Injunctions from the dioceses of Exeter, Salisbury, and Worcester in the south-west, and Chichester, Canterbury, and Norwich in the south-east; a parson in Suffolk refused to preach against the pope, and waved the Ten Articles before his congregation warning, 'Beware, my friends, of the English books!' There was even more widespread hostility to the second Injunctions; they were dismissed by a London rector as 'a thing to make fools afraid withall'.[52] There was a general assumption that the introduction of parish registers was in preparation for taxes on christenings, weddings, and funerals. The clergy attacked the order to have an English Bible in each church for the people to read: a priest at Wincanton denounced 'these new-fangled fellows which read the new books, for they be heretics and knaves and pharisees'; and the vicar of Enfield victimized those who read the Bible, 'the book of Arthur Cobbler'.[53] Parishes were slow to buy the required Bibles; very few outside London and the cathedral cities had done so within two years, and it was only after the threat of fines in 1541 that most parishes grudgingly complied.

The Injunctions had favoured heresy, by promoting the English Bible and attacking the use of images. In 1538 the vicar of Newark warned against English books licensed by the king, and the heretics who took down images. In Chesterfield a hermit noted, 'if a man will pluck down or tear the king's arms he shall be hanged, drawn, and quartered. What shall he do then that doth pluck down churches and images?'[54] Change had gone far enough—too far—and a reversal was expected. A London Bible-reader was threatened that she and her kind would soon be 'tied together, sacked, and thrown into Thames' by the bishop. Thomas Cowley, vicar of Ticehurst in Sussex, told his people of a miracle cure by St Martin and said,

I trust our sovereign lord the king shall be that Martin and take away that disease from you which is the Testament. You botchers, bunglers and cobblers which have the Testament in their keeping, ye shall deliver it to us gentlemen which have studied therefore.

Cowley was a sharp observer: 'Lor, lor masters, I said we should have the old fashion again; ye may see it comes a little and a little.'[55] All would be as before within four years, he said; he was wrong, but only just.

❧ 9 ❧

Reformation Reversed, 1538–1547

ON 16 November 1538 Henry VIII stopped the Reformation dead. His personal involvement in the trial of John Lambert and the proclamation against heresy showed his mind; he would no longer let Cranmer and Cromwell have their way: they must follow his way, or pay for their disobedience. It is a measure of Henry's determination that he threw his support behind the conservative bishops just when diplomatic calculation suggested a Lutheran alliance. Also in November, the pope had finally published his excommunication of the king, and then sent Cardinal Pole off to persuade Francis I and Charles V to mount a crusade against England. In January 1539, by the Treaty of Toledo, France and the Empire agreed not to ally with Henry, and then recalled their ambassadors. For a time at least, England was ringed by a Catholic alliance: France, the Empire, and Scotland. Frantic missions were dispatched to Saxony, Hesse, and Denmark—though by now the Lutherans were somewhat sceptical of Henry's intentions. Thomas Cromwell floated the project of a marriage between the widowed Henry and the sister of the half-Lutheran duke of Cleves, and a treaty was eventually signed in October 1539.

At home, Henry began a massive building programme to strengthen fortifications against the expected invasion, but he did not make theological concessions to the Lutherans, as he had done before when danger had threatened. Lutheran emissaries arrived late in April 1539, but Henry allowed Norfolk, Suffolk, and Bishop Tunstall to impede Cromwell's negotiations.[1] The international situation now moved in the conservatives' favour, as the risk from abroad diminished and the Lutherans became expendable. To stiffen the king's reactionary resolve, conservative councillors warned him of the progress of heresy in Calais; Henry apparently agreed that the terms of the heresy proclamation should be given statutory force. Cromwell and his allies tried to block this proposal by having it shunted off to a committee of bishops, on which the reformers had a narrow majority. But Henry would not wait. On 16 May the duke of Norfolk asked the House of Lords to consider six controversial issues: transubstantiation, communion in one kind, vows of chastity, votive masses, clerical celibacy, and auricular confession, thus including the very problems which had wrecked negotiations with the Lutherans in September 1538.[2]

Norfolk must have had Henry's approval for this move, which asked Parliament to endorse the beliefs and practices demanded by the November proclamation. After debate and negotiation, the two Houses of Parliament and the two of Convocation gave the expected Catholic answers, and the Six Articles were enshrined in statute. Denial of transubstantiation was to be punished by burning without opportunity for recantation; denial of any of the other articles was to be punished by hanging or life imprisonment. Communion in one kind, clerical celibacy, vows of chastity, and votive masses were declared acceptable by God's law (though Henry himself vetoed a claim that auricular confession was demanded by divine law). Cromwell's dialogue with the Lutherans now collapsed; since the religious questions under discussion had been decided by Henry, Parliament, and the law of God, Cromwell had no room for theological manœuvre, and once more Lutheran emissaries went resentfully home. Latimer and Shaxton, the two bishops who had fought hardest against the Six Articles, were forced to resign, leaving Cranmer with few allies on the episcopal bench.[3]

The Act of Six Articles was a disaster for Cranmer and Cromwell. The archbishop's theological advice had been rejected by the king, and he had to pack his secret wife off to Germany for fear of discovery. Cromwell's policy of advancing evangelical doctrines by alliance with Lutheran states had been hamstrung, for it would be much more difficult to repeal the statute than to replace the November proclamation. Cromwell's only hope lay in international pressures on Henry, and for a while they assisted. The expected breach between Charles and Francis did not happen—yet—and the projected German marriage went ahead in January 1540. Henry was not much impressed by Anne of Cleves: on his way to the wedding he told Cromwell, 'My Lord, if it were not to satisfy the world and my realm, I would not do that I must do this day for none earthly thing.'[4] But Henry had no choice: Charles and Francis were fêting each other in Paris, and England needed German allies. Fortunately for Henry, and probably for Anne, relief was soon at hand: Charles and Francis fell out over Milan, the German princes patched up some of their quarrel with Charles, and Henry no longer needed his new wife.

For a while, diplomatic circumstance had protected Cromwell from some of the political consequences of the Act of Six Articles, and he tried to bolster his authority by packing the Privy Chamber with allies.[5] But his position was soon challenged. On a mission to France, the duke of Norfolk apparently persuaded King Francis that an English alliance would be available if Cromwell was overthrown.[6] In London, Bishop Gardiner mounted a Lenten sermon campaign against justification by faith.[7] This had been allowed to influence the Bishops' Book in 1537, but Henry had rebutted it in his revisions. Gardiner probably hoped to take advantage of Henry's detestation of solifideism by provoking a confrontation on the issue, which would discredit English Lutherans and embarrass Cromwell. Robert Barnes (who had been used by Cromwell in the Cleves negotiations) played into Gardiner's hands. He preached a retort at St Paul's Cross, and mocked Gardiner for sowing weeds 'in the garden of Scripture'.[8] Gardiner complained to the king, and secured an order that Barnes, Garrett, and Jerome should abjure their views; when the recantations were inadequate, the three were sent to the Tower.

The political tide was now flowing against Cromwell. On 5 April 1540 the commission which had investigated heresy in Calais reported, and hinted that Cromwell would not enforce the Six Articles. On 12 April committees to advise on doctrine and ceremonies were named, and they were heavily dominated by conservative bishops and scholars.[9] As it became clear that Henry could safely abandon Anne, Norfolk trailed his seductive niece Katherine Howard before the frustrated king. Though Cromwell fought for his life through the spring of 1540, he really had no chance. Henry divorced Anne, married Katherine, and allowed Cromwell to be arrested on charges of treason and heresy.[10] He was said to have defended Barnes and other heretics, and vowed to uphold their doctrine whatever the king did. It is hard to know whether Henry believed these allegations; they seem far-fetched, but they played on his fear of betrayal by those he trusted and on his hatred of sacramentaries. Probably the king did not care whether the accusations were true or not: Cromwell had got him into a mess—diplomatic, marital, political, and theological—and Cromwell paid the penalty.

On 28 June 1540 Cromwell was executed, and on 30 June Barnes, Garrett, and Jerome were burned for heresy, to prove that Henry's flirtation with Lutheranism was over. Barnes did not understand their deaths; he complained that all they had done was in support of the royal supremacy.[11] Lest any should suppose the king meant to abandon his supremacy, three prominent conservatives were also executed for alleged papalism. It was a gruesome symmetry, as three Protestants and three Catholics went to their deaths, just to show where Henry stood. The policy reversal which had begun in September 1538 was complete. Henry had abandoned negotiations with the German Lutherans, and prohibited by law some of the beliefs they had advanced. He had appointed a committee to revise the Bishops' Book, and packed it with guaranteed Catholics who would recommend deletion of the concessions to Lutherans. He had allowed the conservative bishops to begin a drive against heresy, and permitted a tighter definition of heresy than hitherto. He had married into the conservative faction at Court, and he had sanctioned the execution of Cromwell, who had pressed him into semi-Protestant policies. The first Reformation was over.

But that was not enough for Tunstall, Gardiner, and their allies, and perhaps not enough for the king. They wanted some of that Reformation reversed, and old orthodoxies re-enforced. The fall of Thomas More in 1532 had been followed by the release of heretics from custody; the fall of Cromwell in 1540 was followed by a wave of arrests. The authorities of the city of London were quick to display their loyalty to the new policy. Juries were empanelled under the Act of Six Articles, and at least 190 laypeople and sixteen priests were arrested and imprisoned.[12] Certainly fifty of them were clear heretics, followers of Barnes, Latimer, and other Protestant preachers, but the others were mainly critics of ceremonies or irregular attenders at church. Views and conduct which had been tolerated in Cromwell's time were now being penalized, though those arrested were soon released, and after the king had made his point the hunt was called off. There was a further drive against heresy in London early in 1541, though this time Bishop Bonner and the clergy were the activists; a youth named Richard Mekins was hounded to death- by Bonner, to show the fate awaiting those who held to Barnes's teachings.[13]

There was a new political and theological climate. With the execution of Cromwell, the cowing of Cranmer, and the clear demonstration of Henry's new-found conservatism, the balance of opinion among councillors and bishops had shifted. In the theological debates of 1536–8, the evangelicals had made the running and usually got their way, and the conservatives had given in when they supposed the king wanted agreement along reformist lines. But now they knew that Henry was behind them, and they used their majority on the committee for revision of the Bishops' Book. The committee's working papers and reports show sharp differences on the sacraments in general and confirmation, confession, orders, and extreme unction in particular. But out of twenty members only Cranmer, two bishops, and one theologian argued a consistently evangelical position.[14] The king approved of the conservative conclusions, and doubted only the claims on confirmation and consecration of bishops; 'ubi hoc?' he scrawled in the margin of the report on consecration[15]—prove it! Henry retained his high view of the powers of princes against prelates, but for the rest he would now support the conservatives.

The international position also favoured reaction. The breach between France and the Empire became irrevocable in October 1541, when Charles V made his son duke of Milan—which was claimed by France. Now Charles needed all the friends he could get, and summoned a conference at Regensburg to try to heal religious divisions in Germany. Henry feared that if the Germans reached agreement he would be left out in the diplomatic and theological cold; so in November 1540 he sent Gardiner off to Regensburg with a watching brief.[16] When the imperial chancellor offered to mediate between Henry and the pope, Gardiner was instructed to accept the proposal. No doubt Henry was playing for time, but he had indicated— to Gardiner and to the emperor—that ecclesiastical supremacy was negotiable, that the break from Rome was not *necessarily* final.[17] In the event, Henry's gamble paid off: the colloquy at Regensburg foundered on the issue of transubstantiation and Henry did not have to swallow his pride or his supremacy. Gardiner was recalled in June 1541, though not before he had negotiated an alliance with Charles V against France; it was an alliance which would keep Henry Catholic.

Henry had ditched the Lutherans, he was ditching the Bishops' Book, and he wanted to ditch Cromwell's Bible, the version based on Protestant translations by Tyndale and Coverdale. He announced his determination to have the 1539 Great Bible corrected, and in February 1542 Gardiner led the campaign in Convocation.[18] Cranmer tried to protect the reformist translation and block revision, but was voted down by his fellow bishops. The bishops and the Lower House produced lists of mistranslated words, and Cranmer had to establish committees to work on the two Testaments. But Cranmer was able to out-manœuvre Gardiner: he persuaded Henry to commit the project to the two universities, where, no doubt, it would be lost in the intricacies of scholarly debate. This success prompted him to try to bypass revision of the Bishops' Book too: he proposed that he should supervise production of model sermons for use in churches. Gardiner argued that a set of homilies by different authors would bring disunity, and that a single agreed formulary was needed; Henry agreed.[19] The conservative-dominated committee on doctrine would have its way, not a bunch of reformist writers recruited by Cranmer.

The reversal in religion had been a reassertion of Henry's own fundamental conservatism: it had been political necessity which had taken him so far down the reformist road, and now that it was safe to do so he turned back. The risk of imperial invasion had forced Henry to suppress monasteries and court Lutherans; now the dispute over Milan had pressed the emperor into his arms, and he could cement alliance against France with a Catholic policy. But the counter-revolution had also been a response to the widespread popular hostility to religious change, both to heretical preaching and Cromwellian reform. By the Act of Six Articles Henry had rejected just those opinions which many priests and parishioners found repellent: on the eucharist, clerical celibacy, confession, and votive masses. The conservative crowd had been given its sacrificial victim: the rebels in the Pilgrimage had asked for Cromwell's head, and in 1540 they got it. And if the conservatives succeeded at the political centre, they did so too in the localities. Conventional parish religion, disrupted by Cromwell's Injunctions, now revived with only minor concessions to reform.

The 1538 Injunctions had ordered the destruction of images that had been objects of particular devotion, and forbade the burning of candles before images. The surviving churchwardens' accounts show that payments for votive candles ceased almost immediately, and testamentary bequests for them petered out soon after. Revenues from the parish funds which had supported such candles were transferred to other church uses. At Ashburton the money was used to buy a new organ and vestments, and for the painting of the rood-loft; at Morebath there were extensive repairs to the church, the tower, the church house, and its brew-house. But the end of saints' candles does not mean that devotion had been shallow or in decline; everywhere images were cleaned and painted as before, the permitted rood and sacrament lights and Paschal candles were burned, and at Cranbrook in Kent and Eye in Suffolk new rood-lofts were set up. But through the abandoning of candles, images were preserved; disobedience risked having images classed as 'superstitious' and liable to destruction. No images were removed from churches with surviving accounts: the tactic of cleaning up devotion to keep the authorities quiet had worked.

Where, as in the diocese of Canterbury, an officious commissary tried to have images removed on grounds of superstition, there was trouble.[20] Christopher Nevinson had the image of St James at Elmstead pulled down because there had been offerings made and candles before it, but the parishioners petitioned Cranmer that there had been no lights since the king's Injunctions; a local knight had the image replaced. At St George's Canterbury, Nevinson had the image of St George removed on the grounds that it had been carried in procession on the saint's day; the wardens protested to the Council that this was no way to treat the patron of England, and got their image set up again. At Milton and at Sholden, images pulled down by Nevinson were restored by the locals when the commissary moved on. At Chilham, Eastwell, and North Mongeham images which ought to have been removed were retained by the parishes, and at Chartham and St Peter's Canterbury there were protests when images were taken down. At Chilham the vicar continued to declare that prayers to images could aid the sick, and elsewhere images were honoured with garlands in place of forbidden candles.

Parishes were also reluctant to set up English Bibles in churches for the laity to read. Perhaps some of the objection was to cost, but there was also a suspicion that Bible-reading led to heresy. Six months after the 1538 order, 80 per cent of the churches in three Lincoln deaneries had not bought Bibles, and diocesan officials were doing nothing to enforce them. In 1540 the rector of Hastingleigh in Kent asked for cash help for a Bible, 'for we have but one that can read it and but sixteen householders', all poor.[21] Wardens' accounts suggest that by the end of 1540 few churches outside London and the cathedral cities had their Bibles, and even Lincoln cathedral did not buy for its dependant churches until 1541. In May 1541 a proclamation complained, 'His royal Majesty is informed that divers and many towns and parishes within this his realm have negligently omitted their duties in the accomplishment thereof, whereof his Majesty marvelleth not a little.'[22]

Parishes were given six months to comply, on pain of a £2 fine. Now it was cheaper to have a Bible than not, there was grudging obedience: Ashburton and Boxford in Suffolk and Great Hallingbury in Essex bought Bibles soon after the proclamation, and most churches had them by the end of 1545. But some country parishes only obeyed when forced to do so by royal commissioners in 1547.

So parishes had to give up saints' candles, and slowly they installed their Bibles. Some of the guilds dwindled away, though usually it was those which had supported candles before images, and had now lost much of their purpose. Some endowments for prayers were 'privatized', usually to forestall expected royal seizure, as the villagers of Davidstow in Cornwall admitted after selling their chantry oxen in 1545.[23] But it seems that parish religion had not changed very much under the impact of the first Reformation. At Ashburton the guild of the forbidden St Thomas Becket survived, by transmogrification into the guild of St Thomas the Apostle. John Hooper complained in 1546 that the mass, prayers to saints, Lenten fasts, and prayers for the dead 'were never before held by the people in greater esteem than at the present moment'. John Foxe later remembered these years as

those days of King Henry when the mass most flourished, the altars with the sacrament thereof being in their most high veneration, that to man's reason it might seem impossible that the glory and opinion of that sacrament and sacramentals, so highly worshipped and so deeply rooted in the hearts of many, could by any means possible so soon decay and vanish to nought.[24]

The communal and liturgical round of the parish year continued, and local support for churches and their functions declined only slightly. Though there was wariness about bequests to guilds and endowed prayers, gifts to parish churches were fairly well sustained. In a large sample of northern wills, for example, 75 per cent of testators had left money to their churches in 1525–40, and 71 per cent did so in 1540–7.[25] The parish church at Morebath received thirty-three gifts in 1530–8, and twenty-seven in 1539–47. At St Andrew's Canterbury and many other parishes there were the usual collections by the men and the women at Hocktide, and collections to maintain the Paschal candle and the light before the sacrament. In country parishes receipts from church ales held up well, though Boxford's profits from the 'Hockpot' slumped. Church bells were rung at the feast of Corpus Christi, and Corpus Christi plays at Sherborne and Ashburton and the Christmas Robin Hood play at Ashburton were performed as before. Things were not quite the same, but there was no sign yet of the collapse of parochial religion which was to come in King Edward's reign.

The parochial consequences of the Cromwell years were not all bad, and some churches benefited from the suppression of monasteries. At Cartmel in Lancashire the parishioners took over the church they had shared with the priory. At Wing in Buckinghamshire in 1538 the parish bought an organ, stained glass, 'ornaments', and service equipment from Woburn Abbey, and paid for them partly through a voluntary collection. In 1541 the parishioners of Peterborough raised over £7 by a collection and put it towards purchase of 'the great bell of the abbey of Leicester'.[26] In 1542 the people of Sherborne abandoned their church, and purchased instead the great abbey church, and bought an image from Cerne Abbey to put in it. There had been a confiscation scare in 1536–7, but parishes had kept their plate and vestments; new purchases were now made with apparent confidence for the future. At Morebath there was a new cope in 1539, two rochets in 1541, new surplices in 1541 and 1545, and in 1547 the parishioners bought the black vestments and cope for which they had been saving since 1528; 'I pray God that it may be for their souls' health that gave any gift unto it', wrote the vicar.[27]

After Cromwell's fall it seemed that Reformation was not only stoppable but reversible. In 1541 the mayor of Sandwich forbade reading of the Bible by laymen, and imprisoned two who protested, including one who showed him the Injunctions. In the following year the vicar of Faversham took down the Bible which had been set up in his church. At Canterbury the great procession and pageant which had been suppressed as superstitious in 1538 were restored in 1542. One of the city priests compiled a list of 'favourers of evil opinions and common readers of the Bible', in the hope of prosecutions.[28] Even in Cranmer's own diocese, it seemed that conservatives had the evangelicals on the run. Late in 1542 an alliance of cathedral prebendaries, leading parish clergy, and some of the county justices conspired against the archbishop, either to ruin him and have him replaced, or to frighten him into prosecuting heretics.[29] They collected evidence of heresy in the diocese, and argued that Cranmer was tolerating and even encouraging heretics. In March 1543, they took their dossier to sympathizers at Court, just as the Privy Council was beginning a major investigation into heresy in the royal household and at Windsor. This can hardly have been a coincidence.

Information about Windsor heresy had come from Dr John London, warden of New College, Oxford, and a canon of Windsor. There were charges against one of the gentlemen of the Privy Chamber, other Household officers, the dean of Exeter, various choristers, the king's barber, and his cook, William Snowball. Soon there were arrests of London printers for publishing heretical books, examinations of butchers for selling meat in Lent, and heresy trials of preachers from London and Kent. It all looks like a carefully orchestrated campaign to make Henry feel surrounded and threatened by heretics, in the knowledge that when faced by heresy he would have to prove his orthodoxy to his ally Charles V. If the aim of Gardiner and his allies was to destroy the Court evangelicals, they failed. Henry intervened to protect Cranmer, though in a way which warned the archbishop to take care in future.[30] The investigations in the Household were called off, and there were few casualties: three preachers recanted on 8 July 1543, and three lesser figures were burned on 28 July. But if the conservatives sought to make ideological gains while their rivals were on the defensive, they were triumphantly successful.

The heresy investigations were conducted during the final negotiations and drafting for a new formulary of religion, one to replace the Bishops' Book which Henry had refused to endorse in 1537. A small group of bishops and theologians (mainly moderate conservatives) had been working on the king's own revisions of the Book and the reports of the 1540 committee. Their draft incorporated many of Henry's amendments, and was a much more conservative compilation than the 1537 version. The importance of the Bible was played down, and there was stronger emphasis on the mass, transubstantiation, confession, and the ceremonies of the Church. Images were commended, provided they were used without superstition, and Henry himself reworked the text of the second Commandment (on 'graven images') to moderate its criticism.[31] Above all, there was a continuing emphasis on the need for obedience and good works for salvation; there was no justification by faith. The central Reformation doctrine—which Henry had rejected in 1537, and against which Gardiner had campaigned in 1540—was now formally rebutted. Only on purgatory and prayers for the dead was there any reformist revision; perhaps Henry, at war on two fronts, had his eyes on mass endowments.

The draft was discussed in Convocation late in April 1543, and its sections were examined in detail by committees of bishops.[32] Cranmer tried to salvage justification by faith, insisting that though true faith was accompanied by works (faith was not *alone*) it was the faith *only* which justified.[33] It may have been at this point that Gardiner and his allies on the Privy Council tried to break Cranmer's authority; they agreed to have him arrested, and some of them showed Henry the evidence collected in Kent. Cranmer was saved by the persuasions of evangelicals in the Privy Chamber, and perhaps by Henry's determination to maintain a counterweight to the conservatives.[34] The king would not permit the imprisonment of his archbishop, but he rejected his theology: Henry insisted that the new formulary should stress the role of good works and explicitly reject justification by faith. The draft was altered to read that faith justified 'neither only nor alone'. Cranmer gave in, and the draft was passed by Convocation on 30 April; on 6 May it was approved by a special meeting of the nobility,[35] and soon published as *A Necessary Doctrine and Erudition for any Christian Man*.

The *Necessary Doctrine* did not only differ in theology from the Bishops' Book, it differed in status: it was 'the King's Book', drafted under his supervision and issued under his authority. It was also enforced by law. On 8 May 1543 the Lords began consideration of a bill which imposed the King's Book as the official standard in religion, and imposed penalties for publishing or reading books or Bible translations which contradicted the Book's doctrine. The final Act also restricted the reading of the Bible to the upper ranks of society: 'no women nor artificers, prentices, journeymen, serving men of the degrees of yeomen or under, husbandmen, nor labourers' were to read the Scriptures, on pain of a month's imprisonment, though a proviso allowed noble and gentry women to read privately.[36] The statute was designed to exclude perhaps 90 per cent of the population from Bible-reading. Its impact is still reflected on the flyleaf of a copy of Polydore Vergil's history, endorsed

At Oxford, the year 1546, brought down to Saintbury [Gloucs] by John Darbye, price 14*d*, when I keep Mr Latimer's sheep. I bought this book when the Testament was abrogated, that shepherds might not read it. I pray God amend that blindness. Writ by Robert Williams, keeping sheep upon Saintbury Hill, 1546.[37]

The limitation of Bible-reading was a tragedy for Robert Williams; it was a triumph for the conservative bishops and their supporters. They had now undone almost all that Cromwell had achieved between 1536 and 1538. They had taken advantage of Henry VIII's own conservatism, his fear of popular protest, and his wish for an imperial alliance against France. They had imposed transubstantiation and confession in the Six Articles; they had killed Cromwell and frightened Cranmer into compliance. They had promoted heresy hunts, which were not severe enough to destroy heresy but were regular enough to contain its expansion, and they had convinced the king that orthodoxy must be maintained by force. In 1543 they had got the King's Book, which had rejected justification by faith and defended the traditional sacraments, and they had gained a prohibition of Bible-reading by the majority of the people. Cranmer had saved the English Bible from revision in 1542, but in the next year he lost a more important fight. By the spring of 1543 the Protestant elements of the first Reformation had been reversed; only the break with Rome and the suppression of the monasteries survived.

Some historians have suggested that the conservatives lost control of the king in the summer of 1543, and that Reformation was renewed. Certainly Henry changed his matrimonial alliance: Katherine Howard had been executed for adultery in 1541, and Henry married Katherine Parr in July 1543. It seems, though, that Katherine's Protestant commitment has been antedated and exaggerated.[38] Certainly Henry's friend Anthony Denny had secured the appointment of Cambridge evangelicals as tutors to Prince

Edward and the Lady Elizabeth, though it is doubtful if Henry knew how reformist they were (or were to become). Certainly there was some jockeying for political position, as Henry's health declined, though none would risk serious offence to a king still in his early fifties. Certainly the military achievements of the reformist earl of Hertford made him a rising star at Court, and he formed an alliance with Denny and Lord Admiral Lisle against the Howards and Bishop Gardiner. Certainly there was an attack on Gardiner early in 1544, a mirror version of the 1543 plot against Cranmer, though Henry completed the parallel, and saved Winchester as he had saved Canterbury.

As Gardiner had sought to remind Henry of the dangers of heresy in 1543 and discredit the reformers, so the Hertford group reminded Henry of the dangers of papalism in 1544 and sought to discredit the conservatives. A dozen priests and laymen, several of them members and friends of the More family, were arrested and charged with conspiracy against the royal supremacy. On 7 March 1544 seven were executed; they included Germaine Gardiner, nephew and secretary of the bishop. It seems that Hertford and Lisle tried to persuade Henry that Stephen Gardiner must have known of Germaine's activities and shared his views. But Gardiner was tipped off by his allies in the Privy Chamber, and was able to clear himself before the king. Henry would not throw Gardiner to the evangelical wolves, just as he would not throw Cranmer to the conservatives.[39] For the conservatives had not lost control of Henry in 1543: they had never *had* control. Though Gardiner, Tunstall, and others had played on Henry's fear of heresy, the king had not been duped into reaction: he had unravelled Cromwell's Reformation because he had never liked it in the first place, and had only permitted it from diplomatic necessity.

Nor had the evangelicals gained control of the king. Even when the international situation made a Catholic stance less advantageous, Henry did not abandon the ecclesiastical policy he had pursued since 1538. In September 1544 Charles V deserted Henry and left him to fight France and Scotland alone; an anti-imperial group on the Privy Council began to advocate peace with France and another Lutheran alliance, but Henry offered no theological carrots to the Germans. He endorsed an English *Litany* published in May 1544, with a reduction in the invocation of saints, and a book of vernacular prayers, but these were in the tradition of Richard Whitford, designed 'for stirring the people to more devotion'.[40] In May 1545 Henry authorized a new *Primer* in English, and ordered its use in schools; though attention to saints was again diminished, the volume was a collection of traditionalist devotions. It was an instant success, selling sixteen editions in the next two years; the schoolmasters formed a mandatory market, but sales of the *Primer* suggest a continued vitality in conventional religion.

If it is hard to see the *Litany* and the *Primer* as decisive doses of further Reformation, it is impossible so to see the Chantries Act. Henry's threat to the chantries was not a principled attack on endowed prayers or a theological assault on purgatory, it was a precautionary financial measure introduced in necessity. The war against France cost more than two million pounds; Henry had to sell confiscated monastic lands to the gentry, debase the coinage, raise a forced loan, borrow from Antwerp, collect several subsidies—and still there was not enough. By November 1545 the king was virtually bankrupt, living from hand to mouth as funds trickled in. The Privy Council wanted Henry to cut his losses and get out of France, but he refused. So more money had to be raised, and it was to come, when needed, from chantry endowments. A bill on chantries was introduced to Parliament in December 1545, and was considered alongside another subsidy bill; the lesson was not lost on members. The bill transferred to the king all the chantry and guild endowments which had been illicitly privatized since 1536, and empowered him to survey the remaining chantries and to seize such property as he wished.[41]

The bill was right that chantries were being suppressed anyway, and the profits might as well go to the empty Crown coffers. Chantries had always been at risk from the greedy descendants of founders, and there had been occasional resumptions. But after the dissolution of the monasteries and the threat of more royal confiscations, patrons and parishes made their own pre-emptive seizures, often for church or village needs. From 1541 Henry picked off the secular colleges one by one, and from 1543 a handful of chantries were 'surrendered' to him. Perhaps he already envisaged a selective suppression of chantries, since he prepared his theological ground in advance, or perhaps he was justifying the dissolution of monasteries as he sold off their land. In 1543 the King's Book, which had retreated from the Bishops' Book on almost every other issue, undermined endowed prayer: it argued that none could know the fate of the departed or the efficacy of prayers for them, and insisted that masses should be said for the dead in general rather than for specific souls.[42] The burgesses of Richmond in north Yorkshire read the writing on the theological wall, took over the property of six chantries, two chapels, and ten obits, and paid the priests out of town funds.[43]

The Chantries bill passed the Lords without evident trouble: Gardiner and Tunstall were abroad on diplomatic missions, and the chancellor had already threatened praemunire charges against bishops. There was serious difficulty in the Commons, however, and the bill passed only on a division, despite the explicit argument that the king needed the profits from chantries to finance defence expenditure. No doubt the limited intention of the Act made it bearable: it did not envisage the wholesale suppression of chantries, but the survey and seizure of property the king needed. In fact, the peace with France in June 1546 brought the chantries a temporary reprieve. A national survey of endowments was complete by May 1546, but in the eight months more before the king's death the rate of suppression was no faster than before the Chantries Act. Those who would know were confident that chantries had a future. In October 1545 Robert Burgoyne, auditor of Augmentations, endowed a chantry-school for forty years; in July 1546 his brother (auditor of the Duchy) paid for three years of masses, and in January 1547 Henry VIII left £600 for two priests to pray for his soul for ever.[44]

So the English *Litany*, the English *Primer*, and the Chantries Act were not new pieces in a piecemeal Reformation; they were not steps towards the abolitions of the mass and endowed prayers which were to come with the next reign. The attack on the chantries was limited in scope and purpose, a practical response to pressing financial need. The *Litany* and the *Primer* were not victories for the evangelicals, but cautious measures of conservative reform, supportive rather than subversive of traditional religion. Henry had rejected Reformation in 1538, but he had not altogether rejected reform: in 1541 he had abolished the 'superstitious and childish observations' of the Boy Bishop and Holy Innocents, and had repeated Cromwell's order for the removal of relics and shrines from churches.[45] As Henry told Parliament in 1545, he opposed reactionary adherence to 'old mumpsimus' as much as urgent demands for 'new sumpsimus'.[46] Late in 1545 he was persuaded to allow three bishops to report on 'enormities and abuses' in ritual, and then he instructed Cranmer to suppress bell-ringing at Hallowe'en, covering of images in Lent, and the ceremony of 'creeping to the cross' on Good Friday.[47]

But the king changed his mind almost immediately, and reversed the January 1546 directive to Cranmer. He seems to have feared that even such minimal measures might be misinterpreted by Charles V, and so jeopardize Gardiner's negotiations with the emperor. There is a later story that Gardiner himself wrote from Bruges to warn that any shift in religion would wreck his mission, and it is likely that the king retained the ceremonies as a result of political persuasions.[48] For Catholics, there was always a risk that the supreme head's zeal for conservative reform might allow evangelicals to lead him towards radical change, as had happened in Cromwell's time. Even 'creeping to the cross' was worth defending to keep Henry from the arms of the evangelicals, who were small minorities among bishops and councillors, but a dangerous presence in the Household. Henry's doctor William Butts had been a patron of Protestants, as was his successor Thomas Wendy, and Anthony Denny acted as link-man between the king and Cranmer.[49] Perhaps it was the episode of the ceremonies (or perhaps it was the king's failing health) which convinced the conservatives that Henry (and his son) must be saved from the heretics.

It was the London preacher Edward Crome who gave the conservative group its chance, as Robert Barnes had done in 1540. In a series of provocative sermons in March and April 1546, Crome had denied the real presence of Christ in the eucharist, defended the Protestant doctrine of justification, and argued that the king's suppression of chantries showed there was no purgatory—not a lesson Henry wished to be drawn from his actions! Crome was arrested and ordered to recant, but his sermon on 9 May was a defiant refusal to withdraw.[50] Now Crome was called before the Council, and forced to give the names of his allies and supporters. There followed a wave of arrests and interrogations: of the former bishops Latimer and Shaxton, one of Henry's doctors, other preachers, and the courtiers George Blage and John Lascelles. There were enquiries under the Act of Six Articles in Essex and Suffolk, and five men were burned in May. But this was more than a hunt for heretics, it was a search for valuable political scalps. Conservative councillors, Lord Chancellor Wriothesley, Rich, Browne, Gardiner, and Tunstall, conducted the examinations, and sought to incriminate their rivals.

The interrogation of Lascelles led to his associate Anne Askew, a Lincolnshire gentlewoman and friend of evangelical Court ladies. She was pressed to recant her heresies by reformist councillors, who probably feared what she might reveal under pressure, but she held firm. After conviction on 28 June for heresy on the eucharist, she was sent to the Tower. There Wriothesley, Rich, and Sir John Baker questioned her on her relations with the duchess of Suffolk and the wives of Hertford, Denny, and the earl of Sussex, and when she failed to provide the information they wanted, she was tortured by Rich and Wriothesley. Anne Askew was burned at Smithfield with John Lascelles and two others on 16 July; a broken Shaxton preached at the execution.[51] Still the hunt went on. It seems that, from Anne or elsewhere, Wriothesley got wind of heresy among the ladies of Queen Katherine's circle, and he may have obtained Henry's permission to arrest her. But Katherine was apparently warned by Dr Wendy and, like Cranmer in 1543 and Gardiner in 1544, she saved herself by submission to the king's mercy. This brought an end to the persecution, and the remaining heretics were pardoned or quietly dismissed.

Though Wriothesley and his allies failed to ruin their leading rivals, they had seized the political initiative. While the Court reformers struggled to preserve their reputations and to save their friends from the flames, the conservatives took advantage of their own strength. The pulpit at St Paul's Cross was manned by a succession of the most effective Catholic preachers, and books of Catholic propaganda and piety streamed from the London presses. William Peryn's sermons on the eucharist were printed three times in 1546, as was one of Richard Smith's defences of the mass. The voice of heresy was silenced. In July 1546 the conservatives secured the issue of a proclamation against heretical books, the first since 1538: the works of

Barnes and ten others were banned, as were any books teaching contrary to the King's Book; 'I see the death of all godliness and religion', lamented Hooper.[52] In September there were searches for heretics and their books in London, by a royal commission under the Act of Six Articles. On 26 September Bishop Bonner presided at a great conflagration at St Paul's Cross, when piles of books and Bibles confiscated in the searches were tossed into the flames.[53] It was like the good old days of Wolsey and Fisher!

If Henry VIII had died in September 1546, when conservatives were still in the ascendant and reformers had their backs to the stake, English history would have been very different. A regency Council would have been dominated by Norfolk, Wriothesley, Gardiner, and Tunstall. There would have been no second Reformation under the boy King Edward; rather there would have been an Edwardian, not a Marian, reaction. But Henry did not die in September 1546: he was very ill (and pushed about in a wheelchair), but he did not die. Instead, he lived on for another four months, and by then it was all different: Norfolk was in the Tower, Gardiner in disgrace, and Hertford in control.[54] Hertford had already made his political dispositions: he had formed alliances with Lord Lisle and the queen's brother Essex, with Secretary Paget, and with Sir Anthony Denny; in October Sir William Herbert joined Denny (and the alliance) as a chief gentleman of the Privy Chamber. Between them these men could control the business of the Privy Council, access to the king in his private apartments, and use of the facsimile of Henry's signature with which official documents were stamped.

By November 1546 it was clear that Henry was dying, and the factional gloves were off; indeed, Lord Lisle struck Bishop Gardiner in the Council chamber, and was dismissed from Court for a time. But despite Lisle's fisticuffs, it was the conservatives who had to attack, for Hertford now had Henry in his pocket. The duke of Norfolk and his son Surrey campaigned for a Howard regency after the king's death, in a desperate attempt to prise control of young Edward from his uncle Hertford. But those about the king were able to present the Howard case as a direct challenge to the Tudor dynasty. Bishop Gardiner, who might have protected the Howards, was skilfully neutralized. Secretary Paget handled the negotiations for an exchange of lands between Gardiner and the king, and forced the bishop into an apparent refusal of Henry's request, by making impossible demands or exaggerating Gardiner's reluctance.[55] Gardiner pleaded for a personal interview with the king to clear himself, but was kept away from Court. On 12 December Norfolk and Surrey were sent to the Tower; on the following day, Henry altered his will to remove Gardiner and Norfolk from the projected regency Council.[56]

Hertford's triumph, impossible six months earlier, was now almost complete. On 26 December, Henry summoned him, Lisle, Paget, and

Denny to his bedside, and dictated a final version of the will, naming a regency Council of sixteen to rule in Edward's name: a Council which could be dominated by the Hertford group, so long as they held together. On 13 January Surrey was tried and convicted of treason, and executed six days later. His father had thrown himself on Henry's mercy, and found none. Parliament passed an attainder against Norfolk, which was given the royal assent (with the stamp of Henry's signature) on 27 January, and on the 28th, at two in the morning, the king died. He left his will unsigned. It was probably doctored by Paget, who added two crucial clauses: one gave the regency Council power to make any necessary provision for the government of the kingdom, the other allowed it to make gifts to Henry's servants. The first addition empowered the Council to make Hertford regent; the second permitted him to buy support for his bid. Hertford now had all he needed: the will was signed, by the dry stamp of a dead king.[57]

Henry VIII had died a Catholic, though a rather bad Catholic. In an individual and eclectic preamble, his will asked for intercession by Mary and the saints, and insisted on the reality of Christ's presence in the eucharist. He left £666 to the poor to pray for his soul, and another £600 for a chantry of two priests at Windsor and four solemn obits each year.[58] Henry did not envisage or intend what followed in his son's reign, when the assumptions of his will were overthrown one by one. He had not deliberately constructed a Protestant regency; he excluded Gardiner and Norfolk, but he did not know how far Lisle and Hertford would go in religion or how much support they had secured. He had not deliberately given his son a Protestant education; he employed humanist tutors, but he did not know (and we do not know) how evangelical they were while Henry lived. After all, Lisle, Essex, and one of the tutors had co-operated in the anti-heresy drive of 1546, no doubt to conceal their sympathies. So there was nothing predetermined about the Edwardian second Reformation, as there had been nothing predetermined about the Henrician first. Henry did not will his son's Reformation, any more than he had willed his own.

10

Edward's Reformation, 1547–1553

It is easy to suppose that, with Hertford's seizure of power, the Reformation was all over bar the Marian burnings. On 31 January 1547 the regency Council named Hertford protector of the realm and governor of the young king; on 12 March he was commissioned as virtual regent with near-sovereign powers. Then there was a clockwork Reformation. In 1547 there were new reformist Injunctions and new evangelical *Homilies*; endowed prayers were suppressed, and the laity allowed communion in both bread and wine. In 1548 church images were pulled down, and an Order of Communion introduced English prayers to the Latin mass. In 1549 the Latin rites were replaced by a half-Protestant Book of Common Prayer, and the clergy were permitted to marry. In 1550 altars were exchanged for communion tables, and a new Ordinal provided Protestant pastors rather than Catholic priests. In 1551 the episcopate was remodelled and a corps of missionary preachers created. In 1552 there was a decisively Protestant second Prayer Book. In 1553 redundant mass equipment was confiscated, the Protestant theology of the Church defined in Forty-Two Articles, and a Catechism published to teach the new religion.

From the simplifying perspective of historical hindsight, it all seems planned, or at least predetermined. The death of Henry gave power to Protestants; naturally there was a second, a truly Protestant, Reformation. Certainly the tone of the Court changed dramatically: rituals and beliefs demanded by the old king were now derided, evangelical piety was the fashion, and Latimer was installed as Court prophet. The first Parliament of the new reign repealed the heresy Acts and moderated the treason laws. In a more permissive atmosphere, hitherto-banned books were printed freely: in 1547–9, three-quarters of the books published were on religion, and half of these were by Protestants. The repeal of the 1543 Act allowed unrestricted Bible-reading; sixty editions of the Bible were printed in Edward's reign, and by 1549 versions for the poor could be bought in parts.[1] Preachers who had been harried under Henry now declared their views openly; some parishes with evangelical élites began their own liturgical experiments. For Protestants, the times were better even than the golden days of Cromwell's rule: a cautious political Reformation permitted a more determined popular Reformation.

But the inexorable march of the Henrician first Reformation is an illusion concealing compromise and confusion, and so it is with the Edwardian second Reformation. Religious change again proceeded by spasmodic fits, uncertain starts, and threats of reversal. Hertford established his power only with a struggle, and he remained reluctant to risk it in an uncertain cause. His governorship of the king was challenged by his brother Thomas Seymour, who had to be bought off by admission to the Privy Council. In February Hertford became duke of Somerset, but Lord Chancellor Wriothesley continued to dispute his authority as protector and was dismissed from the Council. Lisle (now earl of Warwick) was manœuvring in his own interest, and Paget's attachment to the reformist cause was never more than tactical.[2] Somerset himself had evangelical inclinations, and he cultivated a Protestant mode: he ran a Protestant household, and became a correspondent of Calvin. But his stylized pious pose was probably adopted for political advantage. It attracted supporters against Wriothesley, it drove Gardiner to opposition and imprisonment for disobedience, and it justified assault on Church endowments.

Somerset might promote reform, but only in ways which carried few dangers. By the summer of 1547, Cranmer had concluded that the death of Henry was a disaster, for the Council was now so afraid of popular resistance that it did not dare to enforce change.[3] He was too pessimistic. Somerset's military ambitions in Scotland persuaded him against radical innovation in religion,[4] which might bring rebellion (as in 1536) or imperial invasion. But change was accelerated by interaction between Somerset's reticent reform and the minority clamour for radicalism, as the fate of the images shows. Cranmer and Nicholas Ridley preached before Edward VI against images, and this led to some unofficial iconoclasm, as at Oxford and Southampton. But the removal of images was not yet official policy. The royal Injunctions issued in July 1547 were based on the Cromwellian orders of 1538; the third injunction repeated the prohibition of veneration of images, and clearly intended that images should remain in the churches. But a loosely drafted injunction against shrines to miracles was interpreted by energetic visitation commissioners (and some parishioners) as justification for total suppression.[5]

In September 1547 the London commissioners pulled down images in St Paul's and other churches; there and elsewhere there was a good deal of opposition. With Somerset away campaigning in Scotland, the Council was afraid of disorder and commanded the restoration of images which should not have been removed; but this caused more trouble, with disputes over whether images had been venerated. First conservatives had been offended by removal of images (as at Hull), then evangelicals were angered by replacement (as at St Neots).[6] The regime was having the worst of both worlds, and the restoration of images was provocative to its most fervent supporters. On his return to London, Somerset seems to have decided to make the reformist best of a confused job. On the night of 16 November the visitation commissioners supervised the dismantling of the rood and remaining images in St Paul's. Some of the workmen were injured, which was cited by priests as evidence of God's wrath.[7] The images in other London churches were taken down soon after, but again there was criticism. On 27 November Bishop Barlow preached at St Paul's Cross against idolatry, with a display of images which were smashed after the sermon.

Somerset had blundered into a total ban on images in London, and he had got away with it. In February 1548 the order was extended to the whole kingdom. The Council complained to Cranmer that some parishes had removed all their images, some none; some had restored those which had properly been removed, and almost all had seen disputes. To avoid further trouble, the bishops were to have all images taken down, though they were warned to proceed circumspectly.[8] It seems that images were removed from most churches in 1548, usually without fuss; churchwardens hired carpenters and masons to take down images and clean up the mess afterwards. Some parishes had to be badgered, as at Ashburton; many sold their images into private custody, as at Ludlow; some were slow to obey, even in Canterbury. There was dissension at Farnham, but Gardiner counselled obedience and the images came down.[9] In many places images were hidden away, in hope of future restoration. At Stratton in Cornwall the statues were taken down in 1548, replaced during the rebellion of 1549, and then removed once more; at Bainton in Yorkshire the image of Our Lady of Pity was concealed, and set up again in the reign of Mary.

The early measures of the Somerset regime were no deliberate first stages of an earnest Reformation. The most offensive of the royal Injunctions, to the Catholic curate Robert Parkyn, was the prohibition of processions. Bishop Gardiner protested against their order that parishes must acquire Erasmus's commentaries on the New Testament and a set of model sermons. Gardiner claimed that the sermons, or *Homilies*, were illegal, as they taught justification by faith alone, against the King's Book;[10] but the Council sent him to prison, and demolished his argument by repealing the statute of 1543. Though those homilies which Cranmer himself wrote asserted that salvation came by faith, their restraint made the doctrine less objectionable to critics and guarded against extremist interpretation: good works were not irrelevant, but the necessary fruits of living faith. The *Homilies* were tracts for troubled times rather than aggressive Protestant propaganda; some were on uncontentious moral subjects, and some had been written by reliable conservatives, such as Bishop Bonner.[11] In truth, Gardiner had fretted unduly; parishes were reluctant to buy the new books, and many failed to do so.

When Somerset did strike determinedly against traditional religion, his motives were secular. It had not been intended that chantries would be abolished, and the royal Injunctions ordered that chantrists were also to be teachers. But by the end of 1547 Somerset was in need of money for the Scots war, and reluctant to raise it by further unpopular taxation. The result was the Chantries Act, which authorized the immediate seizure of mass and other endowments. The Council had the greatest difficulty in getting its legislation through Parliament; there was a clamour from the town burgesses, anxious to protect their guild lands, and King's Lynn and Coventry were bought off by land grants. The first bill seems to have been dashed in the Commons, and the Council had to produce a second version which protected some special interests and exempted the charitable activities of secular fraternities. The bill was eased through by its promise that the king would endow schools and charities, and its provision of pensions for redundant priests. The pensions were paid, but the profits of suppression went to the war, as had probably always been intended,[12] and as Cranmer had feared.

The Chantries Act was doubtless a shock to the angry heirs of those who had recently founded chantries, such as the Burgoynes in Bedfordshire. For others it can have been no worse than they expected: endowed prayers had been challenged by preachers for a decade, fraternities were already in decline, and there had been pre-emptive private suppressions; perhaps some chuckled at their foresight. To the Protestants it was a triumph: the Act denounced the doctrines of purgatory and masses satisfactory, and confiscated all those endowments, large and small, which had provided prayers for souls. The Crown's commissioners set out to seize some 4,000 chantries and stipendiary foundations, and an unknown number of petty guilds and obits, from about half the parishes of England. At least a quarter of the chantry priests had been making important contributions to pastoral care, especially in the sprawling parishes of the north, where outlying chapels were served by endowed stipendiaries; about a twelfth of them had also served as schoolmasters, though most of the schools were saved.[13] Some chapels were commandeered, and Duchy of Lancaster officials cheekily sold chapels back to their congregations.

The confiscation of property proved difficult to enforce, and there were numberless tussles between royal commissioners and local interests. At Blackrod, Eccles, and Eccleston in Lancashire, chantrists refused to surrender their land and the tenants continued to pay rents to the priests. The tenants of five other Lancashire chantries staged rent-strikes and refused to pay up to the Duchy or its lessees. There were many attempts to conceal chantry lands and equipments from commissioners, and by 1560 the Duchy had mounted seventeen follow-up investigations to track down losses. At Lancaster the almshouse chantry was hidden from successive inquiries, and the priest continued his praying until final discovery in 1560.[14] In Huntingdonshire the bailiffs of Godmanchester had the deeds of two guilds burned, and converted the endowments to the borough's use; at St Neots the lands of the Jesus fraternity were concealed, but informers frustrated both schemes. Other parishes did better; at Elton Our Lady's guild lands were concealed until 1567, and those at Brampton till 1628.[15] But the need of the Crown and the greed of would-be purchasers won through in the end; endowed prayer ground to a halt.

The suppression of chantries and fraternities was not a sudden and final cataclysm. The Act killed off institutions and devotions which were already waning. Endowment of prayers and recruitment to fraternities had been less popular in London after the 1520s; in Devon and Cornwall the suppression of monasteries had shaken confidence in the security of endowments, and bequests for obits and masses declined.[16] The Chantries Act did not now sweep away priests and prayers. Many ex-chantrists and stipendiaries treated their new government pensions as salaries, and continued to work in churches and chapels; in Lancashire, almost two-thirds served on. A few testators made conditional bequests for masses ('if it so may be'), but there was a massive shift in the pattern of benefactions. In London, the West Country, and the north many testators now left money to the poor, in expectation of prayers in return. In a sample of northern wills, the proportion making bequests to the poor increased from about a quarter under Henry VIII to about half under Edward VI. At Eye in Suffolk in 1552, John Manestrye asked his executors to give to the poor 'as they shall think it most meetest and meritorious to my soul'.[17] There were no more chantry masses, but the poor are always with us.

Somerset had not dashed headlong into reform, but pressures from Protestant enthusiasts and financial necessities had pushed him to dangerous innovations. By the spring of 1548 resentful parishioners were enduring removal of images, restriction of ceremonies, seizure of endowments and equipment from chantries and guilds, and, ominously, the compiling of official inventories of church plate and vestments. It is not surprising that there was trouble, and it is slightly surprising there was not more. At Ashburton the property of the St Lawrence guild was defended by violence in the market square, and there was worse further west. A priest from St Keverne in Cornwall led a mob from the surrounding area to Helston; there, on 5 April 1548, they murdered William Body, the official who had been tearing down images in heavy-handed fashion. A rebel proclamation was read in the market place: they would have the laws kept as they had been under Henry VIII, and those of the new religion would be punished. The mob at Helston swelled to about 3,000, and the quarter sessions had to be cancelled. But the rising was put down by the gentry of east Cornwall, and the ringleaders executed.[18]

It was the Protestants who really made the running in 1548, forcing the pace of change by their books, sermons, and agitation. Somerset was reluctant to appear to countenance extremism, and sought publicly to restrain liturgical innovation and mockery of the eucharist. But he and his allies probably promoted the call for reform; there were at least thirty-one printed tracts against the mass in 1548, two of them by William Turner, Somerset's chaplain.[19] The preachers at St Paul's and the Cross denounced the mass, though one London chronicler claimed respectable citizens would not listen, and the congregations were 'boys and persons of little reputation'.[20] Any conservative protest was gagged: Richard Smith was forced to recant his traditionalist defence of the mass, and sacked from his divinity chair at Oxford; Miles Huggarde's ballad against 'The abuse of the blessed sacrament' was suppressed. Soon there was a conservative ballad lamenting 'little John Nobody, that durst not speak': the Catholic voice, silenced by the regime.[21] In London and Ipswich the public call was for change; the sacrament of the altar was derided as 'Jack of the box', and priests mocked as 'godmakers'.[22]

Like it or not (and like it he did) Somerset had to make some concessions to the campaign he had encouraged. In March 1548 the Council promised there would be further reformation, and in the meantime asked the people to be content with a new Order of Communion; this was a set of English exhortations and prayers to be included in the mass, drafted by Cranmer from the eirenic services of Cologne. Soon after Easter full English services were being allowed at St Paul's and some London parish churches; they were probably from the English translation of the Cologne order. In September Cranmer's draft for a new English service was presented to a loaded committee of bishops and divines, from which the conservative leaders had been excluded. The evangelical majority overruled Bishops Day, Skip, and Thirlby.[23] In December the draft was debated in the Lords; perhaps Cranmer had tried to produce an acceptable compromise, but it was rejected by Heath, Tunstall, and others on the grounds that the new communion implied denial of transubstantiation. Cranmer and Ridley asserted the spiritual presence of Christ in the eucharist, and there were crude interventions from Somerset, Warwick, and Secretary Smith.[24]

The Uniformity bill, which abolished the Latin services and substituted the Book of Common Prayer, finally passed the Lords on 15 January 1549; eight bishops and three lay peers registered formal dissent.[25] There was much less difficulty in the Commons, and the bill was through by 21 January. It was to come into force on Sunday 9 June. The Book of Common Prayer was on sale in London early in March, and some parishes introduced its services immediately; almost all had bought their books by June, though some made do with manuscript copies for a while. The Prayer

Book was an attempt to give Protestants an English service cleansed of gross superstition, without driving Catholics to resistance by abandoning the structure of the mass. Its communion service was much more than a translation of the mass: the consecration was retained, but there was no suggestion of sacrifice and elevation of the bread and wine was forbidden. The 1549 Prayer Book was a theological and liturgical compromise, and a compromise which apparently pleased no one but Bishop Gardiner (whose endorsement from prison wrecked any chance the Book had of being accepted by Protestants!).[26]

The response from the parishes was hostile, especially as the Prayer Book was introduced amid widespread grievances about taxation and agrarian change. On 6 June a town meeting at Bodmin agreed to protest against the new services, and on 10 June the parishioners of Sampford Courtenay in Devon forced their priest to say mass, declaring 'that they would keep the old and ancient religion as their forefathers before them had done'.[27] On 11 June Somerset warned that priests were taking advantage of economic discontents to turn people against the new services. Soon there were riots against the Prayer Book in Hampshire, Oxfordshire, Buckinghamshire, and north Yorkshire, as well as more serious rebellion in the West Country, where some of the gentry were sympathetic and failed to contain disorder. Large contingents from Cornwall and Devon converged on Exeter, but the aldermen were afraid the city would be plundered and refused to admit the rebels. When the insurgents laid siege to Exeter, the aldermen found it hard to restrain citizens who wished to join them:

Come out these heretics and two-penny book men!—where be they? By God's wounds and blood, we will not be pinned in to serve their turn! We will go out and have in our neighbours; they be honest, good and godly men.[28]

The motives of the western rebels were mixed: 'Kill the gentlemen, and we will have the Six Articles up again and ceremonies as they were in King Henry VIII's time!', cried the men of Bodmin.[29] There was certainly economic discontent, and a hostility against the gentry who had co-operated with government policy. But religion was at least the common grievance which held the rebels together, and the Prayer Book was the issue which turned local disorder into regional rebellion. The articles produced on behalf of the rebels camped at Exeter[30] demanded the Latin mass: 'we will not receive the new service because it is but like a Christmas game.' They wanted the old ceremonies and images, reservation of the host, prayers for the dead, even monasteries, and no English Bibles: 'for we be informed that otherwise the clergy shall not of long time confound the heretics.' Somerset claimed the commons had been duped by the clergy into supporting a campaign against Reformation, and the Exeter articles were apparently edited by priests. But the Catholic cry was not confined to clergy, and rebel leaders would hardly have sanctioned a programme focused on a fringe issue.

The western rising was a determined protest against Somerset's policies—especially, but not exclusively, on religion. In East Anglia, where lay–clerical relations were being soured by tithe conflicts, it was different: there the protest was against the landlords, and the rebels ostentatiously demonstrated their loyalty to the regime by holding Prayer Book services. The rebels outside Norwich pleaded for Somerset's aid against oppressive gentry: 'We pray your grace that no lord of no manor shall common upon the commons.' At Exeter, the tone was harsher: 'We will have the mass in Latin as was before.'[31] But the outcome was the same. Though the government and the gentry were unable to cope promptly with such widespread troubles (which convulsed twenty-three counties in 1549), one by one the separate disorders were crushed. Lord Grey dealt with the Oxfordshire malcontents in mid-July, and had the leaders hanged, including four priests. Early in August, Lord Russell's royal army, stiffened by Italian mercenaries, cleaned up Devon and Cornwall with considerable slaughter. And on 27 August the earl of Warwick led another army against the Norfolk rebels at Dussindale, and cut them down.

It is not surprising that Somerset's colleagues on the Council blamed him for the troubles of 1549. Paget had been warning him for months that his overbearing pursuit of the Scottish war and religious reform provoked opposition, and that his sympathy for the poor invited protest. The country was in turmoil with too much change, and old values had not been replaced: 'The use of the old religion is forbidden by a law, and the use of the new is not yet printed in the stomachs of eleven of twelve parts of the realm.'[32] A coalition of Council conservatives and *politiques* plotted over the summer, and in October they moved against Somerset. They sought support by hinting that Princess Mary would become regent and the mass might come back; Somerset tried to rally the radicals by crying that the Reformation was in danger—as indeed it was. In October 1549 the plotters forced Somerset to resign, and sent him and his cronies to the Tower. The earls of Southampton and Arundel manœuvred to pack Council and Court with their conservative allies, and it seemed that Somerset's Reformation was to be undone. There were Catholic riots in Oxford, and the mass was celebrated in some college chapels.[33]

Withdrawal of the Prayer Book would probably have secured wide support from the new government, since hostility to its services had not been confined to the rebellious areas. Robert Parkyn, curate of Adwick-le-Street near Doncaster, was shocked that 'holy mass was utterly deposed', and 'Christ's body and blood' no longer worshipped. The king had complained on 23 July that the new liturgy was being ignored in many places, and on 10 August the Council protested that in the diocese of

London people were staying away from the novel services.[34] As Hooper and Bucer soon reported, many priests tried to make the Prayer Book communion as much like a mass as they could, repeating the old rituals and chanting the English as if it were old Latin. At his visitation in 1550, Bishop Ridley forbade a list of ceremonies used by his clergy to 'counterfeit the popish mass': kissing the altar, ringing a sacring bell, elevating the host, and so on.[35] In the diocese of Ely a curate was in trouble at the 1549 visitation for not following the Book of Common Prayer properly, and in Gloucester there were many such cases at the summer visitation of 1551—fourteen priests in the deanery of Campden alone.[36]

The clockwork Reformation had stopped in the autumn of 1549, but not for long. Like Cromwell in 1536, Warwick had joined a conservative coup to protect his career, but he then saw himself marginalized. He faced the likelihood of a regime nominally headed by Mary and run by Southampton and Arundel, perhaps including his enemy Gardiner, and with no place for him. So Warwick allied with Cranmer and the reformers, brought new supporters into the Privy Chamber and the Council, and bought off some of the conservatives with titles. On 2 February 1550, after five months of intense political conflict, Warwick was made Lord President and Arundel and Southampton were dismissed from the Council.[37] There is not much evidence that Warwick ever really cared about formal religious allegiance; he was to change his faith when Mary seized power in 1553, and die a public Catholic. But in 1550 Protestantism was a useful policy: it attracted essential allies in the struggle with Southampton (especially Cranmer and Edward VI); it bought the support of Somerset (who was readmitted to the Council as counterweight to conservatives), and of London Protestants (whose significance Warwick probably exaggerated);[38] and it provided ideological justification for a further onslaught on Church property.

Warwick soon paid the price for Protestant backing. On 25 December 1549 the Privy Council denied rumours that the mass was to be reinstated, and ordered the destruction of Latin service books.[39] In January 1550 a committee was appointed to devise an English ordination service; it approved a draft prepared by Cranmer, which simplified the medieval rite along lines suggested by Martin Bucer, and the Ordinal was published in March. But the most public break with the past was the replacement of altars by communion tables, when Warwick's hand was forced by the Protestants. Altars had been removed by local initiative in a few places in 1549, and this had become more frequent in London in December, though there was no wave of popular iconoclasm. In his Lenten sermons of 1550 Hooper denounced altars, and by the spring Ridley in London and Barlow in Bath and Wells were campaigning for removal. Ridley's primary injunctions ordered churchwardens to take down altars, and in May and June they were removed from St Paul's and the city churches. At St Paul's trouble was avoided by dismantling altars at night, but throughout the diocese there was resentment and contention; the sheriff of Essex had to be enlisted to enforce obedience there.[40]

It seems that other bishops followed Ridley's example, for the accounts of many churches across the country show the costs of taking down altars in 1550, often after wardens had been summoned to visitation. The laconic entries make the process seem routine: at Morebath the wardens paid 3s. for dismantling the altars, at Yatton in Somerset 7s. 10d.; at Prescot in Lancashire, removing the altar and setting up a communion table cost 5s., at St Michael's in Worcester 13s. 4d. Sometimes costs were covered by selling off altar stones, as at Sherborne or at St Mary at Hill (where a stone was sold for a grave). But there was much dissension and some refusal, as the Council soon complained. In Sussex Bishop Day and others preached in defence of altars, and Richard Cox had to be sent down to justify destruction. In Carmarthen Bishop Ferrar had altars restored, because of 'the grudge of the people'.[41] Rather than risk such local arguments, the Council was drawn into the attack on altars, as it had been drawn into the attack on images in 1548. In November 1550 it ordered the bishops to bring an end to the disputes by enforcing the removal of all altars and the erection of communion tables; in the expectation of trouble they were supplied with notes for sermons in support of tables.[42]

Bishop Day refused to enforce the instruction in his diocese of Chichester, and when several appearances before the Council failed to change his mind he was sent off to the Fleet prison. Other bishops did their duty, and, now armed with direct commands from the Council, they seem to have secured widespread, if reluctant, obedience. Robert Parkyn reported that altars were taken down 'from Trent northwards' in December 1550, blaming 'Edward Seymour and the earl of Warwick, two cruel tyrants and enemies to God and holy Church'.[43] In a parish near Winchester the lawfulness of such destruction was angrily debated; conservatives argued that the young king had been led astray by wicked advisers: 'But when he cometh once of age, he will see another rule, and hang up an hundred of such heretic knaves!'[44] At Ludlow, the altar was taken down in 1551, and the stones laid carefully in the paving of the nave, where they would be available if needed. In Lincolnshire, Richard Troughton bought the altar stone of his church, and kept it safe.[45] Some parishes were repeatedly hassled by officialdom before they followed suit; four Lancashire churches kept their altars at least until the autumn of 1552, and Thame near Oxford did not replace its altar by a table until Christmas 1552.

The balance of ecclesiastical power was now shifting rapidly. Hitherto, a predominantly conservative episcopate had been a brake upon the reforming designs of Cromwell, Cranmer, and Somerset. But the bench of bishops was gradually remodelled, as one by one conservatives refused to conform. Stephen Gardiner had been in prison since June 1548, after giving only the most half-hearted endorsement of official policies when ordered to preach in support. Bonner was imprisoned and deprived of the see of London in September 1549, having preached in defence of transubstantiation when ordered to justify the authority of a minor as king. In March 1550 Heath was imprisoned for his failure to subscribe to the new Ordinal; in the summer Tunstall was placed under house arrest; in December Day went to prison for refusing to enforce the order against altars. From December 1550 to February 1551, there was a well-publicized show trial of Gardiner, when he was charged with papalist sympathy and resistance to royal policy. It was an orchestrated attempt to brand Catholicism as disloyalty. Gardiner was deprived of his bishopric in February, Day and Heath in October, and Tunstall in 1552.

These removals, and a couple of (probably forced) resignations allowed another attack on ecclesiastical property, prompted by disastrous royal finances. Somerset had already extracted land grants from bishops for himself and his cronies, but now sees were systematically dismembered before (or even after) being given to reliable Protestants. In 1550 the sees of London and Westminster were combined, and four London manors and half the Westminster property were seized for the Crown. Veysey of Exeter had to make substantial grants to courtiers before he resigned, leaving little for Coverdale. In 1551 Heath's old see of Worcester was joined to Gloucester, and two-thirds of the Worcester estates went to the Crown, with a few manors for Warwick. After Gardiner's removal from Winchester, Ponet agreed to a massive alienation of lands, which were then mainly used to cement Warwick's alliances in Council and Court. In 1553 the Crown took over the extensive property of Durham, with the intention of creating two ill-endowed sees and a profit for itself. Warwick may have wanted a reformed pastoral episcopate to replace the lordly endowed prelacy, but he also wanted profits.[46]

The dismissals and resignations created slots for energetic Protestants. Ridley became bishop of London in 1550, and began the drive against altars. Miles Coverdale went to Exeter, and with his chaplains preached Protestantism through the diocese. John Ponet succeeded Gardiner at Winchester, but a marital scandal weakened his moral authority and he may have achieved little. The most determined of the new bishops was John Hooper; his consecration was however delayed by a struggle with Cranmer over the rituals, which Hooper lost. At Gloucester Hooper sat as judge in his own consistory court, preached frequently, supervised a careful visitation in the summer of 1551, and examined his parish clergy on the Bible and the Creed. But his priests—used to Catholic doctrine and the Latin mass—were useless tools of Reformation. Only seventy-nine of the 311 examined were satisfactory from a reformist point of view: over half could not recite the Commandments, and two-thirds could not support the Creed with biblical texts. Worse still, many were still using forbidden ceremonies to simulate the mass; but with few Protestants available they could not be replaced.[47]

The findings of Hooper's visitation probably fuelled the call for revision of the Book of Common Prayer, to produce services which could less easily be dressed up as Catholic. The 1549 Prayer Book had been overtaken by events: if it had been a compromise to satisfy some conservative bishops, they were soon removed—and so were the altars. Perhaps the first Prayer Book had been intended as an interim measure, all that could safely be achieved in 1549. Cranmer had defended retention of some ceremonies as a necessary expedient, 'lest the people, not having yet learned Christ, should be deterred by too extensive innovations from embracing his religion'.[48] But there were few to justify the Book against the criticisms of foreign Protestants or the contemptuous attacks of Hooper and Knox on any suggestion of a real corporal presence in the eucharist. Martin Bucer, the Strassburg reformer who fled to England in 1549, produced a list of sixty defects in the Book, and the Italian Peter Martyr submitted his own comments to Cranmer. In the Tower, Gardiner drafted a defence of the real presence in which he appealed to the Prayer Book for support; his approval was enough to sink it![49]

In 1548, when the first Prayer Book was finalized, almost all serious theological opinion in England supported a real presence; by 1551, when a new version was under consideration, this was no longer so, and transubstantiation was virtually a proscribed opinion. In Oxford, the influential Peter Martyr had begun to lecture in defence of Zwingli in March 1549, and at a disputation in May he had rejected a corporal presence in the eucharist; some of those who argued against him were imprisoned.[50] At Cambridge Bucer's own eucharistic teaching was less radical, but he too taught only a spiritual presence. The Council forbade the preaching of transubstantiation, so new disobedient clergy could be removed.[51] Bonner's deprivation was partly for this reason, and in April 1550 Bishop Day saved himself only by preaching against the doctrine. Catholics were silenced, and their views discredited. In the autumn of 1551, Secretary Cecil organized a series of formal disputations on the eucharist: conservative theologians were brought from prison to be solemnly trounced by Cambridge Protestants, before approving councillors and officials.[52] The intellectual stage had been set for a reformed communion service.

Although the 1552 Act of Uniformity sought to present the new Book of Common Prayer as a clarification of the 1549 Book, it broke decisively with the past.[53] Most of the ceremonies which had been condemned by Protestants and all those commended by Gardiner were removed: baptism, confirmation, and burial services were rewritten; and, in the communion service, the structure of the mass was abandoned and many of the prayers omitted. The old vestments were forbidden, singing was restricted, and ordinary bread was to be used and given into the communicants' hands. There has been much controversy over the authorship and meaning of the second Prayer Book; its eucharistic doctrine seems to be Calvinist, implying a spiritual but not a corporal presence of Christ at the sacrament. The Book was probably drafted by Cranmer and Ridley with the advice of Martyr, though they may have been under pressure from Hooper and Knox, who had the ear of Warwick (by now duke of Northumberland). When Knox protested against the kneeling of communicants, Cranmer refused to alter the Book; the Council itself ordered insertion of an explanation that kneeling did not imply adoration of the eucharistic elements or a bodily presence.

The new Prayer Book was to come into use on All Saints' Day, 1 November 1552; it generally did. There was delay caused by the late addition of the rubric on kneeling, but most of the surviving parish accounts show the Book was bought at about the right time—though at Prescot in Lancashire, only just in time, on All Saints' Day itself. From Morebath to St Andrew's Canterbury, from Wing to Sheriff Hutton, the wardens paid between 3*s*. and 8*s*. 'for the book of new service'. For Robert Parkyn—and, no doubt, for many more—the Prayer Book was the ultimate blasphemy, 'brought to pass only to subdue the most blessed sacrament of Christ's body and blood, under form of bread and wine'. He listed the horrors in the book: no extreme unction and no prayers for the dead; bread for the communion 'such as men uses in their houses with meat'; the chalice given into the communicants' hands, with the words 'Drink this in remembrance that Christ's blood was shed for thee', and, worst of all, 'straightly forbidding that any adoration should be done thereunto, for that were idolatry (said the book)'. 'Oh, how abominable heresy and unseeming order was this, let every man ponder in his own conscience!'[54]

In 1552 the Church of England was given a reformed liturgy; in 1553 it acquired a reformed theology. But if the Book of Common Prayer was framed to exclude the superstitions of the papists, the Articles of Religion responded to the errors of Anabaptists and Protestant extremists. Cranmer had been drafting new Articles since 1551, apparently working from the abortive 1538 agreement with the Lutherans, altering and adding to it to meet current concerns. His proposals were discussed at meetings of bishops, and in September 1552 he submitted a draft to the Council. It was referred to a group of royal chaplains for comment; after some negotiation and amendment, the Forty-Two Articles were given royal assent in June 1552, with the intention that all the clergy should be made to subscribe to them. The Anabaptist heresies were vigorously condemned, along with the Catholic doctrines on transubstantiation, purgatory, invocation of saints, and the efficacy of good works. On the issues that divided Protestants, however, there was theological compromise and determined ambiguity, especially on predestination and the eucharist; but the overall effect is a restrained Calvinism.[55]

King Edward's Church had come a long way since 1547. The mass was replaced by a reformed communion, the King's Book by the Forty-Two Articles; and in 1553 there was a Protestant Short Catechism by Bishop Ponet, and a book of private prayers. The political interests of Somerset and Northumberland, the influence of Cranmer and Ridley, the pressures of Hooper and Knox, and the demands of grass-roots Protestantism carried Edward's second Reformation very much further than Henry VIII's first. But the committed Protestants remained a self-conscious minority, battling against 'superstitious papists, carnal gospellers, and seditious rebels'. Hooper admitted in 1550 that most councillors 'favour the cause of Christ as much as they can'; 'the people, however, that many-headed monster, is still wincing, partly through ignorance and partly fascinated by the inveiglements of the bishops and the malice and impiety of the mass-priests'. So the second Reformation, like the first, was forced upon hostile parishes: as Bucer complained, 'Things are for the most part carried on by the means of ordinances, which the majority obey very grudgingly, and by the removal of the instruments of the ancient superstition.'[56]

It is clear from both churchwardens' accounts and diocesan visitations that parishes gradually and grudgingly conformed to official orders. But there was a crisis in parochial religion. As services became plainer, plays and ales were suppressed, guilds and special funds were abolished, so churches attracted less affection—and much less money—from their people. In the north of England, more than 70 per cent of testators had left bequests to a parish church in 1540–6, but only 32 per cent under Edward VI. In Lincolnshire and Huntingdonshire, two-thirds of testators made benefactions to their parish churches in 1545, but only 10 per cent in 1550.[57] It was the same everywhere: bequests and gifts of small sums of money, cloths, and silver rings and spoons almost disappear from churchwardens' accounts. At Morebath in Devon, for example, parochial finances collapsed. There were no gifts, the profitable church sheep had been sold, and purchases of Prayer Books and psalters were funded by borrowing; 'no gift given to the church, but all from the church', the vicar complained.[58] At Boxford in Suffolk, Plough Monday and hockpot collections ceased in 1548, ales in 1549; expenses were met from rates, and from interest paid by borrowers of the proceeds from sales of plate.

The disruption of parish finances was partly due to the economic pressures of the mid-century: bad harvests in 1545, 1550, and 1551; debasements in 1544–6, 1549, and 1551; revaluation of the currency; and a slump in the cloth trade. In 1551 the churchwardens of Yatton in Somerset found their running surplus of £7. 6s. 4d. reduced to £4 by 'the fall of money'.[59] High food prices led to conflict over tithe, as parishioners tried to withhold payments in kind and incumbents tried to increase tithe due in cash. There was organized refusal of tithe in Buckinghamshire after the 1549 harvest, and tithe litigation increased in the dioceses of Chester and York. There had been between four and twelve tithe cases a year in the Norwich consistory court in the 1540s, but there were forty-four in 1550 and fifty-four in 1551. Hard-pressed rectors and wardens seem to have neglected the maintenance of church fabric; in both Norfolk and Hampshire there were many more complaints of unrepaired chancels in 1550–1 than had been usual.[60] When the Marian bishops held their first visitations in 1554, they found that many churches had been allowed to decay in the previous reign.

The parish difficulties of the Edwardian Church were more than financial frictions: they reflected a collapse of allegiance. In East Anglia, absence from church services and refusal of communion became serious in 1548–9, with complaints that many of the people would not listen to sermons or Bible-readings. In 1551 the Council condemned poor church attendance in Exeter diocese. By 1552, the preamble to the Uniformity Act was complaining that people 'abstain and refuse to come to their parish churches'.[61] Recruitment to the priesthood, which had declined sharply in the 1530s, now almost ceased: there were no ordinations in the dioceses of Chester, Durham, and Exeter; only a trickle at Lichfield, Lincoln, and York; and in Canterbury a fall in the number of serving priests suggests there were few new recruits.[62] Only in London, where Bishop Ridley ordained priests licensed from other dioceses, was there a continuing flow of candidates. By the end of Edward's reign, there were signs of a clerical manpower shortage. The suppression of the chantries and guilds had reduced the demand for priests; more seriously, the persistent royal attacks on parish religion had undermined the supply.

There was more to come. The parish inventories, which were demanded from 1547, suggested that the Crown had its greedy eyes on church plate and valuables. Many parishes liquidated their assets: three-quarters of the surviving churchwardens' accounts show sales of equipment under Edward. At Thame silver plate was sold for £70 in 1548, a silver cross for £22 in 1549, two chalices and other things for £28 in 1550, another cross and a bell in 1551; when an inventory was ordered in 1552 there was almost nothing left, and it was said that £300 had been raised by sales.[63] At St Margaret Moses in London, the parish leaders agreed in 1549 to start selling plate 'for diverse and needful urgent causes': they sold in lots in 1549, in 1550, and in 1551, when they raised £103.[64] There was a huge sale of copes, vestments, and altar-cloths at Sherborne in 1550, which yielded almost £40, though much of the plate just disappeared from the accounts. In some parishes, especially in Essex and Suffolk, the proceeds were spent on church, bridge, or highway repairs, or so it was claimed when royal commissioners investigated the losses. Elsewhere, it seems the profits simply passed into the pockets of parishioners. 'All things were put to the spoil', Michael Sherbrook remembered much later.[65]

But not everything was sold or stolen, and when, in 1553, the long-expected confiscation was announced, there was a general campaign of concealment. It was claimed that about £700 worth of equipment was hidden from the commissioners in Somerset, and the Kent commissioners could find little to seize. In April 1553 the parson of Radnage in Buckinghamshire was in trouble,

for the words spoken by him to his neighbours, whereby he did comfort them to keep a good portion of their church plate, saying that a time would come that they should have need of it, and the old ceremonies be restored to the church again.[66]

So when Edward VI died in July 1553, his government was embroiled in a bitter struggle with the parishes over church property; he could hardly have gone at a worse time. Northumberland's attempt to make the Protestant Jane Grey queen was crippled by the intense unpopularity of his confiscations, and within a month of gaining the throne Mary was ordering the return of plate to the parishes.[67] It was poetic justice: the second Reformation was made possible by the accidental timing of Henry's death, and halted by the accidental timing of Edward's.

PART III

Political Reformation and Protestant Reformation

11

The Making of a Minority, 1530–1553

ON 19 November 1530, four men did public penance through the city of London. They were led through the streets sitting backwards on horses, wearing paper hats inscribed 'For crimes against the king's proclamations' and with copies of Tyndale's heretical books pinned to their clothes. At Cheapside Cross they were made to throw the books into a bonfire, and were set in the pillory to be mocked by fellow citizens.[1] Henry VIII's earlier proclamations against heretics and their books were being enforced, a month after the Hampton Court meeting and Henry's decision to coerce the clergy by praemunire. Though the king had begun what became a political Reformation, a Protestant Reformation was still contained by the power of the state. But not for long. The four men in the pillory were all friends of Thomas Cromwell, royal councillor and protector of heretics. As the king's determination to achieve his divorce led him to adopt drastic solutions, Cromwell's influence increased; so did his ability to advance (and shield) those who shared his evangelical preferences, and those who were useful in his attack on the clergy, their wealth, and the ideas which validated their authority.

English Lollardy had been an underground sect, surviving by silence; the early Lutherans had worked among known sympathizers, or were arrested for indiscretion. But, under the protection of Cromwell, Cranmer, and Anne Boleyn, Protestantism soon came out of the closet and into the pulpit. Cromwell and Cranmer controlled the issue of preaching licences, and the bishops found radical preachers brandishing their permits. As broker for the Crown's ecclesiastical patronage, Cromwell suggested reformers for bishoprics and other posts; as archbishop, Cranmer appointed officials and incumbents in his own diocese; as queen, Anne advanced the careers of Barlow, Crome, Latimer, Shaxton, Skip, and probably others,[2] and all three patrons intervened to save Protestants from Henry's intermittent wrath. After the executions of Anne and Cromwell, Denny and Butts protected vulnerable preachers, and in 1543 Cranmer was able to deflect a campaign against heresy in Kent. Under Edward VI, Knox, Latimer, and Lever preached on the great public occasions, and Catholics went to prison; persecution of Protestants virtually ceased. As the duchess of Suffolk told Gardiner in the Tower, 'It was merry with the lambs now the wolf was shut up.'[3]

Ministers, prelates, and courtiers provided the political environment in which Protestantism could expand; it was the two universities which provided the preachers to do the leg-work. The White Horse tavern group in Cambridge and the Cardinal's College set in Oxford had produced the first academic evangelists. The royal visitations of 1535 had promoted study of the Scriptures in place of the schoolmen, and tended to shift power towards supporters of reform, especially when Cromwell was chancellor of Cambridge and high steward of Oxford. At Cambridge, John Cheke was a highly successful teacher, with an evangelical influence over a generation of St John's students, including the men who were to dominate the university in the reign of Edward VI.[4] The impact of Martin Bucer, the Strassburg Protestant who became regius professor of divinity in 1549, was brief but even greater: to John Bradford he was 'God's prophet and true preacher', and a crowd of 3,000 attended his funeral in Cambridge in 1551. Their Cambridge experience was crucial in the conversion of future preachers to Protestantism; before his burning in 1555, Bradford wrote a 'farewell' to 'my mother, the university'.[5]

At Oxford the key influences were Richard Cox, imported from Cambridge as chancellor and dean of Christ Church, and Peter Martyr, the Italian regius professor of divinity from 1548 to 1553. Martyr's lectures and sermons, and his weekly disputations in Christ Church, were effective: the future martyr Bartlet Green was certainly converted by hearing him.[6] His 1549 lectures on the eucharist caused a furore, as did those on justification in 1550. The vigorous response of the Oxford conservatives prompted Northumberland's intervention, to imprison Martyr's opponents and secure the election of reformist heads of houses. Protestants did not manage to establish the control over Oxford which they exercised in Edwardian Cambridge, but students at Christ Church and Magdalen came under Protestant influence, and at Brasenose a string of young men from Lancashire was converted.[7] About sixty Oxford-educated Protestants went into exile under Mary, and almost eighty from Cambridge. The evidence is unsatisfactory, but roughly 340 university men are thought to have become Protestants by 1558; more than 10 per cent of the known Protestants, when only a tiny percentage even of males attended university.[8]

Many of the university Protestants became preachers, and took their new faith to the parishes. By the mid-1530s, there were energetic evangelists working in London: John Bale, Robert Barnes, Edward Crome, and Hugh Latimer from Cambridge, and George Browne, Richard Champion, and Thomas Garrett from Oxford. The London heresy juries of 1540 complained that Barnes, Garrett, Jerome, Latimer, Wisdom, and others 'of the new learning' were busy in the city; groups of supporters were named from five parishes, and some had organized meetings in their homes. Two hundred Londoners from thirty-six parishes were accused of heresy in 1540;

though many were mere sceptics and scoffers, at least a quarter of them were sacramentarians or associates of the preachers.[9] Though the preachers were denounced by some, their message was welcomed by others: Gerard Frise had said 'he had rather go to hear a sermon than to hear a mass'. In his 1537 will Humphrey Monmouth had asked for a sermon by Crome at his funeral instead of a requiem, and left money for sermons by Crome, Barnes, Latimer, and John Taylor. Thereafter several Londoners asked for series of sermons from their favourite preachers, in place of masses.[10]

The efforts and impact of the preachers are plain. In 1536 William Broman admitted he had learned from Dr John Barrett (of Cambridge) that the eucharist was only a memorial, and from John Bale (also Cambridge) that Christ was in men's hearts, not in churches. Henry Goderick, the Oxford-educated rector of Hothfield in Kent, had taught him to put his trust in Christ's passion, not the consecrated host. Goderick's sermons were said to have persuaded a hundred more to share his views.[11] A succession of Protestants—Rose, Shaxton, Rivet, and, most important, Dr Rowland Taylor—served as rectors or curates of Cranmer's jurisdiction at Hadleigh in Suffolk. They catechized children and servants, and promoted Bible-reading among the clothworkers; some parishioners learned Paul's epistles by heart.[12] In Kent some of Cranmer's preachers, especially Ridley and Scory, were tireless evangelists. In 1541–3 Scory preached justification by faith and denounced Latin prayers, invocation of saints, and church ritual and decoration. Thomas Hancock preached against the real presence in Hampshire and Salisbury in 1547, and some of his people at Poole 'were the first that in that part of England were called Protestants'.[13]

It was in the reign of Edward VI that the preachers really made their pitch. In London there was as remarkable a group of evangelists as can ever have been seen: John Bradford, Thomas Becon, John Cardmaker, Edward Crome, Hugh Latimer, Thomas Lever, John Rogers, Lawrence Saunders, and sometimes Miles Coverdale, John Knox, and Rowland Taylor. Probably the most energetic and effective was John Hooper, who preached twice a day after his return from exile in 1549—at the Court, St Paul's, and through the City. Large crowds turned out to hear him, at times too many for the churches, and he reported in 1550 that 'God was with them, for he opened their hearts to understand'.[14] Elsewhere, there were sermon-tours by the great preachers: John Rough on the northern borders in 1547, paid by Somerset; Dr Tongue through Devon and Cornwall in 1548, at the Council's expense; John Bradford several times through his native Lancashire, concentrating on the cloth towns of the Manchester area; Hugh Latimer through Lincolnshire in 1550 and 1552, under the patronage of the duchess of Suffolk; John Hooper across Gloucestershire, during his episcopal visitation in 1551. It was a considerable, though rather haphazard, effort.

And its impact is clear. John Newman of Maidstone described in 1555 what must have been common, at least in south-eastern England. Through Edward's reign Protestant preachers had attacked the real presence, and in time their views were accepted as having the backing of king and Council, especially since contrary teaching had been silenced. Rejection of the presence was a difficult step for many, taken only after much prayer and discussion with friends, but Newman finally took it. The seven who were burned at Smithfield on 27 January 1556 told a similar (though less apologetic) story: 'during the time of King Edward VI they, hearing the gospel preached and the truth opened, followed the order of the religion and doctrine then used and set forth.' Isabel Foster, the 55-year-old wife of a London cutler, admitted that she had followed the Catholic faith 'as other common people did, howbeit blindly and without knowledge, till the reign of King Edward VI, at which time she, hearing the gospel truly preached and opened to the people, received thereupon the faith and religion then taught and set forth'.[15]

It was assumed by Marian ecclesiastics that the heretics who came before them were recent converts. In the diocese of London many of the accused faced charges that they had been brought up to believe in the real presence, and had lately abandoned it.[16] It was an easy defence for Protestants to claim they had gone with the crowd under Edward (and a polemical gain to remind their judges that their religion had been official), but many described their conversion with pride and sometimes precision. John Judson, a London apprentice, had been converted in 1547; John Went, an Essex shearman, in 1548. Agnes George, an Essex husbandman's wife, admitted that in Edward's reign 'she went from her old faith and religion and believed in the faith that was then taught and set forth'; John Hallingdale told Bishop Bonner he had been converted by Edwardian preachers. Roger Holland, a London merchant tailor, had been conservative in beliefs till late in the reign of Edward, when a servant girl persuaded him to read the Bible and Prayer Book and go to sermons at St Paul's and All Hallows.[17] All five held firm to their new faith, and were burned for heresy.

Of course, not all Protestants were converts from Catholicism. Some had first learned religion in the increasingly Protestant atmosphere of parts of Edwardian London, or Essex, or Kent; when the Protestant preachers could set the doctrinal agenda, young people learned the new religion as their parents had learned the old. Joan Lashford, the daughter of a London cutler, had 'misliked the sacrifice of the mass' since 1547, when she was 11; Joan Horns from Billericay had begun 'to learn the faith set forth in King Edward's days', when she too was about 11 years old.[18] Many of the Marian martyrs were young people, who had presumably acquired their Protestantism in Edward's reign. Of fifty-two whose ages were recorded by Foxe, eight were aged 19 or 20 when they suffered in 1555–8, and twenty more were under 30, besides others described as 'young maid' or 'young man'. When thirteen men and women (mainly from Essex) were burned in the same fire at Stratford-le-Bow in 1556, nine were 30 or under: Charles Searles was 21, Lawrence Pernam 22, William Halliwell and Ralph Jackson 24, and Agnes George and John Routh 26. These were true Edwardian Protestants.[19]

In 1556 John Careless drafted a confession of faith for Henry Aldinton, a prisoner in the Lollard's Tower and soon to be one of the 'Stratford-le-Bow thirteen'. Aldington had asked for advice; he was to tell his judges,

Be it known unto you that I in all points do believe as it becometh a true Christian, and as I have been truly taught in the days of that good King Edward, of such godly preachers and prophets sent of God, as have sealed their doctrine with their blood and from whom I dissent in no point.[20]

Many Marian martyrs—and many whose Protestantism was tested less severely—could have made such an affirmation. It is true that Protestants tried to maintain a united credal front against their Marian oppressors, and true too that John Foxe later suppressed evidence of deviance from official Edwardian lines. But the Edwardian theme is strong and authentic in confessions made under Mary. 'The declaration of Robert Wade's faith' was produced with the help of two neighbours for his trial at Norwich in 1555; it was impeccably Edwardian, and seems to have been compiled from the Book of Common Prayer.[21]

Protestant unity was not complete. The Edwardian leaders had not agreed over ceremonies and the eucharist; among those influenced by Zurich theologians there was contempt for any who held to some form of 'carnal' presence in the sacrament, and such 'Lutherans' were thought little better than papists.[22] At the popular level Protestantism had its militant tendencies: old Lollards and sceptics who distrusted any form of clerical authority, individualists who had formed their own faith from the Bible, and radicals who drew conclusions the preachers had not intended. There were still those who could not be persuaded—by Protestant clergy any more than by Catholics—that Christ took his flesh from the Virgin, or that the eucharist could be more than a 'bare memorial'. The Protestant preachers had attacked Catholic symbolism and the sacralization of physical things, so some laypeople objected to all ritual, and to any reverence for bread or wine. Preachers had pressed the supremacy of Scripture and the primacy of faith, against Catholic tradition and the authority of the Church, so some of the laity bandied texts with churchmen and expected spiritual freedom.

At Bocking in Essex, in 1550, there was a group of perhaps sixty people who met to discuss Scripture and church ceremonies, and some of its members had refused to attend the 'superstitious' official communion.

Some of them were probably old Lollards; a few had come from Kent, where their leader, Henry Hart, had taught them to reject the errors of 'learned men'.[23] Hart's own study of the Bible had led him to distrust 'those bishops, pastors and lawyers, of what place and name soever they be, which boast of power and authority to rule and govern other, and yet have no respect to their own souls'. He developed his own brand of fundamentalist moralism, and, against the preachers' doctrine of predestination, argued that God had promised salvation to all who lived in virtue: 'work out your salvation and, as the Apostle Peter saith, make calling and election sure through good works'.[24] Worried by the size of the meetings and the apparent evidence of organization, the Privy Council tried to silence the 'freewillers' by imprisonment in 1551; in 1554, predestinarian leaders tried to silence them by argument, as they shared the hospitality of Queen Mary's prisons.

Catholic judges and propagandists drew delighted attention to the Protestants' prison squabbles, and to the disputes among the Marian exiles over liturgy. But, in truth, there was a remarkable level of agreement among the heretics dealt with by the Marian courts. There were a few Kentish anti-Trinitarians, and more who expressed their views in earthy neo-Lollard scorn; some may have maintained old heresies without benefit of Protestant clergy. But the vast majority were Edwardian Protestants, often converted and almost always influenced by the preachers. The young John Leaf had gone from Yorkshire to London, to be apprenticed as a tallow-chandler; there he became a 'scholar' of the preacher John Rogers. After his arrest in 1555, he affirmed his belief in the doctrines of Rogers, Hooper, Cardmaker, and the other clerical martyrs; he was burned with John Bradford at Smithfield. Bradford was the mentor (probably the creator) of the Protestant circle in his native Manchester. He had preached to them and sent books in Edward's reign; from prison he wrote letters of encouragement and 'The Hurt of Hearing Mass' to keep them steadfast. The preachers had produced a community which could withstand persecution.[25]

The appeal of the preachers had not been universal, of course. There was much hostility in Suffolk in 1536 to Bale's sermons against saints and ceremonies, and Latimer's preaching caused bitter divisions in Bristol and London; 'Latimer many blameth, and as many doth allow', it was reported.[26] Though crowds flocked to hear Latimer in the towns, country people were less curious; when once he arrived to preach, he was politely told that the parish was celebrating a local festival: 'Sir, this is a busy day with us, we cannot hear you; it is Robin Hood's day.' The sermons of Lancelot Ridley and John Scory caused alehouse contention in the Canterbury area in 1542, and 'the more part of the people were offended with their preaching'.[27] When Thomas Hancock preached at Twinham

(Hampshire) and Salisbury in 1547, there were walk-outs led by the clergy; at Hancock's own church at Poole, the merchant Thomas White attempted a boycott of his sermons: 'Come from him, good people; he came from the devil, and teacheth unto you devilish doctrine!'[28] Preachers had a hard time of it in Exeter: Dean Heynes was 'marvellous hated and maligned at', Bishop Coverdale was 'hated of the adversaries of the gospel', and William Alley had to be escorted to the cathedral pulpit by armed guards.[29]

The preaching of Protestantism remained limited and patchy. In 1537 Cranmer complained that the bishop of Norwich blocked the advance of the gospel by refusing licences to preachers 'of right judgement', and in Lincoln diocese Longland tried to restrict preaching to a corps of reliable Catholics. In the reign of Edward Protestant bishops were in control, but there were few to preach the Word. 'And how shall they hear without a preacher?', asked Latimer.[30] Peter Martyr observed in 1550 that there were plenty of preachers in London, 'but throughout the whole kingdom they are very rare'; Bucer told Calvin there were parishes which had not had sermons in years.[31] In Lincolnshire in 1552 there were no sermons at all in ten of sixty-one parishes; in Buckinghamshire none in twenty-five out of forty-nine. Careful studies of the parish clergy in East Anglia, London, and York show that they responded very slowly to Protestant ideas; they were useless as agents of change, unless their dour conservatism prompted some disillusioned laymen to seek novelty elsewhere. Thomas Becon proposed teams of itinerant evangelists for regions without 'learned curates',[32] and in 1551 there was a plan for six new royal chaplains to tour the land; but (to economize) the six were reduced to four, and they worked mainly in London.

But Protestantism was the religion of the Word printed as well as preached, and books might go where preachers rarely appeared. In 1533 a priest in Furness had a copy of *Unio dissidentium*; in 1537 a Rotherham chaplain had some printed ballads mocking church ceremonies, and by 1540 he had read Frith on the eucharist. Some were converted by reading, especially when Protestant preaching was banned: Rose Hickman said that in the 1540s her mother 'came to some light of the Gospel by means of some English books sent privately to her by my father's factors beyond sea'.[33] George Tankerfield turned Protestant under Mary: dislike of persecution led him to the Bible, then to Protestantism and, in 1555, the stake. Julius Palmer, fellow of Magdalen in Oxford, was a vigorous Catholic until the burning of Latimer and Ridley and his reading of the Bible, Calvin, and Martyr changed his religion.[34] Bible-reading was central to the appeal and practice of Protestantism: there were public readings to large crowds or small groups in London and Wotton in Gloucestershire in 1540, Canterbury and Laneham in Kent in 1543, Lowick in Northamptonshire in 1546, and, no doubt, in many other places too.

After the 1538 Injunctions, which ordered that English Bibles be set up in parish churches, a few poor men in Chelmsford bought a New Testament. They met in the church on Sundays, and other parishioners gathered round to hear them read. William Maldon, aged about 20, was one of those who went to listen, but several times his angry father hauled him off to recite Latin matins. William determined to learn to read for himself, and studied a primer through the winter; in May 1539 he and an apprentice bought a New Testament, which they hid in their bedding and read in secret. Soon William was reading John Frith, and trying to persuade his mother not to kneel to the crucifix. 'Wilt thou not worship the cross?' she cried; 'It was about thee when thou wert christened, and must be laid upon thee when thou art dead!' When father Maldon was told of the heresy, he dragged William out of bed by the hair and beat him, and then pulled him about by a halter, declaring, 'I will surely hang him up, for as good I hang him up as another should!'[35] This story (told proudly by William years later) suggests the impact of Bibles and books, but also the importance of literacy, and the outrage which converts might face.

William Maldon's conversion shows that illiteracy was no bar to Protestantism; he was attracted by hearing the Bible read, then taught himself to read, and formed his faith by Frith and the New Testament. The devotion to the gospel of Thomas Hodgesham of Aylsham in Norfolk preceded his literacy; he had learned to read in 1551 from local Protestants, and in 1558 he read the Bible aloud until his neighbours called the constable to have him arrested. Derick Carver, a Swedish-born brewer of Sussex, held meetings in his house in 1554 at which the Prayer Book service was read, but Carver himself only learned to read when in prison.[36] However, these efforts by mature men to learn reading indicate that illiteracy was a handicap for Protestants, leaving them as dependent on readers as Catholics were on priests. Joan Waste, a blind Derby girl, was converted by Edwardian preachers: she saved up for a New Testament, got others to read to her, and sometimes had to pay them. Rawlins White, fisherman, began to turn against Catholicism in the reign of Edward; he sent his young son to school to learn to read, and the boy read the Bible to him each night after supper. White learned Scripture by heart, and became a Protestant proselytizer: he was burned at Cardiff in 1555.[37]

There were illiterate Protestants, and there were some whose Protestantism prompted literacy; but they were few. Protestants were readers; that was what their leaders expected, and that was how their enemies identified them: 'heretics and two-penny book men'.[38] So it is likely that the spread of Protestant allegiance followed the spread of literacy. There has been much dispute on the extent of literacy, especially about the use of ability to sign a name as an indicator of reading, but perhaps those who could read but not sign were balanced by those who could sign but not read. If signatures to court depositions are any guide, there was no significant increase in literacy until the generations educated after 1580; before then, possibly 30 per cent of men and 10 per cent of women could read. It seems that literacy followed social status and occupational need. In the middle of the sixteenth century, virtually all gentlemen and merchants were literate, about half the yeomen, a third of the craftsmen, a tenth of the husbandmen, and hardly any labourers.[39] Since a bibliocentric religion was much more accessible to the literate, it would be surprising if Protestantism's social distribution did not reflect reading.

Protestants were recruited from throughout the social scale, but disproportionately from the middling and prosperous sectors, those more likely to be literate and more able to afford books. The Londoners accused of heresy in 1540 were usually richer than other laypeople; over half of the heretics (but probably a tenth of all Londoners) were assessed for tax as worth £20 or over, but only 28 per cent of heretics (as against 80 per cent of all Londoners) were worth less than £5.[40] The difference was not so marked at Canterbury in 1543: the median subsidy payment of the probable Protestants was 10s., that of conservatives 8s. But a fifth of the Canterbury Protestants were professional men, lawyers, and scriveners, and it was much the same at Sandwich.[41] In Devon the early Protestants were almost all townsmen, and many of them were merchants. Among benchers of the Inns of Court, perhaps a quarter were Protestants by the reign of Edward.[42] A creed which came from the universities and stressed individual Bible-reading appealed to the educated élite. We know the status of some of the men who went into exile in Mary's reign: 37 per cent of them were gentlemen, 41 per cent were clergy and students, and 12 per cent were merchants and lay professionals.[43] But the exiles are a weighted sample: richer Protestants could afford to flee; the less affluent had to stay and risk punishment.

Clothworkers were especially well represented among the Marian heretics, as were other artisans and tradesmen. In 1555 the constables of Coggeshall in Essex arrested six men for refusing the sacrament at Easter. All were weavers or fullers; three recanted and three were burned. The heretics proceeded against in the diocese of Norwich under Mary were drawn mainly from the clothing trades: Edmund Poole, John Denny, Richard Crashfield, and Philip Umfreye were tailors; Robert Bayocke, Alexander Gooch, and John Dale were weavers; Roger Coo and John Davye were shearmen; and Cecilia Orme was daughter of a tailor and wife of a weaver.[44] We know the occupations of sixty-four of those hounded for heresy in Marian Suffolk: nine were clothworkers, and fifteen were from the leather trades, especially shoemakers. John Foxe recorded the occupations of seventy-eight of the Marian laymen martyrs: twenty-six had worked in the cloth trades, eleven in building, and five in leather.[45] Such artisans were more likely to be literate than were labourers, and their work gave them the wider contacts and greater independence which could lead them to encounter and accept new ideas.

It seems that the Marian exiles came predominantly from the upper ranks of society, and that the Marian heretics came mainly from the middling sorts. But these social statistics are far from conclusive. The exiles were a self-selecting sub-set of Protestants, and the rich and educated were more likely to afford and to face life among foreigners. The persecuted were selected by their enemies, who may have paid less attention to the very poor, and harassed high-profile Protestant leaders. However, the scarcity of victims from the gentry and lay professions suggests that jurors concealed the more prosperous and turned in the less. The large number of heretics whose social status is not known weakens any calculation, especially as higher ranks were more likely to be recorded, and the unknown may have been poor. For those below the gentry it was occupation rather than rank which was usually reported. We do not yet know whether Edmund Poole, John Denny, and the others were rich tailors or poor tailors, prominent in their communities or peripheral figures. But almost all the evidence points roughly in the same direction: the Protestants were gentry, professionals, yeomen farmers, and, above all, artisans.

Those known to have attended illegal Protestant meetings in Mary's reign may offer a fair cross-section of the committed core; mainly they had been noticed by spies or caught in raids, rather than presented by priests, churchwardens, or malicious neighbours. There were few gentlemen or merchants among them, but such were a small proportion of the population anyway. Most were artisans, and over a third of the total were from the textile trades.[46] Only some of those detected had their occupations recorded, but there are few signs of the mass of the English population: labourers, farm workers, servants. There certainly were poor Protestants, but proportionately they were rare. Since so few of the poor could read, and probably fewer still could buy Bibles, perhaps positive Protestantism had little to offer them; some might mock the eucharist or avoid confession, but not many of them met in conventicles or went determinedly to the martyrs' fire. Nine of the 'Stratford-le-Bow thirteen' burned in 1556 were tradespeople and small farmers; the only lesser figures were three labourers and one servant, Ralph Jackson of Chipping Ongar.[47]

Protestantism was socially top-heavy, but not a class-based creed: its adherents were all sorts and conditions of men—but, it seems, rather fewer women. Only two of the Stratford thirteen were women, one of them the pregnant Elizabeth Pepper. In all, just over fifty of the 280 Marian martyrs were women. It may be that there was more reluctance to report female heretics, or that women were more likely to recant, though there is plenty of evidence of cruelty to women and endurance by them. Perhaps, like the illiterate poor, women had found less to attract them in a Bible-based religion. In 1540, 190 laypeople had been presented for heresy and irreverence in London: only twenty-six were women, and seventeen of these were presented with their husbands. Though Margaret Ambsworth was in trouble 'for instructing of maids and being a great doctress',[48] it appears that women were less likely than men to be convinced Protestants. In August 1556 twenty-two heretics were taken together in Colchester (probably at a meeting); eight were women. Of the 152 laypeople known to have attended heretical conventicles under Mary, forty-three were women, though when an Islington meeting was discovered in 1558, the women managed to escape, leaving only men to be listed.[49]

The geographical distribution of mid-Tudor Protestantism reflects a number of interacting influences.[50] Some of the most energetic of Protestant bishops had served in the south-east: Cranmer, Hilsey, Ridley (though Latimer, Hooper, and Coverdale had been busy briefly in the west); the long episcopates of Gardiner, Longland, and Tunstall had slowed change in their dioceses. It seems that the Protestant preaching effort had been concentrated in the south-east, close to London and the universities, more prosperous and densely populated areas. Perhaps preachers chose to work in areas where they could hope for sympathy from old Lollards, or perhaps they worked widely but succeeded better in Lollard districts. When Protestantism was spread by the laity, it seems to have been along trade routes to ports, market towns, and manufacturing centres. Perhaps, too, Protestantism was built best where there were concentrations of those most likely to respond: the literate artisans who worked in cities and towns of all sizes, and the clothworkers who were most common in smaller towns and upland hamlets.

The most trustworthy evidence of Protestant allegiance comes from persecutions under Henry VIII and Mary, and from occasional records of enthusiasm under Edward VI and at the beginning of Elizabeth's reign. It seems fairly clear. By 1553 Protestantism was strongest in some of the largest towns, especially London, Norwich, Ipswich, Bristol, and Coventry, and in smaller towns which were ports or cloth towns. The market and cloth towns of Suffolk (especially Hadleigh and Mendlesham), of Essex (notably Colchester and Coggeshall), and of Kent (especially Maidstone and Sandwich) had established Protestant groups, which vigorous repression failed to crush. There were some Protestants almost everywhere in England, but most in a sweep from Norfolk round to Sussex, and in a spur from London up the Thames valley. There were certainly Protestant circles in Wiltshire, Gloucestershire, Huntingdonshire, Northamptonshire, north Warwickshire, south-east Lancashire, and west Yorkshire (especially in Halifax and Leeds), but they were probably smaller and certainly less numerous than in the south-east.[51] The new religion had infiltrated generally, and established a substantial presence in some places, but it had not swept the country.

In 1555 Henry Orinel, a Cambridgeshire husbandman, went to Colchester in search of Protestant counsel, which he found at a meeting in an inn. He reported later that he had chosen Colchester because

this town for the earnest profession of the gospel became like unto a city upon a hill, and as a candle upon a candlestick gave great light to all those who for the comfort of their conscience came to confer there.

The seeds of true religion 'by the preaching of the Word has been sown most plentifully in the hearts of Christians in the days of good King Edward'; but, despite such efforts, even Colchester Protestantism was still the sub-culture of a minority in 1553.[52] At Canterbury the patronage of Cranmer and the efforts of cathedral preachers had created Protestant loyalties among some of the lawyers and merchants and in the leather trades, especially in Northgate ward. But the Protestants were only an activist cell, the Northgate poor were 'blind and ignorant', and moderate civic leaders were alienated by Protestant extremists. John Twyne, the reformist schoolmaster, later bewailed the heresy and selfishness which had discredited Edwardian policy.[53]

Even in the towns of greatest Protestant success, the signs in mid-century are of religious division rather than Reformation victory. In London in 1549, some parishes celebrated Corpus Christi day and others did not; some laypeople observed the holy day and others ostentatiously worked. In 1550 the Corpus Christi and St Barnabas feasts and processions were suppressed by the mayor, 'and the Assumption of Our Lady was such division through all London that some kept holy day and some none. Almighty God help it when his will is!', cried the Greyfriars chronicler.[54] In Bristol the Catholic preacher Roger Edgeworth complained,

Here among you in this city some will hear mass, some will hear none by their good wills; some will be shriven, some will not, but for fear or else for shame; some will pay tithes and offerings, some will not, in that worse than the Jews which paid them truly, and first fruits and many other duties beside. Some will pray for the dead, some will not; I hear of much dissension among you.[55]

In each of these towns, Colchester, Canterbury, London, and Bristol, there were to be Catholics and conformists enough in Mary's reign to mount intense persecutions of the Protestant minorities.

The evidence has sometimes been interpreted differently.[56] It is said that the records of Protestantism survive patchily and by accident, so we can tell where Protestants were but not where they were not. It is suggested that burnings of martyrs and presentments of heretics reflect only the bravery of unusual individuals and the determination of persecutors: the known Protestants may be just the visible tip of a very large iceberg. All this is true—up to a point. Our evidence across the country is uneven at any particular time, but it is fairly comprehensive over a period; it is only for the far north-east that our knowledge is poor, and only for the far north-west (and Wales) that our ignorance is almost total. It is most unlikely that major Protestant groupings were unrecorded by contemporaries and unknowable by historians. Only brave Protestants showed their religion publicly under Mary, but heretics were unpopular and often reported by hostile neighbours, and sometimes by vengeful spouses.[57] Some Catholic bishops were more eager to burn Protestants than were their colleagues, but all wished to harass heretics and many have left court books and visitation records. The evidence is not perfect, but it is not poor.

We do not know about all mid-Tudor Protestants, or even all the Protestant cells. The Protestant iceberg certainly had a submerged section, but how large was it? What proportion of all Protestants were the 3,000 possibles discovered by combing the records from 1525 to 1558, or the 280 known to have been burned between 1555 and 1558? One in ten? One in a hundred? One in a thousand? We cannot tell, but even the biggest multiplier would create only a small fraction of the total population. And, for all their defects, Catholic detection and surviving records can hardly have missed 999 in every 1,000 Protestants. Hatred of heresy probably produced a higher detection-rate than 'iceberg' arguments suppose. However, we cannot assess the scale and distribution of early Protestantism by the evidence of Protestant commitment alone; it has to be interpreted in the context of the realities of the Reformation process and the evidence of conservative attitudes. Is it likely, given the shortage of Protestant preaching and the common hostility of popular response, that Protestants became even a large minority in only a short period? Could even a Latimer or a Bradford or a Knox shatter old loyalties and create a new consciousness by occasional evangelical forays?

Some historians have tried to reach beyond the evidence for Protestant groups and Marian victims, and towards a comparative assessment of the strengths of reformist and conservative allegiances. They have often studied the introductory preambles of surviving last wills in particular areas. Almost all sixteenth-century wills began with a religious formula: 'I bequeath my soul to God . . .'; but then the preambles vary. There were three broad categories: 'I bequeath my soul to God, the blessed Virgin Mary, and all the holy company of heaven'; 'I bequeath my soul to God', or 'to God, my maker and redeemer'; and 'I bequeath my soul to God, trusting to be saved by the merits of Christ's passion', or, sometimes, 'trusting to be numbered among the elect'. Such formulae have been assumed to reflect the religious opinions of the testator, and have been tackled in two ways. The older, and perhaps cruder, method is to treat the first formula as an expression of Catholic confidence in intercession by saints, and the others as showing rejection of the old scheme of salvation, being 'non-traditional', 'reformist', or 'Protestant-type'.

This approach, applied to wills from many parts of England, shows a similar chronology of movement.[58] The traditional formula was heavily dominant everywhere until about 1545; the alternative forms increased rapidly under Edward VI, declined under Mary, and soon became almost universal under Elizabeth. But there were huge regional variations.[59] Late in Edward's reign (the precise dates differ), the traditional formula was used in only 5 or 6 per cent of wills in Kent and the city of Norwich, but in 58 per cent of Northamptonshire and Rutland wills, and in 61 per cent in the city of York. In Mary's reign, about 40 per cent of Kent wills had the traditional preamble, and 43 per cent in the city of London, but 56 per cent in Herefordshire and 75 per cent in the diocese of York. If conservative attachment was broken by the Edwardian preachers, it was only in the south-east of England, it seems. But we must be cautious. Many wills were ambiguous: 'I bequeath my soul to God etc.' was common in London, and in Suffolk in years of high mortality: does it show Protestantism, uncertainty, or the laziness of the scribe or registrar? Testators might abandon reliance upon saints without abandoning Catholicism entirely: many who employed the non-traditional preambles nevertheless asked for prayers for the soul.

A more elaborate approach is to categorize the three sorts of preamble as 'traditional', 'neutral', and 'Protestant'; this enables us to examine positive commitment to central Protestant ideas as well as the decline of the appeal to saints. It is striking that everywhere the shift is from traditional to neutral formulae, and Protestant preambles were used in only a small minority of wills. In London, it is true, 32 per cent of Edwardian wills used the Protestant form, but only about 7 per cent in Kent and in Herefordshire, 9 per cent in York city, and 17 per cent in Northamptonshire and Rutland. In the diocese of York, only fifteen out of 323 wills from Edward's reign and eighteen out of 330 from Mary's used the Protestant appeal to Christ's merits for salvation. It appears that if the new preachers (and the propaganda of the reformist regimes) undermined devotion to the saints, they did not manage to recruit many new Protestants. Mid-century Protestants were, as our earlier evidence suggests, a small—in many places a tiny—minority movement. The negative, mocking aspects of the Reformation message had far more impact than the new slogans of justification by faith and election.

However, we would be wise not to attach much (perhaps not any) significance to will preambles. They form a heavily weighted sample of opinion, and what they have to tell us is far from clear. Wills were generally left by the richer, male members of Tudor society, those somewhat more likely to be Protestant. They were usually drawn up when the testator was dying, and so for the more aged. But do the sudden swings in use of formulas (mainly in line with official religious policy) really reflect the changed opinions of the elderly, or shifts at some unknown earlier dates? Preambles were not a deliberate declaration of religious allegiance; they must be treated with care, not crammed into categories. For contemporaries did not see such clear distinctions between formulas. The duke of Suffolk was silent on saints and appealed to Christ's merits, but wanted masses and prayers for his soul. Henry VIII mentioned both redemption by Christ and prayers from the saints, and left over £1,200 for masses for his soul. Bishop Gardiner, doughty critic of justification by faith alone, trusted to be saved by both the mediation of Christ's passion and the intercession of saints, and endowed a chantry.[60]

But testators did not usually produce their own idiosyncratic preambles. It has been shown that most wills were written by scribes, each usually employing the same formula, often drawn from a precedent book; preambles reflect the habits of scribes rather than the loyalties of the dying.[61] A minor change to the introductions of Halifax wills in 1537 suggested scribal practice; the surviving reformist wills of the 1540s from Thornbury in Gloucestershire are all in the same hand. We know from Kent and Herefordshire that definite Catholics left wills with neutral or even 'Protestant' preambles: in one Lancashire case a scribe added a florid Protestant formula after the testator himself had died. Some will-makers followed local fashion, others official policy. Traditional preambles declined under Edward VI, and recovered dramatically under Mary. Geoffrey Toms of Herefordshire made two wills on 15 June 1559, with the same executors and witnesses: the copies were identical in every respect, save that one had a traditional preamble, the other a Protestant.[62] He, or his scribe, was determined to submit the right sort of will for probate.

So it is hard to know what to make of the evidence of will formulas. At worst, what it shows is insignificant: between 1540 and 1570 scribes abandoned one meaningless formality and took up others, as in our century businessmen (and the writers of manuals for secretaries) gave up 'I remain, Sir, your obedient servant' in favour of 'Yours faithfully'. At best, it shows propaganda against the saints was successful in the south-east, but much less so elsewhere; that the popularity of saints recovered when the campaign against them ceased; and that committed Protestants were few. In 1559–60, 3 per cent of York city wills had Protestant preambles, 6 per cent of those from Kent, 12 per cent of those from Northamptonshire and Rutland, and 14 per cent from east Sussex. The Protestants could come out of the closet after Mary's death, but it had not been very crowded in there. Perhaps the truth lies in neither the worst case nor the best: preambles tell us something, but not very much. They do not offer superior hard evidence for systematic treatment; they supply uncertain impressions for use alongside other sources for the progress of Protestantism and response to the Reformation.

Protestant preachers and proselytizers spread their faith and gained new supporters, especially in Edward's reign, but they were always an unpopular minority. In 1546 young John Davis was living with his apothecary uncle in Worcester; when it was discovered that he lent others a Bible and mocked shaven-crowned priests, his uncle handed him over to the bailiffs as a heretic. In Edward's reign, Edward Underhill of Stepney had been mocked as 'the hot gospeller' who 'is all of the spirit'; he was hated for his public support of Hooper's preaching and Northumberland's religious policy. When he took down the reserved host from above the altar at Stratford-le-Bow, there was a plot among the local women to murder him.[63] When Julius Palmer asked his mother for her blessing in 1556, she retorted, 'Thou shalt have Christ's curse and mine, wheresoever thou go!' She told him he was a heretic because he believed Edwardian doctrine, and not as she, his father, and their forefathers believed: 'Faggots I have to burn thee; more thou gettest not at my hands!'[64] The Marian persecution was possible only because such responses remained commonplace, for Edwardian Protestants had failed to swing opinion in their favour.

There was little in the Protestants' experience to alter their self-image as the 'persecuted little flock of Christ'. Despite the opportunity given them by the reign of Edward VI, they were still assaulted by 'superstitious papists, carnal gospellers, and seditious rebels', as Lever complained in 1550.[65] The truth did not change England. So it came as no great surprise when their young Josiah was taken from them in 1553; Lawrence Saunders announced at Northampton that popery would again be inflicted on the realm as punishment for its lukewarm response to the preaching of the gospel.[66] The preachers had tried: Latimer, Lever, Becon, Bradford, and Knox had done their strenuous best. The Edwardian regime had abolished chantries and the mass, and pulled down images and altars; its people conformed to the new services, and, with much muttering, they mainly did as they were told. But theirs was an external obedience only, for official Protestantism was still a minority faith. As Ridley lamented, 'For the most part they were never persuaded in their hearts, but from the teeth forward and for the king's sake, in the truth of God's Word.'[67]

Catholic Restoration, 1553–1558

ON the night of 4 July 1553, Mary Tudor fled in darkness from her house at Hunsdon in Hertfordshire. She had been warned that her half-brother Edward VI was about to die, and she followed a pre-arranged plan. Her small party rode through the night, and on to Sawston Hall in Cambridgeshire; on 6 July she travelled in disguise to the earl of Bath's house, Hengrave Hall in Suffolk, and on the 7th to Lady Burgh at Euston Hall. Probably on 8 July, she was told of Edward's death; she moved on to her own house at Kenninghall, and next day she received firm confirmation that the king was dead.[1] Mary then wrote to the Privy Council in London, claiming the throne by statute and her father's will and ordering the councillors to proclaim her queen, 'not failing hereof, as our very trust is in you'. But on 10 July Jane Grey, granddaughter of one of Edward's aunts, was proclaimed queen in London; a young tapster who defended Mary's right was nailed by the ears to the pillory. On 11 July the Council's reply to Mary dismissed her claim, and warned her to 'surcease by any pretence to vex and molest any of our sovereign lady Queen Jane her subjects from their true faith and allegiance due unto her grace'.[2]

Probably in May 1553, the duke of Northumberland and the sickly Edward had planned to alter the royal succession established by Henry VIII, to preclude the accession of Catholic Mary, overthrow of the duke, and reversal of the Reformation.[3] Their intention had been to settle the crown upon a future son of the Protestant Jane Grey, but as Edward's health worsened Jane herself was designated successor. With some difficulty, Edward and Northumberland secured the assent of the Council and the judges, and formal letters patent were drawn up on 21 June: Mary (like her sister Elizabeth) was barred from the throne because she was illegitimate and might compromise English independence by marriage to a foreign prince; Jane, safely English, married, and Protestant, was to be queen—and, when Edward died on 6 July, it seemed certain that she would be. For the foreign ambassadors, there was no question: Northumberland controlled the Council, the Crown's military and naval forces, and the central administration. The duke was in charge, and orders to the counties and cities for proclamation of Jane were often obeyed, though officials tried to conceal their actions later.

On 12 July in Rutland, Richard Troughton reported that Mary had been proclaimed queen in Suffolk. He was told, 'The duke had made himself strong, for he had gotten the Tower and all the ordinances of artillery, and all the treasure into his own hands.' 'Fie of money, in comparison to men's hearts!', declared Troughton, and he was right.[4] To the surprise (and embarrassment) of those politicians and local leaders who had supposed there was no choice but to obey Northumberland, Mary was swept to power by a revolution. In part, it was her own doing. She had escaped to Suffolk, and immediately summoned some reliable supporters to join her and others to prepare to tackle any opposition; she had sent out copies of her letter claiming the crown, and written to towns across England for support. In response, major figures such as Sir Robert Southwell, Sir John Mordaunt, Sir William Drury, Sir John Shelton, Sir Henry Bedingfield, and the earls of Bath and Sussex rallied to her. She was proclaimed queen in Buckinghamshire by Sir Edward Hastings and Lord Windsor, in Oxford-shire by Sir John Williams, and in Northamptonshire by Sir Thomas Tresham; in the north the earl of Derby and Lord Dacre raised their force, and marched to Mary's aid.

But it was popular support for Mary's bid which determined the outcome. Parkyn noted that the nobles were divided, 'but the whole commonalty (certain heretics excepted) did apply unto the said Lady Mary'.[5] In East Anglia it was 'the countryfolk' who first joined her cause; the Cratfield churchwardens prepared arms for their contingent to Mary's army. There were protests from 'the common people' of Ipswich as the sheriff and Lord Wentworth proclaimed Jane queen. When Northumber-land sent a naval squadron to prevent either Mary's escape or foreign assistance, the crews mutinied and declared for Mary. Ten thousand men flocked to Peckham and Hastings in Middlesex, to march on Westminster in her name. In north Essex it was the earl of Oxford's household servants who forced him to defect to Mary, and imprisoned the gentry who had been trying to organize aid for Northumberland.[6] Elsewhere, as an account written from the Tower reports, 'the noblemen's tenants refused to serve their lords against Queen Mary'. The Lincolnshire JPs and constables tried to muster recruits for Northumberland's army, with threats that 'if they went not and the duke had the upper hand, he would hang all that would not go'; but there was a boycott.[7]

On 13 July Northumberland led a small but well-equipped force out from London to march against Mary; he raised few allies as he advanced, and on 18 July he retreated from Bury St Edmunds to Cambridge. In his absence the Council deserted him. On 19 July Mary was proclaimed queen at Cheapside: 'Great was the triumph here at London; for my time I never saw the like', wrote one chronicler. After *Te Deum* at St Paul's there were 'bonfires in every street in London, with good cheer at every bonfire, the bells ringing in every parish church, and for the most part all night till the next day to noon'.[8] It was the same everywhere. When Mary was proclaimed at Grantham on 20 July, the crowd threw up their hats, called 'God save the queen!', sang *Te Deum*—and turned to the serious business of drinking. On 21 July she was proclaimed at York, and at other towns on the 22nd, 'whereat the whole commonalty in all places in the north parts greatly rejoiced, making great fires, drinking wine and ale, praising God'. Next day, she was proclaimed at Bridgnorth fair, 'after which proclamation finished the people made great joy, casting up their caps, lauding, thanking, and praising God Almighty with ringing of bells and making of bonfires in every street'.[9]

There had been a mass rejection of Northumberland ('villain', 'cruel tyrant', and 'vile traitor'), and approbation of Mary, 'so noble, godly, and rightful a queen'.[10] Poor Jane Grey was hardly an issue. When historians supposed that Protestantism was popular and widespread, there was no real alternative to the view that it was Mary's Tudor blood which gained her the crown, though it was not obvious that the claim of the bastard Mary should appeal to legitimist Protestants more than that of legitimate Jane. The English had not cared much for legitimism when it did not suit them, or when weaker claimants had stronger force, as in 1327, 1399, 1461, 1471, 1483, and 1485 (or later in 1689, 1714, and 1936). The Tudor name certainly meant something in 1553; it meant an end to the rule of Northumberland, exercised first under Edward Tudor and then under Jane Grey. And among the reasons for opposition to the duke were his recent imposition of the second Prayer Book and confiscation of service equipment from churches. Since many of the Reformation changes had been resented in the parishes, and Protestants were a small though militant minority, religion may now be recognized as one of the elements in Mary's appeal.

Mary was obviously the Catholic candidate. On 15 May 1551 she had ridden through London escorted by 130 knights, gentlemen, and ladies, each with a set of black rosary beads, in pointed contempt for Ridley's campaign against rosaries.[11] After Edward's death, Mary was presented, in London sermons and in Council declarations and circular letters, as a threat to reformed religion: the Council warned that as queen Mary would bring 'the bondage of this realm to the old servitude of the Antichrist of Rome, the subversion of the true preaching of God's word and of the ancient laws, usages, and liberties of this realm'. Such slogans did not mobilize Protestant support for Jane, but they did encourage Catholics to move for Mary. The activists in Mary's coup were Catholic nobles and gentlemen, while the Protestant and neutral gentry waited, and flocked to her cause only when it was clear that she would win anyway. Those who joined Mary in Suffolk or proclaimed her across England were almost exclusively Catholic; the peers had opposed religious change in Edward's reign, and many of the gentry were soon to be enthusiasts for the persecution of heretics or later recusants under Elizabeth.[12]

For many of Mary's supporters, her triumph was the victory of the old religion, and certainly the defeat of the new. In London and Grantham at least, announcement of her accession was followed by singing of the Latin *Te Deum*; in the north 'the common people' now derided married clergy, and 'would point them with fingers in places when they saw them'.[13] At Mary's proclaiming in Oxford there was great celebration, and threats to Protestants that they would soon be burned. When the defeated Northumberland was taken through London to the Tower on 25 July, 'all the people reviled him and called him traitor and heretic, and would not cease for all they were spoken to for it'.[14] When Mary herself passed through the London streets on 3 August, the crowds shouted 'Jesus save her grace!' and images and pictures of the Virgin Mary and saints were displayed in windows.[15] Edmund Bonner, former bishop, now became a somewhat improbable (and temporary) popular hero in the city; after his release from the Marshalsea prison on 5 August, 'all the people by the way bade him welcome home, both man and woman, and as many of the women as might kissed him'; again, as on 19 July and 3 August, 'the people rang the bells for joy'.[16]

The rising for Mary was soon followed by the restoration of her religion. At Melton Mowbray the altar was rebuilt immediately and mass and *dirige* said for Edward VI. At Oxford the chalices were brought out and masses celebrated. In Yorkshire there were masses from the beginning of August, though with some nervousness by the priests. Catholic nobles and gentry encouraged masses, but 'such as was of heretical opinions' protested at the flouting of the law.[17] Then Mary gave a cautious lead. On 10 August she and her ladies attended an illegal requiem for Edward, and the news was leaked; the following day, mass was said at St Bartholomew's in Smithfield, though there were scuffles after the service. The lord mayor and aldermen were told on 13 August that Mary 'meaneth graciously not to compel or constrain other men's consciences'.[18] On 18 August an ambiguous royal proclamation declared that the queen hoped others would follow her religion, and forbade contention. And then, on 21 August, mass was celebrated in the Tower for Northumberland and his associates, to signal their repudiation of heresy.[19] The lord mayor and leading citizens were summoned to witness this dramatic apostasy, and the story was soon around the city. The mass was back.

Now London parishes lost little time. An altar and cross were set up at St Nicholas Cole Abbey on 23 August, and mass was said; next day, half a dozen more London churches followed, 'not by commandment but of the people's devotion'. St Paul's cathedral joined in on the 27th, when the mass was restored and rebuilding of the high altar started; on the 28th a series of daily requiems for Sir John Harington began at St Helen's in Bishopsgate. Many other London churches joined the rush.[20] The accounts of St Dunstan in the West show the old services back in September; the wardens of St Mary at Hill were soon buying Latin service books, and paying for their altar stone to be carried from the parish kitchen and set up in the church. On 17 September Bonner himself celebrated high mass at St Paul's, and sprinkled the congregation with holy water. By then, illegal masses in parish churches were general, and they were no longer news. The chroniclers now reserved their attentions for the unusual events, such as the occasional protests by outraged Protestants and the arrests of bishops and preachers.

The chronology, and enthusiasm, was much the same outside London. The proclamation of 18 August was seized upon by priests in Yorkshire as official permission for the mass; Parkyn reported that 'there was very few parish churches in Yorkshire but mass was sung or said in Latin' by the beginning of September. During the next month, altars, images and crucifixes were set up, and traditional processions began again, 'and yet all these came to pass without compulsion of any act, statute, proclamation, or law'. On 3 September the clergy of Shropshire began to celebrate mass, *auctoritate excellentissime Mariae Reginae nostrae Angliae*,[21] claiming permission of the proclamation. John Hooper wrote dolefully from the Fleet prison on the same day, 'The altars are again set up throughout the kingdom.' At Canterbury the suffragan bishop, Richard Thornden (called 'Dick of Dover' by his many critics), sought to disown his Protestant past and in September celebrated solemn high mass in full pontificals. Other priests were saying mass in Kent by September, and were proceeded against by Justice Hales at the Michaelmas assizes; for this officious piece of law enforcement, he was imprisoned.[22]

Catholic worship was not always restored without trouble. At Crowland (Lincolnshire) the bailiff pressed for the mass after the August proclamation; when parish leaders refused to break the law, the bailiff forced the curate at knife-point: 'Buckle yourself to mass, you knave!'[23] After the proclamation the Catholics of Poole demanded the mass, but their minister, Thomas Hancock, refused. They set up the altar, and hired an immigrant French priest to celebrate, but the altar was pulled down at night by Hancock's supporters. So the Catholics erected an altar in a house, and for a while there were masses there and, at church, Prayer Book services, until Hancock preached against the mass and fled abroad.[24] At Adisham in Kent a group of parishioners took down the communion table on 27 August, but in the following week the local Protestants returned the table. After a Prayer Book service on 3 September, there was a furious confrontation between conservative parishioners and the rector, John Bland, and his clerk: 'Ye are both heretic knaves, and have deceived us with this fashion too long, and if he say any service here again I will lay the table on his face!', shouted John Austen, and threw down the table once more.[25]

When the mass was imposed by law on 20 December 1553, there was further difficulty. Thomas Dobson, married vicar of Orwell in Cambridgeshire, was willing to conform, but with no great enthusiasm. 'We must go to this gear', he scoffed as he went to the altar—which so offended some of the congregation that they stumped out of the church.[26] At Hadleigh Rowland Taylor said the Prayer Book services for as long as he could, and preached against the renewed popery of the surrounding area. But John Clerke and William Foster brought in the rector of Aldham to say mass, and set up an altar, and when it was thrown down at night they rebuilt it and set a guard. This liturgical see-saw, with altars going up and down even faster than the Tudor regime changed its religious policy, seems to have been a feature of divided parishes! When mass was said next day, Taylor tried to stop it: 'Thou devil! who made thee so bold to enter into this church of Christ to prophane and defile it with this abominable idolatry?' Taylor was thrown out of the church and the mass continued behind locked doors, but one or two of his parishioners threw stones through the windows to disturb the priest.[27]

The mass was certainly not welcomed by everyone. In August 1553 a Coventry minister had wished 'them hanged that would say mass', and in September the Council ordered the arrest of a Norfolk preacher who had framed an insulting rhyme against 'the blessed sacrament'. In November William Smythe sought signatures in Maidstone to a petition 'for the retaining still of their new religion', and in some Essex towns there were attempts in February 1554 to organize a boycott of Catholic services.[28] Some of the London parishes were slow to restore the mass, and a few failed to do so after 20 December. On 4 January Bishop Gardiner summoned the churchwardens of thirty parishes, and asked why St Mary Magdalen Milk Street and other churches had not done their duty, 'and they answered that they had done what lay in them'. Later there was a petition from Norfolk Protestants for the return of Prayer Book services:

For truly the religion set forth by King Edward is such in our conscience that every Christian is bound to confess to be the truth of God, and every member of Christ's Church here in England must needs embrace the same in heart and confess it with mouth.[29]

But there can be no doubt that in most places Catholic worship returned speedily and—as chroniclers stressed and Protestants ruefully conceded—without compulsion. Though minorities were distressed, large majorities were delighted that the years of heresy had passed. At Stanford in the Vale (Berkshire) a warden wrote in the accounts,

Ye shall understand that in the time of schism when this realm was divided from the Catholic Church, which was in the year of our Lord God 1547 in the second year of

King Edward VI, all godly ceremonies and good uses were taken out of the Church within this realm . . . and then the old order being brought unto his pristine state before this book was written caused me to write with this term.

At Morebath in Devon, the vicar recorded the recovery of giving to the church:

Anno domini 1548 was high warden of this church Lucy Cely, and by her time the church goods was sold away without commission *ut patet postea*, and no gift given to the church but all from the church, and thus it continued from Lucy's time to Richard Cruce . . . and by all these men's time, the which was by the time of King Edward VI, the church was ever decayed, and then died the king, and Queen Mary's grace did succeed, and how the church was restored again by her time after this ye shall have knowledge of it.[30]

Christopher Trychay of Morebath was right, and not only about his own parish: 'the church was restored again by her time.' It is striking just how rapidly parishes put their money where their priest's mouth was, how quickly they paid out good (or rather, after the Edwardian debasements, bad) money to re-equip their churches. In the first six months of Mary's reign, the churchwardens of Sherborne paid 10s. 6d. for labour to rebuild the high altar, and 7s. for the sewing of new vestments and altar cloths; they bought a range of new service-books, vestments, a gilt crucifix, and candlesticks for the altar, spending a total of £11. 17s. 8d. for new equipment, and another £2. 9s. for labour (in all, the equivalent of an artisan's wages for three years, or the parish's ordinary running costs for a whole year). In the same period the wardens of St Martin's in Leicester bought copes, vestments, altar-cloths, banners, service-books of various sorts, a cross, candlesticks and a canopy for the sacrament. The altar stone was carried from the mayor's house, where it had been kept since 1550, and the altar was rebuilt and painted; the image of St George and the church organ were both repaired.

To finance her coup, Mary had plundered Norfolk church plate confiscated by Edward's commissioners; but once safely in power she ordered county commissioners to return goods to the churches.[31] In most counties plate and vestments had already been sold or spoiled, and return of the rest was a lengthy business; the church at Fordingbridge (Hampshire) did not get its silver cross, pyx, censers, and sacring bell back until 1556. In many parishes, those who had bought church goods under Edward now returned them; others gave money. At St Martin's Oxford, vestments, altar-cloths, mass books, candlesticks, and a cross were returned in 1553. At Croscombe in Somerset the wardens were given a silver chalice, a box for the host, a blue velvet cope, vestments, altar-cloths, a copper cross, and £14 'in ready money'. In 1554–5 Morebath church received a box for the host, a mass book, vestments, a picture of St Sidwell, and images of Mary and

John. The wives and the young men had collections for books, 'and of divers other persons here was received pageants and books, and divers other things concerning our rood loft, like true and faithful Christian people this was restored to this church, by the which doings it showeth that they did like good Catholic men'.[32]

It seems from surviving churchwardens' accounts that about a fifth of churches benefited from the voluntary return of goods sold under Edward. Usually, the wardens had to work harder. At Long Melford in Suffolk they complained of things 'scattered abroad and delivered to sacrilegious persons, which paid little or nothing for them, were many of them spoiled and mangled, and some of them that were saved we brought again as it appeareth afterward in the year of our Lord God 1553'.[33] They bought books, cloths, crosses, and candlesticks, set up the altars and images, and had scriptural texts scraped from the church walls. In 1553 the wardens of Stanford in the Vale asked for expenses 'for going abroad to seek for saints and other of the church stuff that was lacking', and the wardens of St Margaret's Leicester charged 'for making search for the chalice'.[34] Some parishioners had to be encouraged to return equipment: John Blenkinsop was forgiven 10s. of the money he owed Sheriff Hutton church (Yorkshire) when he gave back a mass book and an old porteus. Others had to be taken to court; the Norwich consistory heard seven suits for the recovery of goods in 1555, and the Winchester court nine in 1556.[35]

Restoration was a huge job, but, stage by stage, it got done. After their heroic early efforts, in 1554 the Sherborne wardens paid for repairing their rood-beam and rood (obviously not destroyed in the previous reign), setting up the rood and images, making steps up to the high altar, erecting side altars, and buying banners and a holy water pot. In 1555 they financed the purchase of more vestments and books, the decoration of altar-cloths and banners, and the cleaning of Scripture texts from the church walls. In the next year they bought more candlesticks, a cruet, and various cloths, and financed a revival of the Corpus Christi play. In 1557 there were more new vestments, and a collection raised £61. 19s. 10d. for new bells. In Mary's last year the wardens bought a holy water sprinkler, and another mass book; it was soon to be illegal. At Yatton in Somerset the wardens paid 12s. 4d. for building the altar in 1553; £2. 5s. 2d. for service books in 1554; £6 for a cross, 5s. for painting a rood cloth, and 20s. 8d. for a pyx and a pall cloth in 1555; 26s. 8d. for a tabernacle in 1556; 13s. 4d. for a rood in 1557; and £1 for organ repairs in 1558. In a smaller and poorer parish than Sherborne, it was proportionately heavy expenditure.

Almost everywhere there were phased and realistic programmes of restoration, reflecting the developing flow of instructions and the practicalities of getting Catholic worship going again. In 1553 parishes generally set up the high altar, and bought vestments, books, and a cross. In 1554 most paid for plate, candlesticks, side altars, a sepulchre, cloths, and banners. In 1555–6 they bought a rood and images, and then many began fabric repairs. Some churches simply kept pace with the prescriptions of Mary and her bishops; but that in itself is surprising, for this was expensive reconstruction paid for by the whole parish, not cheap Edwardian destruction which could be done by a pair of nervous churchwardens. Others went faster than official demands; surviving churchwardens' accounts suggest that perhaps 75 per cent of churches had an altar before 20 December 1553; about 45 per cent set up a rood before the order of October 1555, and about 35 per cent had images before the command in Lent 1556. Sometimes there were stop-gap measures. At Harwich in 1554 a crucifixion was painted on cloth for use as a rood, while the parish was paying for altars, books, and vestments; then, in July 1556, an Ipswich carver was paid £1. 6s. 8d. for a wooden rood.

It is sometimes suggested there was a cheapjack restoration of Catholicism, a grudging and token fulfilment of orders from above.[36] Expenditure on roods and images was often less than on such statuary in Henry's reign, and the roods at Harwich and Yatton must have been mean things. But parishes were not now buying optional extras as the mood took them and funds allowed, they were financing crash revival programmes at heavy cost. Pride might be indulged in populous and prosperous London parishes. In 1556 St Mary at Hill paid £7 (the going rate in London) for a rood with images of Mary and John, and another £4 for images of the patron saints. St Michael Cornhill spent £8. 10s. on a rood, Mary, and John, and 17s. more for a supporting beam; the whole monument was winched into place with a crane and rollers. But even poor parishes expected value for their money. The people of Cockerham in north Lancashire refused to pay the carver of their new rood, complaining that

the rood we had before was a well-favoured man, and he promised to make us such another, but this that he hath set us up now is the worst favoured thing that ever you set your eyes on, gaping and grinning in such sort that none of the children dare once look him in the face or come near him![37]

When Mary's bishops held visitations of their dioceses, there were defects in many parishes, but almost everywhere had seen serious efforts to re-establish Catholic worship. In the diocese of Bath and Wells, thirty-six out of 266 churches had no proper altar by April 1554, and twenty-nine were still using the communion table; the faults were soon corrected. In 1554, 51 per cent of parishes had fully satisfied the requirements on books and altars; by 1557, 86 per cent had done so, and all but thirty churches had set up a rood with Mary and John. The wardens at Huish Champflower were still struggling to get their chalice and ornaments back, but in most parishes the Edwardian ravages had been corrected. In the diocese of Chester in 1554, 85 per cent of the churches and chapels visited apparently had their altar, cross, and images, and in 1557, 91 per cent had their rood and other ornaments.[38] In Lincoln diocese in 1556, only five out of 235 churches seem to have lacked altar, rood, or ornaments, and only St Ives had serious omissions. In the archdeaconries of Salisbury and Wiltshire in that year, a fifth of churches had some shortage of ornaments, usually because parishioners refused to return what they had bought; but only two churches out of 197 had no altar and two more no rood.[39]

The position seems worse in the diocese of Canterbury in 1557, partly because the examination of wardens was much more exact. Of the churches visited, 19 per cent had no proper altar, 25 per cent no crucifix for the altar, 10 per cent no chalice, and 9 per cent no rood; a quarter of the parishes lacked one or more of the required service-books, and a third lacked some vestments. But only one in ten parishes had been really negligent, with two or more serious deficiencies. Marden had no altar, cross, rood, or image of the patron saint, but there were no others as bad. More than 80 per cent of parishes were decently, though not perfectly, equipped[40]—and that in a diocese where Cranmer's commissaries had been pulling down images from 1538 and where the destruction of roods and altars had been rigorously enforced. The Kent churchwardens' accounts suggest that the process of restoration there was particularly costly. There was less question of repairing an old rood, or pulling out an old altar stone, or stitching up old vestments; these had been thoroughly defaced in Edward's reign. Especially in west Kent, there was little make-do-and-mend; it was all new expenditure. But still, in the main, altars and roods went up.

One of the most common features of Marian visitation evidence is the obviously appalling state of church fabric. The financial crises which had afflicted parishes under Edward, and perhaps the need to replace service equipment early in Mary's reign, had led to neglect of church buildings. In Bath and Wells in 1554, a third of churches had defects in the nave or chancel. At a visitation of Canterbury in 1556, two-thirds of the churches were in urgent need of major repair; a year later, half of them. At the Lincoln visitation of 1556, more than half the churches had serious fabric defects, most of them in chancels; these were the responsibility of rectors or their lessees rather than parishes. The churchwardens' accounts suggest that some parishes tackled these problems, especially later in the reign when the new equipment had been paid for. At Prescot in Lancashire, for example, there were extensive repairs in 1556: steeple, bells, and church clock were repaired, church and churchyard walls pointed, and new windows were put in. All in all, there were few parishes where annual outlay for much of the reign was not 50 per cent higher than under Edward, and some where it was double.

How was all this paid for? There were levels of expenditure in almost all parishes which, in real terms, were higher than at any other time in the century, and the demands upon parishioners were correspondingly heavy. In the reign of Mary parishes were asked to provide more money than had been needed since the pre-Reformation burst of church extension, and more than was to be demanded again until the Laudian insistence on 'the beauty of holiness'. Yet the funds were raised, in hard economic times, with remarkably little difficulty. Much of the cost of restoration and refurbishment was met by compulsory rates agreed by parishioners and organized by churchwardens: the rood for St Mary at Hill and the repairs at Prescot were both financed by levies. Such rates were themselves an expression of communal concern for churches, and consistory court records suggest there was no particular resistance to parish demands. There were the usual disputes about the allocation of burdens to different townships in a parish, and there were individuals who did not want to pay their share—or, more commonly, contested the size of their share. But the money came in.

A good proportion of the cash needed was raised by voluntary involvement in activities such as parish ales. At Walton in Lancashire there was a church ale in 1555 'for the new adorning of the church'.[41] At Sherborne the church ales had raised about £10 a year in Henry's reign, but profits had dwindled under Edward and ales were abandoned in 1551. But now an urgent need for revenue and perhaps a resurgence of communal commitment produced a boom: the yield of the 1550 ale had been a paltry £2. 12s. 8d., but it was £18 in 1554, £13 in 1555, and £20 a year in 1556–8. At Pyrton (Oxfordshire) the average profit of the Whitsun ales under Edward had been 24s.; in Mary's reign it was 42s. In some parishes, such as Boxford in Suffolk, abandoned ales were not revived; indeed, Boxford was one of the few places where there really was a cut-price restoration. But usually the traditional means of community fund-raising were again employed, often to considerable effect. There were parish hoggling collections through the winter in the West Country; Plough Monday collections in January, especially in East Anglia; Hocktide forfeits after Easter, especially in southern counties; and church ales all over the country.

Some contemporary observers (and some modern historians) thought there was little more than a surly obedience to Mary's Catholic rules, 'from fear rather than from will', as a Venetian reported. Ralph Allerton of Great Bentley in Essex told Bonner in 1557 that there were three religions in England:

The first is that which you hold; the second is clean contrary to the same; and the third is a neuter, being indifferent—that is to say, observing all things that are commanded outwardly, as though he were of your part, his heart set wholly against the same.[42]

Of course he was right: not all were enthusiasts for Marian religion. The see-saw of Reformation and counter-Reformation must have promoted cynicism, and a suspicion that niceties of belief and ritual could not matter much when they were so easily altered. But, surprisingly, conformism was less common than real (and expensive) involvement in parish religion. In the north of England 32 per cent of testators had made bequests to their churches under Edward; under Mary, 59 per cent did so.[43] Catholic commitment was not universal, but it was common.

In the parishes at least, it is hard to detect the 'religious and cultural sterility' and 'arid legalism' which some historians have seen as the hallmarks of the Marian Church.[44] The rapid restoration of the mass and altars, common anticipation of orders to set up roods and images, high expenditure on replacement of equipment, voluntary giving, and a jovial round of church ales—all are a far cry from the Protestant gloom and Catholic doom prominent in most accounts of Mary's reign or the English Reformation. The unattractive disciplinary side of things—the hounding of heretics and married clergy—will be considered in the next chapter; but it must be kept in perspective. The Marian restoration was not an external act, inflicted on parishes by official decree and enforced by grinding bureaucratic procedure. Rather, it was achieved in the parishes, by the parishes, and with only intermittent (and often unnecessary) official prodding. The *real* hallmark of the Marian Church (shown in court act books, visitation presentments, and churchwardens' accounts, rather than the pages of John Foxe), was local enthusiasm, an enthusiasm which produced large sums of money, raised at great speed in bucolic ways, to devote to popular projects.

Marian England was not merry England—but it was pretty cheerful England, at least until the dearth, defeat, and disease of the last years. Civic festivities on the great feasts of the Church, curtailed under Edward, were commonly restored. York's St George's day procession, with an image of the saint carried through the streets 'according to the ancient custom of this city', was reinstated in 1554 by order of the mayor and aldermen.[45] At Leicester the clergy and parishioners of St Martin's and St Margaret's held their traditional Whit Monday procession until 1548; it too was revived in 1554. The old Corpus Christi plays and pageants were revived at Ashburton, Chester, Coventry, Lincoln, Louth, Norwich, Sherborne, Wakefield, Worcester, and York—not always with their former splendour, since costumes and props had sometimes been sold or destroyed. At New Romney in Kent the town plays were exuberantly restored, and in 1555 the Canterbury pageant and parade (suppressed in 1538) again took place on the feast of Becket's translation. At Norwich in 1556 there was a mayoral show, with a tableau celebrating Mary's restoration of truth.[46] And across the country there were Corpus Christi processions, with garlands of flowers and the consecrated host borne under a canopy.

In London parishes the celebration of St Nicholas's day with pageants and processions began again in 1553; when they were cancelled at the last moment in 1554, several parishes had them anyway. These processions were well established by December 1556, with singing 'after the old fashion' and 'as much good cheer as ever they had'. In 1557 'St Nicholas went abroad in most places, and all God's people received him to their houses and had good cheer after the old custom'.[47] Corpus Christi processions, with garlands and torches, were widely restored in London, though they proved divisive. On the first Corpus Christi day of the reign, 'that some kept holy and some would not', a joiner tried to grab the host from a procession at Smithfield, but he was carried off to Newgate by outraged bystanders. Though Bonner's attempt to establish weekly processions in 1556 was a flop, the annual Whit Monday processions drew 'a great number'. The parishioners of St Peter's Cornhill marched to make offerings at St Paul's, with the Fishmongers, the lord mayor and aldermen, and a hundred priests; those of St Clement's without Temple Bar marched with banners and crosses, carrying white rods and singing *Salve festa dies*.[48]

For all the evident enthusiasm, the world was not quite as it had been. In Henry's reign old usages had been questioned; in Edward's processions had been forbidden, images and altars smashed, and the mass suppressed—but the heavens had not fallen in. There were now Protestants and sceptics; there were also those who had discovered better uses for their money than offering candles to images, and better uses for their time than processions. Marian churchwardens' accounts and will-benefactions suggest there was rather less emphasis on saints and on prayers for the dead, if only because the provisions of centuries could not be renewed in five years, and there was understandable worry for the future of gifts to the Church. But this was an adjustment of Catholic emphasis rather than a decline of Catholic loyalty; official religious books also gave the saints less attention, and the Marian bishops themselves made limited provision for prayers for their own souls.[49] Instead, perhaps, there was more concern for the crucified Christ, in the mass, the rood, and Corpus Christi devotion. It is not surprising that there had been change; what is surprising is that so much had remained the same.

At the parish level English Catholicism recovered under Mary—not everywhere and in all respects, since the past could not be entirely undone, but on the whole. The Church showed signs of health which had not been seen since the 1520s, and promise for the future. In clerical recruitment, for example, twenty-five years of decline were now reversed, though career prospects had not improved very much. Under Edward VI ordinations had almost ceased; in Mary's reign they boomed. In Chester diocese there had been no ordinations in Edward's reign; in Mary's there were ordinations of 12 priests in 1555, 17 in 1557, and 70 in 1558, with growing pressure for priesthood from deacons and subdeacons. There were recoveries too at

Durham and Exeter, but they were not so pronounced. In the diocese of Oxford no priests were ordained in 1551–3; in 1554–7 there were 97. In London diocese 25 or 30 priests a year had been ordained in Edward's reign; under Mary the average was 48, and the numbers were still high at the end of the reign. The London candidates at least were carefully examined, with frequent ordination ceremonies so that the examiners could attend to small numbers on each occasion.[50]

Again, after two decades in which the printing press had been used to undermine traditional religion, there were numerous books of Catholic teaching and devotion. The Catholic books of Mary's reign have usually been considered as propaganda, and compared with Protestant polemic; as attacks on heresy, they have been adjudged ineffective.[51] But the official and semi-official religious publications of the reign did not, in the main, seek to argue against Protestant principles; they sought to recreate Catholic understanding by printed sermons, homilies, and works of instruction. Bonner explained in the preface to *A Profitable and Necessary Doctrine* that he had two aims:

both that errors, heresies, and naughty opinions may be weeded, purged and expelled out of my diocese . . . and also that a very pure, sincere, and true doctrine of the faith and religion of Christ, in all necessary points of the same, may faithfully, plainly, and profitably be set forth within my said diocese, to the good erudition and instruction of all the people within the same.[52]

These were to be achieved not by controversy and contention, but by the clear statement of Catholic truths and standards.

Bonner supervised the production in 1555 of Catholic teaching on three levels. For teachers and children, there was *An Honest Godly Instruction for the Bringing Up of Children*, an attractive volume printed in black and red, which combined the letters of the alphabet, the elements of the faith, prayers, and the responses at mass (with translations). For the uneducated laymen there was *Homilies Set Forth*, a manual of thirteen set sermons to be read by the clergy to their congregations. The collection gave simple, homely explanations of Christian life and belief, with particular attention to the eucharist and papal supremacy. For the clergy and literate laymen there was *A Profitable and Necessary Doctrine*, a heavily revised and expanded version of the 1543 King's Book. The book offered a standard course on what a Catholic must believe and do, by exposition and commentary on the Creed, seven sacraments, Ten Commandments, Lord's Prayer, *Ave Maria*, seven deadly sins, and eight beatitudes. It is not an exciting volume, but it is clear, confident, and readable, backed by quotations from the Bible and the Fathers.

These were, in their various ways, effective books: well judged, well organized, and well expressed. And they sold. In London they were compulsory purchases for clergy and teachers, and Cardinal Pole's 1557 injunctions recommended *A Profitable and Necessary Doctrine* to all parishes; but such instructions had not been obeyed with any enthusiasm in the past. *A Profitable and Necessary Doctrine* was published in six editions in 1555, with the homilies added; there were also ten editions of the homilies alone. Also in 1555 there was *A Plain and Godly Treatise concerning the Mass and the Blessed Sacrament of the Altar*, described as 'for the instruction of the simple and unlearned people': it was an energetic exposition of eucharistic doctrine, illustrated from Scripture, the Fathers, and General Councils, published both separately and as an appendix to the *Primer*. Primers, too, were much in demand: there were thirty-three editions of the Sarum *Primer* and four of the York, and demand could only be met with the help of printings at Rouen. Two-thirds of the primers were in English or English and Latin, and in 1556 there were two editions of *The Primer in English for Children*.

It is impossible to assess the impact of such works; in the three years between their publication and Mary's death, it cannot have been great. We know the *Homilies* and *A Profitable and Necessary Doctrine* were bought by churchwardens, mainly in London diocese, but also elsewhere. We know that *A Profitable and Necessary Doctrine* was studied by the Yorkshire curate Robert Parkyn, who based a sermon on images on its exposition of the Commandments.[53] The books cannot tell us what the Marian Church was like, but they may help us to understand what it was becoming. The authors assert the authority of the Church, but they appeal to Scripture and cite it in English. The authors do not abandon saints, images, and prayers for the dead, but they do not devote much attention to them. The authors do not doubt the autonomous efficacy of the sacraments, but they demand informed and pious participation by Catholics. Both *A Profitable and Necessary Doctrine* and Bishop Watson's *Wholesome and Catholic Doctrine* (1558) emphasize the need for inward contrition as well as external acts of penance.[54] Perhaps these are concessions to years of Protestant criticism; as likely, they reflect the mature Erasmian Catholicism of men educated in the 1520s and 1530s.

The beliefs and practice of the Marian restoration were, in some respects, fashioned by the Reformations. The medieval inheritance of monasteries and chantries had been swept away, and could not be replaced; altars, images, and service equipment had been destroyed, and must be replaced. But much had changed hardly at all. The Marian Church was the Church of the 1520s writ later: a vigorous pastoral episcopate; high levels of clerical recruitment; best-selling works of personal edification and piety; active investment in parish religion—and a troublesome cardinal, distrust of clerical authority, and a heresy problem. The parish religion of the 1520s had been attacked in the Cromwellian years, and had recovered with some vigour in the 1540s. It was confronted more determinedly by both official proscriptions and Protestant evangelism in the Edwardian years, and it emerged slightly damaged but essentially intact. From the parish level at least, it seemed the old religion was invincible. A little before Mary's death a Lancashire JP told the mother of a heretic, 'Thou old fool! I know myself that this new learning shall come again, but for how long?—even for three or four months, and no longer!'[55]

Problems and Persecution, 1553–1558

THE first official sermon of Mary's reign provoked trouble at St Paul's Cross. It was preached by Gilbert Bourne, one of Mary's chaplains, on 13 August 1553. Some of the crowd objected to his prayer for souls departed, or to his condemnation of Edward's government for its imprisonment of Bonner—which, despite the popularity of Bonner's release, may not have been tactful three days after Edward's funeral. 'There was a great uproar and shouting at his sermon, as it were like madpeople, what young people and women as ever was heard, as hurly-burly and casting up of caps', wrote Henry Machyn in his diary. The Privy Council took the view that Protestant agitators were responsible, and it may have been right: leading Protestant clergy were suspiciously on hand to calm the mob, and the alleged ringleaders were soon arrested. The lord mayor and aldermen were warned to keep better control, and there was a round-up of Protestant preachers. On 20 August Thomas Watson preached on the obedience of subjects and the wickedness of false teachers, with 'all the crafts of London in their best livery, sitting on forms, every craft by themself, and my lord mayor and the aldermen, and 200 of the guard, to see no disquiet done'.[1]

There were, as we have seen, some local protests against the reintroduction of the mass. In the House of Commons there was contention over religion in November 1553, and finally about eighty members opposed repeal of Edward's Protestant legislation. Especially in the first year of the reign, there were gestures of contempt for the queen's religion. In March 1554 a ghostly voice in Aldersgate Street criticized the queen and the Catholic Church: it was later found to be from a girl who had been bribed to hide behind a wall. In April a dead cat with a shaven head and a paper disc between its paws was hung on the gallows at Cheapside, in mockery of a priest at mass. The consecrated host was stolen from St Mary's in Hull in May, and from Halifax church in July. When Henry Pendleton, a defector from the Protestant cause, preached at St Paul's Cross in June, he was shot at from the crowd; a tin bullet hit the wall above his head. In July and August there were demonstrations against the mass in Ipswich, apparently organized by two Protestant propagandists; however, the regime was not much alarmed, and the culprits were released after a short spell in the Tower.[2]

It is hard to assess the true scale of hostility to restored Catholicism: malcontents and hooligans may not represent very much, and for every protester thousands paid dutifully towards altars and images. At the 1554 visitation of the archdeaconry of London, ninety people were accused of eucharistic heresy, though two-thirds of them denied the charge. Forty people had indicated their dislike of the mass, such as the six at St Stephen Walbrook who 'use either to hang down their heads at sacring time of the mass, or else to sit in such a place of the church that they cannot see the sacring'. At Easter fifty-seven had failed to make confession or receive communion, and about a hundred had not taken part in processions. But some of these cases, and of the 190 accusations of absence from services, may reflect idleness or indifference rather than disapproval. Though many Protestants had not been presented, the returns do not suggest widespread disaffection. Churchwardens had co-operated in making reports, and the accused sought to excuse themselves and to plead their conformity: 'before the queen's reign that now is, they were maintainers and favourers of such doctrine as was then put forth, but not since.'[3]

Visitations of other areas give much the same impression. Only fifteen heretics were reported at the visitation of the archdeaconry of Chester in 1554, almost all from Manchester deanery. The visitors of Bath and Wells diocese in 1554 and 1557 found just over a hundred heretics, three-quarters of them in the deaneries of Bedminster and Frome. The Lincoln visitation of 1556 produced the names of only twenty suspects: four had fled, and all but one of the others submitted. Nicholas Harpsfield's Canterbury visitation in 1557 discovered twenty-seven heretics, thirty-four people who had missed their Easter communion, and twenty-nine absentees from church; about a third of these had fled, and most of the others appeared and submitted.[4] There were some heavier concentrations of hostility: in 1556 a jury reported from Ipswich that forty-two heretics had fled, twenty-three refused communion, twelve would not take part in ceremonies, and seven had objected to the presentment. But even allowing for concealments, the figures are not very large.[5] There were, it appears, hard cores of Protestant activists, larger numbers who conformed reluctantly to royal requirements, and still more who found the demands of restored Catholicism rather a nuisance.

The queen's marriage plans gave the dissidents an opportunity to pose as patriots and mobilize broader support. In November 1553 it became clear that Mary intended to marry Philip of Spain, and on the 16th a parliamentary delegation asked her not to wed a foreigner; before the end of the month, there was a rebellion plot among some Protestant gentry. The conspirators were forced into action in January, when the Council learned of their intentions. But Sir Peter Carew was unable to raise Devon against an alleged Spanish invasion, Sir James Crofts failed in Herefordshire, and the duke of Suffolk mustered only a hundred tenants in Leicestershire. However, Sir Thomas Wyatt managed to raise a rebellion at Maidstone, saying the realm must be saved from foreign domination. He led a force which grew to about thirty gentry and maybe 3,000 others, a force which, because it reached the gates of London, has been seen as a major threat to Mary's regime.[6] The Wyatt rebellion was, however, a two-week crisis, which recruited less than a tenth of the active support the Pilgrimage of Grace had gained, and which shows that there was little serious opposition to the queen and her policies.

Initially, Wyatt's rising was a failure: he could not raise all his own tenants in the Maidstone area, and there was limited recruitment even in the Medway valley, where Protestant success had been greatest. The rebels mustered by Sir Henry Isley from the Tonbridge area were defeated at Wrotham by Lord Abergavenny and Sir Robert Southwell. As Wyatt marched north, he was caught at Rochester between troops from London commanded by the aged duke of Norfolk, and the Kent loyalists; only the desertion of 500 Londoners to Wyatt, crying 'We are all Englishmen!', saved a flagging cause.[7] Wyatt then advanced to Southwark, where he found London bridge closed; the Tower chronicle suggests that sympathy in the city soon turned to fear,[8] and again Abergavenny and the Kent loyalists threatened Wyatt's rear. As his company began to melt away, Wyatt marched west to Kingston bridge, and then eastward along the north bank of the Thames. The rebels walked right into a trap: at Ludgate their advance was blocked by Lord William Howard, and the earl of Pembroke and Lord Clinton closed in behind. The rebels surrendered, rather than be cut down.

There were certainly points at which the rising almost became dangerous: at Maidstone on 25 January, when Wyatt might have recruited better; at Rochester on 29 January, when the defection of the London whitecoats might have led to a rebellion across north Kent; at Southwark on 3 February, when Londoners might have risen against the queen; and at Holborn on 6 February, when the royal forces might have refused to move against the rebels. But on each occasion wider support did not materialize; Wyatt's slogans did not work. His first proclamation claimed the support of leading Kent nobles and gentlemen, his second that armed Spaniards had already landed at Dover; he concealed the queen's pardon from his followers, and stemmed desertions by declaring that the loyalists were hanging ex-rebels.[9] Wyatt was, to say the least, less than frank with his followers: he protested his loyalty to Mary, but would certainly have deposed her for Elizabeth; he probably intended reversal of religion, but kept quiet on the issue—' "Whist!" quod Wyatt, "you may not so much as name religion, for that will withdraw from us the hearts of many" ', claimed the approved loyalist version of the rebellion.[10]

Wyatt and his gentry allies seem to have been concerned for English independence, Protestant religion, and their own careers; their followers joined from hostility to foreigners, Protestant sympathy, economic distress, and tenurial loyalty.[11] We cannot be sure of the balance between motives, and historians have stressed either patriotism or Protestantism; the two were not yet, as later, much the same. The Protestants had played the Spanish card, and lost. Certainly there was support for Wyatt in London, and worry for the consequences of a Spanish marriage. But the limited support for the rising suggests that even in the south-east the prospects of Habsburg rule and Catholic religion were not hateful, or that, at least, loyalty to the queen was stronger than fear of either. There were to be scuffles in London between Spaniards and citizens, and several murders, but Philip himself was a different case. Christopher Trychay, Henry Machyn, a churchwarden at Minchinhampton (Gloucestershire), and Robert Parkyn recorded the titles of Philip and Mary with evident pride, and Parkyn thought the marriage 'was great joy and comfort to all good people in the realm'.[12] By the autumn of 1554, three months after the marriage, Philip's stock was high and rising.

Revelation of the plotting which lay behind Wyatt's rebellion cast doubt on the loyalty of Elizabeth. She was sent to the Tower for two months, and then carted off by Sir Henry Bedingfield into custody at Woodstock. The journey became a triumphant progress for Elizabeth, and a worry for Bedingfield. He reported that the nobles he consulted along the way 'be fully fixed to stand to the late abolishing of the bishop of Rome's authority',[13] but six months later he was proved wrong. After twenty years of anti-papal propaganda, it is astonishing how easily papal jurisdiction was restored at the end of 1554. In the House of Lords, it seems, no one spoke up for the royal supremacy; in the Commons, only Sir Ralph Bagnall did so, and he was ridiculed. The only sticking point—though a determining one—was the issue of confiscated Church lands now in lay ownership. It took time for political realists to persuade Mary, the pope, and his legate Cardinal Pole that the lands must be abandoned. The pope could have his power if the gentry could have their property; there was, however, some last-minute haggling before the papal dispensation for the new holders of Church lands was incorporated in the reunion statute.[14]

Pole had arrived at Dover on 20 November 1554; as he passed through Kent he was joined by a train of nobles and councillors, and the crowds knelt to receive his blessing. On 30 November, at Whitehall, Pole absolved the members of both Houses, 'with the whole realm and dominions thereof, from all heresy and schism'; the absolution was received with great emotion, and hard-bitten politicians wept as they called 'Amen! Amen!'.[15] There was solemn high mass at St Paul's on 2 December, with great enthusiasm among the congregation; at St Paul's Cross, a crowd of 15,000 knelt to receive absolution, many of them in tears. There were further celebrations on 25 January, the feast of the conversion of St Paul. After a great procession and mass at St Paul's, there were bonfires in every parish 'for joy of the people that were converted likewise as St Paul was converted'.[16] Thereafter, the bishops absolved their diocesan clergy, who in turn absolved their parishioners: 'Now, masters and neighbours, rejoice and be merry', a Kentish rector told his people, 'for the prodigal son is come home. For I know that the most part of you be as I am, for I know your hearts well enough.'[17]

There was genuine relief that the time of schism and religious uncertainty was apparently over. Robert Parkyn told his Yorkshire flock, 'this realm is united and knit again to the Catholic faith as all other Christian realms be, whereof our holy father the pope [is] the supreme head'.[18] At Sheriff Hutton and Yatton the churchwardens bought copies of the absolution documents; at Stanford in the Vale they bought prayers for Julius III. No doubt the Protestants were horrified to see the power of Antichrist restored, but there was little open protest. In April 1555 a woman in St Magnus's church refused to pray for the dead pope, declaring, 'Nay, that I will not, for he needeth not my prayers, and seeing he could forgive us all our sins I am sure he is clean himself.' But those who heard her carried her off to the cage on London bridge. Perhaps the novelty of reunion soon wore off. On 26 August 1555 some of the crowd watching a procession through London scoffed at Pole's blessing, and did not bow to the cross carried before him: 'Such a sort of heretics who ever saw?', asked Gardiner in fury.[19] The first fervour passed, but it was followed by indifference, not hostility.

After the rituals of reconciliation and absolution, Church and state did little to rebuild loyalty to Rome. An account of the ceremonies was published, and there were commemorative sermons on the anniversary of the end of the schism, by Harpsfield in 1556 and Pole in 1557.[20] Harpsfield also contributed two homilies on the papal primacy for Bonner's collection, one on the authority given to Peter and the second on the Fathers and the papacy; so there was to be regular rebuttal of the antipapal arguments of the 1547 Homily on Obedience. But there was surprisingly little attention to the claims of Rome in official propaganda or Catholic polemic. This has been seen as part of a broader intellectual malaise in the Marian Church, and as a failure by the regime to realize the importance of literacy and printing. It has been suggested that, even including proclamations and service books, publications which supported Mary's policies outnumbered critical works by only two to one, and that English Protestants published larger numbers of controversial tracts in secrecy and exile than Catholics managed with the backing of the state. So Marian Catholics lost the battle of the books.[21]

If this was true, it was the product of circumstance and not a failure of imagination. Book production in England had already declined from the peaks of 1548 and 1550, and if there were fewer printers active in Marian England it was because Protestant printers lost their licences and foreigners returned home. Some propaganda opportunities were seized, such as the recantations of Northumberland and Cranmer; others, such as the disputation at Oxford in April 1554 and the recantation of Sir John Cheke, were missed. In the first years of the reign, Catholic sermons and works of instruction were published in good numbers: there were sixty-eight such books by the end of 1555. It was only in 1556 and after, when perhaps the market had been supplied, that publications dwindled. Indeed, though the massive demand for service books and primers had initially been met only with the assistance of printers in Paris and Rouen, by February 1556 the London stationers were seeking to restore their own monopoly. But Robert Caley published three editions of Bishop Watson's *Wholesome and Catholic Doctrine* in 1558, and such was its appeal that Kingston and Sutton produced a pirate version.[22]

It is probably true that Catholic leaders and writers wished to inform rather than to persuade. As we shall see, Mary, Bonner, Gardiner, and Pole thought heresy was a minority problem, to be crushed by a few salutary burnings. The people did not need to be weaned from Protestantism, merely reminded of their lost Catholicism and led back by discipline to their old ways. Pole regarded energetic evangelism as unnecessary and inappropriate: 'I think that it is better to check the preaching of the Word rather than proclaim it, unless the discipline of the Church has been fully restored', he wrote in 1558.[23] But for all Pole's caution, there is plenty of evidence of effective preaching and enthusiastic responses. John Feckenham's London sermons were well liked by Machyn: 'a goodly sermon' on 24 September 1553, and 'the goodliest sermon that ever was heard' on 19 November. When Hugh Weston, dean of Westminster, preached at St Paul's Cross on 22 October 1553, the churchyard was fenced off because of the great crowds; when Gardiner preached there on 30 September 1554, 'there were as great a audience as ever I saw in my life'. It was the same in 1557, with 'great audience' several times, and an estimated 20,000 to hear Pendleton at the Spital on Easter Monday.[24]

Pole was unwilling to accept Loyola's offer of Jesuits for England, and he may have been wise. Controversial preaching by a rigorist order with foreign experience and leadership might have been disruptive, and it would have been some years before English (or English-speaking) Jesuits could be trained. But it is unfair and untrue to accuse the Marian Church of having failed to discover the Counter-Reformation:[25] unfair because there were good reasons for Pole's cautious strategy, and untrue because Pole pursued (and in part presaged) some of the essential features of the Council of

Trent's reforming programme. There was more to the Counter-Reformation than Jesuits; there was, above all, diocesan discipline, and that is what Pole sought to achieve. He told his fellow bishops that England's religious troubles had been the fault of the clergy; ignorance had allowed the growth of heresy, and covetousness had allowed heretics to attract support; so priests must be reformed. Pole's legatine synod, from December 1555 to February 1556, produced twelve decrees on clerical discipline. Some were conventional, against absenteeism, pluralism, simony, and heresy, but there were imaginative measures too.[26]

Seminaries were to be established in the cathedrals, for the training of young men for the priesthood. Candidates for ordination were to provide testimonials from parish priests and tutors, and clergy were to be pious, ascetic, and concerned for the poor. The universities were to provide bishops with lists of men suitable for benefices, and incumbents were to devote part of their revenue to education and charity. There were to be parish sermons on Sundays and feast days (with fines for negligent rectors and vicars), homilies for priests who could not preach, and itinerant preachers chosen and supervised by the bishops. These high standards were to be enforced through visitations by bishops who should themselves be resident, preaching pastors. In fact, the bishops who formulated the decrees were men who, given time, would have made something of them. The new appointees were almost all theologians rather than lawyers, drawn from among senior academics and the chaplains of the older bishops. They proved themselves energetic pastors, and even some of the old-style lawyer-politicians, such as Bonner and Tunstall, caught the new spirit.[27]

Cathedral schools were founded or reformed at Durham, Lincoln, Wells, and York, and Bishop Day left £20 to the school at Chichester for boys to be taught 'according to the decree of the synod'.[28] The Marian bishops almost always conducted their own ordination ceremonies, and personally instituted clergy to benefices; several of them were busy preachers, especially Bourne, Pate, Scot, Watson, and White.[29] Watson wrote thirty model sermons on the sacraments, to meet the synod's call for official homilies. Bonner's diocesan injunctions of 1555 set a pattern for pastors to follow: his clergy were to expound *A Profitable and Necessary Doctrine* and the homilies to their people, explain the ceremonies of the liturgy and the significance of holy days, admonish against blasphemy and immorality, and live sober and respectable lives.[30] Of course, such reforming energy would take time to have an impact, and the Marian bishops did not have much time. The deprived Edwardian bishops were only replaced from April 1554, and there were lengthy diocesan vacancies later—especially from 1557, when sour relations with Pole led Pope Paul IV to refuse to confirm Mary's episcopal appointments.

Another reform with no time to succeed was Pole's scheme to overhaul ecclesiastical finances; potentially it was a better solution to the problems of the parish clergy than anything else attempted in the century. In 1555 Mary returned to the Church the first fruits and tenths and the profits of impropriated benefices seized by her predecessors. But her tactless combination of this surrender of revenue with a plea of poverty and a request for taxation provoked trouble in Parliament. Pole's resources were restricted by the responsibility for pensions for ex-religious, transferred to the Church along with the taxes from which it was to be met, but he proposed to subsidize impoverished benefices, and the sums available would increase year by year as pensioners died. The plan required two massive surveys, one of pensions due and the other of poor benefices, which took eighteen months to complete. An elaborate system of cash transfers between dioceses was then needed, as there were variations in yields of taxes, obligations for pensions, and needs of poor incumbents. It was a huge administrative task, which had barely begun to produce benefits when Queen Elizabeth reclaimed her lost revenues.[31]

Mary's other attempts to re-endow the Church also encountered difficulties. She twice met parliamentary resistance to revival of the dismembered see of Durham, since laymen feared this threatened an assault on their own Church holdings. Financial problems forced her to demand compensation when she returned land to the bishops, and only York and Chester profited very much. She restored six religious houses from Crown resources, notably the Benedictines at Westminster, the Franciscan Observants at Greenwich, the Carthusians at Sheen, and the Bridgettines at Syon. The Savoy Hospital and Manchester College were refounded, but the cost of the war against France from 1557 virtually halted re-endowment; the order of St John was the only major restoration thereafter, and in 1558 Pole gave the surplus left after pensions not to poor incumbents but to the war effort. Mary had done what she could afford, but her conscience over Church property was shared by few of her subjects. Viscount Montague and a handful more returned impropriations, and the earl of Pembroke meant to restore the Southampton Observants.[32] But for others the statutory guarantee of their lands was enough: they had paid for the land, and would keep it, whatever Pole said.

Pole tried to reform the clergy, Mary to re-endow them; in the time available, neither got far. The legacy of schism could not be removed rapidly, especially when vested interests were at stake. But the campaign against married clergy was more successful, because it had the backing of the laity. Marriage of priests had been permitted by Parliament in 1549; about a third had married in London; about a quarter in Essex, Suffolk, and Norfolk; about a tenth in the dioceses of Exeter, Lichfield, Lincoln, and York; and about a twentieth in Lancashire.[33] Whether these figures seem high or low depends on one's view of the attractiveness of marriage! It is clear that marriage was a difficult step for many clergy, because of lay hostility. Parkyn gloated that laypeople in Yorkshire gave married priests a hard time. When in 1549 Hugh Bunbury, priest, proposed to Anne Andrew of Chester, she asked 'that the said Hugh would tarry, and not to marry her until there were some other priests married', and soon she called the engagement off.[34] So clerical marriages happened in local batches: in the Avon valley in Somerset, around Wetheringsett in Suffolk, around Wakefield in Yorkshire, and near Warrington in Lancashire: there was safety in wedded numbers.[35]

Mary's royal injunctions of March 1554 ordered the deprivation of all married incumbents. Diocesan administrations set about the huge task of tracking down married priests, dissolving their marriages, putting them to penance, and depriving the beneficed. In Norwich diocese 243 priests lost their posts, and in Bath and Wells about 90; at least 68 priests were removed in Canterbury, and 29 in Rochester. But after the collapse of new recruitment under Edward, there were few replacements for the once-married; so the curates were usually allowed to continue service, and incumbents were often transferred to new benefices: some priests were allowed to arrange convenient job-swaps! Very few of them were Protestants and almost all now conformed.[36] Among the former leaders, Rudd preached at St Paul's Cross 'and repented that he ever was married', Bird joined the drive against heresy in Essex, and Bush published an effective defence of the real presence, while Holgate claimed he had married only because Northumberland called him a papist. A London rector sold his wife to a butcher, and in November 1553 was driven through the city in a cart for public humiliation—but he soon got a church in Kent.[37]

But some priests struggled to keep their wives. At the Norwich visitation of 1556, two of the clergy were reported for behaving as caring husbands, in visiting their ex-wives and supporting them with food and money. Robert Wright, a chaplain at Warrington, was separated from his wife Janet in March 1555; in the next two years, he was before the courts three times for continuing to see her. Finally the Chester consistory lost patience: he was ordered to do public penance, stay twenty miles from her, and undertake a diet of bread and water as punishment.[38] Robert Thwenge of Beverley told the court at York 'that he had rather continue with his wife and live like a layman, if it might so stand with the law'. But such men could be hounded by the courts only because they were presented by churchwardens, and the enforcement of celibacy was supported by parishioners. At St Keyne in the West Country in 1556, the people hauled their parson and his wife out of bed and set them in the stocks.[39] John Ponet's 1549 *A Defence for Marriage of Priests* had made few converts among the laity. In 1554 Thomas Martin published a treatise 'proving that the pretensed marriage of priests and professed persons is no marriage'. Ponet replied from exile, but Martin's work was sufficiently popular for Robert Caley to seek a monopoly of printing it in 1558.[40]

Perhaps 15 per cent of the English clergy were in trouble for marriage, but few suffered for Protestantism. Twenty-one of the Marian martyrs had been bishops or priests, that is, about a tenth of the males who were burned; a handful of others appeared before the courts, recanted their heresies, and worked as Catholics. Seventy-four of those who fled into exile were clergy, and a score of ministers served secret Protestant groups at home. There was a London congregation with a varying membership of between forty and a hundred (and up to 200 late in the reign), which met clandestinely on ships and at private houses: its ministers were, in turn, Edmund Scambler, Thomas Foule, John Rough, Augustine Bernher, and Thomas Bentham. Another London conventicle was broken up on New Year's Eve 1554, when Thomas Rose was caught saying the Prayer Book service for about thirty men and women. Three Protestant preachers were based at a Colchester inn: John Pullan, Simon Harleston, and 'William, a Scot' worked in London and Essex, and Pullan said the Prayer Book communion in his old parish of St Peter Cornhill at Easter in 1555 and 1556.[41] But the vast majority of the clergy who had served in Edward's Church conformed to Mary's, willingly or not.

Ultimately, the Protestants had three choices, as Elizabeth Longshaw explained her own dilemma to John Bradford: 'either to flee, or to abide and deny my God (which the Lord forbid), or else to be cast in prison and suffer death.'[42] Almost 800 people are known to have gone to the Continent in Mary's reign: 472 men, 125 women, and 146 children, though not all were exiles for religion. They established English Protestant communities at Emden, Frankfurt, Strassburg, Wesel, and Zurich, and later at Aarau, Basel, and Geneva. They proved themselves quarrelsome guests, with those tendencies to sectarianism and self-righteousness which so often characterize exiled ideologues. They found it especially difficult to agree on forms of service, and one Frankfurt faction abandoned the Prayer Book and stumped off to Geneva.[43] From Emden and Wesel they mounted an energetic propaganda campaign against Mary's Spanish marriage and her Roman religion, producing more than a hundred books, some of them powerful indictments of the Marian regime. At first the exiled writers counselled patient endurance by the people of England, but by 1558 Christopher Goodman and John Knox were demanding rebellion against idolatry and tyranny.[44]

As well as those who fled abroad, others—and probably more—escaped from home to other parts of England. In Edward's reign Edward Underhill had been well known as 'the hot gospeller' in Limehouse, so under Mary he moved to another part of London, 'for there was no such place to shift in this realm as London, notwithstanding their great spial and search'. But when things were too hot, Underhill had his books bricked up next to the chimney and fled to a house near Coventry. Thomas Mountain was deprived of his London rectory and imprisoned, but when freed on bail pending trial in 1555 he went into hiding in Essex. Lord Darcy organized a search for heretics, and Mountain fled from St Osyth's to Elmstead, and then on to Dedham; Sir Anthony Browne mounted house-to-house searches in the Colchester area, which forced Mountain back to London and so by sea to Antwerp.[45] As we shall see, the persecution was fierce in Essex and several Protestants were forced into flight. An incomplete inquiry in Essex in 1556 found that two men had gone overseas, six had fled 'unto some secret place within the realm', and seven more had disappeared and the jurors did not know (or would not say) where.[46]

The Protestant leaders tried hard to persuade their fearful followers not to bow before the altars of iniquity. As early as October 1553 an exiled printer at Rouen published *Whether Christian Faith May Be Kept Secret in the Heart?*, which condemned the wicked example given to 'the simple and unlearned' when the godly attended mass. In his London prison John Bradford wrote 'The Hurt of Hearing Mass', and had it circulated among his Lancashire friends.[47] From the King's Bench prison in 1555, John Philpot bewailed 'the faithless departing from the true knowledge and use of Christ's true religion'; he warned that it was sin to consort with papists and appear to have forsaken the truth. Protestants knew what they should do, and poor Richard Wever of Bristol drowned himself in a mill-race rather than conform. Of course, social pressure and fear of punishment led most to church, but some still showed their dissent. At Stoke by Nayland in Suffolk, Protestants went to mass but refused communion, until at Easter 1556 they were given a fortnight to receive; they swore they would stand firm, though two broke ranks when the priest offered them communion by the Prayer Book.[48]

The Protestants of Stoke by Nayland were able to hold out for so long partly because of a sympathetic parish priest and partly because of their numbers, too many easily to be forced before the Church courts or arrested by the constables. As Foxe put it, 'they did so hold together that without much ado none well could be troubled'. After the Easter crisis a number of them (mainly the women) boycotted the church, until they were ex-communicated by the bishop's commissary. Some seem then to have conformed, and others fled from the village, which weakened the group. At that point the authorities appear to have decided to seize control. Arrests were made by royal commissioners, and four men were interrogated before Bishop Hopton and Sir Edward Waldegrave. The four refused to attend services because the mass was 'an abominable idol'; they were also charged with denial of the divinity of Christ, and may have been influenced by radicals at Colchester. They were convicted of heresy in February 1557, and

229

burned at Bury St Edmund's later in the year.[49] But in most places Church and state found persecution rather easier, for heretics were few and opinion was often against them.

Mary and her bishops had only a little difficulty in reviving the old heresy laws. In April 1554 a heresy bill sponsored by Gardiner passed through the Commons, but it was voted down in the Lords on 1 May. The opposition had been led by Paget, a privy councillor; he was determined to get the queen safely married before pursuing a divisive persecution. Paget had argued that the authority of the Church should not be bolstered until the holders of Church lands had been guaranteed immunity, and the peers who supported him protested that they had no desire to protect heretics. In the next Parliament, in December 1554, the heresy bill passed both Houses in less than a week; not a single peer protested.[50] From 20 January 1555, heretics convicted by the Church courts faced death by burning. In the forty-six months which followed, the Marian regime was to burn at least 280 people. The statistics and the stories make horrifying reading. The victims included five bishops and fifty-one women: Joan Waste, young and blind, suffered alone outside Derby on 1 August 1556; Alice Downs, a 60-year-old widow, was burned with five others outside Colchester on 2 August 1557; Agnes Prest went to the flames at Exeter as Mary lay dying.[51]

Such a holocaust had not been intended. Mary's own instruction had been that 'Touching punishment of heretics, me thinketh it ought to be done without rashness, not leaving in the meanwhile to do justice to such as by learning would seem to deceive the simple'.[52] On 22 January 1555 Gardiner summoned the Protestant clergy from the London prisons, and offered them mercy if they would abandon their heresy; two may have submitted.[53] On 28 January the trials began: Hooper, Rogers, and Cardmaker were first, and Cardmaker recanted; 'Thou wilt not burn in this gear when it cometh to the purpose', Sir Richard Southwell told Rogers.[54] Bradford, Ferrar, Taylor, Saunders, and Crome were dealt with next. Crome presumably gave some hint of conformity, for he was given time for consultation and later recanted (he had recanted already under Henry, and could have been burned if victims were wanted). So far, all was going to plan; a few of the Protestant leaders had turned, and the rest could be burned to break the spirit of their followers. But on 4 February, when Rogers was taken through the streets to die at Smithfield, the crowds admired his bravery; at the fire, others wept and prayed God to give him strength. He died heroically, and the Church of Edward VI had its proto-martyr.[55]

In his prison at Oxford, Ridley thought the regime hoped to force the preachers to recant, before proceeding next against demoralized senior bishops. He was much relieved 'since I heard of our dear brother Rogers's departing, and stout confession of Christ and his truth even unto the death'.[56] Gardiner miscalculated: he proceeded first against popular pastors, who were supported by their flocks. Rogers was a hard-working London preacher, met on his way to die by his wife and ten children. Hooper was sent to burn at Gloucester, where he had been a model bishop: tireless preacher, pastoral judge, generous in charity and hospitality. He was met outside the city by a sympathetic crowd of 7,000, and at his execution some prayed for him in tears. It was the same when Rowland Taylor died at Hadleigh. The streets were lined with crowds crying, 'Ah! good Lord! there goeth our good shepherd from us, that so faithfully hath taught us, so fatherly hath cared for us, and so godly hath governed us!' He gave away his clothes and the last of his money to the poor, and those who had gathered to see him die called out, 'God save thee, good Dr Taylor!'[57]

The Catholic bishops wanted converts, not martyrs. In prison at Newgate after conviction, Hooper was visited by Bonner and several of his chaplains, to try to persuade him to conform. After his trial, John Bradford was subjected to a barrage of argument, with visits from three bishops, half a dozen theologians, and friends brought down from Manchester. John Philpot faced thirteen formal examinations and conferences, as well as meetings with Bonner and his chaplains; he was seen by a dozen bishops, three leading theologians, and batches of lawyers, peers, and councillors. The legatine synod sent three bishops to offer him his life if he would just acknowledge the real presence. Even with lesser victims, the process of persecution was not inexorable.[58] Alice Benden in Kent, Richard Woodman from Sussex, and Agnes Prest of Cornwall were released by bishops who might have convicted them at once; however, all refused to conform and were later burned. Elizabeth Folkes of Colchester had denied the real presence, but was passed into her uncle's custody when she agreed there was a Catholic Church of Christ. When she heard she was said to have recanted, she gave herself up, and was burned on 2 August 1557.[59]

The burnings were produced by the determination of ordinary Protestants to witness for the truth, and the determination of ordinary Catholics to destroy error—both mixed, no doubt, with less worthy motives. Though the Crown issued heresy commissions, the bishops conducted visitations and trials, and the lord chancellor issued writs for executions, the persecution was not a political act, imposed upon communities against their will. The drive against heresy was only possible because it had the support—not total, but enough—to carry it through. There had been a backlash against heretics and iconoclasts. At Bonner's visitation of London, those who had taken down the rood-lofts of three churches were reported, and the churchwardens who had co-operated with Edward's regime were harassed with presentments.[60] Christopher Jackson of Leeds was delated in May 1554 'for that he railed against the sacraments and burned the image of Our Lady', though the curate admitted that Jackson and other 'busy fellows of the new sort' had behaved themselves since the mass was restored. At

Wem in Shropshire the parishioners refused to allow the burial of William Glover, whom they suspected of heresy.[61]

There was much fear of, and hostility towards, heresy. When William Hunter, a London apprentice, refused Easter communion in 1554, his master threw him out in case he brought trouble on the household. At about the same time, a haberdasher complained that the heretics wanted Elizabeth to be queen, 'but she and they (I trust) that so hope shall hop headless, or be fried with faggots, before she come to it!' Richard Woodman was freed from prison by Bonner in December 1555, but was soon turned in again by his family and neighbours. On a visit to Norwich in 1556 Simon Miller asked in the street where he might hear a Protestant service, and was led off to the diocesan chancellor.[62] In 1557 Bonner released three heretics of Great Bentley in Essex, but villagers soon petitioned Lord Darcy to arrest them for blasphemy against the eucharist. After three days of psalm-singing by Thomas Hudson of Aylsham (Norfolk) in April 1558, his neighbours called the constable to have him arrested. John Lithall refused to kneel before the rood in St Paul's, and a hostile crowd gathered; some spat on him, some called, 'Fie on thee, heretic!', and some said 'It was pity I was not burned already'.[63]

The erratic chronological and geographical incidence of persecution shows there was no sustained national campaign, masterminded from the centre: arrests and burnings fluctuated according to local initiatives.[64] The royal heresy commissions for Canterbury, London, and Norwich dioceses had their information from juries and constables; there were complaints of concealment, but names kept coming in.[65] Visitations received presentments from churchwardens as well as clergy, and the persecution was sustained by lay rather than clerical effort: by justices, jurors, constables, wardens, neighbours, and families. John Fetty of Clerkenwell was twice reported by his own wife, and Alice Benden of Staplehurst by her own husband.[66] In Kent the main activists against heresy were Sir John Baker, Sir Thomas Moyle, and Sir Robert Southwell; in Essex Anthony Browne, Lord Darcy, and Edmund and Sir Henry Tyrrel; and in Suffolk Sir Clement Higham, Sir John Sulyard, and Sir John Tyrrel. Other county and civic officials co-operated in persecution as in other forms of law enforcement; in April 1558 Bonner's commissaries reported from Colchester, 'The officers of this town be very diligent with us, and the undersheriff.'[67]

There were administrative disruptions and delays. In July 1557 the Privy Council asked the sheriffs of Essex, Kent, Suffolk, and Staffordshire, the mayor of Rochester, and the bailiffs of Colchester why certain executions had not yet been carried out.[68] The explanation probably owed more to a declaration of war against France in June than to any unusual reluctance to burn heretics. Local officials were busy levying troops and the second instalment of the subsidy, as well as coping with the consequences of successive harvest failures. In August the sheriff of Essex was fined after his deputy had reprieved a convicted heretic, probably Margaret Thurston, who had recanted when taken to burn. In July 1558 Thomas Bembridge recanted in the pain of the fire, and the sheriff of Hampshire was rebuked for halting the execution.[69] Of course individual gaolers and officials had sympathy for victims, and some may have allowed escapes. The number of burnings in 1558 fell to half the level of previous years, perhaps because of the savage influenza epidemic. But the presentments and punishments continued; five were burned in Suffolk in the last fortnight of the reign.

There were recriminations later, but little disruption and discontent at the time. There was sympathy from the crowds for the great Protestant pastors; when Cardmaker revoked his recantation and was executed on 30 May 1555, some cried, 'The Lord strengthen thee Cardmaker! The Lord Jesus Christ receive thy spirit!' There was protest if several victims burned together before their friends; when five Londoners and two Essex men were to die in the same fire at Smithfield on 27 January 1556, the Council expected difficulty and ordered that young people should be kept at home. As six from the Colchester area died outside the town on 2 July 1557, a large crowd called 'The Lord strengthen them! The Lord comfort them! The Lord pour his mercies upon them!'[70] But there was less compassion for strangers: thirteen people from various parts of south-east England were burned together at Stratford-le-Bow before a crowd of 20,000 on 27 June 1556, apparently without trouble. Families must have been tormented and fellow Protestants outraged by the sufferings, but for the curious mass it was drama: the country people flocked to Dartford for the burning of Christopher Wade in July 1555, and fruiterers brought loads of cherries to sell to spectators.[71]

Examples of public sympathy for heretics come almost entirely from London and other centres of Protestant success: Coggeshall and Colchester, for example. Demonstrations had certainly been organized for the burning of John Rogers in February 1555, and of seven at Smithfield in June 1558.[72] Elsewhere, reactions were mixed or hostile. When George Tankerfield was taken to St Albans to die in 1555, 'some were sorry to see so godly a man brought to be burned'; 'Contrariwise, some there were which said it was pity he did stand in such opinions, and others, both old women and men, cried against him; one called him heretic, and said it was pity that he lived.'[73] When John Hullier suffered on Jesus Green at Cambridge in 1556, a man in the crowd called, 'The Lord strengthen thee!' and some prayed for him, but the Catholics declared he was not to be prayed for and was damned anyway. Rawlins White tried to shout down the preacher at his burning at Cardiff in 1555, so some called, 'Put fire, set to fire!'[74] Officials and bystanders might throw faggots to silence the last speeches of victims —which happened to Christopher Wade at Dartford in July 1555, to three men at Beccles in May 1556, and to Julius Palmer at Newbury in July.[75]

The persecution was not a success. It failed to intimidate all Protestants, and some continued to provoke the authorities and present themselves for martyrdom. It burned the stain of corruption and self-seeking from their religion, now shown as a faith for heroes as well as a front for politicians on the make and the take. The bravery with which heretics met their fate was inspiring; an anonymous letter to Bonner in 1556 claimed that the death of John Philpot harmed the Catholics more than his life, by encouraging Protestants to stand firm.[76] Preachers and writers were forced to counter the argument that the fortitude of heretics showed they died in a good cause. Miles Huggarde displayed the Protestants as 'stinking martyrs', brainsick cranks who deliberately courted burning, not witnesses for their truth.[77] But the persecution was not a disaster: if it did not help the Catholic cause, it did not do much to harm it. The burnings were heavily concentrated in the south-east, nearly half of them in London, Canterbury, and Colchester; elsewhere, the punishment of a few artisan trouble-makers caused little concern. Protestants were horrified, many committed Catholics approved; the rest watched curiously as the law took its course.[78]

The last years of Mary's reign were not a gruesome preparation for Protestant victory, but a continuing consolidation of Catholic strength. In 1556 Margaret Sutton of Stafford had bequeathed 'my fine kerchief to be made a corporas and given to the friars if it go up again'. In 1558 Thomas Witney, last abbot of Dieulacres, left his chalice to the abbey, and Bishop Hopton left half his library to the friars of Norwich, 'if they be restored'.[79] Bishop Griffith made generous gifts of Catholic service equipment to Rochester churches in November 1558.[80] In the parishes, restoration and repair continued, new bells were bought, and church ales produced their bucolic profits. There was, of course, nervousness about the succession, though a London Catholic told a Protestant woman, 'Though the queen fail, she that you hope for shall never come at it, for there is my lord cardinal's grace and many more between her and it.' When Sir Martin Bowes endowed an obit in February 1558, he arranged for an alternative use if the money was 'deemed to be superstitious or ungodly (as God defend)'.[81] It was only chance that made Martin Bowes seem wiser than Maurice Griffith.

✦ 14 ✦

Legislation and Visitation, 1558–1569

ON 17 July 1558 Thomas Bentham wrote from London to the leaders of the Protestant exiles on the Continent. He was minister of the underground Protestant congregation in the city, still grappling with the problems of living under a Catholic regime. He reported on the continuing persecution, and asked for advice: 'Whether the professors of the gospel may prosecute their right and cause in any papistical court?', and whether they might pay tithes to avoid prosecution for refusal. Bentham was planning for the survival of a beleaguered minority, with little realistic hope for a change in its fortunes. There had recently been raging thunderstorms in the Midlands, which he took 'to be a token of God's great displeasure for sin'. The suffering of the godly and the signs of divine wrath were clear enough to Bentham. 'And yet men, for the most part, were never more careless nor maliciously merry than they are now. God amend them!'[1] There was no sign of Catholic collapse, no suggestion that Mary's Church might be in terminal decline. He did not know, and he did not expect, that in four months the trials of the Protestants would be over and their political triumph at hand.

Historians have often regarded Mary's reign as an aberration, an inconvenient disruption of the natural process of Reformation. Henry VIII's breach with the pope and Edward VI's breach with the popish past seem to lead obviously to Protestant success in the reign of Elizabeth; Mary's Catholic regime was seeking to dam the tide of history, and it had to fail: doomed from the beginning and disintegrating at the end. The historical contribution of Mary and her bishops was only to discredit their own religion by cruelty, and dignify their opponents by giving them martyrs. The inexorable forces of modernization which had been generated under Henry and strengthened under Edward were tested under Mary, and they triumphed under Elizabeth. Or so it may seem. But we have already seen that the demand for religious change had been weak, and loyalty to old ways was not destroyed by political diktat; the Protestants had become a significant minority movement, but they had not broken through to mass support. From the perspective of 1558 (if not of 1559), it is the reign of Edward which appears an aberration, disrupting the process of Catholic restoration which had begun in 1538 and was to continue under Mary.

The Marian reconstruction of Catholicism was a success. It was not a total success, for the Protestants could not all be crushed and the indifferent could not all be made enthusiasts—at least, not in five years. But the evidence from the parishes is of considerable and continuing support for traditional services and celebrations, and Pole was leading a promising reform programme which tackled the structural problems of the English Church. The physical consequences of two political Reformations had been repaired as far as political and economic realities allowed, and expenditure on churches was high. In Mary's last year recruitment to the priesthood was better than it had been for thirty years, and the laity's giving to parish religion was probably greater than for twenty. In England, religious division may have been easing; the persecution had slackened, as determination among both heretics and hunters apparently declined. Abroad, Protestant exiles were in dispute and in despair; in 1558 their printed propaganda declined in volume and increased in hysteria, advocating overthrow of Mary before the restoration of Catholicism became irreversible.

If there were failures in Mary's reign, they were political and economic, not ecclesiastical. The disastrous harvests of 1555–7 had pushed food prices to unprecedented levels, and the war against France had brought heavy demands for men and taxes. Philip of Spain had overcome early distrust of a foreign king, but the burdens of a Habsburg war may have revived hostility. The influenza epidemic of 1558 sapped a will to fight which had never been strong, and made it hard for county officials to fill their quotas of recruits.[2] The loss of Calais in January 1558—'the heaviest tidings to London and to England that ever was heard of', Machyn thought— probably undermined the government's prestige and authority. A suspicious Spanish agent claimed that church attendance declined after Calais was taken,[3] but there is no convincing evidence that political problems had neat religious consequences. The Marian regime was not falling apart, any more than the Marian Church. Many political malcontents, supporters of the Northumberland regime and survivors of the Wyatt rebellion, had made their peace with Mary: the officer corps of the armies against France and Scotland was a roll-call of former dissidents who had compromised with reality.[4]

And then Mary made her only serious—her fatal—error: she died on 17 November 1558. Reformation monarchs timed their deaths very badly. Henry VIII died when those who most nearly shared his religious views were in disgrace, and when Protestants and *politiques* controlled Council and Court. Edward VI died when his commissioners were pillaging churches and provoking nostalgia for Catholic ways. Mary died when the political and diplomatic situations made it certain her sister would be queen, and safe for Elizabeth to restore Edwardian Protestantism. Mary had continued to hope for a child who would succeed her, and had made no other provision. In 1558 the most plausible Catholic candidate for the throne, Mary Stuart, was disqualified: as queen of Scots and wife of the French dauphin, she warred with England twice over, and Philip could not have permitted a French pawn to take the English crown. At the last, Mary Tudor reluctantly recognized Elizabeth's claim, as their father had determined: there was no realistic alternative, when the realm was at war and a disputed succession unthinkable. Elizabeth Tudor would be queen, and she would be a Protestant queen.

Elizabeth was herself a Protestant, though an undogmatic one. As a teenage princess, she had cultivated an image of demure evangelicalism; in Mary's reign she had conformed to Catholicism, but with ill-concealed distaste. Some of Mary's councillors had proposed that Elizabeth be executed for treason to preclude a Protestant succession; most would not do away with a daughter of Henry VIII, inconvenient though she might be. She had been the reversionary interest, combining the roles of leading claimant to the throne and figurehead of the opposition, focus of the aspirations of sacked Edwardian politicians, and all opponents of Catholicism at home and a Habsburg alliance abroad. They had maintained discreet contact with Elizabeth, and as Mary's health grew worse they had planned their seizure of power. Elizabeth alerted the commanders of military garrisons, ready to fight for the crown if necessary—but it was not.[5] No one tried to put a Catholic on the throne, and cripple by civil war a country already facing defeat by France. In November 1558 the Marian opposition came to power, just as the Henrician opposition had done in January 1547 and the Edwardian opposition in July 1553.

At Mary's death England was not only at war with France and Scotland, she was effectively at war with Rome, with the fanatically anti-Habsburg Pope Paul IV. In Catholic canon law, Elizabeth was the bastard daughter of an adulterous king; if she was to be a legitimate Catholic queen she would need dispensation from Rome. But there was no guarantee that Paul IV would provide such a decree. He might press for Mary Stuart, as a queen who could swing England into alliance with France; he might seek policy concessions from Elizabeth as the price of recognition. It was technically difficult and diplomatically risky for Elizabeth to be a Catholic queen; in some respects it was safer to be a Protestant queen, who could ignore the pope and fight on for Calais. If her own predilections had not been Protestant, if her most loyal allies had not been Protestant, there would still have been reasons for a Protestant pose in 1558–9. But those reasons were almost entirely foreign, and there was little in the English political climate to dictate a Protestant policy. There were, as we shall see, features which made such a policy possible, but there was nothing which made it necessary, or even wise.

When Elizabeth sought advice from Protestant supporters on how to proceed in religion, they counselled caution. The author of the 'Device for Alteration of Religion' outlined a strategy for renewed Reformation, but warned that the pope would excommunicate Elizabeth, the French would try to invade through Scotland, the Irish would rebel, and English Catholics would cause trouble.[6] The position papers offered by Richard Goodrich, Sir Nicholas Throckmorton, and Armagil Waad recognized that Elizabeth would wish to follow a Protestant policy, but set out the risks and suggested that change should be gradual: 'having respect to quiet at home, the affairs you have in hand with foreign princes, the greatness of the pope, and how dangerous it is to make alterations in religion, especially at the beginning of a prince's reign'.[7] But Elizabeth wanted to break with the past: she aimed to attract popularity by rubbishing her sister's regime, and by claiming to inaugurate a new era of recovery. She wanted to sack Mary's councillors and Mary's bishops, and replace them with ex-Edwardians; and an Edwardian government would have to be a Protestant government.

It is probably Elizabeth's known Protestantism which explains the lukewarm reception she received at her accession. In London there was bell-ringing and some street bonfires, but the celebrations were low key and it was two days before the parishes sang *Te Deum*. It was a week until the news reached Much Wenlock in Shropshire; as the vicar prepared for mass on St Catherine's day, the sheriff arrived to order him to pray for Elizabeth; he did so, and the choir sang *Te Deum*. After mass the congregation went to the market place, where the town crier proclaimed the new queen; on the Sunday after, the bailiffs organized a bonfire with bread and cheese and ale.[8] No doubt the bells were rung in most towns, with 'ale for the ringers, when the queen's grace was proclaimed', as at Leicester.[9] But at Ashburton and Worcester the emphasis was apparently on mourning for Mary rather than joy for Elizabeth. There was some image-smashing in London, and anti-Catholic plays and placards as the Protestant underground came into the open, but traditional Catholic devotion continued and there were great processions on high feasts. When Elizabeth became publicly Protestant, it was not by popular demand.

Elizabeth immediately and obviously threw in her lot with the Protestants. She appointed new Protestant councillors, led by William Cecil.[10] The first sermon of the reign at St Paul's Cross was by the queen's almoner, William Bill, a known Protestant; Richard Cox, who had ruled Edwardian Oxford in the Protestant interest, preached an anti-Catholic sermon at the opening of Parliament; and only Protestants and returned exiles preached at Court.[11] The queen marched out of mass on Christmas day, and issued a proclamation ordering the use of English prayers. There was no elevation of the host in the royal chapel, or at Westminster Abbey when Parliament began. 'Away with those torches, for we see very well',

Elizabeth told the Westminster monks as they bore candles in procession.[12] Elizabeth had embarked upon a Protestant policy, and everyone (except a few confused ambassadors) knew it. Elizabeth and her restored Edwardian government set out to restore Edwardian religion: the royal injunctions of 1547, the Book of Common Prayer of 1552, and the Articles of Religion of 1553.[13] She was going to have a Protestant Church, but the process of getting it turned out to be just as difficult as Goodrich and Waad had warned.

In February 1559 the Council introduced to the Commons a bill to revive the royal supremacy and two bills to revive the church services of Edward's reign. By 21 February these bills had been amalgamated into a single Reformation bill, probably in the hope that those who disliked the pope would stomach Protestantism to get rid of him. The bill passed through the Commons (who had obediently passed Edward's and Mary's religious legislation), apparently helped by the rush to reclaim lands confiscated for the Catholic bishops by Mary.[14] But the composite bill hit trouble in the Lords. John Jewel, just back from exile, complained that

The bishops are a great hindrance to us, for being, as you know, among the nobility and leading men in the Upper House, and having there none on our side to expose their artifices and confute their falsehoods, they reign as sole monarchs in the midst of ignorant and weak men, and easily overreach our little party, either by their numbers or by their reputation for learning.[15]

The bishops were able to appeal to a protest from Convocation, which defended the mass and papal authority, and denied the right of Crown or parliament to alter religious belief.[16]

The lay peers followed the lead of the bishops. They deleted the liturgical provisions from the bill, making it a supremacy bill only, and amended the remainder to allow Elizabeth to claim a royal supremacy if she wished, instead of granting it to her by the authority of parliament. The Elizabethan Reformation had been blocked almost before it got started. The first and the second political Reformations, in the reigns of Henry and Edward, had proceeded by instalments; the third political Reformation, in 1559, was a once-and-for-all affair, and much more objectionable—to nobles as well as Catholic bishops. It was probably at this point, confident of lay support, that the bishops considered threatening the queen with excommunication if she continued in her heretical ways—though they were dissuaded by Archbishop Heath.[17] But Elizabeth had to go on: if she took the royal supremacy she was determined to have, then the Catholic bishops would refuse to serve in her Church; unless she reformed the liturgy, Protestant ministers would not join her episcopal bench. So the power of the bishops had to be broken, and conservative peers brought to heel.

A rigged disputation on religion was staged by the Council, deliberately managed to make the bishops appear obscurantist and obdurate. Afterwards, two of the most outspoken were arrested, reducing their voting-block in the Lords, which was already depleted by death and illness. When Parliament reassembled after Easter, the Council tried Reformation once again, though now more cautiously. Two new bills were introduced into the Commons, one for the supremacy and one for a Protestant liturgy, in the hope that at least the Supremacy bill would pass both Houses. The bills were less offensive to lay conservatives than the original February ones had been. The Supremacy bill was to make the queen 'supreme governor' of the Church, leaving open the question of whether there might be some other 'supreme head', Christ or the pope. The bill got through the Commons without difficulty, but was resisted in the Lords. The bishops argued that there was much more at stake than the power of a foreign pope. If the bill passed, Heath warned, 'We must forsake and flee from the unity of Christ's Church, and by leaping out of Peter's ship hazard ourselves to be overwhelmed and drowned in the waters of schism, sects, and divisions.'[18]

But the bishops could not retain their lay support. Perhaps the change of title made a royal supremacy acceptable to the peers. Perhaps the bishops themselves made the bill more palatable by the amendments they secured, especially that only opinions contrary to Scripture and the General Councils of the early Church could be treated as heresy by royal commissioners, a provision which may have seemed to safeguard Catholic doctrine. Perhaps, too, some peers had been alienated from the bishops by the contentious issue of Church lands, and wanted a supreme governor to keep the clergy in check. Bishop Bonner in particular had made a thorough nuisance of himself by pertinacious defence of the endowments of his see against the claims of those who had been given grants under Edward.[19] Certainly there were conservative lords who voted for the Supremacy bill, but then against the Protestant Uniformity bill. The supremacy went through with only one lay dissenter, though all the bishops present and the abbot of Westminster opposed it. But with the Uniformity bill there was much more difficulty.

The Council had to make major concessions to get its bill past the Lords. The Uniformity bill imposed the 1552 Prayer Book as the prescribed worship of the English Church, but with crucial modifications. The Litany was revised to remove abuse of the pope from its prayers. The words of administration at communion were changed to allow a Catholic under-standing of the real presence of Christ; the vestments and ornaments for the service were to be as for the mass; and the minister in Protestant worship was to stand in church 'in the accustomed place', where Catholic priests had stood. Such tinkering could not satisfy the bishops. Scot of Chester argued against the whole principle of legislating on matters of religion: 'And as for the certainty of our faith, whereof the story of the Church doth speak, it is a thing of all other most necessary, and if it shall hang upon an act of parliament we have but a weak staff to lean unto.'[20] But the gains made by the conservatives were enough to satisfy some of the lay peers; the Prayer Book communion would not be a mass, but at least it would look like a mass. The Lords passed the Uniformity bill, by three votes.[21]

The bill went through by twenty-one votes to eighteen; it was opposed by all the bishops present, and by nine lay peers, two of them privy councillors. And some of the peers then pressed the queen to veto the bill. It was an embarrassing outcome. Elizabeth and her allies had achieved their majority by the intimidation and imprisonment of bishops, and by buying off the nobles; they had been helped by episcopal vacancies, unfilled since 1557 because of Pole's dispute with the pope. If two more peers had voted with the bishops, the bill would have fallen; if Watson and White had not been imprisoned, if Goldwell and Tunstall had not been excluded from Parliament, Uniformity would have been defeated. Once more, Reformation in England proceeded by political accident and tactical manœuvre. The Church of England was established by the merest whisker, a margin of three votes: a margin achieved by political chicanery, and by keeping the Church rather more Catholic than had been planned. Elizabeth and her Protestant advisers had wanted a thoroughgoing Reformation; they had to accept a half-hearted Reformation.

Elizabeth had pursued a radical policy, but was pushed in a conservative direction by the House of Lords. It is sometimes argued that she had pursued a conservative policy, but was pushed in a radical direction by the House of Commons—as J. E. Neale suggested. On the evidence, it is just possible that Elizabeth had tried to impose the 1549 Prayer Book, and that the 1552 Book was forced upon her by the Commons, but it is very unlikely. Neale read Elizabeth's later caution—a caution she learned from the clash of 1559—back to the beginning of the reign, and he exaggerated the political strength of the Protestants. Only nineteen Marian exiles were elected to Parliament, and some of them were not back in time to take their seats.[22] It is true that the constituencies sent few determined Catholic MPs to Westminster, preferring members who would not oppose the intentions of the regime; but in the Commons there was little sign of Protestant militancy (as opposed to the mercenary militance of holders and claimants of Church lands). In 1559 Elizabeth's battle was not with a Protestant House of Commons; it was with a Catholic House of Lords.

Perhaps the route does not much matter: the conclusion was the same. The parliamentary struggles of 1559 produced an ambiguous Book of Common Prayer: a liturgical compromise which allowed priests to perform the Church of England communion in Catholic regalia, standing in the Catholic position, and using words capable of Catholic interpretation. The concessions made to the Lords, and the conservative directions Elizabeth soon gave in her Injunctions, made it much easier for priests to 'counterfeit' the mass, to celebrate communion in ways barely distinguishable from the old service, with minimal risk of arrest. Though Elizabeth had (with some difficulty) achieved an instant Reformation in law, it was to be very different in the churches. There was to be no clear break with the popish past, no sudden rejection of traditional rituals. Instead, there would be local series of minor adjustments, as parish clergy conformed little by little to the pressures of authority, abandoning one by one the movements, gestures, and phrases of the mass. At the centre, the Elizabethan Reformation had been decisive, if difficult; in the parishes, it would be as fudged and fumbling as before.

Elizabeth I was a Protestant (of sorts), but she was also a politician, and she had been badly frightened by her clash with the Lords. She had begun her reign by aligning herself with the Protestants, and discovered the consequences; now she tried to conciliate moderates. When her commissioners proceeded against the Catholic bishops, depriving those who refused an oath to the royal supremacy, they began with the hard-liners: Bonner, Scot, Watson, and White. But Heath, Thirlby, and Tunstall, political bishops who had accepted the 1549 Prayer Book, were left in post for a while, apparently in the hope that they could be brought to conform (which they could not).[23] The royal Injunctions prepared in June 1559 contained significant concessions to conservatives, in modifications and additions to the model Injunctions of 1547. The most important revisions related to church images, for the new Injunctions did not declare them all idolatrous but condemned only superstitious abuse. Though altars were to be removed again, communion tables were normally to stand in the altar's place; the communion was to be with the traditional wafers (rather than ordinary bread as prescribed by the Prayer Book).[24]

If Elizabeth had hoped to please both Catholic and Protestant opinion, the royal visitation of summer 1559 showed that she could not. Six commissions were appointed, each to impose the royal supremacy, the Book of Common Prayer, and the Injunctions on a group of dioceses.[25] The active commissioners were Protestant clergy, often former exiles with no sympathy for the queen's concessions, and, as in 1547, the visitors took a radical interpretation of their instructions. They worked from a set of Articles based on those used in Cranmer's 1548 visitation, when he had enforced the destruction of all images and pictures; they followed his example.[26] Either Elizabeth was playing a very devious game, or her wishes were circumvented by her officials. In London on 24 and 25 August (when the queen was away on summer progress), the visitors organized great bonfires; churchwardens delivered their images to the fire, and 'there they were burned with great wonder'.[27] In Lincolnshire the wardens were sent back to their parishes with orders for burning. At Chichester the great rood from the cathedral was burned in the market-place; at Ashburton the wardens paid 10*d*. 'for their labour that carried the images to be burned, and their drinking'.[28]

But the work of the visitors led to division and disruption. As the Catholics had done after 1553, the Protestants now took their revenge. At Exeter those citizens most noted as devotees of images were made to throw them into the fire before the cathedral. When there was opposition to the demolition of the rood-loft at Throwley in Kent, one man was forced to be present when it was taken down 'for that he was an accuser in Queen Mary's time'.[29] At Bures in Suffolk some of the parishioners hacked down the rood-screen and destroyed the canopy of the Easter sepulchre, but in doing so they damaged some family tombs, and this gave local conservatives their chance. The culprits were indicted at Bury St Edmunds, and reported to the Privy Council. By this stage the queen was apparently worried by the response to the visitation, and Suffolk JPs were ordered to investigate; perhaps it was their report which led to the proclamation of September 1560 against the destruction of tombs and family monuments.[30] But usually, as we shall see, recalcitrance by conservatives was more evident than exuberance by radicals. Many parishes were slow to take down their altars and images, and others hid them away.

The visitation commissioners in each circuit called the clergy before them to subscribe to the supremacy, the Prayer Book, and the Injunctions. It proved a difficult task. In the province of York ninety senior clergy were summoned by name, and their responses noted in the visitors' register; 21 appeared and subscribed, 16 sent proxy representatives, 36 appeared and declined to subscribe, and 17 failed to turn up. Only 23 per cent endorsed the new arrangements; 40 per cent refused outright and were deprived. We know very much less about the parish clergy of the north: 312 of them subscribed, but there was no record of refusers or absentees.[31] There were roughly 1,200 parishes in the province, many with subsidiary chapels; even after the influenza epidemic of 1558, there would have been at least a thousand parish priests and assistants, so it seems that only a third subscribed in 1559. Some priests subscribed later, but certainly not all. In 1563 the bishop of Chester summoned his clergy to subscribe, but fewer than 60 per cent did so; the rest refused, or were specifically excused by the bishop.[32] Few of the northern clergy were dismissed from their posts for disobedience, but many evaded formal submission.

Our information for the province of Canterbury is scanty. We have the names of 1,804 clergy from six dioceses who subscribed in 1559, but again we do not know how many ought to have done so. There were about 3,500 benefices in these dioceses, but some were small and held in plurality; it seems likely that two-thirds of the southern clergy subscribed at the visitation, and that others conformed later.[33] The attractions of subscription were obvious and, with benefices vacant, increasing. When the London clergy were called before the visitation commissioners, Thomas Darbyshire and John Kennall met outside St Paul's; Kennall could hardly believe that Darbyshire would refuse to swear: 'I think you are not so very a fool as to refuse to subscribe, and thereby lose so good livings as you have.'[34] Darbyshire declined the oath, lost his benefices, and went off to Rome; Kennall became archdeacon of Oxford, and a less than diligent enforcer of the rules he had accepted. There were, of course, many more Kennalls than Darbyshires. We cannot be sure how many priests would not conform; probably about 300 lost their benefices in the first two years of the reign, perhaps 5 per cent of incumbents. An unknown (but probably larger) number of curates and assistants, with lesser vested interests, quietly disappeared, becoming domestic chaplains, recusant priests, schoolmasters, or secular workers.[35]

Elizabeth seems to have been outraged by the results of the visitation, both by the provocative iconoclasm of the Protestants and the surly disobedience of conservatives. She resolved to enforce the concessions on images that she had made in the Injunctions and that the visitors had ignored. In October 1559 she ordered that a crucifix and candlesticks be set on the communion table of the Chapel Royal, and decided later that roods should be restored in parish churches. She was to find it easier to prescribe for her own chapel than for the churches of her realm. The new Protestant bishops whom Elizabeth had nominated were horrified by what they saw as her revival of idolatry. Early in 1560 some of them sent a protest to the queen, declaring that all images were specifically prohibited by the second Commandment; a few, though, were willing to allow images in their churches if Elizabeth insisted, provided there was no veneration. In February 1560 the Council staged a disputation among the bishops, and Grindal, Jewel, Sandys, and perhaps others threatened to resign if crucifixes were imposed. The queen backed down; having lost a Catholic episcopate, she could hardly risk losing a Protestant one as well![36]

There was a clear, though probably unspoken, compromise. The queen kept her crucifix, as a hint to conservatives that she was really one of them. Henry Machyn was pleased to see 'the cross, and two candles burning, and the tables standing altar-wise' in her chapel.[37] But the bishops did not have to suffer crosses and roods in their churches, and Elizabeth agreed to another phase of official iconoclasm. In 1560 Grindal was allowed to enforce demolition of rood-lofts in London churches, and in October 1561 she herself ordered all lofts to be taken down, at least to the level of the beam.[38] But these measures produced a further round of local dissension. At Uttoxeter there was much squabbling over the pulling down of the rood-loft and the remaining images, and a churchwarden was killed in a fight with an objector. At Cornwood in the south-west parishioners refused to permit removal of their loft in 1562, until they were excommunicated, and then they obeyed only after a debate in church.[39] There was some reluctance to undertake costly work, lest ecclesiastical policy be reversed once again. When one of the wardens was about to remove the loft of an east Kent church, he was warned, 'Let him take heed that his authority be good before it be pulled down, for we know what we have had but we know not what we shall have.'[40]

Parishioners were often slow to obey the orders of the 1559 commissioners and their own bishops. Bentham of Lichfield complained of Shropshire in October 1560 that 'the most part of churches within this part of my diocese hath not only yet their altars standing but also their images reserved and conveyed away, contrary to the queen's majesty's Injunctions, hoping and looking for a new day'.[41] Shropshire was worse than average, but perhaps not by much. The surviving churchwardens' accounts suggest that two-thirds of parishes took down their altars in 1559 as ordered, and that half had removed their images by the end of 1560. Few rood-lofts were demolished before the instruction of 1561, but by the end of 1562 two-thirds of lofts had been tackled. Other churches conformed with great reluctance. At Morebath the wardens removed two side altars in 1559, but kept their high altar and in 1561 simply covered it with a board as a makeshift communion table. At St Mary's in Chester, Stoke Charity in Hampshire, and probably Long Melford in Suffolk the altars were not taken down until 1562, and at Thame they survived until 1564. The last altar stone at Ludlow was removed in 1576, and at Stanford in the Vale in 1587.

Images and pictures caused more trouble than altars. The High Commission at York issued a string of orders for the removal and burning of images, for seven parishes in 1562, five in 1564, two in 1565, and more thereafter.[42] At Masham in north Yorkshire, there were images in church and more hidden in private houses in 1571; when they were burned by order of the archbishop, Leonard Atkinson used his pikestaff to try to stop the destruction and Edward Ripley threatened the curate with his knife.[43] At Great St Mary's in Cambridge, the stained glass pictures of saints were painted over in 1566, and images were sold in 1567. In 1568 the vicar of St Margaret's Leicester 'with consent of his loving parishioners did extirp and pull down all monuments of superstition'[44]—a formula which suggests dispute! At St Martin's Leicester the images on the pulpit were defaced in 1566, a cross was demolished in 1569, and the last images lost their heads in 1570. Pictures in the windows at Bishop's Stortford were defaced in 1573, and in 1575, after the arrival of a new Protestant rector, Minchinhampton (Gloucestershire) paid 6s. 8d. 'for pulling down, destroying, and throwing out of the church sundry superstitious things tending to the maintenance of idolatry'.[45]

There were long tussles between officials and wardens over rood-lofts in churches; parishes tried minimum compliance, since removal was an expensive business, but they were pushed on by bishops and archdeacons. Few lofts were taken down from northern churches until after 1570, even in cathedral cities; the loft of St Martin's Coney Street in York went down in January 1571. At his primary visitation of York diocese in the summer of that year, Grindal supervised a blitz upon rood-lofts, but there was resistance at Huddersfield and Masham. The troublesome Leonard Atkinson declared that 'he trusted to see them that plucked down the roodloft be as glad to set them up again', and the archbishop had no business 'to cause any rood loft to be pulled down there'.[46] At a visitation of Peterborough diocese in 1574, a score of churches were reported to have rood-lofts standing.[47] Even at Lambeth the rood-loft survived until 1570, when the bishop of Winchester ordered it down; the lofts at Stanford and St Andrew's Canterbury remained till 1571, and those at Rayleigh and St Martin's Oxford till 1574. Ashburton's rood-loft was dismantled in four stages, and the job was not completed until 1579.

In March and April 1566 commissioners in Lincolnshire examined the wardens of 152 churches on their compliance with the Articles and Injunctions of 1559. The returns are very detailed. Of the parishes which responded to each of the questions, 39 per cent claimed to have removed their altars in 1559–60, and 58 per cent their images; but 30 per cent admitted they had only just taken down altars, and 13 per cent their images, in response to the bishop's visitation in 1565 and warnings from the commission in 1566. Merely a quarter of the parishes had dismantled rood-lofts by the end of 1561, and 29 per cent did so only under pressure, in 1565–6. On vestments and mass equipment, the position was even worse: the order to destroy them had been obeyed by a quarter of parishes in 1559–60, and half did so only in 1565–6. Out of the 152 churches, sixty had only recently made a serious effort to comply with the rules, and twenty-five had not yet completed the process. Belton-in-Axholme had only just taken down its images, and the altars were still standing. The church-wardens of Kelby and Londonthorpe removed their images the day before they appeared before the commissioners, and half a dozen parishes had destroyed mass books and equipment in the previous week.[48]

Throughout the 1560s the bishops pressurized the parishes, and slowly got their way. Archbishop Parker's metropolitan visitors enforced the demolition of altars in Kent and Staffordshire in 1560. In August 1564 the wardens of twenty Lancashire parishes were summoned before the Ecclesiastical Commission and ordered to ensure conformity by Michael-mas, when the rural deans would report on progress. The archdeacon of Essex dealt with three churches which had not removed rood-lofts and two which had altars in 1565, but 135 other parishes claimed to be in order.[49] In 1567 the archbishop of York's officers proceeded against seventeen Holderness parishes with roods or other images, and by 1569 virtually all churches in the dioceses of Canterbury and Norwich had conformed. There was more difficulty in Chichester dioceses, where in 1569 the metropolitan visitation found that 'in some places the roodlofts still stand', and often parishioners had drawn crosses on church walls in place of roods. There was general reluctance to change chalices for communion cups, with parishes 'looking for to have mass again', and 'they have yet in the diocese many images hidden up and other popish ornaments, ready to set up the mass again'.[50]

Whether from Catholic loyalty or common prudence, parishes held on to mass equipment for as long as they could, or as long as there seemed any chance it might be needed. Some traded in Catholic chalices for Protestant communion cups early in the reign, such as Betrysden in Kent in 1561 and St Andrew's Canterbury in 1562, perhaps in response to pressure from the archbishop. There were campaigns to enforce such exchanges in the archdeaconry of Essex in 1564, and in the dioceses of Winchester and Norwich in 1567; at least 275 Norfolk churches bought new communion cups in 1567–8. But many parishes had to be harried into obedience, and at the 1569 visitation of Norfolk thirty-nine were presented for their failure to comply fully.[51] Many churches gave up their chalices only after 1570, when Elizabeth had been on the throne for a dozen years. The change came in 1571 at Bramley in Hampshire, Sherborne in Dorset, St Ewen's in Bristol, St Michael in Bedwardine, Worcester, and St Martin's in York. In Somerset and Wiltshire few churches had converted from chalices to cups before they were forced by their bishops, in 1572 and 1576 respectively, and around Salisbury many parishes held on to their medieval plate.[52]

The surviving churchwardens' accounts suggest that about half of the parishes kept their vestments and mass utensils for at least a decade. In 1571 the wardens of Crosthwaite in Cumberland were ordered to dispose of chalices, candlesticks, pyxes, censers, banners, vestments, 'and all other monuments of popery, superstition, and idolatry remaining within the said parish'.[53] Others kept their options open for even longer: Bramley and Long Melford sold their Catholic service equipment in 1575, St Martin's Oxford in 1577, Sherborne in 1581, and Stanford in the Vale in 1585. Often equipment had been hidden away in private houses, sometimes on behalf of the parish, sometimes by individual initiative. At Morebath in Devon, for example, the mass book was entrusted to Thomas Borrage in 1560, and the chasuble to Edward Rumbelow. At Masham in north Yorkshire the old service gear was stored for the parish by nine local families in case of future need. Finally, in 1595, the vestry meeting decided to sell up; five sets of vestments, two copes, two sanctus bells, and various altar cloths were disposed of. And there the Reformation ended!

It had taken the bishops ten years and more to clean up the churches, and it was just as difficult to ensure proper Protestant teaching and worship.

Almost all early Elizabethan parish clergy had originally been recruited as Catholic priests, and, even by 1576, 37 per cent of clergy in three Lincoln archdeaconries were men ordained before 1559. The Protestant Anthony Gilbey complained they were 'old monks and friars and old popish priests, notorious idolators, openly perjured persons, halting hypocrites, manifest apostates'.[54] Some made no secret of their true loyalties. In 1574 the rector of Siddington St Mary in Gloucestershire declared that 'he had said mass and did trust to live to say mass again', and in 1575 the curate of Guisburn in Yorkshire 'did say that the pope was and is head of the Church'.[55] In 1586 there were still eighteen former Catholic priests holding benefices in Warwickshire, seven of them active conservatives; they included the rector of Baddesley, 'unsound in religion and a secret persuader of the people to popery, one that prayeth for the dead, a blasphemer of the name of God, vicious and licentious of life, a companion at all games, an alehouse-haunter'.[56]

These relics from the popish past used Elizabeth's liturgical concessions to the full, and many kept as closely as they could to the old ways. They might read the Prayer Book services quietly and quickly to make them sound like the Latin mass, as at Holy Trinity Chester in 1562 and Barmbrough in Yorkshire in 1567;[57] or add Latin prayers or anthems to the English service, as at Driffield in Yorkshire in 1562 and Huyton in Lancashire in 1564;[58] or omit objectionable parts of the Prayer Book service, as at Eastrington, Yorkshire in 1567;[59] or recite services facing east like mass priests, as at Stock in Essex in 1564 and Leyton near London in 1572.[60] Some of them said mass in private, and consecrated hosts which they later distributed at communion services, as at Ripon in 1567 and Preston in Lancashire in 1574.[61] At Whalley (Lancashire) in 1575 the vicar contrasted his hosts with communion bread, 'saying in them was salvation, but in the other there was nothing worthy acceptance'. His parishioners were told that they should take the Protestant communion

but as common bread and wine as they may take it at home or elsewhere, for that it is so, far differing from the word of God; and that this Church of England is a defiled and spotted Church, and that no man may come to it lawfully in time of divine service except he at his coming in heart exempt himself from this service and all that is partaker of it, and make his prayer by himself according to the doctrine of the pope of Rome.[62]

Protestant bishops and ministers thought that such sympathies were widespread among the old clergy, and that popish doctrine and popish ritual were offered in many churches. But there was little they could do about it. Sympathetic parishioners concealed breaches of Protestant rules, and deviant priests went unreported for years. Even when offenders were presented, they were rarely removed from their posts, for there was a serious shortage of clergy. The influenza epidemic of 1558, the deprivations and resignations of 1559, and a continuing wastage as discontented priests abandoned their cures left benefices vacant and churches unserved. There had been 172 priests working in south Lancashire in 1554, but by 1563 there were only ninety-eight; just fifty-one of the 1554 men were still serving in 1563, though only twenty-one of the rest are known to have died.[63] The diocese of Ely had resident ministers for only one-third of its churches in 1561; a fifth of benefices were vacant, and another third were held by absentees. In 1563 a third of Suffolk benefices had no incumbent, and in 1564 there were complaints from Kent of 'the great scarcity of priests and ministers'.[64]

The new bishops plugged the gaps as best they could. They began by dropping qualifications for ordination, and taking as many recruits as they could find. Edmund Grindal was installed as bishop of London on 23 December 1559, and he held his first ordination on the 28th; in the next seven months he ordained 110 priests. But in August 1560 Archbishop Parker advised his suffragans 'hereafter to be very circumspect in admitting any to the ministry'. He recognized that 'occasioned by the great want of ministers, we and you both, for tolerable supply thereof, have admitted unto the ministry sundry artificers and others, not traded and brought up in learning'. But the new men 'are very offensive unto the people, yea and to the wise of this realm are thought to do great deal more hurt than good, the gospel there sustaining slander'.[65] Probably most bishops tightened standards; Grindal ordained only twenty-three in the next four months. But between 1562 and 1569 Downham of Chester ordained 176 men, in an attempt to fill vacancies; none were graduates, and fifty-six were ordained despite apparent inadequacies. Bentham of Lichfield probably did the same, for Lord Burghley claimed that he had ordained indiscriminately.[66] But shortages remained.

In an effort to ensure some services for all parishes, the bishops allowed a large increase in pluralism, that is, clerics holding more than one benefice each. In Norfolk in 1561, more than half the incumbents were pluralists, though this was an extreme case and a quarter or a third was more common. In Gloucestershire the sharing of ministers between parishes was widespread in 1563. At Lassington the parish had services only once a quarter, for their rector was also curate of Maisemore. At Oldbury the rector was absentee, and the curate also served Boxwell and Leighterton, while living at Tetbury. Some churches depended on successions of wandering ministers. The churchwardens of Stroud admitted their register was in disarray 'by the reason of the lack and change of curates, but it shall be better amended if we may have our curate to continue with us'. At Wickwar the wardens complained, 'We are not sure now of any minister, and if we have such as we have had commonly heretofore they will do us more harm than good, for some of them were liars, some drunkards and blasphemers, some borrowers of horse and money and ride away with all.'[67]

With clerical resources thinly stretched and many priests demoralized and confused by change, there was much neglect in the parishes. Pastoral flaws could always be found, but now they were widespread. A thorough visitation of fifty-six parishes in Wiltshire in 1565 found thirty churches without the required service books and Bibles, and twenty-one with defects in fabric. There was no preaching at twenty-five of the churches; often there had been none for four or five years, and at Reniton 'no sermons these twenty years'. Only thirty-one churches had their own resident minister, and the rest shared incumbents or curates, and sometimes both. The rector of Barford held four benefices and was usually away, 'the service not done in due time and most commonly no service at all'. At Whiteparish 'the vicar serveth two cures, the service not in due time, the vicarage in decay, but one communion this twelvemonth, the vicar teacheth not the catechism'. At Figheldean 'the curate serveth two cures, and cannot serve them duly'. The rector of Winterbourne Earls was absent, there was 'no service in due time, the curate serveth three parishes', and there was no catechizing.[68] It was a sorry situation, but it was not unusual.

The visitors of Chichester diocese in 1569 found only seventeen preachers for all Sussex: 'many churches there have no sermons, not one in seven years, and some not one in twelve years'. The consequences were predictable: 'Except it be about Lewes and a little in Chichester, the whole diocese is very blind and superstitious for want of teaching.'[69] There was improvement, but not very much, thereafter. In west Sussex in 1571, many incumbents were absent, and several parishes were served by negligent curates. At Bosham the curate said Sunday services at inconvenient times, missed weekday services, and failed to read the *Homilies* to his congregation; there was only one sermon a year. The curate of Cocking did not catechize or read the Injunctions, and there were no sermons. At Littlehampton 'the parish hath been very ill served by the curate': there had been no catechism classes and no sermons, and some of the books were lacking. There were defects in the fabric of a third of the churches, a quarter had no sermons, and a fifth did not have the prescribed books.[70] It is hard to see how Protestantism could have made much progress in Elizabethan England. Perhaps it did not—at least, not yet.

✥ 15 ✥

From Resentment to Recusancy

In July 1578 the churchwardens of Weaverham in Cheshire compiled their report for the archbishop of York's visitation. We do not know what they concealed; what they admitted was a catalogue of disobedience and omission. The church did not have the Book of Common Prayer for services, or a Bible, or a copy of the *Homilies*; there was no cloth for the communion table, and no chest for the parish register. An altar in the church had not been demolished, and crosses still stood in the churchyard. The parishioners would not join the Rogationtide perambulations, or send their children to catechism classes; some went to alehouses instead of church, and were not fined for absence; those who did attend chattered through the services. None would take communion three times a year, or receive ordinary bread, as prescribed in the Prayer Book; communicants insisted on the traditional wafers. On All Hallows' eve the bells tolled for souls departed, and 'Jane, an old nun, is an evil woman and teacheth false doctrine'.[1] After almost two decades, the ecclesiastical provisions of 1559 were still comprehensively ignored in this mid-Cheshire parish: the third political Reformation had apparently failed.

But not entirely. The Marian vicar, William Holcroft, had been deprived of the benefice by the York High Commission in November 1571; after the brief tenure of Francis Fletcher, Edward Shallcross served from 1575 to 1614 and, despite personal failings, brought Weaverham to conformity.[2] There the political Reformation did not fail; it succeeded very slowly. Old habits and attitudes survived for a time in the worship of the parish church, but they were hard to sustain against an unsympathetic vicar. The Weaverham conservatives eventually succumbed to pressure from the diocesan administration at Chester, and failed to develop an organized Catholic community; they were presented for petty infringements, but not for recusancy, determined refusal to attend the Church of England. It was different in Malpas, only twenty miles away, where in the 1560s John Maddocks had resigned as a schoolmaster to become an influential recusant priest. In 1582 a congregation of two dozen heard a secret mass at the house of Roger Yardley. One priest refused absolution to those who had attended the parish church; another preached on the need for total fidelity 'unto the mass and the ancient Catholic faith'. Malpas produced one-sixth of known Elizabethan Cheshire recusants, Weaverham none.[3]

The accession of Queen Elizabeth and the political struggles of 1559 had given Protestants the leadership of the Church of England, but not control of the parishes, where Catholic priests and traditionalist laity were in large majorities. Thereafter, the bishops and officials of the Church of England had long struggles to impose the Prayer Book and Injunctions on the parishes. It took ten years in most places, more than twenty in Weaverham, over thirty at Masham in north Yorkshire; but finally it was achieved, especially as the old Catholic-trained clergy died and were replaced by new Protestant-educated ministers. For a while, it was possible to sustain an attenuated Catholicism within the parish framework, by counterfeiting the mass, teaching the seven sacraments, preserving images of saints, reciting the rosary, observing feasts, fasts, and customs: by what some historians have called 'survivalism'.[4] But as times changed and generations passed, as memories faded and rosaries were lost, as new ministers cajoled and bishops imposed penances, survivalist Catholicism was diluted by conformity, until, as at Weaverham after 1578, it disappeared completely.

But Catholicism was not destined for inevitable oblivion in 1559. Elizabeth might be persuaded by argument to accept the truth of Catholic theology, the wisdom of Catholic social thought, or the need for Catholic political support, as some of the Marian bishops had believed in 1559, and exiled Catholic writers continued to hope. Elizabeth might die soon (as she almost did in 1562), and be succeeded by a Catholic, as Edward had been succeeded by Mary. Elizabeth might be overthrown by rebellion, and replaced by a Catholic, as Jane Grey had been toppled by Mary. Elizabeth might be pressed by political reality to move in a more Catholic direction, as Henry VIII had been in 1538. Elizabeth might marry a Catholic prince (as she almost did in 1579), and restore or tolerate her husband's religion. And if national policy did not change, if the Church of England remained Protestant and Catholicism remained proscribed, it was not necessary for Catholics to follow the Weaverham way; there was the alternative Malpas model, the organization of a separated underground Church, with its own priests offering sacraments to their own congregations.

In 1559, and for long after, there were few who thought this sectarian solution would be needed; instead, Catholicism would be restored. There were many rumours that the Latin mass would soon be back, in Coventry in 1560, London in 1561, Cumbria in 1562, Lancashire in 1565, and across the north in 1568.[5] In 1565 the provost of King's College Cambridge refused to destroy vestments and mass books, warning 'That which hath been may be again', and in 1569 priests in Sussex were keeping their old chalices, 'looking for to have mass again'. In 1570 the church at Edmonton (Middlesex) was bequeathed gold candlesticks 'should the mass ever be said there again'.[6] A York priest in 1568 'trusted to see the day when he shall have twenty of the heretics' heads that now be in authority under his girdle'; in 1569 Hampshire Catholics were saying, 'I trust ere it be long the queen's majesty herself shall not choose but to alter this religion, and that with her own hands.'[7] There were new rumours of change about 1580, which led a Warwickshire preacher to shave off his beard ready to be a clean-faced priest. At Pateley Bridge in Yorkshire in 1582, the trader Christopher Smith was willing 'to be paid when mass shall be said by lawful authority'[8]—confidence indeed!

So it is not surprising that most Catholics behaved as they, or their parents, had done in the reign of Edward, and bent with the times pending better ones. James Brighouse, a Yorkshire gentleman, married a Protestant and kept his beliefs to himself, until on his deathbed he declared he was a Catholic: 'for worldly respects he had followed the queen in her religion, which was damnable heresy to his utter damnation. "Marvel not", saith he, "that I speak this plain, for I am going to a place where she is nothing feared." '[9] No doubt many more lived as Brighouse had, and were Catholic only in silent preference. Others were less circumspect, and participated when possible in Catholic worship. Many priests who conformed (more or less) to Prayer Book requirements also offered under-the-counter Catholicism to parishioners. Through the 1560s the vicar of Beoley (Worcestershire) said mass in the Lady Chapel as well as communion in the chancel, and three chaplains ran a mass-centre in the 'Lady loft' of Ripon church.[10] The rector of Stuston in Suffolk was still offering mass in his parlour in 1584, and in 1586 the vicar of Nidd (Yorkshire) was performing the English communion like a mass and celebrating the Latin mass too.[11]

In 1559 the Catholic leadership had been more decisive than these liturgical hermaphrodites: then, all but one of the bishops, and high proportions of deans, archdeacons, cathedral canons, and distinguished academics, resigned, or refused the supremacy oath and were deprived. About a hundred fellows of Oxford colleges lost their posts.[12] This response tells us something about the new firmness of Marian churchmen, and perhaps more about the Elizabethan settlement of religion. Under Henry and Edward, changes had been piecemeal and more acceptable; in 1559 there was a wholesale political Reformation, and the senior Catholic clergy rejected it. The deprived bishops were sent to prison or household detention; many of the academics went to exile in Catholic Europe, especially at Rome or Louvain. From Oxford heads of houses and professors such as Francis Babington, Thomas Harding, Henry Henshaw, Morgan Phillips ('Morgan the sophister', from his skill in disputation), and Richard Smith fled abroad, as did several batches of New College fellows. There were fewer exiles from Cambridge, but they included major figures such as Thomas Bailey, George Bullock, and William Soane.

The Louvainists regarded themselves as a Church government in exile. They bombarded their co-religionists at home with advice and instruction, Elizabeth and her councillors with threats and promises, and English Protestants with great tomes of theological controversy. In 1564–8, the exiles published forty-six Catholic books in English. Thomas Harding (formerly Oxford's professor of Greek) threw himself into an interminable literary wrangle with Bishop Jewel, in which each pillaged early Christian history to prove that his was the true faith. Thomas Dorman, John Rastell, Nicholas Sander, and Thomas Stapleton (recently all fellows of New College) joined in the attack on Jewel.[13] In *A Fortress of the Faith* and several other works, Thomas Stapleton sought to show the continuity of Catholic doctrine and the errors of new-fangled Protestantism. Above all, the academic exiles waited for God: for him to change Elizabeth's heart or strike her down. But by 1568 it seemed the wait might be a long one. In that year, Stapleton gave up writing only for an English audience, Harding advised that devotional books were now needed to keep souls from heresy and sin,[14] and William Allen took the lead in founding an exile college.

Allen had resigned as principal of St Mary's Hall Oxford, and after some indecisive shuttling between England and the Continent had settled with the exiled academics at Louvain. In 1568 he was persuaded to move to Douai, and with Phillips and others he established an English college there. The immediate aims were to provide a centre of English Catholic scholarship, and to recruit young Englishmen who wanted a Catholic education; the long-term goal was to supply a new leadership for the English Catholic Church, 'For we thought it would be an excellent thing to have men of learning always ready outside the realm to restore religion when the proper moment should arrive, although it seemed hopeless to attempt anything while the heretics were masters there.'[15] The new college had constant financial difficulties, but it was an instant educational success: flocks of students were attracted from England, and by 1576 there were 236 in Douai. Many of them came from the English universities, especially Oxford, which suffered a serious haemorrhage of talented young dons in 1568–74, as well as a constant loss of students.[16]

The leading churchmen who refused to acknowledge Elizabeth's royal supremacy had not all gone into exile. Some quietly became private chaplains to Catholic nobles and gentlemen; for twenty years Alban Langdale, formerly archdeacon of Chichester, said secret masses for Lord Montague in Sussex.[17] Others made rather a nuisance of themselves. John Ramridge (ex-archdeacon of Derby) and Anthony Draycott (ex-archdeacon of Huntingdon) were soon saying masses for East Anglian gentry and plotting to send an English delegation to the pope's Council of Trent.[18] Robert Purseglove, formerly suffragan of Hull, was 'stiff in papistry and of estimation in the country' in south Yorkshire in 1562; in 1566 he was allowed to move to Tideswell in Derbyshire, on condition that he did not preach or teach 'to the disturbance or hindrance of the queen's majesty's laws concerning religion'—but the local vicar became a recusant priest, and the school Purseglove founded was soon sending recruits to Douai.[19] David Poole, deprived bishop of Peterborough, lived inoffensively near London for a time, but by 1564 he was in Staffordshire and acting as spiritual adviser to Catholic-minded priests; he heard their confessions and absolved them from schism.[20]

Several senior clergy concentrated on stiffening the resolve of Catholics and organizing provision of the sacraments. Richard Marshall resigned the deanery of Christ Church Oxford in 1559, and travelled around Yorkshire persuading his friends among the gentry to retain their faith; he was caught and imprisoned, but freed after signing an acceptance of the Thirty-nine Articles in 1563. By 1568 he was the leading figure in an underground circle of recusant priests in south Lancashire, celebrating mass and encouraging the gentry to reject the Church of England.[21] Working with him was the militant John Murren, formerly a canon of St Paul's and Bishop Bonner's chaplain; he had preached in defence of Catholicism in London in 1559, before fleeing to the north-west; in 1562 he circulated an anti-Protestant tract in Chester, and then served as a roving recusant priest in Cheshire and Lancashire until his arrest in 1583.[22] In 1568 Marshall's cell also included William Smith, deprived fellow of Corpus Christi College Oxford, and John Ashbrooke, lately a fellow of Eton, as well as a clutch of priests who had been local parish clergy in Mary's time.[23]

In Yorkshire, the earliest underground leaders included Thomas Robertson, ex-dean of Durham and 'thought to do much hurt' in 1562; William Carter (former archdeacon of Northumberland) 'to be considered' in 1562, and on the run in 1570 before his flight to Douai; and Thomas Sidgewick, deprived Cambridge professor of Divinity, and busy around Richmond until he was gaoled in 1570.[24] In Herefordshire there was an instant cadre of a dozen priests, supported by local gentlemen, city councillors, and even canons of the cathedral. William Ely had been president of St John's College Oxford, but was busy in Herefordshire by 1561; he was a constant troublemaker until his arrest in 1605. Thomas Arden had been deprived of prebends at Hereford and Worcester, and Gregory Bassett, once a friar and Cambridge scholar, had lost benefices in Devon. John Blaxton had been vicar-general of Exeter diocese and Walter Mugge a prebendary; in 1561 they were banned from Exeter and ordered away to Hereford, where they were welcomed by a torchlight procession and a feast. In 1564 Bishop Scory complained that 'these go from one gentleman's house to another, where they know to be welcome', in 1565 that they were received 'as if they are God's angels'.[25]

There were other early signs of an alternative Church, staffed by recusant priests who rejected the official one. Peterborough diocese in 1564 had 'straggling doctors and priests' who did 'much hurt secretly and in corners': one of the 'doctors' was William Tresham, removed as vice-chancellor of Oxford and imprisoned for a time. In 1564 there were 'romish sectaries' in Lincoln diocese, and 'popish and perverse priests' in Worcestershire, 'kept in gentlemen's houses and had in great estimation with the people'.[26] In Sussex at least four recusant priests were working in 1569, who 'are fostered in gentlemen's houses, and run between Sussex and Hampshire, and are hinderers of true religion'; one was Stephen Hopkins, formerly vice-provost of Eton and chaplain to Cardinal Pole. Some recusant clergy were only peripatetic pastors to the gentry, but many took on wider responsibilities and reports complained of their stock among 'the people'. In the deanery of Blackburn (Lancashire) seven former curates were by 1571 providing masses for their communities, as they had done before in their churches, and in the whole county there were then at least thirty-eight (and probably fifty) recusant priests.[27]

Ten years after its official proscription, English Catholicism was a curious and confused spectrum of attitudes and behaviour. At its untainted clerical extreme, the academic exiles in Douai, Louvain, and Rome were Catholics among Catholics, able to write, teach, and take the sacraments. At home among the heretics, the rest were compromised in some way. The imprisoned prelates had preserved themselves from schism, but lost the opportunity for Catholic worship and fellowship. Many middle-rank clergy and parish priests had refused the supremacy oath; some were now private chaplains, protected by the greatness of their patrons; some were hunted recusant priests, flitting between manor houses; a few served isolated communities, rarely troubled by authority; but all had to be cautious, and could not offend the laymen upon whom they depended. Most parish incumbents had served on, evading the oath if they could and taking it when they must; some said mass in secret, some counterfeited it in church; some taught Catholic doctrine, some avoided teaching novelties; no doubt some simply sighed for better days. But between them they held the line against heresy.

Among the laity a few had been firm recusants from the start: Thomas Brereton in Lancashire, John Middlemore in Worcestershire, and William Myles in Hampshire, who admitted in 1598 that 'in Queen Mary's time he went to church, and not since'.[28] But almost all were 'church papists' who conformed sometimes. Lord Montague went to church, and had mass at home with his priest; Lady Mounteagle and the duchess of Norfolk each had two domestic chaplains, one for the Prayer Book service and one for the mass.[29] Many who attended church refused the communion; 248 were cited in the diocese of Winchester between 1561 and 1569. Some went to church, and sat where they could not hear (as did James Eton), or read from Our

Lady's Psalter (like Sir Thomas Cornwallis), or even sang Latin psalms to disturb the minister (as did Nicholas Gerard).[30] And at the frail end of the spectrum stood James Brighouse, whose Catholicism was no more than a secret preference until on his deathbed he confessed to it. So there were organized groups of Catholics, with their own priests and mass-centres; there were parish communities who conceded as little as they dared to the heretical times; and there were embattled souls who held to what they could remember of a receding faith.

The strengths and weaknesses of this inchoate Catholicism were displayed in the 1569 revolt of the northern earls.[31] The earls' decision to revolt probably owed little to religion, though Westmorland was certainly a conservative and Northumberland had been absolved from schism by his chaplain. They had been rejected for office and ignored for reward by a suspicious queen, and they turned to indecisive plotting with their gentry allies. But when their hands were forced by the government's attempts to arrest them, it was the Catholic cause which raised much of their support. On 14 November, with about seventy followers, the earls entered Durham cathedral, tore up the Protestant books, and ordered a cessation of Prayer Book services. Next day they issued a proclamation seeking wider support 'as your duty towards God doth bind you, for the setting forth of his true and Catholic religion', and it worked.[32] It is usually thought that the five or six thousand Durham and Yorkshire men who joined the rebel army were drawn from the tenants of the earls and other leaders; but fewer than a fifth of the force came from tenants and their families. At least 80 per cent joined the rising for reasons of their own, and religious loyalty was one of the strongest.[33]

The royal commanders blamed the popularity of the earls' cause on their religious slogans. Sir Ralph Sadler thought that 'all Cleveland, Allertonshire, Richmondshire, and the Bishopric are all wholly gone unto them, such is their affection to the cause of religion'.[34] We know that during the rising Protestant service books were destroyed in about seventy churches in Yorkshire and at least eight in Durham; the mass was restored in at least six churches in Yorkshire and nine in Durham. Some of this was done on the orders of the earls, but not all. At Sedgefield a parish meeting decided to reinstate the altar and holy water stoup; thirty people dragged the stone back into the church, and Richard Hartburn said mass.[35] Great crowds attended the masses at Durham cathedral, and when on 4 December William Holmes absolved the congregation from schism 'in the name of Christ and Bishop Pius of Rome', almost all knelt to be reconciled.[36] After the rebellion, more than fifty priests and about 220 laypeople were called before the Church courts at York or Durham for their involvement in Catholic activity. It had been an impressive demonstration of religious enthusiasm.

But the appeal of Catholicism was not enough to bring the rebels success. The earls had struck south with a fast-moving force, probably intending to free the captive Mary Queen of Scots from Tutbury. When they reached Leeds, however, they turned back, perhaps because they heard that Mary was being moved to Coventry, which they could not storm with the men they had brought. So they returned to their bases, with the intention of holding out until help arrived; they seized Hartlepool, where Spanish troops might land, and reduced the royal fortress of Barnard Castle. The earls wrote for aid from northern Catholic nobles, but none came. The rebellion did not spread, whatever sympathy others had for its cause: areas of notable resistance to Elizabethan religion—Holderness and Howden in Yorkshire, West Derby and Amounderness in Lancashire—did not join. There were efforts to restore Catholicism only in the districts protected by the rebels, and relatively few took risks for religion. Royal commanders had little difficulty in recruiting an army in the Midlands, and they were not resisted as they marched north. On 20 December the earls and their close allies fled into Scotland, leaving their followers to pay with lives and fines.

The revolt was the only significant Elizabethan attempt to overthrow Protestant religion, and it was botched. The earls' liaison with their allies at Court was inadequate, and they were caught off-guard when forced to rebel. They were unable to snatch Mary Stuart as a legitimating figurehead, and their plea for papal sanction was too late to be useful. They did not call out their own tenants, or appeal for a general rising of Catholics. It was far from clear that their rebellion was or could be made a realistic opportunity to reverse Reformation. It came after a decade of adjustment to living with heresy, and well before conditions for Catholics were desperate. There was a strong conviction that God would intervene in time, without any need for treason. Even among the exiles there were as yet few committed to violent action. So Protestantism was saved by conservative loyalism; even the earls and their friends debated whether it was moral to rise against their queen, and the levies for the defence of York were commanded by future recusants.[37] But Catholics who did not join the earls were not feeble, any more than Protestants who did not join Wyatt had been: all were English subjects, whose resistance was limited by both conscience and cowardice.

The problem of reconciling religious and political obligation is seen in the growth of recusancy among lay Catholics. A small number of families refused to attend Prayer Book services from their introduction. Sir Thomas Fitzherbert of Staffordshire was in prison for his recusancy by 1562, and when in 1563 he was offered his freedom if he would go to church, without having to take communion, he refused.[38] Young Thomas Fitzherbert, born in 1552, never attended Protestant services, and as a teenager was reluctant even to talk to Protestants. In 1568, when he was a student at Oxford, his confessor advised him it was permissible to hear a Protestant sermon for curiosity, but he turned back in horror as he reached the church door. The Fitzherberts were, however, unusual; Thomas recalled later that 'very few Catholics abstained from attending Protestant sermons', though they refused communion.[39] At first, indeed, the Catholic leadership concentrated on persuading the laity to abstain from communion. In 1562 John Murren circulated a tract arguing that Catholics were not bound to obey Elizabeth's schismatic laws, and must not betray their baptism by receiving the heretics' communion.[40]

But the priests were soon taking a much firmer line. When some English laymen asked Rome for assurance that they were allowed to attend Protestant services to avoid punishment, they did not get the answer they expected. By 1564 the pope, a committee of the Council of Trent, and the Roman Inquisition had all declared that Catholics might not attend the services of the Church of England, and faculties were issued to four priests to reconcile to Rome those who had fallen into schism.[41] In 1566 Pius V formally forbade attendance, and Lawrence Vaux, deprived warden of Manchester College, was sent to England with the instruction. His mission was a great success in Lancashire, where the recusant priests were persuaded to insist that their penitents refused to attend. In 1567 John Murren and other priests asked for oaths of obedience to the pope's decree, and several leading Lancashire gentlemen gave them. Other Catholics were reluctant to risk the wrath of the queen, and challenged Vaux's authority. In 1567 the Inquisition confirmed both the necessity of recusancy and the powers of the priests deputed to absolve from schism.[42]

Though recusancy was to remain a contentious issue among Catholics, refusal to attend church now became much more common. In Hampshire only three recusants had been charged in 1561–5, then there were fifteen in 1566, eight in 1567, and thirteen in 1568; in 1569, 180 were presented in the archdeaconry of Norwich.[43] In 1567 Nicholas Sander denounced attendance in the preface to *A Treatise of the Images of Christ*, and when Humphrey Ely read it at Oxford he became a recusant.[44] In 1567 too the Ecclesiastical Commission at Chester began its long struggle to drive the Lancashire recusant gentry into conformity; sometimes a few of them agreed to make token attendances to avoid prison, before resuming their recusant ways. Until 1568 Anthony Travers of Preston was a complete conformist; then he abstained from communion, and six months later he became a recusant.[45] Before 1569 Edmund Plowden attended church without taking communion, but when as a Berkshire JP he was asked to swear to hear Prayer Book services he refused to do so and turned to recusancy. Thomas Pound was a conformist courtier until 1569, when he withdrew to a life of austerity and recusancy.[46]

It was argued later by Protestants that Catholics had rejected the church services because of the bull *Regnans in excelsis*.[47] In belated response to a plea from the northern rebels, in April 1570 Pius V had excommunicated Elizabeth and absolved her subjects from obedience to her. There was a polemical advantage in ascribing recusancy to treasonous adherence to a foreign command, but it was a misleading charge. Probably the doubts of some scrupulous Catholics were resolved by the bull, but recusancy was already well established and increasing; priests were busily pressing their followers to stand firm. What seems to have been true is that the rebellion and the bull frightened the authorities into better detection of recusants, so revealing offenders who had earlier escaped. In Hampshire 116 recusants were found in the second half of 1570, and a special metropolitan visitation in 1571 discovered fifty-four lay recusants (forty of them gentry) and thirty-eight recusant priests in Lancashire. In the province of York the High Commission began a systematic attack on recusant gentry: the frequency of sessions was increased, and in 1572–4 about fifty gentlemen were summoned.[48]

The move into recusancy continued. Often it was the influence of a particular priest which helped persuade laypeople to abandon church-going. In 1570 Henry Comberford, deprived precentor of Lichfield, was arrested in the house of the old countess of Northumberland. Imprisoned at York, he conducted an effective campaign to persuade his conservative visitors into recusancy; in 1576 the High Commission charged that 'he hath seduced divers of the queen's majesty's subjects, causing them by his persuasion to be disobedient in coming to the church'. He seems to have been assisted by the Catholic physician Thomas Vavasour, who with his wife ran a maternity home for the matrons of York.[49] By 1576 there were about seventy recusants in York, most of them women, and their replies to interrogation suggest they had had the same teacher: 'she cometh not to the church because her conscience will not serve her', and because the new service had 'neither priest, altar, nor sacrifice'.[50] Perhaps the Protestant bishops' campaign to enforce conformity to the Prayer Book was driving into recusancy those who had been willing to attend church when the mass had been counterfeited.

Recusancy was now a matter of conscience for many Catholics, and in religious matters loyalty to their Church was overriding loyalty to the state. In 1567 Nicholas Tichbourne refused an order to attend, declaring 'he would take no other before his conscience was thoroughly resolved therein, because that is a matter of salvation and damnation'.[51] But a decision for recusancy remained difficult; Michael Tirrey wrestled with the issue for ten years, before finally opting for recusancy in 1574. Within six months he was in gaol, where he remained until he died.[52] In 1572 Sir Thomas Cornwallis admitted to the queen that his conscience had 'thus long withdrawn me from coming to church', but agreed to attend to prove his loyalty. When criticized by Catholics for hearing the service, he would reply 'If a man sat at dinner and hear a fool prate, shall he rise and go away and not be counted himself a more fool', but by 1587 he was a recusant again, much affronted that the regime saw a matter of conscience as a test of loyalty. The church papist Lord Stourton never steeled himself to recusancy, despite his guilt; he kept two Catholic chaplains, to ensure one was always available to absolve him from schism before he died.[53]

By 1574 Catholics had organized themselves as a distinct Church, outside the framework of the Church of England. They were conscious members of a Roman Catholic Church, with local congregations worshipping secretly together. They had their own priests and their own sacraments, and their exiles provided encouraging propaganda and works of piety. But this underground Church had three potentially fatal weaknesses: it suffered from leakage as some church papists drifted away into full conformity; there were too few priests to sustain loyalties and provide the sacraments for those who wished them; and the supply of priests was contracting rapidly as the older generation died. However, the Catholic exiles now began to supply new priests for England, at first because it was impossible to maintain them all at Douai. In 1573 the first four Douai students were ordained, and in 1574 six others; three of them sailed to England, and the welcome they received from Catholics persuaded them to encourage William Allen to send more.[54] Seven priests crossed to England in 1575, sixteen in 1576, fifteen in 1577, and twenty in 1578. In return, young Catholics flocked to Douai to become priests for England.

The college which had been founded as a community of scholarly exiles now became a seminary offering crash courses for trainee priests. In 1579 the English hospice in Rome was converted into a second seminary to expand the provision, and later there were two new training colleges in Spain. The syllabus and worship of the colleges were structured to give young priests the zeal and skills needed to serve a proscribed underground Church. As well as direction in liturgy and prayer, the students were taught how to catechize the laity and deal with their moral problems in confession. It was the first formal professional training ever given to English clergy. Allen seems to have used his power to license priests for England to encourage those with some theological expertise to work with the gentry or in towns, and to restrict the less able to 'uplandish places where there is no other better learned than themselves'.[55] Twenty priests were dispatched in 1579, twenty-nine in 1580, and thirty-one in 1581; between 1574 and 1603 about 600 seminary priests were sent over, and about 460 are known to have worked in England.[56] They secured the future of English Catholicism.

The seminary priests were not missionaries. They were sent to sustain and strengthen the faith of existing Catholics, not to convert Protestants from their heresy, though converts would not be rejected if they could be gained without too much risk to the main purpose. William Allen reported to Rome that the priests had gone 'to preach and teach (though not openly but in private houses, after the old example of the Apostles in their days) the Catholic faith, and administer the sacraments to such as had need and were capable of that heavenly benefit', that is, to be pastors to the Catholics.[57] That was task enough: Henry Shaw, one of the first Douai priests in England, reported in 1576 that he was so busy absolving Catholics from schism that he had no time to think of anything else.[58] When, in 1580, the first Jesuit priests were ordered to England, they were forbidden to approach heretics; they were to deal with reconciled Catholics whenever possible, and their aim was 'the preservation and augmentation of the faith of the Catholics of England'. Robert Persons soon described an exhausting daily schedule of preaching, hearing confessions, reconciling schismatics, and dissuading Catholics tempted to conform.[59]

The Jesuits and seminary priests sought to stem leakage to the Church of England by demanding strict recusancy; their people had to decide if they were really Catholics or not. A meeting of priests at Southwark in 1580 agreed that church attendance was a betrayal of the Catholic faith, and 'this should be the sum of that which all priests should teach'.[60] Robert Persons printed *A Brief Discourse Containing Certain Reasons Why Catholics Refuse to Go to Church* at a secret press, warning that church papists risked infection from heresy and damnation if they died in schism. In 1582 a young seminary priest at Malpas refused absolution to conformist Catholics, and at Caius College in Cambridge Catholic students debated whether it was moral to dissemble their religion.[61] The Jesuit John Gerard made little progress with Protestants, but was often able to stiffen church papists into recusants and introduce strict regimes of Catholic observance. Other new priests persuaded conformists such as Lord Montague, the Bellamy family at Harrow, the Yorkshire gentleman William Lacy, and the Flintshire schoolmaster Richard White to recusancy. However, all but the privileged Montague paid a high price for their new rigour.[62]

The seminary priests brought saving sacraments to English Catholics, but they also brought trouble. Official policy towards Catholics before 1574 had hardly been tolerant, but it was certainly cautious. The supremacy oath was not imposed upon laymen systematically, there were no general purges of local government or searches for recusant priests, and the 12*d*. fine for absence from each service was ineffectually enforced. After the bull of 1570 prominent recusant gentlemen were imprisoned for a time, but they were usually released on bonds in the hope that they would conform. It was apparently expected that Catholicism would wither away, especially as the supply of old priests shrank and masses were fewer. But then came the seminary priests, and by 1577 the bishops were complaining that 'the papists do marvellously increase, both in number and in obstinative withdrawing of themselves from the Church and service of God'.[63] When

Lawrence Johnson reached Lancashire from Rheims in 1580, the JP Edmund Fleetwood recognized a new situation: 'We hoped that, these papistical priests dying, all papistry should have died and ended with them, but this brood will never be rooted out.'[64]

Elizabeth's councillors were less pessimistic and more determined. Cuthbert Mayne, a Douai priest, was executed in 1577, and a second, John Nelson in 1578. In 1580 the York High Commission used specially summoned local juries to report Catholics; hundreds of recusants were bound over on sureties to attend church, take communion, and ensure that their families did the same.[65] A new anti-Catholic statute in 1581 was deliberately drawn to limit the impact of the new priests: it was now treason to be absolved from schism and reconciled to Rome, and the recusancy fine was increased from 12d. per service to £20 per month, forty or fifty times an artisan's wage. Then the execution of priests became more frequent: four in 1581, eleven in 1582, two in 1583, six in 1584. In 1585 a Draconian statute made it treason for a Catholic priest ordained abroad to enter the country, and treason for any person to give him aid or shelter. The priests had to deny their vocation or face execution. A petition from leading lay Catholics argued that, as they had to support the priests essential to Catholic life and salvation, they now had a choice between treason and damnation.[66]

The legislation of 1581 and 1585 brought a crisis for the underground Church. A meeting of priests and Catholic gentry decided that it was too dangerous for priests to lodge at private houses (as they had done since 1559): 'all priests should shift for themselves' at inns.[67] When John Brushford arrived from Rheims in 1585, he said, 'I found everybody so fearful as none would receive me into their house.' He was forced to hide away for two years in London garrets and West Country cottages, until he gave up and returned to France.[68] Later in 1585, the war between England and Spain brought greater dangers, since Protestants believed priests were spies recruiting support for a Spanish invasion. Between 1577 and 1585, twenty-seven priests and eight laymen had been executed; from 1586 to 1592, sixty-nine priests and twenty-eight laypeople suffered, thirty-one of them in the second half of 1588, victims of the fears provoked by the Spanish armada. The laity now conformed in droves, as the priests complained. In 1594 Richard Holtby in the north-east predicted that unless the persecution ceased 'the weak and small number of God's servants shall come to ruin, and the little sparkle of Catholic religion, as yet reserved amongst us, shall be quite extinguished'.[69]

Holtby's fears were not fulfilled. Persecution did not cease, but it eased. Thirty-three priests were executed from 1593 to 1603; many more had been arrested, but were held in prison camps until they were banished; some of them returned at once to England. The 1581 fining system, even after it had been revised in 1587, failed: through evasion, collusion, and administrative difficulty, only 142 recusants paid fines to the Exchequer in 1592, most of them at reduced rates.[70] Many heads of gentry households conformed, at least occasionally, to preserve family estates, and the priests came to recognize that this was a necessary expedient. Trainee priests were taught that they had to be realistic, and allow the sacraments to church papists —who otherwise would be driven from the faith, or forced into penury by fines.[71] So the fierce persecution of 1581–92 passed; it had not crushed the Catholics, but it still had long-term significance. It tested the commitment of families and individuals, and those least integrated into the Catholic community fell into permanent conformity to the Church of England. Where there were few priests to sustain Catholic loyalty, it collapsed.

What was left was a seigneurial sect. Early in Elizabeth's reign, recusant Catholicism had been only partly dependent upon the gentry; some priests had served manor houses, others poorer rural congregations. But as the old priests died out and the proportion of seminary priests increased, the balance tilted.[72] Jesuits and seminarians were recruited mainly from among university scholars and the sons of the gentry. Not surprisingly, they often lived and worked with their social equals. The concentration upon gentry households was a deliberate strategy, however, and not a social accident. The Jesuits were instructed to deal 'with the upper classes rather than with the common people', so there could be a Catholic ruling order when the faith was restored, and so Catholic gentry could protect Catholic servants and tenants.[73] When, after the scare of 1585, William Weston and Henry Garnet organized a clerical placement agency for incoming priests, it was built from the southern gentry friends and patrons of the first Jesuits and their allies.[74] Their system of guides and safe houses probably kept many priests from arrest, but it reconstructed the Catholic community in a domestic rather than congregational form.

When new priests arrived in England, most of them were passed through the Jesuit organization to become household chaplains to Catholic gentlemen. Garnet explained in 1596 that 'the greater part of them, as opportunity offers, we place in fixed residences', so that 'a very large number of families' now had their own priest. When James Younger and Richard Blount reached London in 1591, Younger was sent off to Lady Throckmorton and Blount to the Darrells at Scotney Castle, where he stayed as chaplain for seven years. The organization also supplied funds 'to support priests in a number of rather poor places', but it seems that most priests served primarily as domestic chaplains rather than district pastors.[75] For four years William Anlaby worked among poor Catholics in Yorkshire, but in 1582, 'humbly yielding to the advice of his brethren', he smartened himself up and moved south to serve the gentry. William Freeman, who arrived in England in 1587, worked first among the poor in the west Midlands, but he soon settled down as priest and tutor to a gentry family. In Hampshire in

1592 Thomas Stanney combined a domestic chaplaincy with a district circuit; but he lived with the gentry family, and went around the villages once a month.[76]

The priests' routes into England and the Jesuit agency tended to locate them in south-east England. Many crossed from Calais or Dieppe to Dover or Rye, and then made their way to London; they then headed for East Anglia, or were channelled into the Thames Valley and southern counties. In 1580 half of the new priests were serving in Essex, London, and the Thames Valley, though Catholics were fewest there and government surveillance tight.[77] The Jesuit Robert Southwell complained in 1586 that priests 'betake themselves in great numbers to one or two counties, leaving others devoid of pastors'; by 1590 there was a glut of priests in Oxfordshire, so Thomas Stransham had to move north 'for want of harbour and entertainment'.[78] The maldistribution of priests was partly corrected later, especially when some took the route from Flanders to the Tyne, but acute shortages emerged in the north and Wales as the old recusant priests died. Two lovers from Cleveland had to go to Lincolnshire to find a priest to marry them, and in the 1590s Richard Danby of Masham had to baptize his six children himself.[79]

It was perhaps unavoidable that the attentions of the seminary priests would focus primarily on the gentry of southern England; most priests came in from France, and they needed the material support which the rich could more easily provide. But the consequences were the collapse of Catholicism among the lower orders, and its decline in the north, west, and Wales. Robert Persons noted in 1581 that, although Catholicism had remained strong in Wales, 'thanks to shortage of men to work there it has fallen into considerable ignorance', and he was right. In north Wales traditionalist loyalty was being turned into organized recusancy by energetic priests in the 1570s, but thereafter the growth of separated Catholicism was arrested by harsher official persecution and a lack of priests.[80] It was the same in Cumbria, where recusant priests had created a healthy underground Church by the late 1580s. But the old priests were not replaced by seminary men, and recusancy among the peasants was soon in rapid decline. In 1599 the bishop of Carlisle reported that there were few priests in the diocese, the Catholic gentry were moving away, and now his main problem was not popery but ignorance among ordinary people.[81]

Until the middle of Elizabeth's reign, there were many recusants and church papists among the yeomen, artisans, and husbandmen of England. In Suffolk, for example, there were numerous recusants in the small towns of Beccles, Lowestoft, and Mildenhall in the mid-1570s. Twenty years later they were gone, and Catholicism was virtually confined to the households of the gentry. John Gerard described the Catholics of East Anglia in the early 1590s as 'mostly from the better classes; none, or hardly any, from the ordinary people'. He thought this was because persecution had driven the lesser folk into the Church of England, and he was partly right.[82] But the efforts of government were concentrated upon priests and gentry, and other Catholics were not much troubled by fines or prison. Rather, the middling and poorer Catholics conformed because of a shortage of priests and an absence of pastoral support. In the 1620s a woman in Suffolk complained that there were few priests, and they were not allowed by their gentry hosts to serve among the poor; she claimed it took her six months to find a priest who would receive into the Church three converts she had made.[83] It was hard to be a Catholic without a priest.

So English Catholicism became a country-house religion, the faith of the gentry and their dependants. Where there was a Catholic gentleman to give some protection from persecution and to house a priest who could provide sacraments, there might be other Catholics too. In Derbyshire, recusancy was strongest among the Fitzherberts' tenants at Hathersage, in Stafford-shire among those of another branch of the family at Hamstall Ridware.[84] At Barwick in Yorkshire in 1604, the recusants were John Gascoigne, Esquire, and his wife, his mother, his miller, four female servants, his shepherd and wife, two wives of menservants, and other recusants in the parish were probably tenants.[85] There were districts of Yorkshire where recusancy was much less seigneurial, such as Aysgarth, Cleveland, Richmond, Ripon, and York itself. And there was widespread popular Catholicism in south-west Lancashire and on the Herefordshire–Monmouth border, where priests served congregations rather than families. But these areas simply show what was possible outside the Home Counties, if only there were priests to achieve it. Instead, they had hidden away in the manor houses of the south, leaving Catholics elsewhere to drift back to the Church of England.[86]

At the end of Mary's reign, Catholicism had been the religion of a large majority of English people; by the end of Elizabeth's it was the faith of a small sect. In 1603 the bishops reported to their new king that there were 2,250,765 Church of England communicants and only 8,590 adult recusants; this was a massive underestimate, and it excludes the church papists, but it indicates the scale of the Catholic community.[87] Within two generations, the Catholics had dwindled to numerical insignificance. In 1559, the Protestants had seized control of the Church, its assets, and its coercive machine; without political change, time would consolidate their victory. Those for whom religion was what happened in their local church went with the new ways. Older Catholics conformed little by little, and children grew up in a decreasingly Catholic climate. While the priests and people who preferred the old mysteries lived, there were to be vestiges of Catholicism within the Church of England—often in rituals, widely in beliefs. But this was a residual conservatism, which could not last for ever;

as at Weaverham in Cheshire, it died away with the last generation of those born in a Catholic world.

The only future for the Catholics was in a separated Church of their own, and from 1566 they were building one. This was sure to be a minority movement, for relatively few laypeople would break from the parish community and risk the legal penalties of recusancy and mass-going, though many might satisfy the law and their neighbours by token conformity. Through the 1570s the underground Church was growing fast, as the Church of England became more Protestant and, for Catholics, less bearable. Congregations were organized, supply-lines established, and the future secured with the flow of seminary priests. If the Catholics were to be a minority, they were on the way towards a sizeable one. But expansion was checked by the persecution of the 1580s, which helped drive the fledgeling Church into the houses of the gentry, where the new priests were anyway more at home. Many Catholics outside gentry strongholds now lacked the pastoral care needed for loyalty through difficult times, and abandoned their religion. The Catholic community thus contracted, socially and geographically. It had finally lost the long Reformation struggle.

✣ 16 ✣

Evangelists in Action

IN 1574 the earl of Huntingdon appointed Peter Eckershall curate of Measham, a mining village in the archdeaconry of Derby. The new curate was the parish's first Protestant minister, and, as villagers soon admitted, 'at his coming to them they were ignorant and obstinate papists'. Eckershall began a campaign of Protestant evangelism, preaching sermons, holding catechism classes for the young, and teaching the adults the essentials of the faith. Within two years all communicants could recite a basic Protestant confession, and some had been led 'to a comfortable feeling of their salvation in Christ'. In 1576, when Eckershall was threatened with suspension for failing to wear a surplice at services, the parishioners successfully pleaded with their bishop not to remove the minister who had brought them the truth.[1] A Protestant patron had given Measham a Protestant preacher, and 'obstinate papists' had been made into defenders of the gospel. But only a minority of parishes had experienced the evangelistic efforts of a preacher such as Eckershall, for in the mid-1570s about four-fifths of ministers could not preach.[2]

Through the first half of Elizabeth's reign the shortage of Protestant preachers was acute. A survey of the diocese of Peterborough in 1560 found only nine preachers among 166 clergy; even by 1576 there were just forty preachers among 230 clergy—to spread the gospel through 296 parishes. In Wiltshire in 1561 there were twenty preachers out of 220 clergy, to serve over 300 churches—not much chance of widespread evangelism there. There were more preachers in some areas, and fewer in others: in London itself in 1561 almost half the ministers could preach, in Devon and Cornwall only one in fourteen.[3] But virtually everywhere preaching resources were inadequate and over-stretched. The bishops tried to ensure that ministers who could not themselves preach hired substitutes to give at least one sermon every three months, and the preachers were supposed to preach monthly sermons in their own churches and help out elsewhere.[4] But the non-preachers could not always afford or obtain the prescribed sermons; in Wiltshire, for example, the twenty preachers would have to preach eighty sermons each in 1561 to fulfil the bishops' requirements.

So many parishes did not have even the minimal provision which bishops demanded. In the diocese of York in 1575, 150 clergy were presented for failure to secure quarterly sermons: there had been no sermons in six years at Ellerker, none in seven at Skerne, none in ten at Wressle, and none in twenty at Thorp Arch.[5] In west Sussex in 1579 things were not so bad, but they were bad enough: there were thirty-three preachers to provide sermons for 135 parishes. Twenty-five parishes had their own resident preachers and twenty-five more had quarterly sermons from outsiders; but forty-six parishes had fewer than four sermons a year and twenty-three had one a year or none. At Wiston and Woolavington there were sermons every Sunday; at Angmering and Houghton they were fortnightly, but at Barlavington, Coats, East Dean, Ludsworth, Midlavant, and elsewhere there was no preaching at all. Oxfordshire in 1586 was better off, with the university preachers to draw on; but in forty-six parishes only eleven had frequent sermons, thirty had quarterly sermons, and five had no sermons at all.[6]

Protestant leaders were clear that regular sermons were needed for the spread of Protestantism and the saving of souls. 'Public and continual preaching of God's word is the ordinary mean and instrument of the salvation of mankind', Archbishop Grindal told the queen in 1576. But Bishop Sandys, echoing St Paul, had asked the key question: 'If there be no salvation but by faith, no faith but by hearing the word of God, how should the people be saved without teachers?'[7] How indeed! Certainly not by quarterly sermons, argued a tract of 1585: 'Four sermons in the year are as insufficient ordinarily to make us perfect men in Christ Jesus (to which end Pastors and Doctors are given us) as four strokes with an axe are unable to fell down a mighty oak.' Where there was no frequent preaching, it was claimed in 1588, 'what a pitiful thing it is to come into a congregation of one or two thousand souls and not to find above four or five that are able to give an account of their faith in any tolerable manner, whereby it might be said "This is a Christian man", or "He is a child of the Church".' 'Wherefore (good brethren)', cried John More of Norwich, 'if ye will be saved get you preachers into your parishes.'[8]

But where were the preachers to come from? How could they be found and placed? Frustrated godly Protestants wrote as if there was a secret conspiracy by bishops to deprive parishes of sermons, to maintain 'dumb dogs' in benefices when there was an untapped supply of fervent preachers. This was nonsense. Although Elizabeth feared that too many sermons stirred up trouble, few if any of her bishops thought there could be too many. Perhaps they were unwilling to reorganize Church finances to attract qualified men into parish work, though they were probably right that any problem of incentives could only be solved by divesting lay impropriators of the rectories acquired in sales of monastic property.[9] But for half the reign at least, the question of incentives hardly applied; there were few preachers to be had, whatever the reward. The bishops did their best, but preachers could not be conjured up by prayer. There was no quick political fix, no easy ecclesiastical answer, only a patient wait for the effects of Protestant education and training. Where were the preachers to come from? The universities. How could they be found and placed? By Protestant bishops and patrons.

Protestants gained effective, if not exclusive, control of the universities in the first decade of Elizabeth's reign. The influenza epidemic of 1557–8, deprivations by royal commissioners in 1559–60, and resignations by scrupulous Catholics created vacancies for Protestants, though there were domestic struggles in several colleges. The authorities had particular trouble with New College and Merton at Oxford and King's and Caius at Cambridge, but most Catholics were hounded out and Protestants installed. In Oxford there were new and energetic Protestant heads of house, such as Thomas Sampson at Christ Church and, after disputes, William Cole at Corpus; new professors of divinity, Lawrence Humphrey and Herbert Westphaling; and new college tutors, Protestant mentors for future pupils.[10] At Cambridge there was less disruption, but a Protestant leadership was soon established: William Cecil as chancellor, Leonard Pilkington at St John's, Robert Beaumont at Trinity, Matthew Hutton at Pembroke. Above all, there were new Cambridge fellows: twenty new men at Trinity in 1560, and soon many more than half of all college fellows had been students after 1559. By 1568 Bishop Cox could write of the 'abundant crop of pious young men in our universities'.[11]

Theological orthodoxy was soon demanded at Oxford, partly at the insistence of its chancellor, the earl of Leicester. In 1573 the Privy Council ordered the vice-chancellor to deal with those who breached 'the uniformity of matters of religion', and thereafter suspected Catholics were refused their degrees.[12] In 1579 a new university statute prescribed Reformed theological instruction for all students: they were to be taught first from the catechisms of Calvin, Nowell, and the Heidelberg theologians; then from Bullinger, Jewel, Calvin's *Institutes*, and the Thirty-nine Articles, and they were to be examined each term on what they had learned. In 1581 a new matriculation statute imposed a strict religious test on those entering the university: all new students were to subscribe to the royal supremacy and the Thirty-nine Articles.[13] In theory at least, Oxford had been thoroughly protestantized. At Cambridge, it seems such aggressive regulation was unnecessary: the new statutes of 1570 gave the vice-chancellor and heads of colleges authority to expel any man who taught 'anything against religion', but this power was used primarily against disruptive Protestants.[14]

A rising proportion of Elizabethan ministers had experience of these Protestant universities. Since Church leaders wanted a better-educated clergy who could teach Protestant doctrine and scriptural knowledge, they raised standards for ordination, and so made it more likely that candidates would attend university. In 1571 the bishops declared that they would ordain only those who had been educated 'either in the university or some other inferior school', had some competence in Latin and the Scriptures, and had not worked in 'base and handicraft labour'. In 1575 further articles required ordinands to give an account of their faith in Latin, and insisted that new priests should be at least 24 years old. Although these rules did not stipulate that ministers must be graduates, they demanded high educational attainments and, by delaying ordination and prohibiting labour, encouraged tertiary study.[15] Although admission statistics are problematical, it seems there was now a flow of would-be clerics into the universities, where they learned Reformed theology and prepared for the ministry. The universities became training colleges for clergy, and, at Cambridge, Emmanuel (1584) and Sidney Sussex (1596) were founded as Protestant seminaries.[16]

In 1573 John Whitgift claimed that Cambridge had already 'bred' more than 450 preachers since Elizabeth's accession: there were then 102 preachers at the university, 'and no doubt but God will increase the number of them daily more and more'.[17] By the 1570s, the production of graduate clergy was beginning to alter the composition of the parochial ministry, especially in the more prosperous and attractive areas. In Oxford diocese, admittedly an exceptional case, half the ministers were graduates by 1580. In Northamptonshire and Rutland there were only thirty-eight graduate ministers in 1560, but sixty-six in 1576, eighty in 1585, and almost a hundred in 1590; by 1600 over half the clergy there were graduates.[18] In Kent the number of graduate ministers tripled between 1571 and 1603, and by Elizabeth's death probably two-fifths of the English clergy had degrees. Not all graduates were preachers (and not all preachers were graduates), but the supply of educated evangelists boomed. In Kent and Suffolk most of the godly preachers had been to Cambridge; in Lancashire and Cheshire the preachers came more evenly from Oxford and Cambridge; but almost everywhere the activists were university men.[19]

Many of these ministers had been deliberately placed by Protestant patrons. In his years at York, 1570–6, Grindal recruited 'above forty learned preachers and graduates' for the diocese, perhaps using contacts he had made as a fellow and briefly master of Pembroke College, Cambridge. Richard Curteys took twenty learned preachers to Sussex in his first six years as bishop of Chichester, most of them from Cambridge, where he had been president of St John's.[20] But most bishops had limited direct patronage of their own, and were dependent upon leading Protestant laymen to provide benefices for preachers. As lord keeper, Sir Nicholas Bacon managed most of the Crown's ecclesiastical patronage, and presented suitably qualified Protestants where he could, often after petitions from diocesans. The earls of Bedford, Huntington, Leicester, and Warwick were especially busy placers of godly preachers, mainly in the Midlands. And at the county level coteries of godly gentlemen co-operated to build up the supply of preachers: Fitzwilliam, Knightley, and Mildmay in Northamptonshire; Higham, Jermyn, and Lewkenor in Suffolk; Barrington, Rich, and Wroth in Essex.[21]

The bishops could not produce an all-graduate, all-preaching clergy, but they did try to keep out candidates who would not be able to teach the faith. After the frantic recruitment of the early years of Elizabeth's reign, entry standards were raised for ordinands. In the diocese of Ely about one-sixth of ordination candidates were rejected in the 1560s, apparently because of insufficient knowledge of the Scriptures, but with a flow of graduates from Cambridge the examiners there could afford to be choosy. Other bishops could not be so strict until much later, but as the supply of educated ordinands in each area increased so bishops became more demanding. In 1584 Bishop Overton of Lichfield introduced a more formal assessment system for ordination, with candidates appearing before a panel of preachers for interview. Bishops may also have tried harder to block the promotion of uneducated ministers to benefices, though the legal rights of patrons made this difficult to achieve. Overton's examination system was applied to nominees for benefices, who had to appear before his panel and then serve a probationary period before final approval. Year by year, clerical standards improved.[22]

The provision of preaching generally passed through four stages, but the rate of increase varied from area to area and many districts did not reach the highest stage until the 1620s or later.[23] First, at the beginning of Elizabeth's reign, there was barely more than occasional, itinerant preaching; the handful of preachers in each region might preach around main centres to try to reach as many people as possible, but it is unlikely that they could do much more than sustain the loyalty of existing Protestants. In the second stage, a larger number of preachers concentrated their efforts on market and administrative towns, where committed and curious laity might be drawn; which could convert town citizens by constant attention. In the third stage, there were preaching ministers in most towns and in many country parishes, so that sermons would usually be available to those willing to walk; so rural evangelism was possible. Finally, there were preachers in all but the poorest and most isolated parishes, and a regular diet of sermons was available, and only then was virtually everyone subjected to protestantizing pressure.

In the city of London there was an unusually good supply of preaching soon after Elizabeth's accession: in 1561 thirty-seven out of eighty-seven ministers were preachers, and nineteen more could 'interpret' the gospel. But elsewhere it took decades to reach such 'third stage' levels. For 296 parishes in Peterborough diocese there were nine preachers in 1560, forty in 1576 and 144 in 1603, all but nine of them graduates. In Salisbury diocese there were 121 preachers for 352 parishes by 1584, and 200 by 1603.[24] The breakthrough came later in the great diocese of Lincoln: probably one in five of the clergy could preach in 1576, and by 1585 the proportion may have fallen to one in six; but in 1603, 60 per cent of Lincoln ministers held preaching licences. There is, however, evidence that in their nation-wide survey of 1603 some bishops may have cooked the preaching books; new licences to preach seem to have been issued in suspiciously large numbers, to defuse criticism of shortages of sermons. Nevertheless, the increase in preaching was genuine, if exaggerated. But gaps remained: in Staffordshire in 1604 there were still '118 congregations which have no preachers, neither have had (for the most) now more than forty years'.[25]

In many places and for many years, Church leaders had to make the best of a bad preaching job. Some bishops became apostolic preachers themselves. In 1577 a group of Sussex ministers praised Bishop Curteys for having preached through his diocese three times in six years, taking other preachers with him in concentrated missionary drives. As bishop of Worcester, John Whitgift preached every Sunday in churches within riding distance of his cathedral, and Toby Matthew preached 1,271 sermons as dean and then bishop of Durham. Other superiors devised schemes to spread their thin resources of preaching talent more widely. Archbishop Grindal established a preaching rota for York Minster in 1571, and ordered the chapter to hire a preacher for the city churches.[26] In 1577 the dean and chapter of Christ Church ordered the four preachers on the foundation to preach twelve sermons a year each around sixteen Oxfordshire churches. In 1578 Bishop Barnes of Durham introduced a plan for thirty preachers to provide an extra 303 sermons a year for parishes across the diocese, on top of existing obligations; Barnes himself would preach twenty-four more sermons, and leading dignatories twelve each.[27]

There were other forms of missionary initiative within the Elizabethan Church. Some town councils and parish vestries established civic lecture-ships, to attract evangelical preachers to their communities, preachers who would not have come for the low stipends of impropriated benefices. Such lecturers were often men of presence and prestige, who became local spiritual leaders and exercised a form of superintendency over lesser ministers, as did Anthony Gilby, Thomas Lever, John More, and Percival Wiburn. By 1562 there were Wednesday and Friday divinity lectures, as well as Sunday sermons, at St Martin's in Leicester, and the council compelled attendance on pain of fines. In 1564 William Cole became town preacher at Colchester, his salary paid from collections among the councillors and the godly Protestants. There were early lectureships at Coventry and Ipswich, and later they were established at Hull, Northampton, and Norwich. In 1572 the earl of Leicester, Sir Richard Knightley, and Bishop Bentham began a lectureship at Towcester, and about 1574 the mayor and jurats of Rye called in Richard Fletcher to serve as 'their preacher. By far the greatest concentration was in London, and by 1581 almost a third of city parishes had their own lecturers.[28]

A group of preachers might pool their efforts, to sustain an evangelical onslaught, in a joint 'exercise' or 'prophesying'. Exercises were partly clerical conferences, partly in-service training courses for ministers, partly team missions to the market towns of England. Two or three sermons were preached on each occasion, which were then discussed by the assembled ministers under the chairmanship of moderators. There were regular weekly or monthly preaching exercises in many towns by the mid-1570s, sometimes freelance ventures by ministers, sometimes—as in Suffolk and Sussex—formally established or endorsed by bishops. In Sussex there were exercises at eight centres, in Essex six, in Norfolk and in Nottinghamshire four; at Northampton there was a weekly exercise for the ministers of the town and a quarterly one for the whole county. The most successful exercises—at Coventry, Southam, Stamford, Ashby-de-la-Zouch—were great revivalist rallies, presided over by charismatic preachers and backed by county magistrates. The committed Protestants turned out in strength, to display the number, quality, and enthusiasm of their support.[29]

The exercises were educational as well as evangelical occasions, and opportunities for the educated ministers to teach their lesser brethren, who might in time become preachers themselves. The bishops soon concluded that the teaching of the gospel could not wait until the universities had trained a new generation of evangelists: some of the dumb dogs must be given voice. The royal Injunctions of 1559 had ordered that all clergy (except those with Masters and higher degrees) should study the Bible, and submit to examination by their bishop; in 1564 the archdeacons were instructed to prescribe New Testament texts for study, and to examine the clergy at regular meetings.[30] Such training courses were often provided through the exercises: at Chester, Chichester, Lichfield, Lincoln, London, and York the authorities commanded attendance at exercises, and threatened to punish negligent ministers. Bishop Curteys argued in 1576 that the Sussex exercises had increased the number of preachers from three to forty or fifty in six years. In 1577 his leading ministers claimed that Curteys himself had trained forty new preachers, and that almost all incumbents in the diocese could teach the essentials of the faith to their people.[31]

By then there was an energetic campaign to get ministers to hold catechism classes, especially for the young people of their parishes. The Injunctions of 1559 had expected ministers to teach the Creed, the Ten Commandments, the Lord's Prayer, and the short catechism in the Prayer Book, for half an hour every holy day and every other Sunday. But this was a half-hearted programme, and requirements were soon raised. From Bishop Parkhurst's 1561 Injunctions onwards, the bishops pressed increasing demands upon the clergy, until hour-long (and sometimes two-hour) classes were to be held every Sunday and holy day: ministers were then in trouble if they did not hold these Sunday schools, and parents if they did not make their children attend.[32] Schoolmasters were ordered to catechize, and Alexander Nowell produced a textbook for them to use. From about 1570 (and especially from 1576) large numbers of newly devised and recycled catechisms were printed, as authors tried to capture an expanding educational market, and soon there were books of advice on the best methods of teaching Protestant beliefs. Most favoured a question-and-answer approach, and young people were encouraged to learn their Christian duties and Reformed doctrines by heart.[33]

The hierarchical and parochial Church of England was being restructured in missionary fashion. Borough lectureships provided evangelical platforms for leading preachers, who became civic apostles with fervent followings. Market-day lectures and quarterly sermons by visiting preachers broke down parish boundaries, and gave almost all congregations some access to the Word. Exercises brought ministers together in team missions, of which the proto-presbyterian clerical conferences of East Anglia were the most organized. But all this activity worried the queen, who seems to have feared that too much Protestant effort would provoke Catholics to recusancy or resistance. In 1576 she ordered Archbishop Grindal to suppress the exercises and allow only three or four licensed preachers in each diocese. Grindal was outraged by this gagging of the gospel; he gained endorsement of the exercises from most of the bishops, and refused to carry out Elizabeth's commands. The Privy Council defused the conflict by a compromise: the rowdiest meetings would be suppressed and laypeople excluded from the ministers' discussions. The queen dropped her demand for fewer preachers.[34]

Elizabeth had tried to cripple the evangelical impulse of her Protestant subjects, and had failed: neither her bishops nor her councillors would support her. After the crisis of 1576, there were both official and informal exercises; ministers still met together to discuss their common missionary problems; the endowment of new preaching lectureships continued; and supplies of preachers and of printed catechisms boomed. The queen's intervention only briefly disrupted the protestantizing campaign. At the beginning of her reign there had been few Protestant preachers and few graduate Protestant ministers; by its end, the Church was well staffed by both. In 1603 Archbishop Whitgift reported that to serve 9,244 parishes there were 4,830 preachers, all but a thousand of them graduates. Of the twenty-six dioceses, only Bath and Wells, Exeter, Hereford, Lichfield, Norwich, and the Welsh dioceses did not have preachers for half their parishes or better; and in Canterbury, Chichester, Ely, London, and Rochester there were preachers for three-quarters. The Church of England was then a preaching Church; in 1604 the bishops were able to insist on monthly sermons at all churches, and weekly sermons from all preachers.[35]

The success of the missionary campaign was assisted by changes in the provision of schooling, what some have called an 'educational revolution'. There had been heavy investment in new schools in the 1550s, though political and religious disruptions delayed their impact for a decade. Protestant clergy emphasized the role of learning in Christian understanding, and some Elizabethan bishops—Parker, Grindal, Pilkington, Sandys, and others—founded schools themselves. It seems that admissions to universities increased markedly, suggesting that education was now thought important. We know much less about elementary education, but it is likely that there were more teachers than ever before active in the first half of Elizabeth's reign and that they had more pupils.[36] It would otherwise be hard to explain the significant increase in literacy which now took place. Illiteracy among those who had been of school age in 1580 was much lower than among those of school age in 1560, judging from the ability to sign their names later. Among East Anglian yeomen illiteracy fell from 55 per cent to 25 per cent, among tradesmen from 60 per cent to 40 per cent, and among husbandmen from 90 per cent to 70 per cent; and the trend was the same elsewhere.[37]

Overall literacy rates seem to have stagnated after about 1580, and reading among labourers and women remained rare. But two decades of educational advance gave Protestant ministers a brief opportunity: for a time, they confronted a more educated clientele. The preachers regarded scriptural knowledge as essential to the life of faith, and pressed Bible-reading, or at least frequent hearing, as a Christian duty. The influential Richard Greenham taught his people at Dry Drayton in Cambridgeshire that they should read the Bible to prove their faith—and the illiterate 'must use the help of others that can read'. He feared there would be no profit from sermons for those 'that have not been trained up in reading the Scriptures or hearing them read'.[38] He may have been right; certainly other ministers thought regular reading was necessary in the formation of Protestant faith and conscience. So perhaps educational change created conditions for Protestant advance. A religion which stressed Bible-reading had more appeal as literacy grew; those with scriptural knowledge might respond more effectively to the preachers; and the literate had another route to faith; by Protestant books.

Sales of Protestant books were both a reason for and an indicator of the impact of Protestant ideas. By the middle of Elizabeth's reign, there was apparently a heavy demand for Protestant books of all kinds: Bibles, catechisms, collections of sermons, works of moral exhortation, private devotions. Fourteen editions of the English Bible were published in the 1560s, twenty-five in the 1570s, twenty-six in the 1580s, and thirty-one in the 1590s· some, however, were for use in churches.[39] Nine collections of sermons were published in the 1560s, sixty-nine in the 1570s, 113 in the 1580s, and 140 in the 1590s—some bought by ministers, no doubt.[40] Not all books printed were sold, though publishers would not persist with unpopular lines. Not all books purchased were read, and not all those read were understood; but some books influenced some people, and their publication provides some index of Protestant loyalty. By the 1590s, books, usually the Bible, were being mentioned in the probate inventories of about one-third of will-makers in the towns of Kent, mainly the more prosperous members of their communities. Protestants were indeed the people of the book.[41]

The preachers and printers of Elizabethan England offered the message of Christian hope and endurance. Its content was well summarized in John More's best-selling *Brief and Necessary Catechism*, first published in 1572. The catechism was described as 'requisite to be learned by heart', and its conclusion must have become the kernel of faith for tens of thousands:

By the Ten Commandments I see my miserable estate, that I deserve death, damnation, and the curse of God, which must be paid because God is just; and whereas I myself am not able to pay it, the Holy Ghost through the preaching of the Gospel worketh in me faith, which assureth me that the Son of God, being made man for me, hath even in my nature suffered whatsoever my sins deserved and hath made me with him the child of God and heir of everlasting life. Whereof, lest I should doubt or waver, he hath appointed two sacraments, as our outward signs and tokens to be seen and felt of me, that as surely as I see myself a partaker of them outwardly so, the Holy Ghost inwardly instructing me, I should not doubt but inwardly to be a partaker of Christ himself, with all his benefits, his ransom, righteousness and holiness to be mine, that in him and through him I shall have life everlasting. And thus being born anew into this lively hope by the Holy Ghost, my ways should be directed and guided by the same spirit, to walk in holiness and righteousness all the days of my life.[42]

These themes were general in Protestant teaching: sinfulness, faith through preaching, justification by Christ, assurance of salvation, glorification in heaven, and a godly life as the fruit of faith. It was a spiritual package which gained many converts, some by Damascene revelation, some by patient formation of a new Christian conscience. Often it was a minister who had been the means of conversion, as was Peter Eckershall at Measham. When the preacher Arthur Wake was removed from his Northamptonshire rectory for nonconformity in 1574, a dozen of his converts rode to ask the bishop for his reinstatement, carrying a petition signed by twenty more.[43] But laypeople were not simply passive recipients of the ministers' evangelical efforts. The young Cheshire gentleman John Bruen was converted at Oxford about 1578 by a fellow student, John

Brerewood. At Lawshall in Suffolk, where the rector was a crypto-Catholic, the local Protestants established a rival lectureship in 1582; three years of preaching brought a 'stirring of many in that place to seek the Lord'. Bartimeus Andrewes encouraged the godly to play their own missionary role: 'I pray you neighbour', they should say, 'Let us go to such a sermon or such a godly exercise, and I will go with you also.'[44]

Protestant fathers had particular duties in the furtherance of faith. Robert Cawdrey advised that households should be called together two or three times a week for prayers, Bible-reading, psalm-singing and systematic catechizing, led by the 'master of the family'. Josias Nichols wanted families examined each Sunday on their understanding of their minister's sermon, and a two-hour catechism class once a week.[45] Some zealots exceeded these prescriptions. Eusebius Paget described the religious routine of one gentry household (probably John Isham's in Northamptonshire) in the 1570s. The whole household met in the parlour every morning for prayers by the master; there were prayers before and after meals, and 'in meal time some one of the servants readeth a chapter of the Bible'; and there was an hour-long session each evening for prayers, psalms, and learning of catechism. After his father's death in 1587, John Bruen established a godly regime at Bruen Stapleford: there were family prayers, psalms, and Bible-readings each morning; regular catechizing and Bible study for the children; and evening Bible classes for the entire household.[46]

All this evangelical and educational effort had its effect. By the middle of Elizabeth's reign there was mounting evidence from many areas of real Protestant conviction, as well as Protestant conformity. In the 1560s the characteristic parish offences reported at visitation had been those of conservatism and neglect: retaining 'monuments of superstition' and failure to buy Bibles. But by the 1580s, at least in the south-east, the offences of Protestant enthusiasm were more common: gadding to sermons in other parishes; private conventicles for prayer and Bible study; and hostility to popish survivals such as the sign of the cross at baptisms. In Northamptonshire there was very little evidence of Protestant commitment until about 1570, when the new preachers were having an impact. At the Inns of Court, convinced Protestants were in the majority by the 1570s.[47] At Hull and Lewes the Protestant breakthrough came in the 1570s, at Terling in Essex in the 1580s, at Leeds and York in the 1590s.[48] In the towns of south-east Lancashire there was substantial Protestant enthusiasm by the 1580s, and in rural Cambridgeshire by the 1590s.[49] There was, at last, a Protestant Reformation.

Its local successes were assisted by shifts in political power, which put county governments into the hands of Protestant gentry and their backers. In Hampshire the energetic Bishop Horne secured the removal of four Catholic JPs in 1561-2 and three more in 1564; the influence of the conservative Paulet interest dwindled thereafter.[50] In some counties there were dramatic upheavals. After the failure of the revolt of 1569 and the flight of the earls, effective authority in County Durham passed from the Neville family to the bishop, and in Northumberland from the Percys to Sir John Forster and his allies. In Norfolk and Suffolk the fall of the duke of Norfolk, from 1569 to 1572, allowed Protestants to take control, although the conservative gentry were not broken until Privy Council proceedings against them in 1578.[51] In Cornwall there was a coup in 1577, when a coalition of coastal Protestant gentry with privateering interests broke the influence of the old county families, the Arundells and Tregians. In the north-west, however, power passed gradually: the Chester ecclesiastical commission was remodelled in 1568, and an activist bishop arrived in 1579, but the Lancashire JPs were not purged until 1587, and then with only partial success.[52]

In the 1580s England was fast becoming a Protestant nation. The religious rhetoric of its leaders was Protestant, as was the public tone of its ruling order. Convinced Protestants dominated Court and parliament, and controlled the government of the Church. The administration of the law, by judges, lawyers, and justices of the peace, was not yet exclusively Protestant; but in many parts of the country there were vigorous Protestant magistrates who backed Protestant preaching and demanded Protestant social discipline. The parish clergy included some ageing crypto-papists and some younger anti-Calvinists, and there were other ministers who followed the Prayer Book without much consideration of religious allegiance and belief. But there were more and more educated evangelists, men who preached a Reformed gospel and expected informed commitment from their congregations. After forty years of rapid turnover of parish clergy, brought by epidemic disease and policy vacillation, the ministry now settled down to longer lives and longer service.[53] The missionary generation was to have a profound and lasting impact.

The efforts of the ministers were most obvious where they caused trouble, and that was in many places. Enthusiastic converts to Protestantism were scathing of the moral and spiritual laxity of their neighbours, and only too willing to try to enforce improvements. In Essex the preachers provoked clashes between their godly supporters and their 'profane' enemies in a dozen parishes between 1582 and 1591; the town of Maldon was divided for more than a decade, with a 'multitude of papists, heretics, and other enemies to God and her royal majesty' opposing George Gifford and his earnest followers. At Rochdale in 1585 and Peasmarsh, Sussex, in 1588, communities were split into godly supporters of preachers with strong views on morals and sabbath observance, and hostile parties led by local alehouse-keepers.[54] A critic of the Kentish preachers asked, 'Hath not Minge brought Ashford from being the quietest town in Kent to be at deadly hatred and bitter division?', and claimed that others had disturbed Chart, Cranbrook, Tenterden, and elsewhere. Josias Nichols was the champion county nuisance, who did 'offend all the congregations where he cometh'.[55]

Some of the fiercest town conflicts were provoked when the preachers and their followers tried to have Mayday or Whitsun celebrations suppressed as remnants of popery and superstition. At Lincoln in 1584–5 there was a struggle between the godly party, who wanted strict controls on alehouses and sabbath observance, and a rival group defending the cause of maypoles and May games. At Shrewsbury in 1588 the maypole was pulled down by godly magistrates, and resistance by the poor men of the shearmen's guild led to imprisonments.[56] There were notorious troubles at Banbury over maypoles in 1588 and 1589, provoked by the preacher Thomas Bradbridge; there were street demonstrations and counter-demonstrations in 1589, and further disputes over Whitsun ales and morris dancing. The Privy Council intervened to restore calm, and ordered that townspeople be permitted 'those pastimes of recreation'.[57] When the mayor of Canterbury forbade a maypole in 1589, disaffected country people danced a protest morris outside his house. But the preachers were not abashed when accused of divisiveness, and quoted Christ in their own defence: 'I came not to send peace, but a sword.'[58]

The frequent parish disruptions of the 1580s suggest that the preachers were making their mark—right across England, and in places in Wales. It now, and only now, becomes appropriate to identify a true Protestant Reformation: now 'Protestant' because it involved real changes in personal belief, not merely shifts in ecclesiastical policy; now 'Reformation' because there were widespread conversions, not merely the localized persuasions of a Latimer and a Hooper. The two universities had produced preachers, and the preachers had been provided with benefices and lectureships. Their allies among the gentry had control of local government, and could support the preachers' word with the magistrates' sword. Their rival old priests had grown feeble and died; their enemy new Jesuits and seminary men were priest-holed in manor houses. Their congregations had more literate members, and adults might buy catechisms to teach the gospel to their children. The conditions for a successful missionary campaign were being fulfilled by the 1580s—not in the period of Cromwellian reform, not in the reign of Edward VI, not even (except for a few parts of south-east England) earlier in Elizabeth's reign.

So the ministers were creating a Protestant nation, but not a nation of Protestants.[59] That was certainly what they themselves thought. No doubt Calvinist students of New Testament parables were especially prone to evangelical pessimism: the seeds of the truth would fall on stony ground, or be choked by weeds; the godly would be few, the reprobate numberless.

Perhaps the ministers had unreasonably high standards, and would count as good Protestants only those with thorough grounding in Reformed divinity.[60] But it is hard to ignore or overrule their uniform conclusion: the Protestants—by whom most of them meant the informed godly Protestants—were a small minority. In 1572 it was estimated that 'not every fortieth person in England is a good and devout gospeller (unless it be in London)'. In 1617 John Darrell guessed that one-twentieth of the people were 'Christians indeed', the rest mere conformists.[61] 'Tell me how many sound, sincere, faithful and zealous worshippers of God will be found amongst us?', asked Theologus the minister in Arthur Dent's dialogue. 'I think there would be few in every village, town, and city; I doubt they would walk very thinly in the streets, so as a man might easily tell them as they go.'[62]

Few were zealous Protestants, the ministers were sure, and few more were informed Protestants. When George Gifford described the religion of many Essex parishioners, 'the country divinity', in 1581, it was not recognizably Protestant. 'If a man labour all the week truly and honestly, and upon the Sabbath day come to the church and make his prayers, shall we say God regardeth not his prayers because he does not understand what he prayeth?', asked Gifford's 'Atheos', the common man.

His intent is good, he doth his good will, he hath a wife and children to provide for, he must follow the world and let preaching go, or else he shall beg; and so long as he doth hurt no man but deal uprightly, I think God doth require no more at his hands. Such as have nought else for to do, let them seek for knowledge.

This was the 'works religion' which Luther and the Protestants had condemned, a gut conviction that salvation came from prayer and charity, whatever the preachers said. Gifford's 'Zelotes', a Protestant, expected no more: in most parishes, he said, 'ye shall not find five among five score which are able to understand the necessary grounds and principles of religion'. Gifford's book was republished in 1598, still an accurate description of 'the religion which is among the common sort of Christians'.[63]

Two characters in Arthur Dent's fictitious 1601 debate held similar opinions:

If a man say his Lord's Prayer, his Ten Commandments, and his Belief, and keep them, and say nobody harm, nor do nobody no harm and do as he would be done to, have a good faith to God-ward and be a man of God's belief, no doubt he shall be saved without all this running to sermons and prattling of the Scriptures,

insisted 'Asunetus, an ignorant man'. 'Well, I cannot read, and therefore I cannot tell what Christ or what St Paul may say, but this I am sure of, that God is a good man (worshipped might he be), he is merciful, and that we must be saved by our good prayers and good serving of God.'[64] Josias

Nichols found such views common. He reported in 1602 that he had examined Kentish parishioners on their understanding of Protestantism. 'I scarce found ten in the hundred to have any knowledge' of Christ and his role, or sin and its punishment. On justification by faith, core Protestant doctrine, it was worse: 'scarce one but did affirm that a man might be saved by his own well-doing, and that he trusted he did so live, that by God's grace he should obtain everlasting life by serving of God and good prayers, etc.'[65]

Gifford, Dent, and Nichols were, it is true, writing with polemical purpose, and so were Cawdrey, Perkins, and others who supported their claims. They were pleading for more preaching, or excusing nonconforming ministers, or demanding more intense religiosity, or making sales-pitches for catechisms; they sought to frighten their readers with the twin spectres of popery and ignorance. But they were right. A meeting of ministers in 1604 agreed that there were three sorts of people among 'our country congregations'. There were 'those effectually called by the preaching of the Gospel to the more sincere profession of religion'. Others '(as lamentable experience after so many years' preaching of the Gospel doth too plainly witness in most places) are notwithstanding merely ignorant and superstitious', still regretting the loss of the old mass. 'Lastly, other some are either indifferent or plain neuters, of which the last sort greatly regard not of what religion they be'; they simply conformed to the religion of the state.[66] Ministers (and modern historians) disputed whether the second or third group was the largest of the three; none could suppose the first might be.

This is not surprising, for Protestant reformers had set awesome, and perhaps unachievable, standards. The preachers asked a lot of their people: they required an informed interior commitment to the Reformed faith, not merely external obedience to formal rules; they demanded conviction as well as conformity. They wanted religion to be a spiritual experience, not a social practice. They expected sermon-going, home catechizing, and Bible-reading: 'You have no prayers in your family, no reading, no singing of psalms, no instructions, exhortations, or admonitions, or any other Christian exercises!', cried Dent's 'Theologus' to 'Antilegon'. The preachers wished for their people a saving faith which was reflected in Christian life, what Dent summarized as 'a love to the children of God; a delight in his Word; often and fervent prayer; zeal of God's glory; denial of ourselves; patient bearing of the cross with profit and comfort; faithfulness in our calling; honest, just, and conscionable dealing in all our actions among men'.[67] Only the prayers of those with such faith would be answered, Gifford's 'Zelotes' insisted: 'God help us if it be thus; how shall poor men do then?', retorted 'Atheos'.[68]

The ministers seemed to propagate too intellectual and demanding a religion, above the capacities of ordinary people. 'God forbid that all those should be awry which are not learned. Is it not enough for plain countrymen, ploughmen, tailors, and such other for to have their Ten Commandments, the Lord's Prayer, and the Belief? I think these may suffice us, what should we meddle further?', asked 'Atheos' in 1581.[69] Twenty years later, 'Asunetus' used the same dullards' defence: 'We have no leisure, we must follow our business, we cannot live by the Scriptures; they are not for plain folk, they are too high for us, we will not meddle with them. They belong to preachers and ministers.'[70] Certainly 'Atheos' and 'Asunetus' were stereotype bumpkins, setting out their cloddish views for easy demolition by 'Zelotes' and 'Theologus'; but their blunt refusal to learn was apparently common. Robert Cawdrey complained that parishioners would resist religious instruction, arguing, 'It is too much and too hard that you require of us, and we are old and cannot learn.' William Perkins listed 'That a man need not have any knowledge of religion because he is not book-learned' as one of the 'common opinions' of 'ignorant people'.[71]

Those without knowledge and fervour were damned by the godly as papists and atheists; in return, the godly were called 'puritans', 'precise fools', 'not Protestants but pratlingstants, that use to tell lies'.[72] The demands made by ministers led to division and dispute in many parishes. At East Hanningfield in Essex in the 1580s there were two religious groups: the godly, mocked as 'saints and Scripture men' by their critics, met together with their rector for prayer and study; the rest, called 'irreligious' by the godly, were refused communion by the rector and trooped off to West Hanningfield to receive the sacrament there.[73] At Preston Capes in Northamptonshire in 1584–5 there was a struggle between an aggressive godly vicar, John Elliston, and those he branded as 'blasphemers of God's name, profaners of the Sabbath'. Elliston tried to force even adults to attend his catechism classes, and his opponents demanded that he observe the ceremonies of the Prayer Book. By 1604 there was a liturgical stand-off at Preston Capes: the next vicar, Robert Smart, gave communion only to those who stood to receive it, like godly Protestants, while other parishioners would receive only if permitted to kneel, as the Prayer Book prescribed.[74]

The godly were accused of spiritual pride, the less godly of spiritual indifference; perhaps there was something in both charges. But behind the mutual abuse and recrimination were two concepts of Christian life and worship, as George Gifford recognized. The godly minority had been gripped by Protestant doctrines of justification and predestination: they trusted to have been chosen by God to be saved by faith in Christ. So faith must be furthered, by sermon-going, Bible-study, and prayer; faith must be demonstrated, by rejection of the wicked and their ways. For the rest, it was different. The easy-going (but church-going) majority had adjusted to religious change; the Book of Common Prayer had replaced the mass, the queen had replaced the pope. 'What tell ye me of the pope? I care not for him! I would both he and his dung were buried in the dunghill!', snorted 'Atheos' when accused of popery. But 'Atheos', 'Asunetus', and probably millions like them had not been made Protestants. They did not share—they did not even think they should know—the key Protestant beliefs; rather, 'We must be saved by our good prayers and good serving of God': by worship and by works.[75]

CONCLUSION

The Reformations and the Division of England

THE sixteenth century was an age of religion: God mattered. It seems that very few in England doubted the basic tenets of Christianity, and the few kept their queries to themselves, or risked ostracism and punishment. This does not mean that everyone understood and accepted each detail of the Creeds; rather, hardly anyone rejected the Christian belief system entirely. It seems, too, that very few stood permanently outside the framework of organized worship, and the few were in trouble if discovered. This does not mean that everyone went to church every Sunday; rather, hardly anyone never went to church at all. In the churches, the clergy offered prayer and praise to God, rites of social passage, moral teaching, and pastoral support, and their people generally took these provisions seriously. This does not mean that everyone heeded every word; rather, hardly anyone deliberately ignored the authority of God or the ceremonies of his priesthood. Everyone lived within a system of moral laws derived from Old and New Testament prescripts and enforced by Church teaching and Church courts; and fear of God's wrath and public penance limited moral choice. This does not mean that everyone was good; rather, everybody knew how to be good.

As in all ages, there was a range of spiritual involvement and intensity, from those for whom religion was everything to those for whom it was very little. There were, before and after the Reformations, men and women who structured their whole lives around the contemplation of God and his will. There were others who studied and prayed as much as the demands of their workaday world allowed. There were probably more for whom Christian rules and examples were regular points of moral reference, and who found encouragement in the annual cycles of worship. These were all, to a greater or lesser extent, thinking Christians. No doubt they were heavily outnumbered by unthinking Christians, those who habitually observed the customs of their communities in religion as in other aspects of life. There were many who thought little of God or Christ except on Sundays, holy days, and in emergencies, and perhaps not very much even then. But they could follow Christian ways as they had been trained, and join in services as natural and necessary parts of existence. And there were certainly some who were unwilling conscripts to compulsory religious practice, who would rather be almost anywhere than at prayer—but who were at prayer, sometimes.

Before the Reformations, there were modes of Christian living to accommodate all levels of intensity. There was scope for mysticism and contemplation in the religious orders, as best exemplified by the Carthusians. There were patterns of ascetic life available for the fervent who were unable to withdraw from the secular world: Thomas More's Court doublet concealed a hair shirt. Laymen (laywomen somewhat less easily) could join religious guilds, read pious books, give alms to the poor and sick, pray through favourite saints, and attend mass frequently to savour the mystery of bread become God: they could follow the way of Whitford's *Work for Householders*. For the less reflective, there was the way of the *Primer* and the *Lay Folks' Mass Book*, of miracle stories, candles before images, holy water, Paternosters and Aves, prayers for souls departed: the world of many of the parishioners of Morebath in Devon. For the religious minimalists, there was an undemanding scheme of salvation which rewarded decent living and participation in sacraments; the Church would do the rest. And for all there was the worship which meant so much to Roger Martyn of Long Melford: altars, mass, rood, images, processions, singing, bells.

All religious reformers wanted to make unthinking Christians more thoughtful: Bilney and Whitford in the 1520s, Hooper and Bonner in the 1550s, Gifford and Campion in the 1580s. There were those who called for Catholic re-formation as well as those who demanded Protestant Reformation. But Catholic reformers did not doubt that the unthinking could be Christians: less informed Christians, perhaps less secure Christians, but Christians none the less, seeking their way to heaven as best they could. Justification by works incorporated all in an achievable salvation system: the same sacraments could save Thomas More, Roger Martyn, and the people of Morebath. Thus sixteenth-century Catholics did not share the view of some modern historians that the unreflective were really pagans, whose ignorance barred them from true Christianity: there could be doing Christians as well as comprehending Christians. However, the Protestant insistence that justification came from faith in Christ undercut the status and the prospects of the unthinking. Good works and worship could be habitual; saving faith could not: it required understanding, decision, interior conviction; it required informed belief.

The Protestant Reformation advanced an exclusive model of Christian life. There were no alternative patterns of piety, no concessions to variety of talents or opportunities, no choices of ways to the Lord. If the Christian would be saved, he or she must be a thinker: a sermon-goer, a catechism-learner, a Bible-student, an earnest prayer, a singer of psalms; indeed, to be a real Christian at all required sermon, catechism, Bible, prayer, and psalms. It was not enough—it was not much at all—to go to church and recite prayers; it was worthless to live charitably with one's neighbours, unless good living came from right faith. 'For the remainders of popery yet stick in the minds of many of them, and they think that to serve God is nothing else but to deal truly with men and to babble a few words morning and evening, at home or in the church, though there be no understanding', declared William Perkins contemptuously.[1] Protestantism was not a works religion, it was a Word religion: the Word preached, the Word read, the Word sung to the Lord, the Word applied to life, the Word wrestled with in the heart of a sinner yearning for grace.

As Richard Whitford had set the pattern of piety for thinking lay Catholics about 1530, William Perkins set it for thinking Protestants about 1590. His books and sermons expounded Calvinist divinity and applied it to the real world, and they sold as Whitford's had done, with over forty editions printed in the 1590s (and many more thereafter).[2] In 1590 Perkins published his catechism, *The Foundation of Christian Religion*, reprinted at least four times in the decade. It was 'to be learned of ignorant people, that they may be fit to hear sermons with profit and to receive the Lord's supper with comfort'; it was to make them thinking Christians. It expounded 'the principle points of Christian religion in six plain and easy rules': the Trinity, the Fall, Christ's atonement, justification by faith, faith by hearing the Word preached, and the Last Judgement; and it explained the Ten Commandments and the two sacraments. For Perkins, the key issue was assurance of election, 'when a man is verily persuaded by the Holy Spirit of God's favour towards him particularly, and of the forgiveness of his own sins': from assurance came justification before God and sanctification in life.[3]

The new model Christians were to know they were saved, and were to show it in their lives. They were to study the word of God, search their souls, recoil from sin, call upon God's forgiveness, feel the mercy of a loving Father, and be assured of their predestined election to eternal life. 'We must take the anchor of hope, and fasten it in heaven upon the foundation of God's election, which being done we shall pass in safety and rejoice in the midst of all storms and tempests.' After that, it was not quite plain sailing, but it was to be plain living: 'All the elect that live in this world shall be called, justified, sanctified, and lead all their lives in good conscience before God and men', Perkins promised in 1595.[4] There was no way to salvation through Carthusian contemplation, or More's mortification, or Whitford's regime of prayer, or the Morebath reliance on images, or Martyn's devotion to the annual cycle of worship. The Protestant Reformation had established a single route to heaven, through saving faith nurtured by the Word: 'The true testimony of the Holy Ghost is wrought ordinarily by the preaching, reading, and meditation of the word of God'.[5]

Only the Word could lead to God: all else was distraction or downright idolatry, a trap set by Satan to keep the unwary from true faith. 'The images also of the cross, of Christ crucified, and of the saints ought to be abolished out of churches', warned Perkins, and so also should

popish superstitions in sacrifices, meats, holidays, apparel, temporary and bead-ridden prayers, indulgences, austere life, whipping, ceremonies, gestures, gait, conversation, pilgrimage, building of altars, pictures, churches, and all other of that rabble. To these may be added consort in music in divine service, feeding the ears not edifying the mind.[6]

The theological foundation of works-religion was challenged, and the 'ignorant multitude' mocked for its reliance on artificial aids and external acts. Religion as experienced by Roger Martyn and by the people of Morebath was to be overthrown: preached down by Protestants, banned by the state, punished by Church courts. The hallowed routines of the religion of doing were forbidden; the images which had taught the loving sacrifice of Christ were taken down; the altars on which his sacrifice was repeated were removed; piece by pious piece, the church of Long Melford was stripped bare. The ordinary way to God was declared closed.

Habitual Christians were ordered to be thinking Christians. 'It is not sufficient', Perkins told them,

to say all these without book, unless ye can understand the meaning of the words and be able to make a right use of the Commandments, of the Creed, of the Lord's Prayer, by applying them inwardly to your hearts and consciences, and outwardly to your lives and conversations. This is the very point in which ye fail.[7]

It was not enough for a Christian to go to church on Sunday. Before the service he or she must prepare by private prayer and examination of conscience; during it, 'hear reverently and attentively to the Word preached and read'; after it, 'spend the rest of the Sabbath in the meditation of God's word' and in 'the works of charity, as to visit the sick, give alms to the needy, admonish such as fall, reconcile such as are at jar and discord among themselves'. There must not be 'any other thing whatsoever which is a means to hinder or withdraw the mind from that serious attention which ought to be in God's service'.[8] It was a tall order for the unreflective Christians, and many of them were unable or unwilling to fulfil it.

For the Protestant Reformation was much less effective than the political Reformations had been: legislative destruction proved easier than evangelical construction. The endowments and equipment of traditional worship were confiscated by governments, and comfortable old rituals were scrapped, and replaced by the sterilized services of the Book of Common Prayer. The instruments of popish superstition had thus been destroyed, but the attitudes which had sustained them were not. For the unthinking Christians at least, the religion of works was not, and perhaps could not be, replaced by the religion of the Word. Perkins knew that 'ignorant people' had ignored the Protestant message: they still thought 'that faith is a man's good meaning and his good serving of God', 'that a man which cometh at no sermons may as well believe as he which hears all the sermons in the world', and 'that a man eats his maker in the sacrament'. Though the forms of worship had changed, for many the scheme of salvation had not: 'We must be saved by our good prayers and good serving of God.'[9] So the new prayers must now function as the old had done, enlisting Christ's mercy and assuaging the judicial wrath of God.

The political Reformations had succeeded in driving Catholic public worship from the churches; but the Protestant Reformation did not destroy essentially Catholic views of Christian life and eternal salvation. The political Reformations had succeeded in imposing more Protestant ways of worship; but the Protestant Reformation did not generate widespread attachment to Protestant doctrines of justification. So men and women expected to be saved through the Church, as their forebears had been; the external actions of prayer and praise had changed, but the benefits anticipated from them had not. If the parish church could no longer provide salvation through the sacraments of the Church of Rome, it would have to give salvation through those of the Church of England. And in many parishes the new services slowly acquired the appeal of the old. The Prayer Book services were introduced by conforming ex-Catholic priests, often with the movements and vestments of the old mass, which were only abandoned under pressure from bishops or with the succession of new ministers. The Book of Common Prayer thus gained the legitimacy and the assumed efficacy of the mass book.

This was probably one reason why there was so much trouble for Protestant ministers who rejected some Prayer Book ceremonies as popish: how could rituals be effective if the clergy missed them out or got them wrong? In 1574 some parishioners at Cirencester refused to receive communion because it was not administered according to the Prayer Book. In 1583 Edward Fage, gentleman, of Doddington in Essex asked his minister to follow the Book of Common Prayer in services. In return he was abused in sermons, so he took himself off to worship at Stondon Massey.[10] There were demands for surplice, cross, and churchings at Preston Capes in 1584–5, and there parishioners continued to protest against clergy who refused to minister by the book. There were troubles at Flixton in Suffolk in 1588–90 over the nonconformity of the vicar, Thomas Daynes: when members of the congregation followed the services in their Prayer Books to try to keep him to the rubrics, he cried, 'they which would have service said according to the Book of Common Prayer are papists and atheists'; and he was half right, for why should Protestants care much for liturgical accuracy?[11]

There was a particular insistence that baptisms should be properly performed, for otherwise a child's soul might be at risk. Perkins complained of 'the common ignorant sort of people, who think that an infant dying without baptism dies without Christendom'—and the baptism had to be with a sign of the cross, as the Prayer Book, the people of Preston Capes, and many other parishioners demanded. In 1597 the churchwardens of St Cuthbert's Thetford reported that Elizabeth Jenkinson had prevented their minister using the sign of the cross at a christening, 'thereby giving great offence to many those inhabitants of Thetford then and there present'.[12] If ministers could not be trusted for a reliable baptism, people voted with their feet and sought the sacrament elsewhere. In 1598 and 1601 it was complained that the vicar of Leyland in Lancashire did not sign with a cross, 'wherefore many of the parishioners do cause their children to be baptized at other churches'. It was the same at Poulton in 1604 and at Kirkham in 1605, where sixty-one families were presented for having children christened away from their own church.[13] We need to notice the protests of parishioners, as well as the nonconformity of ministers.

The combination of successful political Reformations and less successful Protestant Reformation had established an anomaly: the Church of England was Protestant—not as Protestant as many wished, yet Protestant; but its people—most of its people—were not. They were accused of 'popery and atheism' by godly ministers, but unfairly. Though they retained a works religion, they were certainly not Catholics; they were beyond the reach of Catholic priests, outside and opposed to the institutional Church of Rome. And nor were they atheists, by which the godly meant that they were mere conformists. Perkins thought that 'the world abounds with atheists, epicures, libertines, worldlings, neuters that are of no religion',[14] but he was probably wrong. The majority were conformists, but not *mere* conformists. They conformed to what suited them, the residual rituals of the Prayer Book; they would not conform to what did not suit them, the godly regime of long sermons and truncated ceremonies. They wanted to stand and sing, to bow and kneel, to have rings and crosses, as the Prayer Book gave them leave, and they wanted to receive the communion without officious examination by their minister.

These churchgoers were de-catholicized but un-protestantized. What they were not is a good deal clearer than what they were. Perkins and others claimed they just wanted an easy life: not too much preaching, not too much moral discipline, not too much Sabbath observance, not too much learning of catechism, not too much religion! Perkins had a point. But the binary vision of the predestinarians lumped all worldlings together indiscriminately. Certainly some of them were surly conscripts to matins as they (or their parents) had been surly conscripts to mass; certainly some mocked real devotion, scorned moral lessons, and flouted Church rules, 'swearing, gaming, drinking, surfeiting, revelling, and railing on the ministers of the word'.[15] But those who defended church ceremonies against the nonconformists were hardly (despite Perkins) 'the ungodly', even if they were the not very godly. Perhaps they may be called 'parish anglicans': 'parish', because they stressed communal values of village harmony and worship and objected to the divisiveness of the godly; 'anglican' (but not yet 'Anglican'), because they stressed Prayer Book rituals and objected to the nonconformity of the godly.

Where the Protestant Reformation really succeeded, it made Perkins-style Protestants; where it failed, the political Reformations made 'parish anglicans'. And there were some who resisted (and some who escaped) both Protestant and political Reformations: the Catholics. For recusant papists, the Jesuit Robert Southwell offered a pattern of piety more realistic than that of Perkins: *A Short Rule of Good Life*, 'to direct the devout Christian in a regular and orderly course'. Southwell too asked for self-denial and study, but sought a practical routine rather than a proof of godliness.[16] Each day should have prayer and meditation on waking, rosary in mid-morning ('if company and other more weighty matters will permit'), prayers before and after meals, afternoon prayer, reading of pious books before supper (but reading for relaxation after), examination of conscience at bedtime, prayer and meditation until sleep. If possible there should be confession twice weekly, careful preparation for communion, and communion every Sunday and high festival. And if no priest was available, 'I must notwithstanding at my usual times prepare myself and to almighty God make even in words the same confession that I would to my ghostly father.'[17]

Southwell's *Rule* was a latter-day Whitford's *Work*, perhaps 'A Work for Great Householders'—a model for the recusant gentry to follow. It too sold well, given the difficulties of production and distribution, and this was not surprising. It did not demand the soul-searching and earnestness which Perkins wanted, nor the same righteous rejection of the company of sinners. If private prayers were interrupted by unexpected visitors, a Catholic 'need not be much troubled for omitting the rest', for God would accept the entertainment of guests as a work of merit,[18] as he would accept the efficient management of household and estate as an appropriate offering to him. Servants should be carefully chosen, disciplined, and taught true religion; gambling among them should be restricted, but need not be forbidden. As with Whitford, aids to piety are not rejected; in the absence of images, each room should be dedicated to a saint, and each day given a patron saint who could proffer support. Southwell too wanted his book read regularly; at least once a month was his suggestion. But there were no strict prescriptions: 'thou must not understand that word MUST as though thou were bound to the performance of anything there expressed.'[19]

Southwell wrote his book about 1590, sixty years after Whitford's *Work*, and it was first published in 1595. In the two books the model Catholic lives the same spiritual life, but the Reformations have altered its context, from teeming Catholic London to a hostile countryside, from business household to a gentry mansion. The contrast reflects the eventual retreat of Catholicism across much of England to country-house oblivion. Whitford had wanted his Catholic to flaunt his piety in public devotions, but under persecution Southwell's papist had to be circumspect. His religion was necessarily more individual, more private, and more domestic, a set of interior convictions more than a set of social acts. The Catholic life had lost much of its public dimension, and some of the works which had characterized it had been pruned. In that sense, Southwell's Christian had been forced to become more like Perkins's Christian, and religion had been internalized. But not all Catholics could be thinking Catholics, Southwell Catholics, as not all non-Catholics could be thinking Protestants. There were still habitual Catholics, who followed the old ways without much thought.

The Jesuit John Gerard was impressed by the determination and devotion of the beleaguered East Anglian gentry households where he worked in the 1590s; adversity, education, and a resident chaplain made for an intensive piety of almost monastic dedication. But Gerard was unhappy with the easy-going ways of ordinary Catholics in parts of his native Lancashire, 'where a large number of the people are Catholics and nearly all have leanings towards Catholicism'. There it was easy to get 200 people at mass and sermon: however, 'People of this kind come into the Church without difficulty, but they fall away the moment persecution blows up. When the alarm is over, they come back again.'[20] In west Lancashire, parts of north Yorkshire, and on the Herefordshire–Monmouthshire borders—ill-governed areas with little Protestant preaching—there were pockets of semi-public Catholicism; the Reformations had passed by. In 1600 Richard Cowling, a Jesuit serving in Lancashire, reported that 'Catholics are so numerous that priests can wander through the villages and countryside with the utmost freedom', and laypeople knelt openly for a priest's blessing.[21] In such places (and on some Catholic estates) traditional habits had not been shattered, and 'the old religion' remained viable.

After the Reformations, then, there were four kinds of English Christians: godly Protestants, recusant papists, parish anglicans, and those we might call 'old Catholics', ranging from those most affected by Reformation to those least affected. The godly had found a new route to God; papists had been forced on to a side-track; parish anglicans travelled their usual road but by new transport; and only a few old Catholics used traditional ways. The godly Protestants were most numerous in the towns of the south and east; the old Catholics had been marginalized in the upland north and west. There was a thin scattering of recusant papists in many places, and the parish anglicans were everywhere. Many observers, Catholic and Protestant, thought the godly and the two sorts of Catholic were roughly equal minorities, with a large majority of parish anglicans.[22] We cannot tell if they were right. Perhaps the proportions are less significant than the fact and the perception of division. There had been amicable coexistence between exponents of different forms of religious experience before the Reformations: only a few Lollards stood outside a consensual Catholicism. But after the Reformations there were breaches and bitterness.

The godly Protestants were heretics and sectarians in the eyes of papists, religious maniacs who 'will walk to the fire so long as they find one', persecuting fanatics who harried God's priests to the gibbet. The parish anglicans were also critical of the earnestness and intolerance of the godly. Perkins complained that true Protestantism 'is nick-named with terms of "preciseness" and "purity" ', so people were ashamed to be thought fervent; 'some say that if they should frequent sermons they should be accounted precise and be mocked for their labour'.[23] Both the godly and the papists, enthusiasts all, despised parish anglicans as worthless time-servers: for Perkins, they were those who believed 'it is safest to do in religion as most do'; the papists at Douai thought 'they will turn as the wind, and to the stronger side'. If the godly distinguished at all between papists and old Catholics, it was only to see the former as slightly more traitorous than superstitious, and the latter as slightly more superstitious than traitorous. Both were 'wicked imps of Antichrist', and Perkins was clear that the Antichrist 'as it is now apparent, can be none other than the pope of Rome'.[24]

So the Tudor Reformations had not replaced a Catholic England by a Protestant England: the country was divided, and the Protestants were insecure; popery had not been crushed, the worldlings had not turned to the gospel. For the godly, parish anglicans were not only failed Protestants, they were potential papists; they were still contaminated with Antichrist, unable to reject the devil and his works. Robert Cawdrey feared that if the Crown declared a restoration of the mass, only one in ten would refuse to abandon 'Christ and his religion'.[25] And why should the others not return to popery, for—as Gifford, Perkins, Dent, and more complained—they had never abandoned its essentials? Those who did not feel their salvation assured by faith were vulnerable to false religion, for they had not experienced the security of trust in Christ; those who had not turned to the Lord might be returned to Satan, by the persuasive wiles of Jesuits and seminary priests. The godly were thus surrounded by an infamous coalition against the gospel of Christ: papists, old Catholics, parish anglicans, the irreligious, the sinners rejected by God. No wonder they were nervous, no wonder they cried for ever more preaching, more persecution, more Reformation.

The godly were struck by what little had changed, despite all the efforts of princes and preachers, despite all the attacks on Antichrist. There were still lordly bishops, still officious Church courts, still underfunded parishes, still churches designed for popish worship not gospel sermons, still non-preaching ministers, still popish vestiges in the services, still popish opinions in the pews. 'We in England are so far off from having a Church rightly reformed, according to the prescript of God's word, that as yet we are scarce come to the outward face of the same', wailed the authors of *An Admonition to the Parliament* in 1572. Later, William Perkins thought that things were getting worse, and that the Protestant cause had lost its momentum: 'We are not now that which we have been twenty or thirty years ago', for 'sundry that have heretofore showed some forwardness begin to falter and stagger and look another way.'[26] Of course, there were also preaching bishops, pastoral judges, endowed lectureships, graduate preachers, English service-books, and godly men and women who knew the Lord and read their Bibles; but to admit so much weakened the case for continued Reformation.

To Roger Martyn in Suffolk it all looked different. There were no holy altars, no Latin masses, no saving sacraments, no crucifixes, no gilded images, no paintings in the church, and no processions around it; instead, there were sermons and psalms. The tithe was still demanded, but it seems to have been refused or disputed much more often. Long Melford had no assistant chaplains to pray for souls, its chapels decayed, and there was no abbey at Bury St Edmunds. For a hostile observer such as Martyn, the Church of England had become a diminished thing. In his youth, there had been about 40,000 parish priests in the Church; in his old age, there were fewer than 10,000. There had been 10,000 monks and friars and 2,000 nuns, but now there were none. The thousands of religious fraternities and the thousands of chantries had gone. Well over a thousand churches and chapels were no longer used for worship; most had been monastic churches, and were now converted to secular use; some were city churches made redundant by amalgamations; others were outlying chapels which had no ministers to serve there and no endowments or offerings to support them. Much had been destroyed.

But there remained nearly all the parish churches of England, stripped and scrubbed almost bare. The papists thought Christ had been driven from these buildings, the godly thought Antichrist still ruled there. But for the rest—that is, for most—the churches were as they had always been: community centres, where people met God and their neighbours to mark seasons of the year and stages of life, to be reminded of duties and ask forgiveness for sins, to seek safety in this world and salvation in the next.

Robert Southwell and William Perkins were not much impressed by this unintensive religious regime; nor had Richard Whitford been. But its retention through the disruptive Reformations—'one while popery, another while the Gospel; now peace, and anon persecution'[27]—suggests it met real human needs. When the Protestants offered (and then tried to enforce) a more earnest alternative, that had been widely rejected. Perhaps it was because it was new, perhaps because it was irksome, perhaps also because it gave solace to so few. The continuing religion of worship and works—a little worship and not many good works—sold security for all, at a reasonable price. It was an offer not to be refused.

The Reformations brought drama and excitement. Henry VIII disposed of the pope, the monasteries, four of his wives, and two of his closest advisers. There was constant muttering against religious change, and there were dangerous rebellions in 1536, 1549, 1554, and 1569. The two Edwardian governments were overthrown by force, and both Mary and Elizabeth alienated sections of the aristocracy and many of their clergy. The ecclesiastical policy of the state shifted sharply in 1530, 1538, 1547, 1553, and 1559 (twice); it may almost have done so in 1536, 1549, 1561, and 1579. Protestants marched steadfastly towards the horror of the heretics' fire, Catholics towards the ordeal of the traitors' gallows. There was piety and political calculation, hope and despair, striving and endurance; and there was daily life and worship, year upon year. While politicians were having their hesitant Reformations, while Protestants were preaching their evangelical reform, parish congregations went to church: they prayed again to their God, learned again how to be good, and went off home once more. That was how it had been in 1530; that was how it was in 1590. Some Reformations.

Abbreviations

APC	*Acts of the Privy Council of England*, ed. J. R. Dasent (1890–1907)
BIHR	*Bulletin of the Institute of Historical Research*
BIY	Borthwick Institute of Historical Research, York
BL	British Library
CPR	*Calendar of Patent Rolls*, 1547– (1924–)
CSPD	*Calendar of State Papers, Domestic Series*, ed. R. Lemon *et al.* (1856–72)
CSP Span	*Calendar of State Papers, Spanish*, ed. G. A. Bergenroth *et al.* (1862–1964)
CSP Ven	*Calendar of State Papers, Venetian*, ed. R. Brown *et al.* (1864–98)
EHR	*English Historical Review*
HJ	*Historical Journal*
HMC	Historical Manuscripts Commission
JEH	*Journal of Ecclesiastical History*
LJ	*Journals of the House of Lords*
LP	*Letters and Papers, Foreign and Domestic, of the Reign of Henry VIII*, ed. J. S. Brewer *et al.* (1862–1932)
PP	*Past and Present*
PRO	Public Record Office
RO	Record Office
SP	State Papers
TRHS	*Transactions of the Royal Historical Society*
TRP	*Tudor Royal Proclamations*, ed. P. L. Hughes and J. F. Larkin (1964–9)
VCH	*The Victoria History of the Counties of England*

Notes

Except for the publications of learned societies and works otherwise specified, the place of publication is London.

Prologue

1. W. Parker, *The History of Long Melford* (1873), 70–3.
2. Ibid. 77–87.
3. Ibid. 73.
4. J. Caley (ed.), *Valor Ecclesiasticus* (6 vols., 1810–34), iii. 451–3.
5. Ibid. 459–65.
6. There were two priests for each parish in a county such as Kent (M. L. Zell, 'The Personnel of the Clergy in Kent in the Reformation Period', *EHR* 89 (1974), 517), where the parishes were small, but as many as seven or eight in Lancashire, where parishes were very large (C. Haigh, *Reformation and Resistance in Tudor Lancashire* (Cambridge, 1975), 22, 30–3).
7. My comments on the medieval period depend heavily upon P. Heath, *Church and Realm, 1272–1461* (1988).
8. F. Seebohm, *The Oxford Reformers* (1911 edn.), 230–47. For a discussion of the sermon's context, see C. Harper-Bill, 'Dean Colet's Convocation Sermon and the Pre-Reformation Church in England', *History*, 73 (1988), 191–210. I accept the re-dating of the sermon to 1510; see J. B. Gleason, *John Colet* (Berkeley, Calif., 1989), 181–4, 370.
9. E. Surtz, *The Works and Days of John Fisher* (Cambridge, Mass., 1967), 59.

Introduction

1. Most firmly by M. Powicke, *The Reformation in England* (Oxford, 1941), 1.
2. For discussion of such an approach, see M. Oakeshott, 'Historical Experience', in *Experience and its Modes* (1933).

Chapter 1

1. Editions of Whitford and other authors have been calculated from W. A. Jackson, F. J. Ferguson, and K. F. Pantzer (eds.), *A Short-Title Catalogue of Books, 1475–1640*, 2 vols. (2nd edn., 1976, 1986), with help from J. Rhodes, 'Private Devotion in England on the Eve of the Reformation', Ph.D. thesis (Durham, 1974).
2. R. Whitford, *The Pomander of Prayer* (1531 edn.), sig. Aii.
3. Cf. W. A. Pantin, *The English Church in the Fourteenth Century* (Cambridge, 1955).
4. R. Whitford, *A Werke for Householders* (1530), sigs. Ci, Bi.
5. Ibid., sig. Eiii.
6. Whitford, *Pomander*, sig. Aii.
7. J. J. Scarisbrick, *The Reformation and the English People* (Oxford, 1984), 3–6;

W. K. Jordan, *The Charities of Rural England, 1480–1660* (1961); id., *The Charities of London* (1960); id., *The Social Institutions of Lancashire* (Manchester, 1962); id., 'The Formation of the Charitable Institutions of the West of England', *Transactions of the American Philosophical Society*, NS, 1 (1960); M. Bowker, *The Henrician Reformation: The Diocese of Lincoln under John Longland, 1521–1547* (Cambridge, 1981), 48, 148; L. R. Attreed, 'Preparation for Death in Sixteenth Century Northern England', *Sixteenth Century Journal*, 13 (1982), 46.

8. J. E. Binney (ed.), *The Accounts of the Wardens of the Parish of Morebath* (Devon and Cornwall Notes and Queries Supplement, 1904).

9. A. Hanham (ed.), *Churchwardens' Accounts of Ashburton, 1479–1580* (Devon and Cornwall Record Society, 1970); E. Hobhouse (ed.), *Churchwardens' Accounts of Croscombe, Pilton, Yatton, etc.* (Somerset Record Society, iv, 1890).

10. F. Ouvry, 'Extracts from the Churchwardens' Accounts of the Parish of Wing', *Archaeologia*, 36 (1855), 221–3, 227.

11. *VCH Cambridgeshire*, viii. 26; Dorset RO, P155/CW12–21.

12. C. Cotton (ed.), 'Churchwardens' Accounts of the Parish of St Andrew, Canterbury', *Archaeologia Cantiana*, 32–6 (1917–23).

13. H. Littlehales (ed.), *The Medieval Records of a London City Church (St Mary at Hill)*, (Early English Text Society, 1904–5).

14. R. C. Dudding (ed.), *The First Churchwardens' Book of Louth* (1941), 181; J. Stow, *The Survey of London* (1987 edn.), 131; J. E. Oxley, *The Reformation in Essex to the Death of Mary* (Manchester, 1965), 30–1; Scarisbrick, *Reformation*, 14; Dorset RO, P155/CW22.

15. *VCH Somerset*, iii. 11, 164, 264; iv. 104, 204, 220, 237; v. 51; R. Whiting, *The Blind Devotion of the People* (Cambridge, 1989), 86–9; D. MacCulloch, *Suffolk and the Tudors* (Oxford, 1986), 140 and n.; C. Haigh, *Reformation and Resistance in Tudor Lancashire* (Cambridge, 1975), 66.

16. See especially Scarisbrick, *Reformation*, 19–39; C. M. Barron, 'The Parish Fraternities of Medieval London', in C. M. Barron and C. Harper-Bill (eds.), *The Church in Pre-Reformation Society* (Woodbridge, 1985); S. Brigden, *London and the Reformation* (Oxford, 1989), 36–9; N. P. Tanner, *The Church in Late Medieval Norwich, 1370–1532* (Toronto, 1984), 71–88, 132, 223.

17. J. Foxe, *Acts and Monuments*, ed. G. Townsend (8 vols., 1843–9), v. 364.

18. R. Whiting, ' "For the Health of my Soul": Prayers for the Dead in the Tudor South-West', *Southern History*, 5 (1983), 71, 77, 92.

19. Whiting, *Blind Devotion*, 30; Attreed, 'Preparation for Death', 46; Bowker, *Henrician Reformation*, 177; Scarisbrick, *Reformation*, 5; C. Burgess, ' "By Quick and by Dead": Wills and Pious Provision in Late Medieval Bristol', *EHR* 102 (1987), 855–6.

20. J. A. F. Thomson, 'Piety and Charity in Late Medieval London', *JEH* 16 (1965), 191–2; Tanner, *Norwich*, 101, 104, 220–1; R. B. Dobson, 'The Foundation of Perpetual Chantries by the Citizens of Medieval York', in C. J. Cuming (ed.), *Studies in Church History*, iv (Leiden, 1967), 32–7; A. Kreider, *English Chantries: The Road to Dissolution* (Cambridge, Mass., 1979), 85, 87–90.

21. Tanner, *Norwich*, 107–8.

22. J. H. Moran, 'Clerical Recruitment in the Diocese of York, 1340–1530: Data and Commentary', *JEH* 34 (1983), 19–20, 47, 49, 54.

23. Moran, 'Clerical Recruitment', 49 and n.; A. T. Bannister (ed.), *Register of Charles Bothe* (Canterbury and York Society, 1921), 304–30; Lichfield Joint RO, B/A/1/12, fos. 178–291; B/A/1/14 ii; S. Thompson, 'The Pastoral Work of the English and Welsh Episcopate, 1500–1558', D.Phil. thesis (Oxford, 1984), 179, 184; Bowker, *Henrician Reformation*, 40; Guildhall RO, MS 9531/10, fos. 152–63; R. L. Storey, 'Ordinations of Secular Priests in Early Tudor London', *Nottingham Medieval Studies*, 33 (1989), 122–33.

24. Moran, 'Clerical Recruitment', 51; W. F. Irvine (ed.), 'List of the Clergy in Eleven Deaneries of the Archdeaconry of Chester, 1541–2', *Record Society of Lancashire and Cheshire*, 33 (1896); H. E. Malden and H. Chitty (eds.), *Registers of Gardiner and Ponet* (Canterbury and York Society, 1930), 174–85.

25. Bowker, *Henrician Reformation*, 124; M. L. Zell, 'The Personnel of the Clergy in Kent in the Reformation Period', *EHR* 89 (1974), 517.

26. Kreider, *English Chantries*, 38–70; C. Burgess, ' "For Increase of Divine Service": Chantries in the Parish in Late Medieval Bristol', *JEH* 36 (1985), 50–3, 59–65.

27. Of course, strictly speaking we know only of printings, not sales, but it is reasonable to assume that in a competitive market printers only reprinted works which were selling well.

28. Tanner, *Norwich*, 240–2, 248–51.

Chapter 2

1. S. Brigden, *London and the Reformation* (Oxford, 1989), 62; P. Heath, *English Parish Clergy on the Eve of the Reformation* (1969), 73–4.

2. G. R. Elton, *Star Chamber Stories* (1958), 175–220.

3. C. Jenkins, 'Cardinal Morton's Register', in R. W. Seton-Watson (ed.), *Tudor Studies* (1924), 65–9.

4. Calculated from K. L. Wood-Legh (ed.), *Kentish Visitations of Archbishop William Warham* (Kent Archaeological Society, 1984).

5. M. Bowker, *The Secular Clergy in the Diocese of Lincoln, 1495–1520* (Cambridge, 1968), 3, 110–11, 114, 116, 151–2; ead., *The Henrician Reformation: The Diocese of Lincoln under John Longland, 1521–1547* (Cambridge, 1981), 6–7.

6. T. More, *A Dialogue Concerning Heresies*, ed. T. M. C. Lawler, G. Marc'hadour, and R. C. Marius (Complete Works of St Thomas More, New Haven, Conn., 1981), i. 301.

7. J. H. Moran, 'Clerical Recruitment in the Diocese of York, 1340–1530: Data and Commentary', *JEH* 34 (1983), 50–1.

8. W. Lyndwood, *Provinciale seu constitutiones Angliae* (Oxford, 1679 edn.), 33; S. Thompson, 'The Pastoral Work of the English and Welsh Episcopate, 1500–1558', D.Phil. thesis (Oxford, 1984), 34–6, 178, 181–3.

9. Ibid. 108–9.

10. Ibid. 109; Bowker, *Secular Clergy*, 104–5.

11. Heath, *English Parish Clergy*, 56, 61.

12. N. P. Tanner, *The Church in Late Medieval Norwich, 1370–1532* (Toronto, 1984), 24–6; R. Houlbrooke, *Church Courts and the People during the English Reformation, 1520–1570* (Oxford, 1979), 101–2.

13. *LP* vii. 523(4).

14. Wood-Legh (ed.), *Kentish Visitations*, 97, 176.
15. B. L. Woodcock, *Medieval Ecclesiastical Courts in the Diocese of Canterbury* (1952), 86; Houlbrooke, *Church Courts*, 133–4, 147, 273–4; Heath, *English Parish Clergy*, 152; Tanner, *Norwich*, 6.
16. Houlbrooke, *Church Courts*, 122–3, 127–34, 136, 140.
17. C. Haigh, *Reformation and Resistance in Tudor Lancashire* (Cambridge, 1975), 59–60.
18. Brigden, *London*, 52, 201, 203.
19. S. Brigden, 'Tithe Controversy in Reformation London', *JEH* 32 (1981), 285–301.
20. Brigden, *London*, 50–1; Haigh, *Reformation and Resistance*, 58–9.
21. HMC, *Third Report* (1872), 333.
22. Wood-Legh (ed.), *Kentish Visitations*, 22, 134.
23. Haigh, *Reformation and Resistance*, 57.
24. Bowker, *Henrician Reformation*, 53; Cheshire RO, EDC 1/1–3; Woodcock, *Medieval Ecclesiastical Courts*, 86; Houlbrooke, *Church Courts*, 125; C. St German, 'A Treatise concerning the Division between the Spiritualty and Temporalty', in T. More, *The Apology*, ed. J. B. Trapp (Complete Works of St Thomas More, New Haven, Conn., 1979), 194–5.
25. *LP* xi. 106.
26. Wood-Legh (ed.), *Kentish Visitations*, 122; Bowker, *Secular Clergy*, 30; ead., *Henrician Reformation*, 54–5.
27. R. Wunderli, 'Pre-Reformation London Summoners and the Murder of Richard Hunne', *JEH* 33 (1982), 215 and n.; Woodcock, *Medieval Ecclesiastical Courts*, 100.
28. S. Lander, 'Church Courts and the Reformation in the Diocese of Chichester', in C. Haigh (ed.), *The English Reformation Revised* (Cambridge, 1987), 49–50.
29. D. Crawford, 'The Rule of Law? The Laity, English Archdeacons' Courts, and the Reformation to 1558', *Parergon*, NS, 4 (1986), 155–62, 170–1; Houlbrooke, *Church Courts*, 273–81.
30. M. Bowker, 'The Commons Supplication against the Ordinaries in the Light of some Archidiaconal *Acta*', *TRHS* 5th series, 21 (1971), 62–74; Houlbrooke, *Church Courts*, 42, 95–6, 112, 114–16, 263.
31. Wood-Legh (ed.), *Kentish Visitations*, 258, 85, 267–9.
32. Ibid. 203–5.
33. J. Foxe, *Acts and Monuments*, ed. G. Townsend (1843–9), iv. 580–1.
34. A. Hudson, *The Premature Reformation* (Oxford, 1988), 11–18, 451–3.
35. S. J. Smart, 'John Foxe and "The Story of Richard Hun, Martyr" ', *JEH* 37 (1986), 3; S. Brigden, 'The Early Reformation in London, 1520–1547', Ph.D. thesis (Cambridge, 1979), 87 and n.; W. Farrer (ed.), *Court Rolls of the Honour of Clitheroe* (3 vols., 1897–1913), i. 58; Cheshire RO, EDC 2/2, p. 138.
36. Foxe, *Acts and Monuments*, iv. 222, 233, 237. For Lollard fear of public hostility, see Hudson, *Premature Reformation*, 148, 149, 468, 495.
37. Hudson, *Premature Reformation*, 236, 226; A. Hope, 'Lollardy: The Stone the Builders Rejected?', in P. Lake and M. Dowling (eds.), *Protestantism and the National Church* (1987), 8–11, 13.
38. More, *The Apology*, 115.

39. M. Aston, *Lollards and Reformers* (1984), 72–5, 81–95; J. A. F. Thomson, *The Later Lollards, 1414–1520* (Oxford, 1965), 117–38.
40. Thomson, *Later Lollards*, 173–91; Bowker, *Henrician Reformation*, 59–60, 183.
41. Foxe, *Acts and Monuments*, iv. 227.
42. Ibid. iv. 440 ff.; Hope, 'Lollardy', 3–4; D. Plumb, 'The Social and Economic Spread of Rural Lollardy: A Reappraisal', in W. J. Sheils and D. Wood (eds.), *Studies in Church History* (Oxford, 1986), 121–2.
43. Hope, 'Lollardy', 4–5; Plumb, 'Social and Economic Spread of Lollardy', 113–16; J. Fines, 'Heresy Trials in the Diocese of Coventry and Lichfield, 1511–12', *JEH* 14 (1963), 162; Brigden, *London*, 97–8.
44. Jenkins, 'Cardinal Morton's Register', 47–9; Hudson, *Premature Reformation*, 467–8.
45. Thomson, *Later Lollards*, 226–30; Foxe, *Acts and Monuments*, iv. 243.
46. A. G. Dickens, *Reformation Studies* (1982), 379; id., *Lollards and Protestants in the Diocese of York* (Oxford, 1959), 47.
47. Foxe, *Acts and Monuments*, iv. 222, 237–8; J. F. Davis, *Heresy and Reformation in the South-East of England, 1520–1559* (1983), 27.
48. BL, Cotton MS Cleopatra E. v, fo. 360 (*LP* iv(3). 6385).

Chapter 3

1. J. Foxe, *Acts and Monuments*, ed. G. Townsend (1843–9), iv. 583–4.
2. Ibid. 583, 584–5.
3. J. McConica (ed.), *The History of the University of Oxford*, iii (Oxford, 1986), 123.
4. J. J. Scarisbrick, *Henry VIII* (1971 edn.), 152–6.
5. D. Wilkins, *Concilia Magnae Britanniae* (4 vols., 1737), iii. 690–3; A. T. Bannister (ed.), *Register of Charles Bothe* (Canterbury and York Society, 1921), 102; *TRP* i. 133; M. Bowker, *The Henrician Reformation: The Diocese of Lincoln under John Longland, 1521–1547* (Cambridge, 1981), 58–9.
6. R. Houlbrooke, *Church Courts and the People during the English Reformation, 1520–1570* (Oxford, 1979), 226; P. Clark, *English Provincial Society from the Reformation to the Revolution: Kent 1500–1640* (Hassocks, 1977), 30.
7. N. Harpsfield, *The Life and Death of Sir Thomas More*, ed. E. V. Hitchcock (Early English Text Society, clxxvi, 1932), 84–5; R. M. Fisher, 'Reform, Repression, and Unrest at the Inns of Court, 1518–1558', *HJ* 20 (1977), 790–1, 796.
8. J. F. Davis, *Heresy and Reformation in the South-East of England, 1520–1559* (1983), 41–2.
9. J. A. Muller (ed.), *The Letters of Stephen Gardiner* (Cambridge, 1933), 167.
10. Foxe, *Acts and Monuments*, iv. 635.
11. Ibid. 635, 642; Davis, *Heresy and Reformation*, 46.
12. W. A. Clebsch, *England's Earliest Protestants, 1520–1535* (New Haven, Conn., 1964), 43–7; J. P. Lusardi, 'The Career of Robert Barnes', in T. More, *Confutation of Tyndale's Answer*, ed. L. A. Schuster *et al.* (Complete Works of St Thomas More, New Haven, Conn., 1973), iii. 1371–83.
13. *LP* iv(1). 1962; S. Brigden, *London and the Reformation* (Oxford, 1989), 158–9.
14. Clebsch, *England's Earliest Protestants*, 139–42; Brigden, *London*, 106–8.

15. Brigden, *London*, 159–60.
16. J. Strype, *Ecclesiastical Memorials* (3 vols., Oxford, 1822), i(2). 54–5, 63–5.
17. McConica, *Oxford*, 123–4, 363–4; Foxe, *Acts and Monuments*, v. app. 6.
18. Bowker, *Henrician Reformation*, 62.
19. Davis, *Heresy and Reformation*, 33, 46–52.
20. S. Brigden, 'The Early Reformation in London, 1520–1547', Ph.D. thesis (Cambridge, 1979), 86.
21. S. Thompson, 'The Pastoral Work of the English and Welsh Episcopate, 1500–1558', D.Phil. thesis (Oxford, 1984), 128; Davis, *Heresy and Reformation*, 48–52.
22. Davis, *Heresy and Reformation*, 49.
23. Ibid. 12.
24. The following account is based on Strype, *Ecclesiastical Memorials*, i(1). 113–34; (2). 50–65; Davis, *Heresy and Reformation*, 57–64.
25. Davis, *Heresy and Reformation*, 63.
26. Foxe, *Acts and Monuments*, iv. 688.
27. *CSP Ven*, 1527–33, 271; Brigden, *London*, 183–4.
28. Foxe, *Acts and Monuments*, iv. 659–64.
29. Ibid. 683–5.
30. Ibid. 698–700; Fisher, 'Reform, Repression, and Unrest', 791.
31. Foxe, *Acts and Monuments*, v. 38–9.
32. Davis, *Heresy and Reformation*, 80.
33. Foxe, *Acts and Monuments*, v. 19–26.
34. Davis, *Heresy and Reformation*, 66; J. A. Guy, *The Public Career of Sir Thomas More* (Brighton, 1980), 167–71; D. MacCulloch, *Suffolk and the Tudors* (Oxford, 1986), 150, 154.
35. Foxe, *Acts and Monuments*, v. 25–6; iv. 580–1; H. Latimer, *Remains*, ed. G. E. Corrie (Parker Society, 1845), 224.
36. G. R. Elton, *Policy and Police* (Cambridge, 1972), 353.
37. Foxe, *Acts and Monuments*, iv. 618–19; *LP* iv(2). 4038(3); vi. 99; H. Robinson (ed.), *Original Letters Relative to the English Reformation* (2 vols., Parker Society, 1846), i. 230–2.
38. M. Dowling (ed.), 'William Latymer's Chronickille', *Camden Miscellany*, xxx (Camden Society, 1990), 54–5; A. G. Dickens, *Lollards and Protestants in the Diocese of York* (Oxford, 1959), 38.
39. Foxe, *Acts and Monuments*, v. 33–4.
40. MacCulloch, *Suffolk*, 143–5; T. More, *A Dialogue concerning Heresies*, ed. T. M. C. Lawler, G. Marc'hadour, and R. C. Marius (Complete Works of St Thomas More, New Haven, Conn., 1981), i. 92–4.
41. BL, C 18 e 2. 96; *VCH Hertfordshire*, ii. 385. The incident is discussed, with a rather different emphasis, in M. Aston, 'Iconoclasm at Rickmansworth, 1522', *JEH* 40 (1989), 524–52.
42. Foxe, *Acts and Monuments*, iv. 706–7; MacCulloch, *Suffolk*, 155.
43. Brigden, *London*, 228.
44. Foxe, *Acts and Monuments*, v. 31.
45. e.g. Brigden, *London*, 29–30, 34–42, 380–9; R. Whiting, *The Blind Devotion of the People* (Cambridge, 1989), 20, 30, 60, 63.

Chapter 4

1. S. E. Lehmberg, *The Reformation Parliament, 1529–1536* (Cambridge, 1970), 117, 145, 151; D. Wilkins, *Concilia Magnae Britanniae* (1737), iii. 724, 746; J. Foxe, *Acts and Monuments*, ed. G. Townsend (1843–9), v. 29; G. Burnet, *The History of the Reformation*, ed. N. Pocock (7 vols., Oxford, 1865), iii. 164, 167.

2. Foxe, *Acts and Monuments*, v. app. 3; *LP* vii. 923; E. Hall, *Henry VIII*, ed. C. Whibley (2 vols., 1904), ii. 225.

3. Hall, *Henry VIII*, ii. 210.

4. J. Guy, 'Law, Lawyers, and the English Reformation', *History Today* (November 1985), 16–18; E. W. Ives, 'The Common Lawyers in Pre-Reformation England', *TRHS* 5th series, 18 (1968), 165–7; B. L. Woodcock, *Medieval Ecclesiastical Courts in the Diocese of Canterbury* (1952), 88–90.

5. Guy, 'Law, Lawyers, and the English Reformation', 20; J. H. Baker (ed.), *The Reports of Sir John Spelman* (Selden Society, 1977), ii. 64–5.

6. R. L. Storey, *Diocesan Administration in Fifteenth-Century England* (2nd edn., Borthwick Papers, 1972), 27; W. T. Waugh, 'The Great Statute of Praemunire', *EHR* 37, 173–205; Baker (ed.), *Sir John Spelman*, ii. 66, 237.

7. Storey, *Diocesan Administration*, 30; Baker (ed.), *Sir John Spelman*, 65.

8. Baker (ed.), *Sir John Spelman*, ii. 48, 53–4, 60–1, 237–43.

9. A. Fox and J. Guy, *Reassessing the Henrician Age: Humanism, Politics, and Reform, 1500–1550* (Oxford, 1986), 174–5.

10. R. J. Knecht, 'The Episcopate and the Wars of the Roses', *University of Birmingham Historical Journal*, 6 (1958), 108–10, 120, 129–31; R. G. Davies, 'The Episcopate', in C. H. Clough (ed.), *Profession, Vocation, and Culture in Later Medieval England* (Liverpool, 1982), 57–62.

11. C. Harper-Bill, 'Archbishop John Morton and the Province of Canterbury', *JEH* 29 (1978), 4–5.

12. PRO, SC 1/44, fo. 83 (I owe this reference to Robin Storey). The date of the letter is uncertain, but see Baker (ed.), *Sir John Spelman*, ii. 68.

13. K. L. Wood-Legh (ed.), *Kentish Visitations of Archbishop William Warham* (Kent Archaeological Society, 1984), 82, 86, 133.

14. Storey, *Diocesan Administration*, 20, 24, 32.

15. J. A. F. Thomson, *The Later Lollards, 1414–1520* (Oxford, 1965), 237–8; R. A. B. Mynors, D. F. S. Thomson, and W. K. Ferguson (eds.), *The Correspondence of Erasmus, 1501–1514* (Collected Works of Erasmus, Toronto, 1975), 189, 192.

16. F. Seebohm, *The Oxford Reformers* (1911 edn.), 230–47.

17. BL, Cotton MS Vitellius B. ii. fos. 80–1^v (*LP* i(2). 3033).

18. P. I. Kaufman, 'Polydore Vergil and the Strange Disappearance of Christopher Urswick', *Sixteenth Century Journal*, 17 (1986), 79–81; D. MacCulloch, *Suffolk and the Tudors* (Oxford, 1986), 148–9.

19. His story is now best read in S. Brigden, *London and the Reformation* (Oxford, 1989), 98–103, and R. Wunderli, 'Pre-Reformation London Summoners and the Murder of Richard Hunne', *JEH* 33 (1982), 218–24.

20. Wunderli, 'Pre-Reformation London Summoners', 217–18.

21. S. M. Jack, 'The Conflict of Common Law and Canon Law in Sixteenth-Century England: Richard Hunne Revisited', *Parergon*, NS, 3 (1985), 135–8, 141.

22. S. J. Smart, 'John Foxe and "The Story of Richard Hun, Martyr" ', *JEH* 37 (1986), 4; J. Fines, 'The Post-Mortem Condemnation for Heresy of Richard Hunne', *EHR* 78 (1963), 523–31.
23. Wunderli, 'Pre-Reformation London Summoners', 221–2.
24. D. Hay (ed.), *The Anglica Historica of Polydore Vergil* (Camden Society, 1950), 229; E. J. Davis, 'The Authorities for the Case of Richard Hunne', *EHR* 30 (1915), 477–8.
25. J. G. Bellamy, *Criminal Law and Society in Late Medieval and Tudor England* (Gloucester, 1984), 115–32.
26. The 1515 controversies are helpfully discussed by J. D. M. Derrett, 'The Affairs of Richard Hunne and Friar Standish', in T. More, *The Apology*, ed. J. B. Trapp (Complete Works of Thomas More, New Haven, Conn., 1979), 226–35; Bellamy, *Criminal Law and Society*, 133–7; P. Gwyn, *The King's Cardinal: The Rise and Fall of Thomas Wolsey* (1990), 46–50.
27. W. Ullmann, 'This Realm of England is an Empire', *JEH* 30 (1979), 183 (though Ullmann assumed that the oath was altered in 1509).
28. J. A. Guy, 'Henry VIII and the Praemunire Manœuvres of 1530–1531', *EHR* 97 (1982), 497.
29. Ullmann, 'This Realm of England', 177, 184, 195–6, 200, 203; Baker (ed.) *Sir John Spelman*, ii. 65.
30. *LJ* i. 57.
31. R. J. Schoeck, 'Common Law and Canon Law in their Relation to Thomas More', in R. S. Sylvester (ed.), *St Thomas More: Action and Contemplation* (New Haven, Conn., 1972), 41–2. Cf. A. G. Dickens, *The English Reformation* (2nd edn., 1989), 116.
32. R. Fiddes, *The Life of Cardinal Wolsey* (1724), Collections, 179.
33. The best discussion of Wolsey as churchman is now Gwyn, *King's Cardinal*, 265–355, 464–80.
34. R. Bayne (ed.), *The Life of Fisher* (Early English Text Society, extra series, xxvii, 1921), 34–5.
35. M. Bowker, *The Secular Clergy in the Diocese of Lincoln, 1495–1520* (Oxford, 1968), 124–6.
36. P. Clark, *English Provincial Society from the Reformation to the Revolution: Kent, 1500–1640* (Hassocks, 1977), 32.
37. Seebohm, *Oxford Reformers*, 240.
38. C. Haigh (ed.), *The English Reformation Revised* (Cambridge, 1987), 3, 23, 38–46, 78; R. Houlbrooke, *Church Courts and the People during the English Reformation, 1520–1570* (Oxford, 1979), 10–11; S. Thompson, 'The Pastoral Work of the English and Welsh Episcopate, 1500–1558', D.Phil. thesis (Oxford, 1984), 34–6, 105–9, 181.
39. M. Bowker, *The Henrician Reformation: The Diocese of Lincoln under John Longland, 1521–1547* (Cambridge, 1981), 11.
40. Thompson, 'Pastoral Work', 125, 210–20.
41. Guy, 'Law, Lawyers, and the English Reformation', 16–17.
42. J. A. Guy, *Christopher St German on Chancery and Statute* (Selden Society, suppl. series, 1985), 19–21; C. St German, *Doctor and Student*, ed. T. F. T. Plucknett and J. L. Barton (Selden Society, 1974), 230–1, 242–3, 309, 313–14.

Chapter 5

1. J. A. Guy, *The Political Career of Sir Thomas More* (Brighton, 1980), 136–8 (an interpretation I find more convincing than J. A. Guy, 'Henry VIII and the Praemunire Manœuvres of 1530–1531', *EHR* 97 (1982), 482–8).

2. For the rise of Anne, I follow, in the main, E. W. Ives, *Anne Boleyn* (Oxford, 1986), 77–182, but cf. R. M. Warnicke, *The Rise and Fall of Anne Boleyn* (Cambridge, 1989), 43–99. The best overall treatment of the divorce campaign is still J. J. Scarisbrick, *Henry VIII* (1971 edn.), 218–316, but there is important new material in V. M. Murphy, 'The Debate over Henry VIII's First Divorce', Ph.D. thesis (Cambridge, 1984).

3. Scarisbrick, *Henry VIII*, 202–7.

4. Ibid. 267–9. P. Gwyn, *The King's Cardinal: The Rise and Fall of Thomas Wolsey* (1990), 537, suggests Wolsey never believed this scheme would work.

5. Ives, *Anne Boleyn*, 102, 106–9.

6. Ibid. 122–4, 131–2.

7. D. Starkey, *The Reign of Henry VIII: Personalities and Politics* (1985), 94–100.

8. M. D. Knowles, ' "The Matter of Wilton" in 1528', *BIHR* 31 (1958), 92–6.

9. R. Fiddes, *The Life of Cardinal Wolsey* (1724), Collections, 175.

10. *LP* iv(2). 3913, p. 1742.

11. Scarisbrick, *Henry VIII*, 282–3, 286.

12. Ives, *Anne Boleyn*, 136–7, 161–3.

13. *LP* iv(3). 5476, 5481; Ives, *Anne Boleyn*, 139–41.

14. Scarisbrick, *Henry VIII*, 294. For the divorce hearing, see H. A. Kelly, *The Matrimonial Trials of Henry VIII* (Stanford, Calif., 1976), 75–131; Murphy, 'Debate over Divorce', 58–137.

15. E. Hall, *Henry VIII*, ed. C. Whibley (1904), ii. 153.

16. *LP* iv(3). 5749, quotation at p. 2551.

17. Guy, *More*, 106, 206–7.

18. Ives, *Anne Boleyn*, 141–50. Cf. Gwyn, *King's Cardinal*, 51–3.

19. *LP* iv(3). 6075.

20. S. E. Lehmberg, *The Reformation Parliament, 1529–1536* (Cambridge, 1970), 81–2.

21. Hall, *Henry VIII*, ii. 164–5.

22. Ibid. 166–7.

23. S. Brigden, 'Tithe Controversy in Reformation London', *JEH* 32 (1981), 294–6.

24. Scarisbrick, *Henry VIII*, 279.

25. R. Houlbrooke, *Church Courts and the People during the English Reformation, 1520–1570* (Oxford, 1979), 114–15; Hall, *Henry VIII*, ii. 166. It is most unlikely that Wolsey really had demanded a thousand marks for probate of a will worth £4,485 (G. W. Bernard, 'The Rise of Sir William Compton, Early Tudor Courtier', *EHR* 96 (1981), 772), as Sir Henry Guildford claimed; that would have been fifteen times the usual rate, and would surely have been recorded and resisted.

26. Guy, *More*, 117–21; Hall, *Henry VIII*, ii. 167.

27. R. Bayne (ed.), *The Life of Fisher* (Early English Text Society, extra series, xxvii, 1921), 68–70; C. Haigh (ed.), *The English Reformation Revised* (Cambridge, 1987), 60–2.

28. See, for example, M. Bowker, *The Secular Clergy in the Diocese of Lincoln, 1495–1520* (Oxford, 1968), 90, 104–5; P. Heath, *English Parish Clergy on the Eve of the Reformation* (1969), 56, 67.

29. K. L. Wood-Legh (ed.), *Kentish Visitations of Archbishop Warham* (Kent Archaeological Society, 1984), 64, 66, 70–1, 83–5, 105, 106–7, 117, 124, 129, 132, 192–4, 217, 290–2.

30. Lehmberg, *Reformation Parliament*, 89–91, 97–9.

31. *CSP Span*, 1529–30, 349–50.

32. E. Surtz and V. Murphy (eds.), *The Divorce Tracts of Henry VIII* (Angers, 1988), pp. viii–xxvi; A. Fox and J. Guy, *Reassessing the Henrician Age: Humanism, Politics and Reform, 1500–1550* (Oxford, 1986), 154–6; Ives, *Anne Boleyn*, 159–60.

33. J. McConica, *The History of the University of Oxford*, iii (Oxford, 1986), 124–5.

34. *LP* iv(3). 6256.

35. *CSP Span*, 1529–30, 510–11.

36. Ives, *Anne Boleyn*, 164; Scarisbrick, *Henry VIII*, 339.

37. *LP* iv(3). 6638; Lehmberg, *Reformation Parliament*, 107.

38. G. Nicholson, 'The Act of Appeals and the English Reformation', in C. Cross *et al.* (eds.), *Law and Government under the Tudors* (Cambridge, 1988), 19–26; Fox and Guy, *Reassessing the Henrician Age*, 156–61.

39. Scarisbrick, *Henry VIII*, 341–3, 350–2; *CSP Span*, 1529–30, 734.

40. *CSP Span*, 1529–30, 758–9.

Chapter 6

1. J. A. Guy, *The Political Career of Sir Thomas More* (Brighton, 1980), 141–7.

2. For conflicting interpretation of the praemunire crisis, see J. J. Scarisbrick, 'The Pardon of the Clergy, 1531', *Cambridge Historical Journal*, 12 (1956), 22–39; J. A. Guy, 'Henry VIII and the Praemunire Manœuvres of 1530–1531', *EHR* 97 (1982), 481–503; G. W. Bernard, 'The Pardon of the Clergy Reconsidered', *JEH* 37 (1986), 258–87. I follow Guy for detail, but not for argument.

3. Scarisbrick, 'Pardon', 32.

4. Ibid. 33–5.

5. S. E. Lehmberg, *The Reformation Parliament, 1529–1536* (Cambridge, 1970), 112–15.

6. J. J. Scarisbrick, *Henry VIII* (1971 edn.), 362–3.

7. D. Wilkins, *Concilia Magnae Britanniae* (1737), iii. 745; A. G. Dickens, *Lollards and Protestants in the Diocese of York* (Oxford, 1959), 156–8.

8. E. Hall, *Henry VIII*, ed. C. Whibley (2 vols., 1904), ii. 200–1.

9. J. A. Guy, *Christopher St German on Chancery and Statute* (Selden Society, supplementary series, 1985), 21–2; C. St German, *Doctor and Student*, ed. T. F. T. Plucknett and J. L. Barton (Selden Society, 1974), 327.

10. Guy, *More*, 157–8; Hall, *Henry VIII*, ii. 185–95.

11. E. Surtz and V. Murphy (eds.), *The Divorce Tracts of Henry VIII* (Angers, 1988), pp. iv–ix.

12. Guy, *More*, 159–60; E. W. Ives, *Anne Boleyn* (Oxford, 1986), 169–76; *LP* v. 216.

13. *CSP Span*, 1529–30, 555.

14. Ibid. 1531–33, 384.

15. Lehmberg, *Reformation Parliament*, 137–8.
16. For the 'Supplication' crisis, see especially G. R. Elton, *Reform and Reformation* (1977), 150–5; and Guy, *More*, 186–201. Cf. C. Haigh (ed.), *The English Reformation Revised* (Cambridge, 1987), 62–6.
17. Hall, *Henry VIII*, ii. 203.
18. M. Kelly, 'The Submission of the Clergy', *TRHS* 5th series, 15 (1965), 103.
19. Wilkins, *Concilia*, iii. 750–2.
20. H. Gee and W. J. Hardy (eds.), *Documents Illustrative of English Church History* (1896), 154–76.
21. Hall, *Henry VIII*, ii. 209.
22. Wilkins, *Concilia*, iii. 753–4.
23. Ibid. 749.
24. Kelly, 'Submission', 107.
25. J. A. Muller (ed.), *The Letters of Stephen Gardiner* (Cambridge, 1933), 48–9; G. Redworth, *In Defence of the Church Catholic: The Life of Stephen Gardiner* (Oxford, 1990), 37–8.
26. Hall, *Henry VIII*, ii. 210–11.
27. Kelly, 'Submission', 115–17.
28. Guy, *More*, 198–200.
29. G. R. Elton, *Studies in Tudor and Stuart Politics and Government* (3 vols., Cambridge, 1974, 1983), ii, 82–106.
30. Guy, *More*, 207–8.
31. For this group, see pp. 137–9.
32. G. R. Elton, *Policy and Police* (Cambridge, 1972), 180–1, 206–7.
33. Lehmberg, *Reformation Parliament*, 192.
34. Elton, *Policy and Police*, 222–3.
35. E. F. Rogers (ed.), *St Thomas More: Selected Letters* (New Haven, Conn., 1961), 217.
36. S. Brigden, *London and the Reformation* (Oxford, 1989), 222–4; Elton, *Policy and Police*, 225, 120.
37. *Statutes of the Realm*, ed. A. Luders, T. E. Tomlins, *et al.* (11 vols., 1810–28), iii. 492.
38. W. Roper and N. Harpsfield, *Lives of Saint Thomas More* (1963), 50.

Chapter 7

1. G. R. Elton, *Policy and Police* (Cambridge, 1972), 400–20.
2. E. F. Rogers (ed.), *St Thomas More: Selected Letters* (New Haven, Conn., 1961), 249.
3. P. Janelle (ed.), *Obedience in Church and State: Three Political Tracts by Stephen Gardiner* (Cambridge, 1930), 68–171, quotation at p. 157.
4. Ibid., p. lvi.
5. J. Foxe, *Acts and Monuments*, ed. G. Townsend (1843–9), viii. 110.
6. The acceptance of royal supremacy by 'les Catholiques schismatiques' is discussed in J.-P. Moreau, *Rome ou l'Angleterre? Les réactions politiques des catholiques anglais au moment du schisme (1529–1553)* (Paris, 1984), 123–76.
7. R. Bayne (ed.), *The Life of Fisher* (Early English Text Society, extra series, xxvii, 1921), 108. The story may be aphocryphal.

8. Elton, *Policy and Police*, 232–40.
9. M. Bowker, 'The Supremacy and the Episcopate: The Struggle for Control, 1534–1540', *HJ* 18 (1975), 227–43.
10. E. W. Ives, *Anne Boleyn* (Oxford, 1986), 303–4; M. Dowling, 'Anne Boleyn and Reform', *JEH* 35 (1984), 38–9. Cf. R. M. Warnicke, *The Rise and Fall of Anne Boleyn* (Cambridge, 1989), 154–62.
11. J. G. Nichols (ed.), *Narratives of the Days of the Reformation* (Camden Society, 1859), 277–8.
12. E. G. Rupp, *Studies in the Making of the English Protestant Tradition* (Cambridge, 1947), 92–9.
13. For the fall of Anne, I follow Ives, *Anne Boleyn*, 335–408, and D. Starkey, *The Reign of Henry VIII: Personalities and Politics* (1985), 108–21, rather than Warnicke, *Rise and Fall of Anne Boleyn*, 191–233.
14. *CSP Span*, 1536–8, 81, 84–5, 106, 107–8.
15. J. E. Cox (ed.), *Miscellaneous Writings and Letters of Thomas Cranmer* (Parker Society, 1846), 324.
16. W. D. Hamilton (ed.), *Wriothesley's Chronicle* (2 vols., Camden Society, 1875, 1877), i. 33–5; J. Ridley, *Thomas Cranmer* (Oxford, 1962), 97–8. Tunstall and Longland also preached, apparently to prove their obedience to Henry's supremacy.
17. *CSP Span*, 1536–8, 84.
18. D. Wilkins, *Concilia Magnae Britanniae* (1737), iii. 805–7, discussed in P. Hughes, *The Reformation in England* (1963 edn.), ii. 24–9.
19. C. Lloyd (ed.), *Formularies of Faith* (Oxford, 1825), p. xvi.
20. Rupp, *English Protestant Tradition*, 106–14.
21. Lloyd, *Formularies*, pp. xxi, xxv.
22. Ibid., pp. xxvi–xxvii.
23. H. Gee and W. J. Hardy (eds.), *Documents Illustrative of English Church History* (1896), 269–74.
24. Some versions of the 1536 Injunctions omit the bible clause altogether, but by 1537–8 diocesan injunctions were quoting it.
25. *Statutes of the Realm*, iii. 575–8.
26. J. Youings, *The Dissolution of the Monasteries* (1971), 33–46.
27. S. Lehmberg, *The Reformation Parliament, 1529–1536* (Cambridge, 1970), 227.
28. See pp. 143–9.
29. Youings, *Dissolution*, 49–71; E. M. Hallam, 'Henry VIII's Monastic Refoundations of 1536–7 and the Course of the Dissolution', *BIHR* 51 (1978), 130–1.
30. P. J. Holmes, 'Tudor Great Councils', *HJ* 33 (1990), 10–12.
31. Ridley, *Cranmer*, 118–21.
32. J. A. Muller (ed.), *The Letters of Stephen Gardiner* (Cambridge, 1933), 351.
33. Rupp, *English Protestant Tradition*, 133–47.
34. Lloyd, *Formularies*, 123–5.
35. Cox (ed.), *Writings of Cranmer*, 350.
36. Ibid. 469–70.
37. Ibid. 83–114, discussed in J. J. Scarisbrick, *Henry VIII* (1971 edn.), 523–37.
38. Cox (ed.), *Writings of Cranmer*, 84.
39. Rupp, *English Protestant Tradition*, 115–18.

40. Hamilton (ed.), *Wriothesley's Chronicle*, i. 76, 79–80, 83.
41. Gee and Hardy, *Documents*, 275–81.
42. Elton, *Policy and Police*, 254.
43. Ridley, *Cranmer*, 161–5; G. Burnet, *The History of the Reformation*, ed. N. Pocock (Oxford, 1865), iv. 373–91.
44. Rupp, *English Protestant Tradition*, 117.
45. Foxe, *Acts and Monuments*, v. 227–8.
46. *TRP* i. 270–6, discussed in Elton, *Policy and Police*, 255–7.

Chapter 8

1. J. Foxe, *Acts and Monuments*, ed. G. Townsend (1843–9), v. 234.
2. The story of Elizabeth Barton is told by A. D. Cheney, 'The Holy Maid of Kent', *TRHS* 2nd series, 18 (1906), 108–39, and A. Neame, *The Holy Maid of Kent* (1971).
3. J. E. Cox (ed.), *Miscellaneous Writings and Letters of Thomas Cranmer* (Parker Society, 1846), 273.
4. *LP* vi. 1470.
5. Ibid. 1468 (5).
6. E. F. Rogers (ed.), *St Thomas More: Selected Letters* (New Haven, Conn., 1961), 184–5, 193–201.
7. *LP* vi. 835.
8. E. J. Devereux, 'Elizabeth Barton and Tudor Censorship', *Bulletin of the John Rylands Library*, 49 (1967), 94, 99–102.
9. *LP* vi. 1468 (7).
10. *CSP Span*, 1534–5, 610, 441.
11. G. Mattingley, *Catherine of Aragon* (1950 edn.), 286–90.
12. G. R. Elton, *Policy and Police* (Cambridge, 1972), 113–17.
13. Ibid. 14–18; Cox (ed.), *Writings of Cranmer*, 326–8.
14. Elton, *Policy and Police*, 58, 278–80, 137; T. N. Toller (ed.), *Correspondence of Edward, Third Earl of Derby* (Chetham Society, 1890), 11–12.
15. Elton, *Policy and Police*, 86, 208, 358.
16. *LP* xiii(1). 981; Elton, *Policy and Police*, 131, 20, 27.
17. PRO, SP 1/102, fos. 73–4 (*LP* x. 346).
18. PRO, SP 6/6, no. 6 (*LP* vii. 146), dated by Elton, *Policy and Police*, 352–3.
19. PRO, SP 1/92, fo. 128 (*LP* viii. 626).
20. *LP* viii. 661.
21. Ibid. 609.
22. Elton, *Policy and Police*, 318.
23. R. Whiting, *The Blind Devotion of the People* (Cambridge, 1989), 75; Elton, *Policy and Police*, 321–5.
24. J. Raine (ed.), *The Priory of Hexham* (Surtees Society, 1863), App., pp. cxxviii–cxxix.
25. *VCH Hampshire*, ii. 55; *VCH Staffordshire*, iii. 265, 254; C. Haigh, *The Last Days of the Lancashire Monasteries* (Chetham Society, 1969), 41–4; J. Youings, *The Dissolution of the Monasteries* (1971), 50 (to which should be added Cockersand, which paid to the Duchy).
26. D. Knowles, *The Religious Orders in England*, iii (Cambridge, 1959), 307–8.

27. G. W. O. Woodward, 'The Exemption from Suppression of Certain Yorkshire Priories', *EHR* 76 (1961), 397–8; Knowles, *Religious Orders*, iii. 310–11; *LP* x. 1191; C. Haigh, *Reformation and Resistance in Tudor Lancashire* (Cambridge, 1975), 127.

28. This account of the Lincolnshire rising owes much to M. Bowker, *The Henrician Reformation: The Diocese of Lincoln under John Longland, 1521–1547* (Cambridge, 1981), 148–56; ead., 'Lincolnshire 1536: Heresy, Schism, or Religious Discontent?', in D. Baker (ed.), *Studies in Church History*, ix (Cambridge, 1972), 195–212.

29. *LP* xi. 585.

30. Ibid., xii(1). 70(9).

31. Ibid., xi. 552.

32. M. H. and R. Dodds, *The Pilgrimage of Grace 1536–1537 and the Exeter Conspiracy 1538* (2 vols., 1971 edn.), i. 114.

33. Aske's own account of the rising is printed in *EHR* 5 (1890), 331–43.

34. Toller (ed.) *Derby Correspondence*, 50.

35. Dodds, *Pilgrimage*, i. 177.

36. *EHR* 5, 337.

37. *LP* xi. 1246. The formulation of the articles was described by Aske in *EHR* 5, 339–41, and their contents are assessed in Dodds, *Pilgrimage*, i. 346–73.

38. A. G. Dickens, *Reformation Studies* (1982), 71–82; G. R. Elton, *Studies in Tudor and Stuart Politics and Government* (Cambridge, 1983), iii. 201–7.

39. G. W. O. Woodward, *The Dissolution of the Monasteries* (1966), 94, implied that 55 monasteries had been suppressed, and this has often been repeated; but see S. M. Jack, 'Dissolution Dates for the Monasteries Dissolved under the Act of 1536', *BIHR* 43 (1970), 169–79.

40. *LP* xii(1). 192.

41. Ibid. 841(2), 1259, 1018, 393; Dodds, *Pilgrimage*, i. 222, 232–3; A. C. Tempest, 'Nicholas Tempest, a Sufferer in the Pilgrimage of Grace', *Yorkshire Archaeological Journal*, 11 (1890), 253.

42. Dodds, *Pilgrimage*, i. 259–60.

43. Elton, *Policy and Police*, 387, 389.

44. E. Hall, *Henry VIII*, ed. C. Whibley (1904), ii. 277.

45. Elton, *Policy and Police*, 296, 142–50; C. E. Moreton, 'The Walsingham Conspiracy of 1537', *Historical Research*, 63 (1990), 29–43; *LP* xiii(1). 194.

46. Elton, *Policy and Police*, 70.

47. A. Kreider, *English Chantries: The Road to Dissolution* (Cambridge, Mass., 1979), 155–60; *LP* xiii(1). 477.

48. Elton, *Policy and Police*, 10, 363.

49. Ibid. 24–5.

50. *LP* x. 1099; Elton, *Policy and Police*, 30, 36, 121–2.

51. *LP* xii(1). 530; xiii(1). 715.

52. Ibid., xi. 1393; xiii(1). 1492(2).

53. Elton, *Policy and Police*, 25, 26–7.

54. *LP* xiii(1). 604, 1345.

55. Ibid., (2). 820(1); (1). 1199(2).

Chapter 9

1. G. Redworth, 'A Study in the Formulation of Policy: The Genesis and Evolution of the Act of Six Articles', *JEH* 37 (1986), 49–50.
2. Ibid. 53–4.
3. J. Ridley, *Thomas Cranmer* (Oxford, 1962), 178–84.
4. J. J. Scarisbrick, *Henry VIII* (1971 edn.), 481.
5. D. Starkey (ed.), *The English Court* (1987), 114–15.
6. G. R. Elton, *Studies in Tudor and Stuart Politics and Government* (Cambridge, 1974), i. 213–14.
7. G. Redworth, *In Defence of the Church Catholic: The Life of Stephen Gardiner* (Oxford, 1990), 109–15; S. Brigden, 'Popular Disturbance and the Fall of Thomas Cromwell and the Reformers, 1539–1540', *HJ* 24 (1981), 263–6; J. Foxe, *Acts and Monuments*, ed. G. Townsend (1843–9), v. 430.
8. J. A. Muller (ed.), *The Letters of Stephen Gardiner* (Cambridge, 1933), 170.
9. *LJ* i. 129.
10. Discussed in Elton, *Studies*, i. 220–7.
11. Foxe, *Acts and Monuments*, v. 435–6.
12. Ibid. 443–9; S. Brigden, *London and the Reformation* (Oxford, 1989), 320–2.
13. E. Hall, *Henry VIII*, ed. C. Whibley (1904), ii. 311.
14. G. Burnet, *The History of the Reformation*, ed. N. Pocock (Oxford, 1865), iv. 443–96; vi. 241–8; Ridley, *Cranmer*, 207–11.
15. Burnet, *History of the Reformation*, vi. 247.
16. Redworth, *Gardiner*, 130–5.
17. Foxe, *Acts and Monuments*, vi. 578; Redworth, *Gardiner*, 136–8, 145–50.
18. Redworth, *Gardiner*, 160–4.
19. Ibid. 164–7; Muller (ed.), *Letters of Stephen Gardiner*, 302–3.
20. *LP* xviii(2). 548, pp. 317, 307, 309, 297, 299, 296, 303.
21. Ibid., xiv(2). 214; xv. 454.
22. M. Bowker, *The Henrician Reformation: The Diocese of Lincoln under John Longland, 1521–1547* (Cambridge, 1981), 170; *TRP* i. 296.
23. R. Whiting, *The Blind Devotion of the People* (Cambridge, 1989), 178.
24. H. Robinson (ed.), *Original Letters Relative to the English Reformation* (Parker Society, 1846), i. 36, 41; Foxe, *Acts and Monuments*, viii. 580.
25. L. R. Attreed, 'Preparation for Death in Sixteenth Century Northern England', *Sixteenth Century Journal*, 13 (1982), 46.
26. W. T. Mellows (ed.), *Peterborough Local Administration* (Northamptonshire Record Society, 1939), 143.
27. J. E. Binney (ed.), *The Accounts of the Wardens of the Parish of Morebath* (Devon and Cornwall Notes and Queries Supplement, 1904), 155.
28. *LP* xviii(2). 546, pp. 299, 308, 358; P. Clark, *English Provincial Society from the Reformation to the Revolution: Kent 1500–1640* (Hassocks, 1977), 41, 64.
29. M. L. Zell, 'The Prebendaries' Plot of 1543: A Reconsideration', *JEH* 27 (1976), 241–53.
30. *LP* xviii(2). 546, pp. 319–78; Redworth, *Gardiner*, 176–202.
31. J. E. Cox (ed.), *Miscellaneous Writings and Letters of Thomas Cranmer* (Parker Society, 1846), 100; C. Lloyd, *Formularies of Faith* (Oxford, 1825), 130, 295.

32. *LP* xviii(1). 365; Christ Church, Oxford, MS 306, p. 72.
33. Muller (ed.), *Letters of Gardiner*, 336–7; Redworth, *Gardiner*, 173.
34. J. G. Nichols (ed.), *Narratives of the Days of the Reformation* (Camden Society, 1859), 252–8; Ridley, *Cranmer*, 236–9.
35. *LP* xviii(1). 365, 507.
36. S. E. Lehmberg, *The Later Parliaments of Henry VIII, 1536–1547* (Cambridge, 1977), 186–7.
37. A. G. Dickens, *The English Reformation* (2nd edn., 1989), 214.
38. M. Dowling, *Humanism in the Age of Henry VIII* (1986), 66–8, 235–7.
39. Redworth, *Gardiner*, 205–6; Foxe, *Acts and Monuments*, v. 690–1.
40. J. K. McConica, *English Humanists and Reformation Politics under Henry VIII and Edward VI* (Oxford, 1965), 233.
41. A. Kreider, *English Chantries: The Road to Dissolution* (Cambridge, Mass., 1979), 168–77.
42. Lloyd, *Formularies*, 373–6.
43. Kreider, *English Chantries*, 158.
44. M. McGregor (ed.), *Bedfordshire Wills* (Bedfordshire Historical Record Society, 1979), 167, 173; *LP* xxi(2). 634.
45. *TRP* i. 301–2.
46. Foxe, *Acts and Monuments*, v. 535.
47. Cox (ed.), *Writings of Cranmer*, 414–15.
48. Foxe, *Acts and Monuments*, v. 562–3.
49. Dowling, *Humanism*, 62–5, 68.
50. Foxe, *Acts and Monuments*, v. 537; Brigden, *London*, 363–6.
51. Brigden, *London*, 370–6; Foxe, *Acts and Monuments*, v. 544, 547, 550.
52. *TRP* i. 373–6; Robinson (ed.), *Original Letters*, i. 41.
53. J. G. Nichols (ed.), *Greyfriars' Chronicle* (Camden Society, 1852), 52.
54. I follow D. Starkey, *The Reign of Henry VIII: Personalities and Politics* (1985), 154–9.
55. This seems the most plausible version of events, despite the criticisms of Redworth, *Gardiner*, 239–45.
56. J. Guy, *Tudor England* (Oxford, 1988), 198.
57. Ibid. 198–9; Starkey, *Henry VIII*, 159–66.
58. *LP* xxi(2). 634.

Chapter 10

1. J. N. King, *English Reformation Literature* (Princeton, NJ, 1982), 88–9, 127, 129.
2. For these difficulties, see D. E. Hoak, *The King's Council in the Reign of Edward VI* (Cambridge, 1976), 34–46, 231–9.
3. J. Foxe, *Acts and Monuments*, ed. G. Townsend (1843–9), v. 563–4.
4. M. L. Bush, *The Government Policy of Protector Somerset* (1975), 100–26.
5. Cf. M. Aston, *England's Iconoclasts: Laws against Images* (Oxford, 1988), 254–63.
6. Hoak, *King's Council*, 215; *APC* ii. 140–1, 518; A. G. Dickens, *Lollards and Protestants in the Diocese of York* (Oxford, 1959), 183.
7. W. D. Hamilton (ed.), *Wriothesley's Chronicle* (2 vols., Camden Society, 1875, 1877), ii. 1; J. G. Nichols (ed.), *Greyfriars' Chronicle* (Camden Society, 1852), 55.

8. J. E. Cox (ed.) *Miscellaneous Writings and Letters of Thomas Cranmer* (Parker Society, 1846), 510.

9. Foxe, *Acts and Monuments*, vi. 211.

10. A. G. Dickens (ed.), 'Robert Parkyn's Narrative of the Reformation', *EHR* 62 (1947), 66; J. A. Muller (ed.), *The Letters of Stephen Gardiner* (Cambridge, 1933), 362, 370–1, 373, 380–7.

11. R. B. Bond (ed.), *Certain Sermons or Homilies (1547)* (Toronto, 1987), 26–36.

12. A. Kreider, *English Chantries: The Road to Dissolution* (Cambridge, Mass., 1979), 186–202; Bush, *Government Policy*, 33, 43 and n., 142.

13. Kreider, *English Chantries*, 13–19, 42–64.

14. C. Haigh, *Reformation and Resistance in Tudor Lancashire* (Cambridge, 1975), 147–8.

15. Kreider, *English Chantries*, 158; J. J. Scarisbrick, *The Reformation and the English People* (Oxford, 1984) 98–9; *VCH Huntingdonshire*, iii. 13, 166.

16. R. Whiting, *The Blind Devotion of the People* (Cambridge, 1989), 30–2.

17. L. R. Attreed, 'Preparation for Death in Sixteenth Century Northern England', *Sixteenth Century Journal*, 13 (1982), 46, 48, 50; M. A. Cook, 'Eye (Suffolk) in the Years of Uncertainty, 1520–1590', Ph.D. thesis (Keele, 1981), 28.

18. Whiting, *Blind Devotion*, 76, 110; A. L. Rowse, *Tudor Cornwall* (1941), 257–9.

19. King, *English Reformation Literature*, 89, 287.

20. Nichols (ed.), *Greyfriars' Chronicle*, 56.

21. King, *English Reformation Literature*, 216–17.

22. Nichols (ed.), *Greyfriars' Chronicle*, 55; A. G. Dickens, *The English Reformation* (2nd edn., 1989), 247.

23. G. J. Cuming, *A History of Anglican Liturgy* (2nd edn., 1982), 45–7.

24. F. A. Gasquet and E. Bishop, *Edward VI and the Book of Common Prayer* (1891), 395–443.

25. *LJ* i. 331.

26. Cuming, *History of Anglican Liturgy*, 51–9; G. Redworth, *In Defence of the Church Catholic: The Life of Stephen Gardiner* (Cambridge, 1990), 287 and n.

27. J. Vowell (*alias* Hooker), *The Description of the City of Excester* (3 vols., Devon and Cornwall Record Society, 1919), ii. 57. The fullest recent account of the Western Rebellion is in J. Cornwall, *Revolt of the Peasantry, 1549* (1977); the significance of the rising is disputed by Whiting, *Blind Devotion*, 34–8.

28. Vowell, *Description*, ii. 75.

29. F. Rose-Troup, *The Western Rebellion of 1549* (1913), 127.

30. Ibid. 492–4.

31. F. W. Russell, *Kett's Rebellion in Norfolk* (1859), 48; Rose-Troup, *Western Rebellion*, 492.

32. J. Strype, *Ecclesiastical Memorials* (Oxford, 1822), ii(2). 431.

33. J. Berkman, 'Van Der Delft's Letter: A Reappraisal of the Attack on Protector Somerset', *BIHR* 53 (1980), 247–52; Hoak, *King's Council*, 53, 241–5; H. Robinson (ed.), *Original Letters Relative to the English Reformation* (Parker Society, 1846), i. 69, 71; ii. 464.

34. Dickens (ed.), 'Parkyn's Narrative', 69–70; Foxe, *Acts and Monuments*, v. 726, 729–30.

35. Robinson (ed.), *Original Letters*, i. 72, 547; E. Cardwell, *Documentary Annals* (2 vols., Oxford, 1844), i. 93–6.
36. F. Heal, 'The Parish Clergy and the Reformation in the Diocese of Ely', *Proceedings of the Cambridge Antiquarian Society*, 66 (1975), 152; F. D. Price, 'Gloucester Diocese under Bishop Hooper', *Transactions of the Bristol and Gloucestershire Archaeological Society*, 60 (1938), 119–21.
37. Hoak, *King's Council*, 55–9, 245–58.
38. S. Brigden, *London and the Reformation* (Oxford, 1989), 502–3.
39. G. Burnet, *The History of the Reformation*, ed. N. Pocock (Oxford, 1865), v. 287–8.
40. Robinson (ed.), *Original Letters*, i. 72, 79; Brigden, *London*, 462–4; Hamilton (ed.), *Wriothesley's Chronicle*, ii. 41; Nichols (ed.), *Greyfriars' Chronicle*, 67; W. K. Jordan (ed.), *The Chronicle and Political Papers of King Edward VI* (1966), 37.
41. Foxe, *Acts and Monuments*, vii. 12.
42. Ibid., vi. 5.
43. Dickens (ed.), 'Parkyn's Narrative', 72–3.
44. J. Bale, *An Expostulation agaynste a Franticke Papyst of Hampshyre* (1552), sig. Bi.
45. F. Madden (ed.), 'Petition of Richard Troughton, Bailiff of South Witham', *Archaeologia*, 23 (1831), 46.
46. F. Heal, *Of Prelates and Princes* (Cambridge, 1980), 139–46.
47. Price, 'Gloucester Diocese', 57–61, 72, 101, 119–21. The Gloucester figures have often been used to argue that parish clergy were uneducated and stupid; they show rather that priests did not yet know the English Bible.
48. Robinson (ed.), *Original Letters*, ii. 535–6.
49. Cuming, *History of Anglican Liturgy*, 72–4.
50. J. McConica, *The History of the University of Oxford*, iii (Oxford, 1986), 370–4.
51. *TRP* i. 410–12.
52. W. S. Hudson, *The Cambridge Connection and the Elizabethan Settlement of 1559* (Durham, NC, 1980), 85.
53. Cuming, *History of Anglican Liturgy*, 75–86.
54. Dickens (ed.), 'Parkyn's Narrative', 74–6.
55. E. Cardwell, *Synodalia* (2 vols., Oxford, 1842), i. 18–33, discussed in Dickens, *English Reformation*, 280–2.
56. T. Lever, *Sermons, 1550*, ed. E. Arber (1871), 56; Robinson (ed.), *Original Letters*, i. 76; ii. 543.
57. Attreed, 'Preparation for Death', 46; M. Bowker, *The Henrician Reformation: The Diocese of Lincoln under John Longland, 1521–1547* (Cambridge, 1981), 177.
58. J. E. Binney (ed.), *The Accounts of the Wardens of the Parish of Morebath* (Devon and Cornwall Notes and Queries Supplement, 1904), 200.
59. E. Hobhouse (ed.), *Churchwardens' Accounts of Croscombe, Pilton, Yatton, etc.* (Somerset Record Society, iv, 1890), 162.
60. R. Houlbrooke, *Church Courts and the People during the English Reformation, 1520–1570* (Oxford, 1979), 273, 159 and n.
61. Ibid. 243–4; Whiting, *Blind Devotion*, 166; *Statutes of the Realm*, iv. 130.
62. M. L. Zell, 'The Personnel of the Clergy in Kent in the Reformation Period', *EHR* 59 (1974), 517–18.

63. Oxfordshire RO, Par. Thame b. 2; F. G. Lee, *The History of the Prebendal Church of Thame* (1883), 67–70, 531–2.
64. G. Huelin, 'A Sixteenth Century Churchwardens' Account Book of St Margaret Moses', *Guildhall Studies in London History*, 1 (1973), 2–3.
65. D. MacCulloch, *Suffolk and the Tudors* (Oxford, 1986), 169; J. E. Oxley, *The Reformation in Essex to the Death of Mary* (Manchester, 1965), 167–77; Dickens, *Lollards and Protestants*, 208.
66. *APC* iv. 257, 283; P. Clark, *English Provincial Society from the Reformation to the Revolution: Kent 1500–1640* (Hassocks, 1977), 75.
67. *APC* iv. 329, 338, 348, 354–5, 360, 361, 371, 376.

Chapter 11

1. S. Brigden, 'Thomas Cromwell and the "Brethren" ', in C. Cross, D. Loades, and J. J. Scarisbrick (eds.), *Law and Government under the Tudors* (Cambridge, 1988), 33.
2. M. Dowling, 'Anne Boleyn and Reform', *JEH* 35 (1984), 38–9; E. W. Ives, *Anne Boleyn* (Oxford, 1986), 303–4.
3. J. Foxe, *Acts and Monuments*, ed. G. Townsend (1843–9), viii. 570.
4. W. S. Hudson, *The Cambridge Connection and the Elizabethan Settlement of 1559* (Durham, NC, 1980), 53–5.
5. H. C. Porter, *Reformation and Reaction in Tudor Cambridge* (Cambridge, 1958), 54–5; *The Writings of John Bradford* (2 vols., Parker Society, 1848–53), i. 445, 442.
6. Foxe, *Acts and Monuments*, vii. 731, 739.
7. J. McConica, *History of the University of Oxford*, iii (Oxford, 1986), 368–74, 380; C. M. Dent, *Protestant Reformers in Elizabethan Oxford* (Oxford, 1983), 7–13; C. Haigh, *Reformation and Resistance in Tudor Lancashire* (Cambridge, 1975), 162, 163–4.
8. Figures from J. Fines, 'Register of Early British Protestants, 1520–1558' (unpublished); McConica, *History of Oxford*, 144.
9. Foxe, *Acts and Monuments*, v. 443–9.
10. Ibid. 448; W. D. Hamilton (ed.), *Wriothesley's Chronicle* (2 vols., Camden Society, 1875, 1877), i. 72; S. Brigden, *London and the Reformation* (Oxford, 1989), 391.
11. J. Strype, *Ecclesiastical Memorials* (Oxford, 1822), i(1). 441–2; *LP* xiv(1). 1052–3.
12. D. MacCulloch, *Suffolk and the Tudors* (Oxford, 1986), 163, 170–1; Foxe, *Acts and Monuments*, vi. 676–8.
13. *LP* xviii(2). 546, pp. 302, 304–5; J. G. Nichols (ed.), *Narratives of the Days of the Reformation* (Camden Society, 1859), 72–3, 77.
14. Brigden, *London*, 460–2; H. Robinson (ed.), *Original Letters Relative to the English Reformation* (Parker Society, 1846), i. 80.
15. Foxe, *Acts and Monuments*, vii. 335, 716–17.
16. Ibid., vi. 730–1, 373–8.
17. Ibid., vii. 717; viii. 152, 433–4, 473–4.
18. Ibid., vii. 717, 749; viii. 142.

19. S. Brigden, 'Youth and the English Reformation', *PP* 95, 65 n.; Foxe, *Acts and Monuments*, viii. 153.
20. Foxe, *Acts and Monuments*, viii. 187.
21. J. F. Davis, *Heresy and Reformation in the South-East of England, 1520–1559* (1983), 39–40.
22. Robinson (ed.), *Original Letters*, i. 89, 320, 322–3; ii. 662.
23. *APC* iii. 196–9, 206–7; C. Burrage, *The Early English Dissenters* (2 vols., Cambridge, 1912), ii. 1–14.
24. J. W. Martin, *Religious Radicals in Tudor England* (1989), 51–2, 78, 80.
25. Foxe, *Acts and Monuments*, vii. 192–3; Haigh, *Reformation and Resistance*, 170–2, 188; *Writings of Bradford*, ii. 236, 297–351.
26. *LP* xii(1). 40; M. St Clare Byrne (ed.), *The Lisle Letters* (6 vols., Chicago, 1981), i. 581.
27. G. E. Corrie (ed.), *Sermons by Hugh Latimer* (Parker Society, 1844), 208; *LP* xviii(1). 546, p. 365.
28. Nichols (ed.), *Narratives of the Reformation*, 72–3, 78.
29. R. Whiting, *The Blind Devotion of the People* (Cambridge, 1989), 168–9, 254; J. Hooker, 'Life of Sir Peter Carew', in *Calendar of Carew Manuscripts, 1515–74*, p. cxiv.
30. J. E. Cox (ed.), *Miscellaneous Writings and Letters of Thomas Cranmer* (Parker Society, 1846), 336; Corrie (ed.), *Sermons by Latimer*, 200.
31. Robinson (ed.), *Original Letters*, ii. 485, 546.
32. T. Becon, 'The Jewel of Joy', in *The Catechism of Thomas Becon*, ed. J. Ayre (Parker Society, 1844), 422.
33. A. G. Dickens, *Lollards and Protestants in the Diocese of York* (Oxford, 1959), 42–3; M. Dowling and J. Shakespeare, 'Religion and Politics in Mid-Tudor England Through the Eyes of an English Protestant Woman: The Recollections of Rose Hickman', *BIHR* 55 (1982), 97.
34. Foxe, *Acts and Monuments*, vii. 343–4; viii. 204–8.
35. Nichols (ed.), *Narratives of the Reformation*, 349–50.
36. Foxe, *Acts and Monuments*, viii. 463–4; vii. 322–5.
37. Ibid., viii. 247–8; vii. 29.
38. J. Vowell (*alias* Hooker), *The Description of the City of Excester* (Devon and Cornwall Record Society, 1919), ii. 75.
39. D. Cressy, *Literacy and the Social Order: Reading and Writing in Tudor and Stuart England* (Cambridge, 1980), esp. 142–68.
40. Brigden, *London*, 410–12, compared with figures from 1522 in W. G. Hoskins, *The Age of Plunder* (1976), 38, and from 1582 in S. Rappaport, *Worlds within Worlds: Structures of Life in Sixteenth Century London* (Cambridge, 1989), 166 and n.
41. P. Clark, 'Reformation and Radicalism in Kentish Towns, *c*.1500–1553', in W. J. Mommsen (ed.), *Stadtbürgertum und Adel in der Reformation* (Stuttgart, 1979), 118–19, 123.
42. Whiting, *Blind Devotion*, 260; R. M. Fisher, 'The Reformation in Microcosm? Benchers at the Inns of Court, 1530–1580', *Parergon*, NS, 6 (1988), 44–5.
43. C. H. Garrett, *The Marian Exiles* (Cambridge, 1938), 41.
44. Foxe, *Acts and Monuments*, vii. 139; Davis, *Heresy and Reformation*, 114, 115, 117, 120–1, 122–3.

45. MacCulloch, *Suffolk*, 172; P. Hughes, *The Reformation in England* (1963 edn.), ii. 259–60 and n.
46. Martin, *Religious Radicals*, 133.
47. Foxe, *Acts and Monuments*, viii. 153.
48. Ibid., v. 448.
49. Martin, *Religious Radicals*, 33, 133; Foxe, *Acts and Monuments*, viii. 468–9.
50. D. M. Palliser, 'Popular Reactions to the Reformation during the Years of Uncertainty, 1530–70', in C. Haigh (ed.), *The English Reformation Revised* (Cambridge, 1987), 94–113.
51. A. G. Dickens, 'The Early Expansion of Protestantism in England, 1520–1558', *Archiv für Reformationsgeschichte*, 78 (1987), 187–221; id., *The English Reformation* (1989 edn.), 325–34.
52. M. Spufford, *Contrasting Communities: English Villagers in the Sixteenth and Seventeenth Centuries* (Cambridge, 1974), 246; J. C. Ward, 'The Reformation in Colchester, 1528–1558', *Essex Archaeology and History*, 15 (1983), 84–95; P. Collinson, *The Birthpangs of Protestant England* (1988), 37.
53. P. Clark, *English Provincial Society from the Reformation to the Revolution: Kent 1500–1640* (Hassocks, 1977), 38–44; *LP* xviii(2). 546, p. 300.
54. J. G. Nichols (ed.), *Greyfriars' Chronicle* (Camden Society, 1852), 59, 67.
55. R. Edgeworth, *Sermons very fruitfull, godly and learned* (1557), fo. ccix.
56. See especially Dickens, 'Early Expansion', 192–7; id., *English Reformation*, 326, 330–1.
57. Foxe, *Acts and Monuments*, viii. 510–11.
58. See the summary in Dickens, 'Early Expansion', 213–16.
59. Clark, *Kent*, 58, 76; E. M. Shepperd, 'The Reformation and the Citizens of Norwich', *Norfolk Archaeology*, 38 (1983), 56; W. J. Sheils, *The Puritans in the Diocese of Peterborough, 1558–1610* (Northamptonshire Record Society, 1979), 15–16; D. M. Palliser, *Tudor York* (Oxford, 1979), 250–1; Brigden, *London*, 485–6, 629, and more precise information from Dr Brigden; M. Moir, 'Church and Society in Sixteenth Century Herefordshire', M.Phil. thesis (Leicester, 1984), 92; Dickens, *Lollards and Protestants*, 215, 220.
60. J. G. Nichols and J. Bruce (eds.), *Wills from Doctors' Commons* (Camden Society, 1863), 28–9, 42–3; *LP* xxi(2). 634.
61. C. Cross, 'The Development of Protestantism in Leeds and Hull, 1520–1640: The Evidence from Wills', *Northern History*, 18 (1982), 233; J. D. Alsop, 'Religious Preambles in Early Modern English Wills as Formulae', *JEH* 40 (1989), 20–1.
62. Dickens, *Lollards and Protestants*, 172; K. G. Powell, 'The Social Background to the Reformation in Gloucestershire', *Transactions of the Bristol and Gloucestershire Archaeological Society*, 92 (1973), 119; M. L. Zell, 'The Use of Religious Preambles as a Measure of Religious Belief in the Sixteenth Century', *BIHR* 51 (1978), 248–9; Moir, 'Herefordshire', 93, 89.
63. Nichols (ed.), *Narratives of the Reformation*, 62–5, 157–60.
64. Foxe, *Acts and Monuments*, viii. 209.
65. C. Davies, ' "Poor Persecuted Little Flock" or "Commonwealth of Christians": Edwardian Protestant Concepts of the Church', in P. Lake and M. Dowling (eds.), *Protestantism and the National Church* (1987), 79, 86–7.

66. Foxe, *Acts and Monuments*, vi. 613.
67. Ibid., vii. 573.

Chapter 12

1. The best reconstruction of these early events is D. Hoak, 'Two Revolutions in Tudor Government: The Formation and Organization of Mary I's Privy Council', in C. Coleman and D. Starkey (eds.), *Revolution Reassessed: Revisions in the History of Tudor Government and Administration* (Oxford, 1986), 94–5 and n. Mary's seizure of power is described in D. M. Loades, *Mary Tudor: A Life* (1989), 174–85, and J. Loach, *Parliament and the Crown in the Reign of Mary Tudor* (Oxford, 1986), 1–12.
2. R. Tittler, *The Reign of Mary I* (1983), 84–6; J. G. Nichols (ed.), *The Diary of Henry Machyn* (Camden Society, 1848), 35–6.
3. S. T. Bindoff, 'A Kingdom at Stake', *History Today*, 3 (1953), 642–8.
4. F. Madden (ed.), 'Petition of Richard Troughton Bailiff of South Witham', *Archaeologia*, 23 (1831), 29.
5. A. G. Dickens (ed.), 'Robert Parkyn's Narrative of the Reformation', *EHR* 62 (1947), 77–8.
6. D. MacCulloch (ed.), 'The *Vita Mariae Angliae Reginae* of Robert Wingfield of Brantham', in *Camden Miscellany*, xxviii (Camden Society, 1984), 188, 253, 255, 258, 263–4; *APC* iv. 293.
7. J. G. Nichols (ed.), *The Chronicle of Queen Jane, and of Two Years of Queen Mary* (Camden Society, 1850), 9; Madden (ed.), 'Petition of Richard Troughton', 32–7, 45.
8. Nichols (ed.), *Chronicle of Jane and Mary*, 11; C. L. Kingsford (ed.), 'Two London Chronicles', in *Camden Miscellany*, xii (Camden Society, 1910), 27; J. G. Nichols (ed.), *Greyfriars' Chronicle* (Camden Society, 1852), 80.
9. Madden (ed.), 'Petition of Richard Troughton', 43–4; Dickens (ed.), 'Parkyn's Narrative', 78; C. H. Hartshorne (ed.), 'Extracts from the Register of Sir Thomas Butler, Vicar of Much Wenlock in Shropshire', in *Cambrian Journal* (1861), 93.
10. Madden (ed.), 'Petition of Richard Troughton', 39, 41.
11. Nichols (ed.), *Machyn's Diary*, 4–5.
12. Loach, *Parliament*, 7–10.
13. Dickens (ed.), 'Parkyn's Narrative', 79.
14. Nichols (ed.), *Greyfriars' Chronicle*, 81.
15. Ibid. 81–2; W. D. Hamilton (ed.), *Wriothesley's Chronicle* (2 vols., Camden Society, 1875, 1877), ii. 95; S. Brigden, *London and the Reformation* (Oxford, 1989), 525.
16. Nichols (ed.), *Greyfriars' Chronicle*, 82.
17. Dickens (ed.), 'Parkyn's Narrative', 79.
18. Hamilton (ed.), *Wriothesley's Chronicle*, ii. 96–7; Kingsford (ed.), 'Two London Chronicles', 29; Nichols (ed.), *Chronicle of Jane and Mary*, 16; *APC* iv. 317–18.
19. *TRP* ii. 5–8; Nichols (ed.), *Chronicle of Jane and Mary*, 18–19; Hamilton (ed.), *Wriothesley's Chronicle*, ii. 100.
20. Nichols (ed.), *Machyn's Diary*, 42–3; Hamilton (ed.), *Wriothesley's Chronicle*, ii. 101–2; Kingsford (ed.), 'Two London Chronicles', 29.

21. Dickens (ed.), 'Parkyn's Narrative', 79–80; Hartshorne (ed.), 'Register of Sir Thomas Butler', 93.

22. H. Robinson (ed.), *Original Letters Relative to the English Reformation* (Parker Society, 1846), i. 100; J. Foxe, *Acts and Monuments*, ed. G. Townsend (1843–9), vi. 712–13; vii. 297.

23. Foxe, *Acts and Monuments*, viii. 632–3.

24. J. G. Nichols (ed.), *Narratives of the Days of the Reformation* (Camden Society, 1859), 80–4.

25. Foxe, *Acts and Monuments*, vii. 289.

26. M. Spufford, *Contrasting Communities: English Villagers in the Sixteenth and Seventeenth Centuries* (Cambridge, 1974), 244–5.

27. Foxe, *Acts and Monuments*, vi. 678–9.

28. *APC* iv. 340, 369, 373, 375, 395.

29. Nichols (ed.), *Chronicle of Jane and Mary*, 34; Foxe, *Acts and Monuments*, viii. 122–3.

30. W. Haines (ed.), 'Stanford Churchwardens' Accounts (1552–1602)', *The Antiquary*, 17 (1888), 70; J. E. Binney (ed.) *The Accounts of the Wardens of the Parish of Morebath* (Devon and Cornwall Notes and Queries Supplement, 1904), 200.

31. *APC* iv. 295, 329, 338, 348, 354–5, 360, 361, 371, 376.

32. Binney (ed.), *Morebath Accounts*, 185.

33. W. Parker, *The History of Long Melford* (1873), 100.

34. Haines (ed.), 'Stanford Accounts', 118; J. Nichols, *The History and Antiquities of the County of Leicester* (4 vols., 1815), i. 560.

35. R. Houlbrooke, *Church Courts and the People during the English Reformation, 1520–1570* (Oxford, 1979), 167.

36. R. Whiting, *The Blind Devotion of the People* (Cambridge, 1989), 68–9.

37. Foxe, *Acts and Monuments*, vi. 564–5.

38. Somerset RO, D/D/Ca 22, 27; Cheshire RO, EDV 1/1–2.

39. J. Strype, *Ecclesiastical Memorials* (Oxford, 1822), iii(1). 482–6; (2). 389–413; Wiltshire RO, Salisbury Diocesan Records, Visitation Detecta Book 2.

40. L. E. Whatmore (ed.), *Archdeacon Harpsfield's Visitation, 1557* (2 vols., Catholic Record Society, 1950–1). The figures in P. Hughes, *The Reformation in England* (1963 edn.), ii. 237 are sometimes inaccurate and in general misleading.

41. J. A. Twemlow (ed.), *Liverpool Town Books, 1550–70* (Liverpool, 1918), 51.

42. *CSP Ven*, 1555–8, 1018; Foxe, *Acts and Monuments*, viii. 407.

43. L. R. Attreed, 'Preparation for Death in Sixteenth Century Northern England', *Sixteenth Century Journal*, 13 (1982), 46.

44. A. G. Dickens, *The English Reformation* (1989 edn.), 309, 311.

45. A. Raine (ed.), *York Civic Records, 1548–58* (Yorkshire Archaeological Society, 1946), 105.

46. A. M. Bartholomew, 'Lay Piety in the Reign of Mary Tudor', MA thesis (Manchester, 1979), 101–3; P. Clark, *English Provincial Society from the Reformation to the Revolution: Kent 1500–1640* (Hassocks, 1977), 98–9.

47. Nichols (ed.), *Machyn's Diary*, 75, 77–8, 121, 160.

48. Nichols (ed.), *Greyfriars' Chronicle*, 89, 97; id., *Machyn's Diary*, 62, 63–4, 89, 138–9.

49. Whiting, *Blind Devotion*, 69, 42; Bartholomew, 'Lay Piety', 93–4; S. Thompson, 'The Pastoral Work of the English and Welsh Episcopate, 1500–1558', D.Phil. thesis (Oxford, 1984), 196, 198.

50. Thompson, 'Pastoral Work', 184–7; C. Haigh, *Reformation and Resistance in Tudor Lancashire* (Cambridge, 1975), 200–1; Guildhall RO, MS 9535/1, fos. 14–74.

51. E. J. Baskerville, *A Chronological Bibliography of Propaganda and Polemic Published in English between 1553 and 1558* (American Philosophical Society, 1979), 6–11; J. W. Martin, *Religious Radicals in Tudor England* (1989), 107–23; D. M. Loades, *The Reign of Mary Tudor* (1979), 338–43; Dickens, *English Reformation*, 310–12. But cf. J. Loach, 'The Marian Establishment and the Printing Press', *EHR* 101 (1986), 135–48.

52. E. Bonner, *A Profitable and Necessarye Doctryne* (1555), sig. Aii.

53. A. G. Dickens, *Reformation Studies* (1982), 271–2.

54. Bonner, *Profitable and Necessarye Doctryne*, sigs. P–Sii; T. Watson, *Holsome and Catholyke Doctryne Concerninge the Seven Sacramentes* (1558), fos. cv–cxxxv.

55. Foxe, *Acts and Monuments*, viii. 563.

Chapter 13

1. J. G. Nichols (ed.), *The Diary of Henry Machyn* (Camden Society, 1848), 41, for the passages quoted; W. D. Hamilton (ed.), *Wriothesley's Chronicle* (2 vols., Camden Society, 1875, 1877), ii. 97, 99–100; *APC* iv. 317–18, 320; J. Foxe, *Acts and Monuments*, ed. G. Townsend (1843–9), vi. 391–4; D. MacCulloch (ed.), 'The *Vita Mariae Angliae Reginae* of Robert Wingfield of Brantham', in *Camden Miscellany*, xxviii (Camden Society, 1984), 272–3.

2. Nichols (ed.), *Machyn's Diary*, 58–60, 65–6; C. L. Kingsford (ed.), 'Two London Chronicles', in *Camden Miscellany*, xii (Camden Society, 1910), 36–7; M. Huggarde, *The Displaying of the Protestantes* (1556), fos. 119ᵛ–20ᵛ; A. G. Dickens, *Lollards and Protestants in the Diocese of York* (Oxford, 1959), 225; *APC* v. 49, 70, 88.

3. M. Jagger, 'Bonner's Episcopal Visitation of London, 1554', *BIHR* 45 (1972), 306–11; G. Alexander, 'Bonner and the Marian Persecutions', in C. Haigh (ed.), *English Reformation Revised*, 168–9. For a different emphasis, cf. S. Brigden, *London and the Reformation* (Oxford, 1989), 562–9.

4. Cheshire RO, EDV 1/1; Somerset RO, D/D/Ca 22; R. B. Walker, 'Reformation and Reaction in the County of Lincoln, 1547–58', *Lincolnshire Archaeological and Architectural Society Reports and Papers*, 9 (1961), 58–9; P. Hughes, *The Reformation in England* (1963 edn.), ii. 242.

5. Foxe, *Acts and Monuments*, viii. 598–600.

6. D. M. Loades, *Two Tudor Conspiracies* (Cambridge, 1965), 15–76; Brigden, *London*, 536–45.

7. J. Proctor, 'The History of Wyat's Rebellion' (1555), in A. F. Pollard (ed.), *Tudor Tracts* (1903), 230.

8. J. G. Nichols (ed.), *The Chronicle of Queen Jane and of Two Years of Queen Mary* (Camden Society, 1850), 43.

9. Proctor, 'History', 208–9, 212–13, 216, 237–8.

10. Ibid. 210.

11. Loades, *Two Tudor Conspiracies*, 55–6, 76–88; M. R. Thorp, 'Religion and the Wyatt Rebellion of 1554', *Church History*, 47 (1978), 363–80; W. B. Robison, 'The National and Local Significance of Wyatt's Rebellion in Surrey', *HJ* 30 (1987), 769–90; P. Clark, *English Provincial Society from the Reformation to the Revolution: Kent 1500–1640* (Hassocks, 1977), 88–96.

12. J. E. Binney (ed.), *The Accounts of the Wardens of the Parish of Morebath* (Devon and Cornwall Notes and Queries Supplement, 1904), 181; Nichols (ed.), *Machyn's Diary*, 34, 67; J. Bruce (ed.), 'Extracts of Accounts of the Churchwardens of Minchinhampton, Gloucestershire', *Archaeologia*, 35 (1853), 423; A. G. Dickens (ed.), 'Parkyn's Narrative of the Reformation', *EHR* 62 (1947), 82.

13. D. M. Loades, *The Reign of Mary Tudor* (1979), 168.

14. J. Loach, *Parliament and the Crown in the Reign of Mary Tudor* (Oxford, 1986), 106–15.

15. *CSP Span*, 1554–8, 121; Foxe, *Acts and Monuments*, vi. 569, 572; Loades, *Reign of Mary Tudor*, 326.

16. Nichols (ed.), *Machyn's Diary*, 77, 80–1; Kingsford (ed.), 'Two London Chronicles', 41; *CSP Span*, 1554–8, 112, 122; Hamilton (ed.), *Wriothesley's Chronicle*, ii. 126; J. G. Nichols (ed.), *Greyfriars' Chronicle* (Camden Society, 1852), 93–4.

17. R. H. Pogson, 'Reginald Pole and the Priorities of Government in Mary Tudor's Church', *HJ* 18 (1975), 12; Dickens (ed.), 'Parkyn's Narrative', 83; Foxe, *Acts and Monuments*, vii. 38.

18. A. G. Dickens, *Reformation Studies* (1982), 271.

19. Foxe, *Acts and Monuments*, vii. 37; J. G. Nichols (ed.), *Narratives of the Days of the Reformation* (Camden Society, 1859), 209–10.

20. J. Elder, *The Copie of a Letter Sent into Scotlande* (1555), reprinted in Nichols (ed.), *Chronicle of Jane and Mary*, 136–66; J. Harpsfield, *A Notable and Learned Sermon or Homilie* (1556); J. Strype, *Ecclesiastical Memorials* (Oxford, 1822), iii(2). 482–510.

21. See p. 216 and refs.

22. J. Loach, 'The Marian Establishment and the Printing Press', *EHR* 101 (1986), 136–7; E. J. Baskerville, *A Chronological Bibliography of Propaganda and Polemic Published in English between 1553 and 1558* (American Philosophical Society, 1979), 7–8, 13, 35, 68, 83.

23. Pogson, 'Pole and the Priorities', 16.

24. Nichols (ed.), *Machyn's Diary*, 44, 48, 46, 69, 131, 139–40.

25. A. G. Dickens, *English Reformation* (2nd edn., 1989), 309–10, 311. Cf. Pogson, 'Pole and the Priorities', 3–6.

26. W. Schenck, *Reginald Pole, Cardinal of England* (1950), 142–4; D. Wilkins, *Concilia Magnae Britanniae* (1737), iv. 121–6.

27. R. H. Pogson, 'The Legacy of the Schism', in J. Loach and R. Tittler, *The Mid-Tudor Polity, c.1540–1560* (1980), 125–6; P. Hughes, 'A Hierarchy that Fought', *Clergy Review*, 18 (1940), 25–39.

28. S. Thompson, 'The Pastoral Work of the English and Welsh Episcopate, 1500–1558', D.Phil. thesis (Oxford, 1984), 217 and n.

29. Ibid. 179, 185–6, 69, 172–4.

30. G. Burnet, *The History of the Reformation*, ed. N. Pocock (Oxford, 1865), v. 393–401.

31. R. H. Pogson, 'Revival and Reform in Mary Tudor's Church: A Question of Money', in Haigh (ed.), *English Reformation Revised*, 139–56; Loach, *Parliament*, 131, 133–8.

32. Loach, *Parliament*, 80–1, 94–5; F. Heal, *Of Prelates and Princes* (Cambridge, 1980), 150–61; Loades, *Reign of Mary Tudor*, 352–5, 439.

33. D. M. Palliser, 'Popular Reactions to the Reformation during the Years of Uncertainty, 1530–70', in Haigh (ed.), *English Reformation Revised*, 100; R. Whiting, *The Blind Devotion of the People* (Cambridge, 1989), 232; A. M. Johnson, 'The Reformation Clergy of Derbyshire, 1536–1559', *Derbyshire Archaeological Journal*, 100 (1980), 57–8.

34. Dickens (ed.), 'Parkyn's Narrative', 79, 82; Cheshire RO, EDC 2/4, 119.

35. Somerset RO, D/D/Vc 66; D. MacCulloch, *Suffolk and the Tudors* (Oxford, 1986), 177; Dickens, *Reformation Studies*, 112–21; C. Haigh, *Reformation and Resistance in Tudor Lancashire* (Cambridge, 1975), 179–82.

36. R. Houlbrooke, *Church Courts and the People during the English Reformation, 1520–1570* (Oxford, 1979), 181–2; G. R. Baskerville, 'Married Clergy and Pensioned Religious in Norwich Diocese', *EHR* 48 (1933), 44; *VCH Somerset*, ii. 65–6; Clark, *Kent*, 99.

37. Nichols (ed.), *Machyn's Diary*, 69, 48; Foxe, *Acts and Monuments*, vii. 104–5; P. Bush, *A Brefe Exhortation Set Fourthe* (1556); Dickens, *Reformation Studies*, 355, 357.

38. Houlbrooke, *Church Courts*, 182; Haigh, *Reformation and Resistance*, 180–1.

39. Dickens, *Lollards and Protestants*, 191–2; Whiting, *Blind Devotion*, 143.

40. Baskerville, *Chronological Bibliography*, 44–5; Loach, 'Printing Press', 140–1.

41. Hughes, *Reformation in England*, ii. 199, 259; J. W. Martin, *Religious Radicals in Tudor England* (1989), 125–36; Dickens, *English Reformation*, 301–6.

42. *The Writings of John Bradford* (2 vols., Parker Society, 1848–53), ii. 227.

43. C. H. Garrett, *The Marian Exiles* (Cambridge, 1938), 40–2; Dickens, *English Reformation*, 339–49.

44. Baskerville, *Chronological Bibliography*, 8, 16–30.

45. Nichols (ed.), *Narratives of the Reformation*, 149, 157, 159, 171, 209–12.

46. D. M. Loades, 'The Essex Inquisitions of 1556', *BIHR* 35 (1962), 93.

47. *Writings of Bradford*, ii. 228, 236, 297–351.

48. Foxe, *Acts and Monuments*, vii. 686–90; viii. 556–7; Nichols (ed.), *Narratives of the Reformation*, 31.

49. Foxe, *Acts and Monuments*, viii. 556–7; MacCulloch, *Suffolk*, 179–80; J. F. Davis, *Heresy and Reformation in the South-East of England, 1520–1559* (1983), 146–7.

50. Loach, *Parliament*, 97–102, 115.

51. Hughes, *Reformation in England*, ii. 259; Foxe, *Acts and Monuments*, viii. 247, 388, 392, 503.

52. Burnet, *History of the Reformation*, v. 440.

53. Nichols (ed.), *Machyn's Diary*, 80; Foxe, *Acts and Monuments*, vi. 589; H. Robinson (ed.), *Original Letters Relative to the English Reformation* (Parker Society, 1846), i. 171. These early proceedings are described in D. M. Loades, *The Oxford Martyrs* (1970), 148–56.

54. Foxe, *Acts and Monuments*, vi. 596.
55. Ibid. 611; *CSP Span*, 1554–8, 138.
56. H. Christmas (ed.), *The Works of Nicholas Ridley* (Parker Society, 1841), 378.
57. Foxe, *Acts and Monuments*, vi. 611, 650–9, 696–8.
58. Ibid. 650; vii. 645, 674; Haigh, *Reformation and Resistance*, 189–90.
59. Foxe, *Acts and Monuments*, viii. 326–8, 333, 496–503, 389–92.
60. Brigden, *London*, 568.
61. Dickens, *Lollards and Protestants*, 224; Foxe, *Acts and Monuments*, vii. 401.
62. Foxe, *Acts and Monuments*, vi. 723; viii. 623, 333, 380.
63. Ibid., viii. 382, 464, 533.
64. Hughes, *Reformation in England*, ii. 283 n.
65. *CPR*, 1555–7, 24–5; Burnet, *History of the Reformation*, v. 469–74; Houlbrooke, *Church Courts*, 233; Foxe, *Acts and Monuments*, viii. 387–8, 598–600.
66. Hughes, *Reformation in England*, ii. 268–71, 274; Foxe, *Acts and Monuments*, viii. 510–11, 326–7.
67. Strype, *Ecclesiastical Memorials*, iii(2). 128.
68. *APC* vi. 135.
69. Ibid. 144, 361, 371–2; Foxe, *Acts and Monuments*, viii. 420–2, 491–2.
70. Foxe, *Acts and Monuments*, vii. 82, 715; viii. 392; Nichols (ed.), *Machyn's Diary*, 99–100.
71. Nichols (ed.), *Machyn's Diary*, 108; Foxe, *Acts and Monuments*, viii. 153; vii. 319.
72. Foxe, *Acts and Monuments*, vi. 611; viii. 559; Strype, *Ecclesiastical Memorials*, iii(2). 133–4.
73. Foxe, *Acts and Monuments*, vii. 345–7.
74. Ibid., viii. 379–80; vii. 33.
75. Ibid., vii. 319; viii. 147, 218.
76. Ibid., vii. 713–14.
77. Loades, *Oxford Martyrs*, 159–61; Huggarde, *Displaying of the Protestantes*, fos. 43ᵛ–52, 62ᵛ–3, 69ᵛ, 127.
78. For a different view, see Loades, *Oxford Martyrs*, 148–66, 234–42; id., 'The Enforcement of Reaction, 1553–1558', *JEH* 16 (1965), 58–66.
79. *VCH Staffordshire*, iii. 137; MacCulloch, *Suffolk*, 181.
80. Thompson, 'Pastoral Work', 209.
81. Foxe, *Acts and Monuments*, viii. 530; D. M. Palliser, *Tudor York* (Oxford, 1979), 243.

Chapter 14

1. J. Strype, *Ecclesiastical Memorials* (Oxford, 1822), iii(2). 134–5.
2. D. M. Loades, *The Reign of Mary Tudor* (1979), 241–3, 379, 384–5, 468; C. S. L. Davies, 'England and the French War, 1557–9', in J. Loach and R. Tittler (eds.), *The Mid-Tudor Polity c.1540–1560* (1980), 179–80.
3. J. G. Nichols (ed.), *The Diary of Henry Machyn* (Camden Society, 1848), 162–3; *CSP Span*, 1557–9, 351.
4. Davies, 'England and the French War', 163.
5. J. E. Neale, *Essays in Elizabethan History* (1958), 49.
6. H. Gee, *The Elizabethan Prayer Book and Ornaments* (1902), 195–202.

7. N. L. Jones, *Faith by Statute: Parliament and the Settlement of Religion, 1559* (1982), 17–22; Gee, *Elizabethan Prayer Book*, 210.

8. Nichols (ed.), *Machyn's Diary*, 178; C. H. Hartshorne (ed.), 'Extracts from the Register of Sir Thomas Butler, Vicar of Much Wenlock in Shropshire', in *Cambrian Journal* (1861), 96–7.

9. J. Nichols, *The History and Antiquities of the County of Leicester* (4 vols., 1815), i. 573.

10. W. MacCaffrey, *The Shaping of the Elizabethan Regime* (Princeton, NJ, 1968), 26–36.

11. Nichols (ed.), *Machyn's Diary*, 178, 189, 190, 192; *CSP Ven*, 1558–80, 22–3.

12. Jones, *Faith by Statute*, 43–6, 83; *TRP* ii. 102–3.

13. Hereafter I follow (with adjustments) Jones, *Faith by Statute*, 47–50, 83–159, rather than J. E. Neale, *Elizabeth I and Her Parliaments, 1559–1581* (1953), 51–84.

14. Jones, *Faith by Statute*, 104–12.

15. H. Robinson (ed.), *Zurich Letters* (2 vols., Parker Society, 1842, 1845), i. 10.

16. D. Wilkins, *Concilia Magnae Britanniae* (1737), iv. 179–80.

17. R. Persons, 'A Story of Domestical Difficulties', *Catholic Record Society, Miscellanea*, 2 (1902), 59–60; Jones, *Faith by Statute*, 127–8.

18. J. Strype, *Annals of the Reformation* (4 vols., Oxford, 1824), i(2). 400.

19. G. Alexander, 'Bishop Bonner and the Parliament of 1559', *BIHR* 66 (1983), 169–79.

20. Strype, *Annals*, i(2). 439–40.

21. *CSP Span*, 1558–67, 67; Jones, *Faith by Statute*, 150.

22. P. W. Hasler (ed.), *The House of Commons, 1558–1603* (3 vols., 1981), i. 102–4.

23. H. Gee, *The Elizabethan Clergy and the Settlement of Religion, 1558–1564* (Oxford, 1898), 30–8; W. P. Haugaard, *Elizabeth and the English Reformation* (Cambridge, 1968), 36–42; J. Bruce and T. T. Perowne (eds.), *Correspondence of Matthew Parker* (Parker Society, 1853), 77–8.

24. E. Cardwell, *Documentary Annals* (2 vols., Oxford, 1844), i. 210–42, esp. 212, 234.

25. C. G. Bayne, 'Visitation of the Province of Canterbury, 1559', *EHR* 28 (1913), 658–9.

26. M. Aston, *England's Iconoclasts: Laws against Images* (Oxford, 1988), 298–301.

27. Nichols (ed.), *Machyn's Diary*, 207–8.

28. E. Peacock (ed.), *English Church Furniture, Ornaments and Decorations at the Period of the Reformation* (1866), 61, 87–9, 114–15, 150, 158 (45% of Lincolnshire parishes obeyed the order in 1559); *VCH Sussex*, ii. 23; A. Hanham (ed.), *Churchwardens' Accounts of Ashburton, 1479–1580* (Devon and Cornwall Record Society, 1970), 143.

29. R. Whiting, *The Blind Devotion of the People* (Cambridge, 1989), 80; P. Collinson, *Godly People: Essays on English Protestantism and Puritanism* (1983), 406.

30. D. MacCulloch, *Suffolk and the Tudors* (Oxford, 1986), 182–4; *TRP* ii. 146–8.

31. C. J. Kitching (ed.), *The Royal Visitation of 1559: Act Book for the Northern Province* (Surtees Society, 1975); Gee, *Elizabethan Clergy*, 71–88.

32. C. Haigh, *Reformation and Resistance in Tudor Lancashire* (Cambridge, 1975), 209–11.

33. Gee, *Elizabethan Clergy*, 94–129.
34. Persons, 'Domestical Difficulties', 61.
35. Gee, *Elizabethan Clergy*, 236–47, 251 (Gee put the total for beneficed men at between 200 and 480, and preferred the lower figure); Haigh, *Reformation and Resistance*, 213–16.
36. Haugaard, *Elizabeth and the English Reformation*, 185–200; Cardwell, *Documentary Annals*, i. 268–73; Collinson, *Godly People*, 123–8.
37. Nichols (ed.), *Machyn's Diary*, 226.
38. Ibid. 241; Gee, *Elizabethan Prayer Book*, 273–4.
39. J. Foxe, *Acts and Monuments*, ed. G. Townsend (1843–9), viii. 156; Whiting, *Blind Devotion*, 81, 183–4.
40. P. Collinson, *The Birthpangs of Protestant England* (1988), 52.
41. R. O'Day and J. Berlatsky (eds.), 'Letter Book of Thomas Bentham' in *Camden Miscellany*, xxvii (Camden Society, 1979), 168.
42. BIY, HC.AB 1–2.
43. Ibid., AB 6, fos. 54ᵛ–55.
44. Nichols, *History of Leicester*, i. 560.
45. J. Bruce (ed.), 'Extracts of Accounts of the Churchwardens of Minchinhampton, Gloucestershire', *Archaeologia*, 35 (1853), 430.
46. BIY, HC.AB 6, fo. 54ᵛ.
47. G. Anstruther, *Vaux of Harrowden* (1953), 77.
48. Peacock, *English Church Furniture*, 47–8, 66–7, 95–6, 109–10, 114–15, 139–40, 148–9, 151–2.
49. P. Clark, *English Provincial Society from the Reformation to the Revolution: Kent 1500–1640* (Hassocks, 1977), 162; *VCH Staffordshire*, iii. 47; Cheshire RO, EDA 12/2, fos. 76ᵛ, 77, 79ᵛ; F. G. Emmison, *Elizabethan Life: Morals and the Church Courts* (Chelmsford, 1973), 180–4.
50. BIY, V.1567–8/CB 2, fos. 186ᵛ–212; R. Hutton, 'The Local Impact of the Tudor Reformations', in C. Haigh (ed.), *The English Reformation Revised* (Cambridge, 1987), 135; *VCH Sussex*, ii. 24–6.
51. Emmison, *Morals*, 257; R. Houlbrooke, *Church Courts and the People during the English Reformation, 1520–1570* (Oxford, 1979), 170.
52. *VCH Somerset*, ii. 35; *VCH Wiltshire*, iii. 32 n.
53. *VCH Cumberland*, ii. 79–80.
54. C. W. Foster (ed.), *The State of the Church in the Reigns of Elizabeth and James I* (Lincoln Record Society, 1926), 457; *A Parte of a Register* (Middelburg, 1593), 62.
55. F. D. Price (ed.), *The Commission for Ecclesiastical Causes in the Dioceses of Bristol and Gloucester, 1574* (Bristol and Gloucestershire Archaeological Society, 1972), 111; W. J. Sheils (ed.), *Archbishop Grindal's Visitation, 1575* (Borthwick Institute, 1977), 54.
56. A. Peel (ed.), *The Seconde Parte of a Register* (2 vols., Cambridge, 1915), ii. 165–74, quotation at p. 169.
57. Cheshire RO, EDA 12/2, fo. 1ᵛ; BIY, HC.AB 3, fo. 106ᵛ.
58. BIY, HC.AB 1, fo. 95; Cheshire RO, EDA 12/2, fo. 80.
59. BIY, HC.AB 3, fo. 176.
60. Emmison, *Morals*, 195; W. H. Hale, *A Series of Precedents and Proceedings* (1847), 153.

61. BIY, HC.AB 3, fos. 176, 182, 185, 189, 190; V.1567–8/CB 1, fo. 105; Cheshire RO, EDC 5/1574.
62. Haigh, *Reformation and Resistance*, 217–18.
63. Ibid. 215.
64. F. Heal, 'The Parish Clergy and the Reformation in the Diocese of Ely', *Proceedings of the Cambridge Antiquarian Society*, 66 (1975), 156–7; MacCulloch, *Suffolk*, 184; Clark, *Kent*, 162–3.
65. J. Strype, *The History of the Life and Acts of Edmund Grindal* (Oxford, 1821), 53–73; Bruce and Perowne (eds.), *Parker Correspondence*, 120–1.
66. Haigh, *Reformation and Resistance*, 239; C. Read, *Lord Burghley and Queen Elizabeth* (1960), 303; R. O'Day, 'Thomas Bentham: A Case Study in the Problems of the Early Elizabethan Episcopate', *JEH* 23 (1972), 138–9.
67. J. I. Daeley, 'Pluralism in the Diocese of Canterbury during the Administration of Matthew Parker', *JEH* 18 (1967), 40–6; Houlbrooke, *Church Courts*, 188; C. W. Field, *The State of the Church in Gloucestershire* (Robertsbridge, Sussex, 1971), 14, 17, 22, 27.
68. Wiltshire RO, Salisbury Diocesan Records, Visitation Detecta Book 4, quotations at fos. 5, 3^v, 1^v, 1, 2.
69. *VCH Sussex*, ii. 24–6.
70. West Sussex RO, Ep. I/23/1, examples at fos. 6–6^v, 2^v, 25.

Chapter 15

1. BIY, V.1578/CB 3, fo. 29^v.
2. Ibid., HC.AB 6, fos. 57, 127^v; AB 11, fo. 296^v; G. Ormerod, *History of the County Palatine and City of Chester*, ed. T. Helsby (3 vols., 1875–82), ii. 117; K. R. Wark, *Elizabethan Recusancy in Cheshire* (Chetham Society, 1971), 80–1.
3. Wark, *Elizabethan Recusancy in Cheshire*, 42–4, 81, 132.
4. See especially A. G. Dickens, *Reformation Studies* (1982), 163–71, 182–3.
5. H. Robinson (ed.), *Zurich Letters* (2 vols., Parker Society, 1842, 1845), i. 85; BL, Additional MS 48023, fo. 355 (I am grateful to Dr G. W. Bernard for showing me his transcript of this chronicle); H. N. Birt, *The Elizabethan Religious Settlement* (1907), 311; Cheshire RO, EDA 12/2, fo. 93^v; BL, Lansdowne MS 7, fo. 212; *CSPD*, Addenda 1547–65, 567.
6. M. D. R. Leys, *Catholics in England, 1559–1829* (1961), 7; *VCH Sussex*, ii. 25; A. Dures, *English Catholicism, 1558–1642* (1983), 7.
7. J. C. H. Aveling, *Catholic Recusancy in the City of York, 1558–1791* (Catholic Record Society, 1970), 166; Birt, *Elizabethan Religious Settlement*, 419.
8. A. Peel (ed.), *The Seconde Parte of a Register* (Cambridge, 1915), ii. 166; BIY, HC.AB 10, fo. 157.
9. J. C. H. Aveling, *Northern Catholics: The Catholic Recusants of the North Riding of Yorkshire, 1558–1790* (1966), 91.
10. V. Burke, 'Catholic Recusants in Elizabethan Worcestershire', MA thesis (Birmingham, 1972), 39; BIY, HC.AB 3, fos. 176, 182.
11. J. H. Pollen (ed.), *Unpublished Documents relating to the English Martyrs, 1584–1603* (Catholic Record Society, 1908), 72; BIY, HC.AB 11, fo. 64.
12. J. Bossy, *The English Catholic Community, 1570–1850* (1975), 12; C. M. F. J.

Swan, 'The Introduction of the Elizabethan Settlement into the Universities of Oxford and Cambridge', Ph.D. thesis (Cambridge, 1955), apps.

13. A. F. Allison and D. M. Rogers, 'A Catalogue of Catholic Books in English, 1558–1640', *Recusant History*, 3 (1956), 176–7; P. Milward, *Religious Controversies of the Elizabethan Age* (1978), 1–6.

14. M. R. O'Connell, *Thomas Stapleton and the Counter Reformation* (New Haven, Conn., 1964), 61; J. R. Roberts, *A Critical Anthology of English Recusant Devotional Prose, 1558–1603* (1966), 4–5.

15. W. Allen, *An Apologie and True Declaration of the Institution and Endevours of the Two English Colleges* (Rheims, 1581), fos. 21^v–3; T. F. Knox (ed.), *First and Second Douai Diaries* (1878), p. xxvi.

16. A. Morey, *The Catholic Subjects of Elizabeth I* (1978), 101, 106–9, 187; Bossy, *English Catholic Community*, 15–17.

17. *CSPD*, Addenda 1547–65, 523; R. B. Manning, *Religion and Society in Elizabethan Sussex* (Leicester, 1969), 160 and n.

18. Birt, *Elizabethan Religious Settlement*, 528–9; *CSPD*, Addenda 1547–65, 522, 524; *DNB*, *sub* Draycott, Rambridge.

19. *CSPD*, Addenda 1547–65, 521; BIY, HC.AB 3, fo. 46^v; J. M. J. Fletcher, 'Bishop Pursglove of Tideswell', *Derbyshire Archaeological Journal*, 32 (1910), 19–20; G. Anstruther, *The Seminary Priests: Elizabethan* (Ware, n.d.), 60, 126.

20. *CSPD*, Addenda 1547–65, 521; M. Bateson (ed.), 'Letters from the Bishops to the Privy Council, 1564', *Camden Miscellany*, ix (Camden Society, 1893), 40–1; W. R. Trimble, *The Catholic Laity in Elizabethan England* (Cambridge, Mass., 1964), 23.

21. *CSPD*, Addenda 1547–65, 524; J. Strype, *Annals of the Reformation*, i(2). 48–9; W. Allen, *Letters and Memorials*, ed. T. F. Knox (1882), 21; Cheshire RO, EDA 12/2, fos. 118, 124, 127.

22. *CSPD*, Addenda 1547–65, 524; J. Scholefield (ed.), *The Works of John Pilkington* (Parker Society, 1842), 480–6; Allen, *Letters and Memorials*, 21; PRO, SP 12/48, fo. 71; 12/167, fos. 123, 125; BIY, HC.AB 6, fo. 86^v.

23. Cheshire RO, EDA 12/2, fo. 118; BIY, HC.AB 6, fo. 88^v.

24. *CSPD*, Addenda 1547–65, 521, 524; BIY, HC.AB 5, fos. 147, 155, 233^v.

25. *CSPD*, Addenda 1547–65, 522–4; 1547–80, 183; Bateson (ed.), 'Letters from the Bishops', 19–23; BL, Harleian MS 6990, fo. 64.

26. Bateson (ed.), 'Letters from the Bishops', 34–5, 33, 3; *CSPD*, Addenda 1547–65, 523.

27. *VCH Sussex*, ii. 25; BIY, HC.AB 6, fo. 114^v; C. Haigh, *Reformation and Resistance in Tudor Lancashire* (Cambridge, 1975), 254.

28. BIY, HC.AB 6, fo. 83^v; Burke, 'Worcestershire Recusants', 63; J. E. Paul, 'The Hampshire Recusants in the Reign of Elizabeth I', Ph.D. thesis (Southampton, 1958), 131.

29. R. Smith, *An Elizabethan Recusant House*, ed. A. C. Southern (1954), 19; Duke of Norfolk (ed.), *The Lives of Philip Howard Earl of Arundel, and of Anne Dacres his Wife* (1857), 170–1.

30. Paul, 'Hampshire Recusants', 39, 412; 'Diocesan Returns of Recusants for England and Wales, 1577', *Catholic Record Society, Miscellanea*, 12 (1921), 78; P. McGrath and J. Rowe, 'The Recusancy of Sir Thomas Cornwallis', *Proceedings*

of the Suffolk Institute of Archaeology, 28 (1961), 242; H. Foley, *Records of the English Province of the Society of Jesus* (8 vols, 1877–83), ii. 26.

31. The following account relies heavily upon S. E. Taylor, 'The Crown and the North of England, 1559–70', Ph.D. thesis (Manchester, 1981), by far the best study of the origins and course of the 1569 rebellion.

32. C. Sharp, *Memorials of the Rebellion of 1569* (1840), 42 n.–43 n.

33. Taylor, 'Crown and the North', 246–85.

34. A. Clifford (ed.), *State Papers and Letters of Sir Ralph Sadler* (2 vols., Edinburgh, 1809), ii. 337.

35. J. Raine (ed.), *Depositions and Ecclesiastical Proceedings from the Courts of Durham* (Surtees Society, 1845), 182–8.

36. Ibid. 136–7, 143–7, 155.

37. Sharp, *Memorials*, 196–7; Aveling, *City of York*, 36.

38. *CSPD* Addenda 1547–65, 524; Birt, *Elizabethan Religious Settlement*, 518.

39. Foley, *Records*, ii. 210.

40. Scholefield (ed.), *Pilkington's Works*, 480–6.

41. C. G. Bayne, *Anglo-Roman Relations, 1558–1565* (Oxford, 1913), 163–7, 177–80; P. Holmes, *Resistance and Compromise: The Political Thought of the Elizabethan Catholics* (Cambridge, 1982), 84–5.

42. J. H. Pollen, *The English Catholics in the Reign of Queen Elizabeth* (1920), 104–6; A. O. Meyer, *England and the Catholic Church under Elizabeth* (1915), 475–8; Haigh, *Reformation and Resistance*, 249–50.

43. Paul, 'Hampshire Recusants', 39, 412; R. Houlbrooke, *Church Courts and the People during the English Reformation, 1520–1570* (Oxford, 1979), 246.

44. N. Sander, *A Treatise of the Images of Christ* (Louvain, 1567), sigs. A–Avi; H. Ely, *Certaine Briefe Notes upon a Briefe Apologie* (Paris, 1602), 66–7.

45. Haigh, *Reformation and Resistance, 250–3, 260–3*; BIY, HC.CP 1572.

46. G. de C. Parmiter, *Edmund Plowden* (Catholic Record Society, 1987), 105–8; Foley, *Records*, iii. 570–3.

47. W. Camden, *The History of the Most Renowned and Victorious Princess Elizabeth* (1675 edn.), 245; R. Persons, *A Treatise Tending to Mitigation towards Catholic Subjects in England* (St Omer, 1607), 11, attacking Edward Coke's claims.

48. Paul, 'Hampshire Recusants', 47–8; BIY, HC.AB 6, fos. 64–119; AB 7; P. Tyler, 'The Ecclesiastical Commission for the Province of York, 1561–1641', D.Phil. thesis (Oxford, 1965), 150, 235–6.

49. Aveling, *City of York*, 41–2, 45; BIY, HC.AB 5, fo. 233^v; AB 8, fo. 169^v; 'Diocesan Returns, 1577', 4.

50. J. Morris, *Troubles of our Catholic Forefathers* (3 vols., 1872–7), iii. 248–58.

51. Paul, 'Hampshire Recusants', 38.

52. Aveling, *Northern Catholics*, 29–31; BIY, HC.CP 1576; Foley, *Records*, iii. 242.

53. McGrath and Rowe, 'Cornwallis', 237, 242, 247–9; Foley, *Records*, iii. 444.

54. Knox (ed.), *First and Second Douai Diaries*, pp. lxii, 24–7, 98.

55. Ibid., pp. xxxvii–xliii, xlvii–xlviii.

56. Calculated from Anstruther, *Seminary Priests*.

57. R. Persons, 'Of the Life and Martyrdom of Father Edmund Campion', 1, *Letters and Notices*, 11 (1877), 325.

58. Knox (ed.), *First and Second Douai Diaries*, 98.

59. L. Hicks (ed.), *Letters and Memorials of Father Robert Persons* (Catholic Record Society, 1942), 319–21, 59–61.

60. R. Persons, 'Of the Life and Martyrdom of Father Edmund Campion', II, *Letters and Notices*, 12 (1879), 35–6; id., 'A Story of Domestical Difficulties', *Catholic Record Society, Miscellanea*, 2 (1902), 178–81.

61. Wark, *Recusancy in Cheshire*, 42–4; J. Venn, *Early Collegiate Life* (Cambridge, 1913), 84.

62. Smith, *Elizabethan Recusant House*, 19; Dures, *English Catholicism*, 28; R. Challoner, *Memoirs of Missionary Priests*, ed. J. H. Pollen (1924), 66–7, 102–4.

63. 'Diocesan Returns, 1577', I.

64. T. Worthington, *A Relation of Sixteen Martyrs* (Douai, 1601), 57.

65. BIY, HC.AB 10, fos. 3, 10, 20ᵛ, 23, and *passim*; Tyler, 'Ecclesiastical Commission', 254–8.

66. HMC, *Various Collections*, iii. 34–43; A. Pritchard, *Catholic Loyalism in Elizabethan England* (1979), 51–2, 54–5.

67. P. Caraman, *Henry Garnet, 1555–1606, and the Gunpowder Plot* (1964), 35.

68. C. Dodd, *Church History of England*, ed. M. A. Tierney (3 vols., 1839–43), iii. 136 n.–137 n.

69. Morris, *Troubles*, iii. 118–19. The figures for executions are from P. Caraman and J. Walsh, *The Martyrs of England and Wales, 1535–1680* (1960); G. F. Nuttall, 'The English Martyrs, 1535–1680: A Statistical Review', *JEH* 22 (1971), 192–3.

70. F. X. Walker, 'The Implementation of the Elizabethan Statutes against Recusants, 1581–1603', Ph.D. thesis (London, 1961), 248–52, 293–4.

71. Dures, *English Catholicism*, 33–4; Holmes, *Resistance and Compromise*, 101–8.

72. C. Haigh, 'From Monopoly to Minority: Catholicism in Early Modern England', *TRHS* 5th series, 31 (1981), 129–47; but see the debate in *JEH* 35 (1984) and 36 (1985).

73. Hicks (ed.), *Letters of Persons*, 320.

74. W. Weston, *Autobiography of an Elizabethan*, ed. P. Caraman (1955), 28, 72, 77, 79; Caraman, *Garnet*, 32–6, 44–5; C. Devlin, *The Life of Robert Southwell, Poet and Martyr* (1956), 114, 116, 161, 220–1; Dures, *English Catholicism*, 20–6.

75. Caraman, *Garnet*, 45; Devlin, *Southwell*, 225–6.

76. Challoner, *Memoirs*, 232, 592, 594–5; Pollen (ed.), *Unpublished Documents Relating to the English Martyrs*, 345–8.

77. J. Bossy, 'Rome and the Elizabethan Catholics: A Question of Geography', *HJ* 7 (1964), 136–7; Haigh, 'Monopoly to Minority', 133.

78. Pollen (ed.), *Unpublished Documents Relating to the English Martyrs*, 309; A. Davidson, 'Roman Catholicism in Oxfordshire, c.1580–c.1640', Ph.D. thesis (Bristol, 1970), 416–17.

79. Bossy, 'Rome and the Elizabethan Catholics', 138–40; Aveling, *Northern Catholics*, 191.

80. Hicks (ed.), *Letters of Persons*, 108; Haigh (ed.), *English Reformation Revised*, 199–200.

81. Haigh (ed.), *English Reformation Revised*, 200–1; *CSPD*, 1598–1601, 362.

82. D. MacCulloch, 'Catholic and Puritan in Elizabethan Suffolk', *Archiv für Reformationsgeschichte*, 72 (1981), 249; J. Gerard, *Autobiography of an Elizabethan*, ed. P. Caraman (1951), 33.

83. M. C. E. Chambers, *The Life of Mary Ward* (2 vols., 1882, 1885), ii. 28, 35.
84. Bossy, *English Catholic Community*, 175; S. A. H. Burne (ed.), *Staffordshire Quarter Sessions Rolls*, 1581–9 (Staffordshire Record Society, 1929), 36–7, 44–6, 70–1, 87–8.
85. Dickens, *Reformation Studies*, 201–2, 205.
86. Cf. K. J. Lindley, 'The Lay Catholics of England in the Reign of Charles I', *JEH* 22 (1971), 200–7; Bossy, *English Catholic Community*, 78–106.
87. B. Magee, *The English Recusants* (1938), 83–4.

Chapter 16

1. P. Collinson, *Godly People: Essays on English Protestantism and Puritanism* (1983), 102–3.
2. C. W. Foster (ed.), *The State of the Church in the Reigns of Elizabeth and James I* (Lincoln Record Society, 1926), 458.
3. W. J. Sheils, *The Puritans in the Diocese of Peterborough, 1558–1610* (Northampton-shire Record Society, 1979), 20; *VCH Wiltshire*, iii. 33; W. H. Frere, *The English Church in the Reigns of Elizabeth and James I* (1904), 107; A. L. Rowse, *Tudor Cornwall* (1941), 324.
4. E. Cardwell, *Documentary Annals* (2 vols., Oxford, 1844), i. 213.
5. W. J. Sheils (ed.), *Archbishop Grindal's Visitation, 1575* (Borthwick Institute, 1977), pp. vi, 80, 78, 76, 11.
6. West Sussex RO, Ep. I/23/5; A. Peel (ed.), *The Seconde Parte of a Register* (2 vols., Cambridge, 1915), ii. 130–42.
7. W. Nicholson (ed.), *The Remains of Edmund Grindal* (Parker Society, 1843), 379; J. Ayre (ed.), *The Sermons of Edwin Sandys* (Parker Society, 1842), 154.
8. *A Parte of a Register* (Middelburg, 1593), 216, 305; J. More, *Three Godly and Fruitful Sermons* (Cambridge, 1594), 69.
9. C. Hill, *Economic Problems of the Church* (1971 edn.), 132–67; Ayre (ed.), *Sermons of Sandys*, 155.
10. J. McConica (ed.), *The History of the University of Oxford*, iii (Oxford, 1986), 405–18; C. M. Dent, *Protestant Reformers in Elizabethan Oxford* (Oxford, 1983), 17–46.
11. H. C. Porter, *Reformation and Reaction in Tudor Cambridge* (Cambridge, 1958), 101–9; H. Robinson (ed.), *Zurich Letters* (2 vols., Parker Society, 1842, 1845), i. 207–8.
12. *APC* viii. 120; McConica, *History of Oxford*, 387.
13. Dent, *Oxford*, 88–93, 147.
14. Porter, *Cambridge*, 156–7.
15. *A Booke of Certaine Canons, Concernyng Some Parte of the Discipline of the Churche of England* (1571), 5; E. Cardwell, *Synodalia* (2 vols., Oxford, 1842), i. 113–14, 133; R. O'Day, *Education and Society, 1500–1800* (1982), 136–7.
16. R. O'Day, *The English Clergy: The Emergence and Consolidation of a Profession, 1558–1642* (Leicester, 1979), 132–43.
17. J. Ayre (ed.), *The Works of John Whitgift* (3 vols., Parker Society, 1851–3), i. 313.
18. Hill, *Economic Problems*, 207 n.; Sheils, *Peterborough*, 91–2.
19. P. Clark, *English Provincial Society from the Reformation to the Revolution: Kent*

1500–1640 (Hassocks, 1977), 169, 181; R. G. Usher, *Reconstruction of the English Church* (2 vols., New York, 1910), i. 241; P. Collinson, *The Elizabethan Puritan Movement* (1967), 128; R. C. Richardson, *Puritanism in North-West England* (Manchester, 1972), 58–63.

20. Nicholson (ed.), *Remains of Grindal*, 380; P. Collinson, *Archbishop Grindal, 1519–1583* (1979), 207–8; R. B. Manning, *Religion and Society in Elizabethan Sussex* (Leicester, 1969), 64–5, 178–9.

21. O'Day, *English Clergy*, 87–8, 95, 113–16; Collinson, *Godly People*, 455–66; W. Hunt, *The Puritan Moment: The Coming of Revolution in an English County* (Cambridge, Mass., 1983), 100–5.

22. O'Day, *English Clergy*, 49–57, 68–9.

23. P. Collinson, 'The Elizabethan Church and the New Religion', in C. Haigh (ed.), *The Reign of Elizabeth I* (1984), 187.

24. Frere, *English Church*, 107; Sheils, *Peterborough*, 92; M. Ingram, *Church Courts, Sex and Marriage in England, 1570–1640* (Cambridge, 1987), 87.

25. C. W. Foster (ed.), *State of the Church in the Reigns of Elizabeth and James I* (Lincoln Record Society, 1926), pp. lvii, 458; E. J. I. Allen, 'The State of the Church in the Diocese of Peterborough, 1601–1642', B.Litt. thesis (Oxford, 1972), 31–2; A. Peel, 'A Puritan Survey of the Church in Staffordshire in 1604', *EHR* 26 (1911), 352.

26. P. Collinson, *The Religion of Protestants: The Church in English Society, 1559–1625* (Oxford, 1982), 50, 48; id., *Grindal*, 199.

27. Christ Church, Oxford, Chapter Act Book 1549–1645, 229; J. Raine (ed.), *Injunctions and other Ecclesiastical Proceedings of Richard Barnes* (Surtees Society, 1850), 81–91.

28. C. Cross, *The Royal Supremacy in the Elizabethan Church* (1969), 96–9; Collinson, *Elizabethan Puritan Movement*, 50–1; Sheils, *Peterborough*, 26; Manning, *Sussex*, 76–8; P. Seaver, *The Puritan Lectureships* (Stanford, Calif., 1970), 123–9.

29. Collinson, *Elizabethan Puritan Movement*, 171–6, 210–11; id., *Godly People*, 480.

30. Cardwell, *Documentary Annals*, i. 218, 328.

31. Collinson, *Elizabethan Puritan Movement*, 171–3, 210–11; Manning, *Sussex*, 190–1, 64.

32. W. H. Frere and W. M. Kennedy (eds.), *Visitation Articles and Injunctions* (3 vols., Alcuin Club, 1910), iii. 22, 87–8, 99, 166, 275–6; W. M. Kennedy (ed.), *Elizabethan Episcopal Administration* (3 vols., Alcuin Club, 1924), ii. 42–3, 71–2, 93, 113; iii. 211, 320, 338; C. Haigh, *Reformation and Resistance in Tudor Lancashire* (Cambridge, 1975), 245–6.

33. I. Green, ' "For Children in Yeeres and Children in Understanding": The Emergence of the English Catechism under Elizabeth and the Early Stuarts', *JEH* 37 (1986), 397–425; R. Cawdrey, *A Short and Fruitfull Treatise of the Profit and Necessitie of Catechising* (1604 edn.); T. Sparke and J. Seddon, *A Catechisme, or Short Kind of Instruction, Whereby to Teach Children and the Ignoraunter Sort the Christian Religion. Whereunto is Prefixed a Learned Treatise of the Necessity and Use of Catechising* (Oxford, 1588).

34. Collinson, *Grindal*, 233–52; C. Haigh, *Elizabeth I* (1988), 39–41.

35. Usher, *Reconstruction*, i, 241; Cardwell, *Synodalia*, i. 273.

36. L. Stone, 'The Educational Revolution in England, 1560–1640', *PP* 28 (1964),

41–80; D. Cressy, *Literacy and the Social Order: Reading and Writing in Tudor and Stuart England* (Cambridge, 1980), 165, 167–9; O'Day, *Education and Society*, 25–42, 81–105.

37. Cressy, *Literacy and the Social Order*, 160, 163, 162.
38. R. Greenham, *The Workes of the Reverend and Faithfull Servant of Jesus Christ* (1601), 212, 203.
39. Calculated from W. A. Jackson, F. J. Ferguson, and K. F. Pantzer (eds.), *Short Title Catalogue of Books, 1475–1640*, 2 vols. (2nd edn., 1976, 1986), i. 87–90.
40. A. F. Herr, *The Elizabethan Sermon: A Survey and a Bibliography* (Philadelphia, 1940), 27.
41. Clark, *Kent*, 209–11.
42. J. More, *A Bryefe and Necessary Catechisme or Instruction* (1577), sig. Ciiii.
43. Sheils, *Peterborough*, 29.
44. W. Hinde, *A Faithful Remonstrance of the Holy Life and Happy Death of John Bruen* (1641), 16–17; BL, Additional MS 38492, fos. 107–8; Collinson, *Religion of Protestants*, 242–3.
45. Cawdrey, *Short and Fruitfull Treatise*, 23–4; J. Nichols, *An Order of Household Instruction* (1596), sig. B4.
46. E. Paget, *Short Questions and Answeares, conteyning the Summe of Christian Religion* (1583), sig. A4; Hinde, *Faithful Remonstrance*, 50–74.
47. Sheils, *Peterborough*, 14–24; R. M. Fisher, 'The Reformation in Microcosm? Benchers at the Inns of Court, 1530–1580', *Parergon*, NS, 6 (1988), 55–60.
48. C. Cross, *Urban Magistrates and Ministers: Religion in Hull and Leeds from the Reformation to the Civil War* (Borthwick Papers, 1985), 16–19; Manning, *Sussex*, 41, 192, 213; K. Wrightson and D. Levine, *Poverty and Piety in an English Village: Terling, 1525–1700* (1979), 155–6; C. Cross, 'Priests into Ministers: The Establishment of Protestant Practice in the City of York, 1530–1630', in P. N. Brooks (ed.), *Reformation Principle and Practice* (1980), 222–3.
49. Haigh, *Reformation and Resistance*, 296–300; M. Spufford, *Contrasting Communities: English Villagers in the Sixteenth and Seventeenth Centuries* (Cambridge, 1974), 262–3, 334–44.
50. R. H. Fritze, 'The Role of Family and Religion in the Local Politics of Early Elizabethan England: The Case of Hampshire in the 1560s', *HJ* 25 (1982), 278–9.
51. M. E. James, *Family, Lineage and Civil Society: A Study of Society, Politics and Mentality in the Durham Region, 1500–1640* (Oxford, 1974), 51, 67–70, 78–9, 147; S. J. Watts, *From Border to Middle Shire: Northumberland, 1586–1625* (Leicester, 1975), 96; A. H. Smith, *County and Court: Government and Politics in Norfolk, 1558–1603* (Oxford, 1974), 48–53, 82–3, 207–8, 218; D. MacCulloch, *Suffolk and the Tudors* (Oxford, 1986), 95–104, 195–7.
52. Rowse, *Tudor Cornwall*, 347–55; Haigh, *Reformation and Resistance*, 212–13, 285.
53. O'Day, *English Clergy*, 10–11.
54. Hunt, *Puritan Moment*, 146–7, 153–4; C. Haigh, 'Puritan Evangelism in the Reign of Elizabeth I', *EHR* 92 (1977), 57; J. J. Goring, 'The Reformation of the Ministry in Elizabethan Sussex', *JEH* 34 (1983), 359.
55. Peel (ed.), *Seconde Parte of a Register*, i. 238.
56. C. Hill, *Society and Puritanism in Pre-Revolutionary England* (1969 edn.), 178–9.

57. A. Beesley, *The History of Banbury* (1841), 242–4, 615–16; *CSPD*, 1581–90, 586, 601, 602, 605; *APC* xvii. 202.
58. Clark, *Kent*, 157; Matthew 10: 34. Cf. *A Dialogue Concerning the Strife of our Churche, wherein are Aunswered Divers Accusations wherewith the Godly are Falsely Charged* (1584).
59. Cf. P. Collinson, *The Birthpangs of Protestant England* (1988), 1–27.
60. Collinson, *Religion of Protestants*, 190–1, 199–200.
61. H. N. Birt, *The Elizabethan Religious Settlement* (1907), 435; J. Darrell, *A Treatise of the Church Written against Them of the Separation* (1617), 28 (I owe this reference to Patrick Collinson).
62. A. Dent, *The Plaine Man's Path-way to Heaven* (1601), 287.
63. G. Gifford, *A Briefe Discourse of Certaine Points of the Religion Which is Among the Common Sort of Christian, Which May Be Termed the Countrie Divinitie* (1598 edn.), 116–17, 78.
64. Dent, *Plaine Man's Path-way*, 27, 30.
65. J. Nichols, *The Plea of the Innocent* (1602), 212–13.
66. HMC, *Montague of Beaulieu* (1900), 37.
67. Dent, *Plaine Man's Path-way*, 274, 33–4.
68. Gifforde, *Briefe Discourse*, 111–13.
69. Ibid. 45–6.
70. Dent, *Plaine Man's Path-way*, 29.
71. Cawdrey, *Short and Fruitfull Treatise*, 94; W. Perkins, *The Workes of that Famous and Worthy Minister of Christ* (3 vols., 1612, 1609), i. sig. A2.
72. Dent, *Plaine Man's Path-way*, 26; W. H. Hale, *A Series of Precedents and Proceedings* (1847), 168.
73. Collinson, *Godly People*, 11.
74. *Seconde Parte of a Register*, i. 291–6; Sheils, *Peterborough*, 37–8, 68–9.
75. Gifford, *Briefe Discourse*, 34; Dent, *Plaine Man's Path-way*, 30.

Conclusion

1. W. Perkins, *The Workes of that Famous and Worthy Minister of Christ* (3 vols., Cambridge, 1612, 1609), i. 670.
2. Calculated from W. A. Jackson, F. J. Ferguson, and K. F. Pantzer (eds.), *A Short Title Catalogue of Books, 1475–1640*, 2 vols. (2nd edn., 1976, 1986), ii. 227.
3. W. Perkins, *The Foundation of Christian Religion, Gathered into Six Principles* (1636 edn.), 22.
4. Perkins, *Workes*, i. 292, 283.
5. Ibid., ii. 22.
6. Ibid., i. 36, 38.
7. Ibid., sig. A2.
8. Ibid. 48–9.
9. Ibid., sig. A2; A. Dent, *The Plaine Man's Path-way to Heaven* (1601), 30.
10. F. D. Price (ed.), *Commission for Ecclesiastical Causes in the Dioceses of Bristol and Gloucester, 1574* (Bristol and Gloucestershire Archaeological Society, 1972), 65; F. G. Emmison, *Elizabethan Life: Morals and the Church Courts* (Chelmsford, 1973), 77.
11. M. Spufford, *Small Books and Pleasant Histories* (1981), 34.

12. Perkins, *Workes*, ii. 87; J. F. Williams (ed.), *Bishop Redman's Visitation, 1597* (Norfolk Record Society, 1946), 69.
13. Cheshire RO, EDV 1/12a, fo. 96; 1/2b, fo. 122; 1/13, fo. 198ᵛ; 1/14, fos. 186–7.
14. Perkins, *Workes*, ii. 260.
15. Ibid., i. 311.
16. R. Southwell, *A Short Rule of Good Life* (1595), 45–66.
17. Ibid. 61.
18. Ibid. 53.
19. Ibid., sig. A5.
20. J. Gerard, *Autobiography of an Elizabethan*, ed. P. Caraman (1951), 32–3.
21. P. Caraman (ed.), *The Other Face: Catholic Life under Elizabeth I* (1960), 121.
22. E.g. H. Foley, *Records of the English Province of the Society of Jesus* (8 vols., 1877–83), ii. 140; HMC, *Montague of Beaulieu*, 212–13.
23. Foley, *Records*, ii. 140; Perkins, *Workes*, ii. 354; i. 710.
24. Perkins, *Workes*, i. sig. A2, 31; Foley, *Records*, ii. 140.
25. R. Cawdrey, *A Short and Fruitfull Treatise of the Profit and Necessitie of Catechising* (1604 edn.), 93–4.
26. W. H. Frere and C. E. Douglas (eds.), *Puritan Manifestoes* (1954 edn.), 9; Perkins, *Workes*, ii. 260.
27. W. Burton, *The Rowsing of the Sluggard in 7 Sermons* (1595), 68.

Bibliographical Survey

Introduction

THE modern historiography of English Reformations was revolutionized in 1964, when A. G. Dickens published *The English Reformation*. Professor Dickens told the familiar stories of parliamentary statutes, English Bibles, and Protestant Prayer Books, but he added the men and women who experienced religious change, and showed how and why new religions appealed to some of them. His book was a formidable achievement, and since then it has stood as the best all-round survey of Reformation in England. But no historical study will go unchallenged for ever, no matter how good it is. Historians are always debating among themselves, asking each other questions, trying to sort things out. Some later work, especially that based on local archives, began to suggest that Dickens might have exaggerated what was wrong with the old Catholic Church and exaggerated the appeal of new Protestantism. Some of this work was collected together in C. Haigh (ed.), *The English Reformation Revised* (Cambridge, 1987), in an attempt to revise the English Reformation, rather than *The English Reformation*! But in 1989 Dickens published a second, revised edition of his book, in which he attempted to rebut criticism; I do not believe he succeeds.

The great strength of Dickens's book was its portrayal of (and sensitive sympathy for) evangelical Protestants; its weakness was its treatment of Catholics and conservatives, those who did not want Reformation. In 1984 J. J. Scarisbrick plugged some of the gaps with *The Reformation and the English People* (Oxford), which looked at the popularity of conventional Catholicism before the Reformations, and at the adjustments which people were forced to make during them. Dickens offered a Reformation without Catholics, which made it hard to understand why Reformation was slow and difficult; Scarisbrick offered a Reformation without Protestants, which made it hard to understand why it happened at all. We need a version of religious conflict and transformation which includes both sides of the religious fence—and those who sat on the fence, those who could not find it, and those who did not see why there was such a fuss about the fence. It is easy for those of us who write about Reformation to assume that religion was always the dominating issue in Tudor England, that everyone (or almost everyone) cared passionately about the disputes, and that all Reformation decisions were taken on religious grounds. But we would probably be wrong.

Professor Dickens insisted that the Reformation was about religion, and so it was. But it was not *only* about religion: it was also about government and politics, because sixteenth-century governments insisted on ideological uniformity, and because ideology was subject to political calculations and pressures. Our understanding of government and Reformation was hugely increased by G. R. Elton's *Policy and Police* (Cambridge, 1972). Elton showed how much hostility there was to Henry VIII's (or Thomas Cromwell's) Reformation in the 1530s, and how Cromwell used the weapons of early modern government to overcome that hostility. Elton showed that Reformation was not only a struggle between Catholics and Protestants: it was also a struggle between government and governed; it was a question of enforcement. So we have to consider the mechanisms of government and the responses of the localities, if we are to see Reformation realistically. It may be that, working from the records of what Cromwell tried to do, Professor Elton exaggerated the success of enforcement. Cromwell, for all his efforts, did not break opposition to religious change, as Somerset, Northumberland, Elizabeth Tudor, and William Cecil were to find. Reformation was hard to achieve.

Reformation was also complicated by the machinations of politicians. In political history, the major advances in recent years have been made by Eric Ives and David Starkey. In *Faction in Tudor England* (Historical Association, 1979), Ives suggested that Tudor politics should be understood as group competition for office and reward; in *Anne Boleyn* (Oxford, 1986), Ives showed how one female politician rose and fell in a cut-throat Court, and lost her head when she lost support. David Starkey has drawn attention to the importance of easy access to the monarch, and to the political role of the royal Privy Chamber and its Gentlemen; see especially D. Starkey (ed.), *The English Court* (1987), and D. Starkey, *The Reign of Henry VIII: Personalities and Politics* (1985). Other historians (notably Simon Adams, George Bernard, Peter Gwyn, Glyn Redworth, and Retha Warnicke) have objected that the Ives–Starkey approach reduced kings and queens to mere pawns, and have argued that there were no fixed factional alliances fighting pitched political battles. But, in the high-risk atmosphere of the Court, fortunes and even lives were at stake. Personal influences, political manœuvering, and the calculation of individual advantage made the development of policy (including religious policy) a matter of chance. So religious change in Tudor England was fragmented and episodic: there were English Reformations!

This bibliographical survey is not a comprehensive listing of important studies of Reformation subjects. Rather, it seeks to indicate areas of recent controversy and progress, and to draw particular attention to formative and new work, especially work which has contributed to the approach adopted in this book.

Part I: A Church Unchallenged

Recent studies of the English Church before Reformation have, in the main, shown it as a viable institution with reasonable (though not uncritical) community support. For general surveys, see P. Heath, *Church and Realm, 1272–1461* (1988), and, more briefly, C. Harper-Bill, *The Pre-Reformation Church* (1990), and his 'Dean Colet's Convocation Sermon and the Pre-Reformation Church in England', *History*, 73 (1988). Religious belief and practice are sensitively discussed in J. Rhodes, 'Private Devotion in England on the Eve of the Reformation', Ph.D. thesis (Durham, 1974); J. J. Scarisbrick, *The Reformation and the English People* (Oxford, 1984); and K. Thomas, *Religion and the Decline of Magic* (1971); there are local studies by R. Whiting, *The Blind Devotion of the People* (Cambridge, 1989) on the West Country; by S. Brigden, *London and the Reformation* (Oxford, 1989); and by N. P. Tanner, *The Church in Late-Medieval Norwich, 1370–1532* (Toronto, 1984). It is sometimes said that my own view of Reformation in England is too much influenced by C. Haigh, *Reformation and Resistance in Tudor Lancashire* (Cambridge, 1975).

Reassessment of the Church was really begun with studies of the parish clergy, especially M. Bowker, *The Secular Clergy in the Diocese of Lincoln, 1495–1520* (Cambridge, 1968) and P. Heath, *English Parish Clergy on the Eve of the Reformation* (1969). Some of the best new work is in thesis form; see especially P. Marshall, 'Attitudes of the English People to Priests and Priesthood, 1500–1553', D.Phil. thesis (Oxford, 1990), a balanced and realistic study. Margaret Bowker also led the re-evaluation of the Church courts, in 'The Commons Supplication against the Ordinaries in the Light of Some Archidiaconal *Acta*', *TRHS* 5th series, 21 (1971); more generally, see R. Houlbrooke, *Church Courts and the People during the English Reformation, 1520–1570* (Oxford, 1979), and R. H. Helmholz, *Roman Canon Law in Reformation England* (Cambridge, 1990); and, for important detail, S. Lander on the Chichester courts in C. Haigh (ed.), *English Reformation Revised* (Cambridge, 1987) and D. Crawford, 'The Rule of Law? The Laity, English Archdeacons' Courts and the Reformation to 1558', *Parergon*, new series, 4 (1986). The most helpful survey of the work of the bishops is S. Thompson, 'The Pastoral Work of the English and Welsh Episcopate, 1500–1558', D.Phil. thesis (Oxford, 1984); for particular cases, see M. Bowker, *The Henrician Reformation: The Diocese of Lincoln under John Longland, 1521–1547* (Cambridge, 1981), and B. Bradshaw and E. Duffy (eds.), *Humanism, Reform and the Reformation: The Career of Bishop John Fisher* (Cambridge, 1989). There has not been much recent attention to the monasteries, beyond a few local studies; perhaps D. Knowles, *The Religious Orders in England*, iii (Cambridge, 1959), seemed to have solved all the problems. In showing that the monasteries were not a great scandal, Knowles demoted them from being a major cause of Reformation; they may have been innocent (or not very guilty) victims.

While some historians have been rehabilitating the Church before Reformation, others have stressed the significance of its enemies. A. Hudson, *The Premature Reformation* (Oxford, 1988) works primarily from early Lollard texts; D. Plumb, 'The Social and Economic Spread of Rural Lollardy: A Reappraisal', in W. J. Sheils and D. Wood (eds.), *Studies in Church History*, xxiii (Oxford, 1986), looks at the densest Lollard communities; A. Hope, 'Lollardy: The Stone the Builders Rejected?', in P. Lake and M. Dowling (eds.), *Protestantism and the National Church* (1987), is realistic. J. F. Davis, *Heresy and Reformation in the South-East of England, 1520–1559* (1983), suggests links between Lollardy and Protestantism; the best recent examination of early Protestants is in Brigden, *London*. Common lawyers were not necessarily enemies of the Church, but some of them came into conflict with it. The most important new work is rather technical; see especially J. H. Baker's introduction to *The Reports of Sir John Spelman* (Selden Society, 1977), and E. W. Ives, *The Common Lawyers in Pre-Reformation England* (Cambridge, 1983). For an accessible introduction to the issues, see J. Guy, 'Law, Lawyers, and the English Reformation', *History Today* (November 1985). Some historians have supposed that the Church's worst enemy was Cardinal Wolsey: by his corruption and arrogance, he may have made ecclesiastical authority objectionable and precipitated a crisis which his Church could not survive. Such a view is contested by P. Gwyn, *The King's Cardinal: The Rise and Fall of Thomas Wolsey* (1990). Perhaps Gwyn applies just a touch too much whitewash.

Part II: Two Political Reformations, 1530–1553

The best account of politics in these years is in G. R. Elton, *Reform and Reformation* (1977), but several of the crises have since been re-examined. J. A. Guy, *Tudor England* (Oxford, 1988), incorporates much of the latest research. The clash over praemunire has been debated by J. A. Guy, 'Henry VIII and the Praemunire Manœuvres of 1530–1531', *EHR* 97 (1982) (who thinks the aim was financial), and G. W. Bernard, 'The Pardon of the Clergy Reconsidered', *JEH* 27 (1986) (who thinks Henry wanted to force the clergy to acknowledge his authority); I suspect that neither is right. The work of G. Nicholson on the 1530 *Collectanea* has been influential, and is most easily found in his 'The Act of Appeals and the English Reformation', in C. Cross *et al.* (eds.), *Law and Government under the Tudors* (Cambridge, 1988). Some important new emphases have come through political biographies, especially J. A. Guy, *The Political Career of Sir Thomas More* (Brighton, 1980); S. Gunn, *Charles Brandon, Duke of Suffolk* (Oxford, 1988); and G. Redworth, *In Defence of the Church Catholic: The Life of Stephen Gardiner* (Oxford, 1990). J. J. Scarisbrick, *Henry VIII* (1968), remains crucial. There has been argument over the significance of Anne Boleyn. Eric Ives, *Anne Boleyn* (Oxford, 1986), presents her as a skilful politician with evangelical loyalties; R. M. Warnicke, *The Rise and Fall of Anne Boleyn* (Cambridge, 1989) protests that she was a sweet little victim of nasty men. The reviews suggest that Ives will prevail.

There has been a growing recognition of the importance of international relations (a high priority for rulers) in the formation of religious policy, especially shown in Redworth, *Gardiner*; G. Redworth, 'A Study in the Formulation of Policy: The Genesis and Evolution of the Act of Six Articles', *JEH* 37 (1986); and, a little later, M. L. Bush, *The Government Policy of Protector Somerset* (1975). But foreign policy has been examined in detail only by D. L. Potter, 'Diplomacy in the Mid-sixteenth Century: England and France, 1536–1550', Ph.D. thesis (Cambridge, 1973). The political calculations of John Dudley are revealed in D. Hoak, 'Rehabilitating the Duke of Northumberland', in J. Loach and R. Tittler, *The Mid-Tudor Polity, c.1540–1560* (1980). An understanding of Edwardian politics can, with effort, be extracted from D. E. Hoak, *The King's Council in the Reign of Edward VI* (Cambridge, 1976).

The suppressions, confiscations, and destructions are best considered by J. Youings, *The Dissolution of the Monasteries* (1971); A. Kreider, *English Chantries: The Road to Dissolution* (Cambridge, Mass., 1979); J. J. Scarisbrick, 'The Dissolution of the Secular Colleges' in Cross *et al.* (eds.), *Law and Government under the Tudors*; F. Heal, *Of Prelates and Princes* (Cambridge, 1980); S. E. Lehmberg, *The Reformation of Cathedrals* (Princeton, NJ, 1988); and M. Aston, *England's Iconoclasts: Laws against Images* (Oxford, 1988). There is an evocation of what it was like to be on the receiving end of this legalized looting in J. J. Scarisbrick, *The Reformation and the English People* (Oxford, 1984).

Opposition to Reformation has received more attention than had been usual: G. R. Elton, *Policy and Police* (Cambridge, 1972) looked at agitators and alehouse critics; clergy and intellectuals were examined by J.-P. Moreau, *Rome ou l'Angleterre? Les Réactions politiques des catholiques anglais au moment du schisme (1529–1553)* (Paris, 1984). Elton argued that the Pilgrimage of Grace was an attempted political coup, in 'Politics and the Pilgrimage of Grace', in his *Studies in Tudor and Stuart Politics and*

Government (3 vols., Cambridge, 1974, 1983), iii; but the primacy of religious concerns was reasserted by C. S. L. Davies, 'Popular Religion and the Pilgrimage of Grace', in A. Fletcher and J. Stevenson, *Order and Disorder in Early Modern England* (Cambridge, 1985). J. Youings, 'The South-Western Rebellion of 1549', *Southern History*, 1 (1979), and R. Whiting, *The Blind Devotion of the People* (Cambridge, 1989), have argued that the Western Rising was not very important and not very religious; I think they are wrong on both counts, if a traditionalist defence of church ceremonies and customs can be counted as religious. In his essay 'The Local Impact of the Tudor Reformations', in C. Haigh (ed.), *The English Reformation Revised* (Cambridge, 1987), Ronald Hutton reported the conclusions of his work on churchwardens' accounts, a study parallel to research for this book. Our observations of events were, happily, much the same, though our explanations are not identical.

Part III: Political Reformation and Protestant Reformation

A. G. Dickens has given an energetic and compressed account of the spread of popular Protestantism in 'The Early Expansion of Protestantism in England, 1520–1558', *Archiv für Reformationsgeschichte*, 78 (1987), summarized in A. G. Dickens, *The English Reformation* (1989 edn.); D. Palliser, 'Popular Reactions to the Reformation during the Years of Uncertainty, 1530–70', in Haigh (ed.), *English Reformation Revised*, is more cautious. There are now many local studies of the impact of Reformations, both political and Protestant, on towns and counties. For the towns, see especially: S. Brigden, *London and the Reformation* (Oxford, 1989); P. Clark, 'Reformation and Radicalism in Kentish Towns, c.1500–1553', in W. J. Mommsen (ed.), *Stadtbürgertum und Adel in der Reformation* (Stuttgart, 1979); G. Mayhew, 'Religion, Faction and Politics in Reformation Rye, 1530–59', *Sussex Archaeological Collections*, 120 (1982); M. A. Cook, 'Eye (Suffolk) in the Years of Uncertainty, 1520–1590', Ph.D. thesis (Keele, 1981); E. M. Shepperd, 'The Reformation and the Citizens of Norwich', *Norfolk Archaeology*, 38 (1983); J. Martin, 'The People of Reading and the Reformation, 1520–1570', Ph.D. thesis (Reading, 1987); C. Cross, 'The Development of Protestantism in Leeds and Hull, 1520–1640: The Evidence of Wills', *Northern History*, 18 (1982); D. M. Palliser, *Tudor York* (Oxford, 1979).

For the counties, see P. Clark, *English Provincial Society from the Reformation to the Revolution: Kent 1500–1640* (Hassocks, 1977)—though there is a rather different picture of the area in M. L. Zell, 'Church and Gentry in Reformation Kent, 1533–1553', Ph.D. thesis (Los Angeles, 1974); G. Mayhew, 'The Progress of the Reformation in East Sussex, 1530–1559: The Evidence from Wills', *Southern History*, 5 (1983); D. MacCulloch, *Suffolk and the Tudors* (Oxford, 1986); M. Spufford, *Contrasting Communities: English Villagers in the Sixteenth and Seventeenth Centuries* (Cambridge, 1974), on Cambridgeshire; J. E. Oxley, *The Reformation in Essex to the Death of Mary* (Manchester, 1965); M. Bowker, *The Henrician Reformation: The Diocese of Lincoln under John Longland, 1521–1547* (Cambridge, 1981); W. J. Sheils, *The Puritans in the Diocese of Peterborough, 1558–1610* (Northamptonshire Record Society, 1979); R. Whiting, *The Blind Devotion of the People* (Cambridge, 1989), on Devon and Cornwall; K. G. Powell, 'The Social Background to the Reformation in Gloucestershire', *Transactions of the Bristol and Gloucestershire Archaeological Society*, 92

(1973); M. Moir, 'Church and Society in Sixteenth Century Herefordshire', M.Phil. thesis (Leicester, 1984); G. Williams, *Welsh Reformation Essays* (Cardiff, 1967); C. Haigh, *Reformation and Resistance in Tudor Lancashire* (Cambridge, 1975); M. E. James, *Family, Lineage and Civil Society: A Study of Society, Politics and Mentality in the Durham Region, 1500–1640* (Oxford, 1974); S. M. Keeling, 'The Reformation in the Anglo-Scottish Borders', *Northern History*, 15 (1979).

The development of Protestant ideas in the Reformation period is a less fashionable topic than it once was, except in the United States. There are interesting suggestions in B. Hall, 'The Early Rise and Gradual Decline of Lutheranism in England', in D. Baker (ed.), *Reform and Reformation: England and the Continent, c.1500–c.1750* (Oxford, 1979); J. N. King, *English Reformation Literature* (Princeton, NJ, 1982); P. Collinson, *Godly People: Essays on English Protestantism and Puritanism* (1983); D. D. Wallace, *Puritans and Predestination: Grace in English Protestant Theology, 1525–1695* (Chapel Hill, NC, 1982); P. Lake, *Moderate Puritans and the Elizabethan Church* (Cambridge, 1983); and J. W. Martin, *Religious Radicals in Tudor England* (1989). For a survey, see H. Davies, *Worship and Theology in England from Cranmer to Hooker, 1534–1603* (Oxford, 1970). There is much robust good sense on this subject (and many others) in D. MacCulloch, *The Later Reformation in England, 1547–1603* (1990). There has been some excellent work on the universities: C. M. Dent, *Protestant Reformers in Elizabethan Oxford* (Oxford, 1983); J. K. McConica (ed.), *The History of the University of Oxford*, iii (Oxford, 1986); H. C. Porter, *Reformation and Reaction in Tudor Cambridge* (Cambridge, 1958).

The politics of Mary's reign is now best approached through D. M. Loades, *Mary Tudor: A Life* (Oxford, 1989), perhaps adjusted in the light of E. Russell, 'Mary Tudor and Mr Jorkins', *BIHR* 63 (1990); D. Loades, *The Reign of Mary Tudor* (1979); and J. Loach, *Parliament and the Crown in the Reign of Mary Tudor* (Oxford, 1986). On the Marian Church, see R. H. Pogson, 'Revival and Reform in Mary Tudor's Church: A Question of Money', in Haigh (ed.), *English Reformation Revised*; R. H. Pogson, 'Reginald Pole and the Priorities of Government in Mary Tudor's Church', *HJ* 18 (1975); and R. H. Pogson, 'The Legacy of the Schism', in J. Loach and R. Tittler, *The Mid-Tudor Polity, c.1540–1560* (1980), though perhaps a concentration on Pole's problems at the Marian centre produces unnecessarily pessimistic conclusions. For a somewhat different approach, see A. M. Bartholomew, 'Lay Piety in the Reign of Mary Tudor', MA thesis (Manchester, 1979); S. Thompson, 'The Pastoral Work of the English and Welsh Episcopate, 1500–1558', D.Phil. thesis (Oxford, 1984); and J. Loach, 'The Marian Establishment and the Printing Press', *EHR* 101 (1986); Marian propaganda is treated less favourably by E. J. Baskerville, *A Chronological Bibliography of Propaganda and Polemic Published in English between 1553 and 1558* (American Philosophical Society, 1979), and Martin, *Religious Radicals*. There is not very much good work on the Marian persecution: perhaps it is not an attractive subject. The best is: D. M. Loades, *The Oxford Martyrs* (1970); G. Alexander, 'Bonner and the Marian Persecutions', in Haigh (ed.), *English Reformation Revised*; and, most notably, Brigden, *London*.

It now seems likely that the interpretation of the Elizabethan settlement advanced by J. E. Neale, *Elizabeth I and Her Parliaments, 1559–1581* (1953), will be superseded by the views of N. L. Jones, *Faith by Statute: Parliament and the Settlement of Religion, 1559* (1982), and W. S. Hudson, *The Cambridge Connection and the Elizabethan*

Settlement of 1559 (Durham, NC, 1980). W. P. Haugaard, *Elizabeth and the English Reformation* (Cambridge, 1968), is also important. The implementation of the settlement is best tackled through the local studies listed above; and R. O'Day, 'Thomas Bentham: A Case Study in the Problems of the Early Elizabethan Episcopate', *JEH* 23 (1972); P. Collinson, *Archbishop Grindal, 1519–1583* (1979); P. Tyler, 'The Ecclesiastical Commission for the Province of York, 1561–1641', D.Phil. thesis (Oxford, 1965); and MacCulloch, *Later Reformation.* The only good account of the revolt of the northern earls is S. E. Taylor, 'The Crown and the North of England, 1559–70', Ph.D. thesis (Manchester, 1981).

There have been controversies over the nature and success of Elizabethan Catholicism. J. Bossy, *The English Catholic Community, 1570–1850* (1975), argued that the old Church died and a new community was created. Continuity has been asserted by C. Haigh, 'The Continuity of Catholicism in the English Reformation', in Haigh (ed.), *English Reformation Revised*; A. D. Wright, 'Catholic History, North and South', *Northern History*, 14 (1978); and P. McGrath, 'Elizabethan Catholicism: A Reconsideration', *JEH* 35 (1984). The impact of the missionary priests has been disputed between the following: C. Haigh, 'From Monopoly to Minority: Catholicism in Early Modern England', *TRHS* 5th series, 31 (1981); McGrath, 'Elizabethan Catholicism'; C. Haigh, 'Revisionism, the Reformation and the History of English Catholicism', and a 'Comment' by McGrath, *JEH* 36 (1985); and A. D. Wright, 'Catholic History, North and South, Revisited', *Northern History*, 25 (1989). The issues are surveyed sensibly by A. Dures, *English Catholicism, 1558–1642* (1983). There are many local studies of Catholicism; among the best are J. E. Paul, 'The Hampshire Recusants in the Reign of Elizabeth I', Ph.D. thesis (Southampton, 1958); V. Burke, 'Catholic Recusants in Elizabethan Worcestershire', MA thesis (Birmingham, 1972); K. R. Wark, *Elizabethan Recusancy in Cheshire* (Chetham Society, 1971); J. C. H. Aveling, *Northern Catholics: The Catholic Recusants of the North Riding of Yorkshire, 1558–1790* (1966); J. C. H. Aveling, 'The Catholic Recusants of the West Riding of Yorkshire, 1558–1790', *Proceedings of the Leeds Philosophical and Literary Society* (Literary and Historical Section), 10(4) (1963); J. A. Hilton, 'Catholicism in Elizabethan Durham', *Recusant History*, 14 (1977). For different aspects of the persecution of Catholics, see: F. X. Walker, 'The Implementation of the Elizabethan Statutes against Recusants, 1581–1603', Ph.D. thesis (London, 1961), and M. Hodgetts, *Secret Hiding Places* (Dublin, 1989). The attitudes of Catholics towards their position are discussed in P. Holmes, *Resistance and Compromise: The Political Thought of the Elizabethan Catholics* (Cambridge, 1982), and A. Pritchard, *Catholic Loyalism in Elizabethan England* (1979).

The indispensable guide to the growth and character of Elizabethan Protestantism is Patrick Collinson. For a survey, see his essay 'The Elizabethan Church and the New Religion', in C. Haigh (ed.), *The Reign of Elizabeth I* (1984). For greater detail, see also Collinson, *Godly People*; Collinson, *The Elizabethan Puritan Movement* (1967); Collinson, *The Religion of Protestants: The Church in English Society, 1559– 1625* (Oxford, 1982); and Collinson, *The Birthpangs of Protestant England* (1988). Some of the mechanisms of protestantization are considered in R. O'Day, *The English Clergy: The Emergence and Consolidation of a Profession, 1558–1642* (Leicester, 1979); J. J. Goring, 'The Reformation of the Ministry in Elizabethan Sussex', *JEH* 34 (1983); D. Cressy, *Literacy and the Social Order: Reading and Writing in Tudor and*

Stuart England (Cambridge, 1980); P. Collinson, 'Lectures by Combination', in his *Godly People*; and I. Green, ' "For Children in Yeeres and Children in Understanding": The Emergence of the English Catechism under Elizabeth and the Early Stuarts', *JEH* 37 (1986). For some of the problems Protestants encountered, see: C. Haigh, 'The Church of England, the Catholics and the People', in Haigh (ed.), *Reign of Elizabeth*; Haigh, 'Puritan Evangelism in the Reign of Elizabeth I', *EHR* 92 (1977); W. Hunt, *The Puritan Moment: The Coming of Revolution in an English County* (Cambridge, Mass., 1983), on Essex; K. Wrightson and D. Levine, *Poverty and Piety in an English Village: Terling, 1525–1700* (1979); and K. Thomas, *Religion and the Decline of Magic* (1971). So English Reformations were not over yet—not by a long way. And nor is the argument about them.

Index